Living in
the Spirit's Fire

Living in the Spirit's Fire

SAINT EUGENE DE MAZENOD

Founder of the Missionary Oblates
of Mary Immaculate

By Alfred Hubenig, O.M.I.

Foreword by René Motte, O.M.I.

Living in the Spirit's Fire: Saint Eugene de Mazenod, Founder of the Missionary Oblates of Mary Immaculate is published by Novalis.

Cover Painting of Bishop de Mazenod by Joseph Dassy, 1833; photo by Alfred A. Hubenig, O.M.I.

Cover design and layout: Suzanne Latourelle

Photos: Alfred A. Hubenig, O.M.I.

© 1995, Novalis

Business Office:Novalis
      49 Front St. East, 2nd Floor,
      Toronto, Ontario, M5E 1B3

Editorial Office:Novalis
      223 Main Street,
      Ottawa, Ontario, K1S 1C4

Legal deposit: 3rd trimester, 1995

National Library of Canada

Bibliothèque nationale du Québec

Printed in Canada.

Canadian Cataloguing in Publication Data

Hubenig, Alfred, 1931-

    Living in the spirit's fire: Saint Eugene de Mazenod, founder of the Missionary Oblates of Mary Immaculate

ISBN: 2-89088-766-9

    1. Mazenod, Charles Joseph Eugène de, 1782-1861.

2. Oblates of Mary Immaculate—Biography.   I. Title.

BX4705.M4575H83   1995   271.76   C95-900862-4

To the memory of
Jean Drouart, O.M.I.

A true son of de Mazenod, who,
through a life lived and constantly
challenged by the Oblate Founder's
charism, was an example for so
many of us;

A happy Oblate with a contagious
smile for everyone, and with a
heart that encompassed the whole
world.

I can hear his hearty laugh echoing
through the corridors of heaven,
meeting all his early-Church friends
from the catacombs of Rome,
meeting Eugene de Mazenod,
and happy to be home.

CONTENTS

FOREWORD

In drawing the spiritual profile of Saint Eugene de Mazenod, the invitation made by one of his episcopal colleagues, Bishop Bertaud of Tulle, still merits emphasizing:

> Go to Marseilles. There is a bishop there whose Congregation is still small, but the man himself has a heart as big as St. Paul's, as big as the world.

These are words that truly convey the enthusiasm felt by those who knew him in life and by those who have come to know him through the works he established and the writings he has left behind.

A heart as big as the world! A young priest who renounced the advantages of his aristocratic origins to become the servant of the poor, who shared his generous zeal with a group of others, young priests like him, so that, becoming the friends of the lowly and unpretentious, speaking their language, visiting them, welcoming them, they journeyed up and down the roads of Provence, often on foot, to rekindle the faith, even in the most remote villages.

A heart as big as the world! Even when he still had only ten companions in his society, the Rule Eugene wrote for the group in 1818 already stated emphatically, "Their ambition will be to encompass in their holy desires the immense breadth of the entire world." That ambitious dream began to take form in 1841 when Bishop de Mazenod sent his first disciples to Canada. It was the beginning of a heroic epic that would see the Oblates of Mary Immaculate spread from pole to tropics: in Canada, Sri Lanka, Southern Africa and today in over sixty countries – wherever the apostolate demands a radical renouncing of self on the part of those whom Pius XI once called "specialists in the most difficult missions." Thousands of Oblates have lived and spent themselves in the radiance of the Founder's "big heart."

A big heart such as his is a gift from God, privileged with abounding sensitivity; indeed, Eugene de Mazenod felt deep distress in the face of any inequality or injustice. That big heart was also and especially the result of an extraordinary grace. On Good Friday, 1807, Jesus caused him forcibly to feel the strength of his love. Eugene wept, he lamented his sins and he felt immense joy at discovering the meaning of his life – that he was destined to give himself totally to Jesus Christ, the Saviour. That was to be the reality inspiring his entire life. Because of his passionate love for Jesus Christ he became unconditionally committed to the Church: "To love the Church," he said, "is to love Jesus Christ, and vice versa." And in loving Christ, he discovered the value of every single soul, ransomed by the blood of the Son of God. That love of Christ was the cement that bound him to his apostolic companions and that continues to give Oblates today the strength to live together as brothers. Christ's love made itself manifest to Eugene in Mary Immaculate. In her he could admire the marvel of Redemption which Christ accomplished:

> We glorify God in the masterpiece of his power and love . . . . It is the Son whom we honour in the person of his Mother.

A heart as big as the world! A gift from Jesus Christ, confided to the maternal protection of Mary Immaculate.

To help me discover the richness of Eugene de Mazenod's heart, I had the good fortune of having Father Henri Tassel as both my first superior and my spiritual director at the scholasticate of La Brosse-Montceaux in France. He was a man who often referred to our Founder, finding in him a model of fidelity to the Spirit. My good fortune continued at the scholasticate in Rome where Father Jean Drouart was my superior. His enthusiasm for our sainted Founder was contagious and he passed it on to me, encouraging me to study his life and spirituality. I cannot thank the Lord enough for having given me those two men as guides in my religious and missionary life. Later, as an Assistant General of the Congregation, I had the singular opportunity of visiting so many missionary Oblates throughout the world; those visits confirmed how vital Eugene de Mazenod's charism remains to this day among those who have committed themselves to follow him.

And now, the Lord's grace gives me the opportunity to pass the flame on to other Oblates who come to Aix-en-Provence from all over the world to let themselves be caught up by the Founder at the very source, where the Oblate Congregation was born. It is to them that I give the conferences that have occasioned this book. Their reactions often spring from their missionary experience and they have helped me tailor my presentations. My thanks go to all of them, especially to Father Frank Santucci who taped my talks and put them in order. And a very special debt of gratitude to Father Alfred Hubenig who put my texts in masterful English, working them over, reorganizing them and adding considerable material to complete them, while adapting the entire work to readers unfamiliar with the details of French history. Without his collaboration, this book could never have come into being. Again, thank you, Al, from the bottom of my heart.

This work was done primarily for the Oblates and it is to them that we wish especially to present it. But we also want it to be a help to all who seek to discover in the spirituality of Eugene de Mazenod the inspiration and support they need in their particular apostolate. Indeed, it has already done that for a good number.

Saint Eugene, whose entire life was directed toward the discovery of Christ's limitless love, today gives us the same message he gave to a young Oblate of his day, "Charity – love – is the pivotal point around which all our existence revolves." To the faithful of his diocese he said:

> Charity embraces everything and, whenever necessary for new needs, it invents new means: spiritual aids, temporal helps, bread for the soul, bread for the body, and all given generously in the name of Jesus Christ.

Could a message be more timely today?

René Motte, O.M.I.   Aix-en-Provence
                            The Feast of Blessed Eugene de Mazenod
                                                May 21, 1995

PREFACE

Early in 1993 it was my privilege to live for four months in the house at Aix-en-Provence in southern France where Saint Eugene de Mazenod founded the tiny society of mission preachers that would soon become the Congregation of the Missionary Oblates of Mary Immaculate. For almost three of those months I lived with a group of fifteen Oblate confrères from all over the world, sharing the richness of their missionary experiences and engrossed by the conferences of a group of outstanding Oblates and guest theologians. Among the former was Father René Motte, who despite his precarious health took us tirelessly in the soft drizzle of Mediterranean winter through the streets and alleys trodden by the Oblate Founder. We also went out into the enchanting Provençal countryside with him, to the towns where those first members of the Congregation preached their parochial missions with such resounding success. We saw the mission crosses that still commemorate those epic moments and, meditating in the stone churches of those villages, I could all but hear the echo of their thunderous words.

But two elements that contributed even more than those outings to make the stay in Provence one of the outstanding experiences of my life were the conferences that René gave our group and the insights he gained through years of studying and meditating on the Founder's life. I thought I had come to Aix with a fairly rounded knowledge of Eugene de Mazenod – after all, I had read Leflon's awesome work and even translated a shorter biography of the Founder. Moreover, the late Jean Drouart, an eternal optimist, a dear friend, a holy Oblate and a happy saint, did much to broaden my acquaintance with de Mazenod on our many walks and drives in and about Rome when I worked there. Indeed, as personal preparation for Eugene's beatification in 1975, Jean and I made a memorable retreat, celebrating the Eucharist early each morning for the eight days leading up to the event, in a succession of places where the Oblate Founder had celebrated Mass while awaiting the outcome of the Congregation's petition for papal approbation in 1826. Before each eucharistic celebration we would read and meditate on an excerpt from his First Roman Journal that mentioned the place where we were, and what Eugene had done on that day. Later, in 1979, I was called back to Rome from missionary work in Mexico to write the Congregation's present Constitutions and Rules, based on the exhaustive work of the Rules Commission.

So, all in all, God's grace has given me a privileged Oblate life, putting me, in many ways, in close proximity to the Founder – yet my grasp of the man really only came together there in Aix, seeing him where he was born, living in the house where he began his little company of Missionaries of Provence, seeing him through René's eyes and in the fire that René's enthusiasm injected into his conferences. It was something for which I shall be eternally grateful to the Lord and to René, his instrument.

Those conferences made me want to share my acquaintance of the Oblate Founder with those who have only a passing knowledge of the man or do not know him at all. Writing a biography seemed to be the answer, yet even as I set out on that course I realized that something more than a straightforward account was needed. For someone born in France, French history may be fundamental, but the rest of us lack some very basic details vital to understanding Eugene de Mazenod's thought and actions. Often we see him out of context and he becomes a caricature of his real self. Thus a different kind of biography was called for.

As a basis for this book, I am deeply indebted to René, whose copious notes in French and English I have used freely, working them over, then setting them into the historical, political and social context of France in the late 18th and the 19th centuries, trying to inform without oversimplifying. For further source material I frequently turned to Eugene de Mazenod's first French biographers, especially to the best of them, Rambert and Rey, making new translations as I went. In the process I discovered a good number of additional rich texts, many of which have been incorporated. Included, too, were facts and insights drawn from the books and articles of several other Oblates, as well as a smattering of texts from the Fathers of the Church. It meant a great deal of seemingly endless researching, sandwiched between other commitments, but it was a labour of love.

The book was written in five countries where work and unrelated investigations carried me: Aix, in France, to begin with, where I had a wealth of original Oblate source material at my disposal (upon running out of time in Aix I lugged ten kilos of photocopies along with me from one place to the other, gradually lightening the load as I committed sheet after sheet to my trusty lap-top computer). The next stop was Seville in Spain, where I continued writing while living with two dedicated Oblates in a poor factory district on the outskirts and doing research in the city centre at the General Archives of the Indies, working with the original letters of the first explorers of the Americas. After that, it was off to Mexico City to close out my fifteen years of missionary work in that country and to find out the details of the exceptional miracle attributed by Rome to the intercession of Saint Eugene (a detailed account is found in the epilogue). That stop was followed by a brief stay in San Antonio, Texas. The journey finally came to an end in Canada, where I have returned to work after a twenty-five-year absence, and where, at last, I finished the final chapter of this book, along with the plans for a new church.

This is the story of a saint: not a plaster saint, but a saint of flesh and blood and bone – a saint of unquenchable fire, called by the Spirit to serve the poor and the most abandoned – an imperfect saint who struggled all his life toward perfection, a saint ground in the mortar of God's silence and purified in the crucible of obedience, a saint who challenges us today as much as he challenged people in the 19th-century, a saint who will keep on challenging us with his charism as long as we allow the Spirit to work through us as it did through him.

And now I want to share Eugene de Mazenod with others. The more I delve into his life, the more I am drawn to that volatile, energetic, explosive and very human saint. I hope the following pages will encourage readers do the same.

My thanks to the many fellow-Oblates and other friends who encouraged me to write this book, who read the manuscript and gave me their helpful suggestions and observations, and to Patricia Murphy for her painstaking editing.

Alfred A. Hubenig, O.M.I   Edmonton, Alberta, Canada
Good Friday
April 14, 1995

I

Vocation as a History of Grace

The French Revolution

On July 14, 1789, when the people of Paris stormed the ancient fortress of the Bastille, a surprised and startled Louis XVI is said to have asked one of his courtiers, the Duc de la Rochefoucauld, "What is happening? Is it a riot?" "No, Sire," came the reply. "It is a revolution."

Eugene de Mazenod was born on the eve of that revolution – on August 1, 1782, at the twilight of the 18th century. It was a century that saw the ideas of Voltaire and the Enlightenment unfold. It was a time when the Western world was shaken to its roots by the impact of a social upheaval that transformed the traditional monarchic order of the ancien régime into a republic and thus became the turning point of modern European history.

The French take their Revolution for granted – after all, they have studied it and lived with its results since birth. In the English-speaking world, however, such terms as Estates General, National Assembly, Constitutive Assembly, Girondists, Jacobins, Montanists, the Convention, the Vendée, the Paris Commune, etc., may imply very little. Ask someone what the French Revolution was all about and the answer will likely be about how the aristocrats lost their heads to the guillotine in the Reign of Terror. Yet, to better comprehend Saint Eugene de Mazenod's origins and thoughts, a fuller understanding of the Revolution is a necessity. That is the reason for this brief and possibly oversimplified history.

The Context of the Revolution

France in 1788 was ruled by an absolute monarch; his ministers were mere advisors and all decrees of the realm emanated from the king himself without having to be passed by any legislative body representative of the nation. The court lived in incredible luxury with no costs spared. When Queen Marie Antoinette's first daughter was born, she "limited" the number of servants attending the baby to *only 80*. Corruption in high places was the norm; the country groaned under the excessive and costly burden of royal functionaries who bought their positions, then collected an infinity of accumulated feudal taxes and customs duties on such minute things as crossing a bridge or taking produce from one town to another.

The national territory was divided into 30 provinces, each ruled by an *intendant*. Since feudal times, the king's subjects were divided into three classes, called *estates*.

The First Estate: "Those Who Pray for the Realm"

In all, some 120,000 persons made up the clergy. The high clergy came from the ranks of the nobility and lived extremely well on tithes and taxes derived from their lands, which constituted a sixth of France. Tithes were paid by commoners and peasants, in addition to the taxes they already had to pay to the nobles. However, the low clergy, mostly country parish priests and vicars, enjoyed neither benefices nor true representation and barely eked out an existence on the stole fees and gifts of their impoverished parishioners. The high clergy paid no taxes on their huge holdings but did make voluntary contributions to the royal coffers from time to time.

The Second Estate: "Those Who Defend the Realm"

The nobility in France represented about 350,000 persons. A privileged few lived at the court of Versailles amidst great splendour and luxury. The majority, however, lived in the provinces, mostly on the income from feudal taxes exacted from their peasants, supplemented by royal grants and pensions. Noblemen themselves were not taxed.

The Third Estate: "Those Who Work the Realm and Obey"

The middle-class (the *bourgeoisie*) were grouped together in the Third Estate with a conglomeration of artisans, servants, labourers and peasants. Over 25 million in all were classed as Third Estate. The bourgeois had become rich through commerce, banking and industry, but chafed at their lack of corresponding political power. Artisans and workers, mostly dependent on the bourgeois for their living, supported the latter's movements. The peasants, who were crushed under the weight of exorbitant taxes, were probably the worst off.

Liberalism and the Monarchy Set to Clash

Despite despotic rule, in many respects France was the most advanced nation of Europe towards the end of the 18th century. Jean-Jacques Rousseau's radical concepts of the social contract and of the inherent good of the common person gave impetus to anti-monarchical republicanism.

The *Encyclopedia* (1751-72), edited by Diderot and d'Alembert and largely devoted to practical technology, was designed as a monument to reason. The Enlightenment and the new theories of the French philosophers circulated widely, their books and periodicals read across the entire continent. In France itself, liberal thinkers, strongly influenced by the writings of Voltaire and by free-masonry, formed clubs where the new ideas were debated and where plans for a new tomorrow were hatched. From these clubs would come the two major and conflicting tendencies that made the Revolution.

The *Girondists*, so named because the majority of their early leaders came from the Gironde region, were mostly moderate republicans with some monarchist leanings. They represented the *grande bourgeoisie* (the upper middle-class) which had grown rich through commerce. Their political outlook was regionalist and federalist. When the Revolution broke, out the Girondists would opt to export their revolutionary principles through a policy of expansion and conquest.

The *Jacobins*, a political club formed in 1789, represented the *petite bourgeoisie* (lower middle-class) as well as the nation's liberal professionals. Politically they were centralists, attempting to base everything in Paris. Quite moderate at the start, they even claimed Count Honoré Mirabeau as an early member. With the onset of the Revolution, however, they sought to limit the power of the king. Splitting with the Girondists, the Jacobins opted to concentrate on changes within the country itself rather than wage war throughout Europe. Supported by the lower classes of Paris, they became increasingly radical and eventually sent most of the Girondists to the guillotine. Maximilien Robespierre, the most notable Jacobin leader, set off the notorious Reign of Terror. As the Terror grew he not only executed "counter-revolutionaries" but most of his former allies as well.

The Assembly of Notables

The dichotomy between the king's despotic rule and the spread of liberal thought pointed to the oncoming cataclysm. The situation reached a crisis in 1788 when a nearly bankrupt France ground to an administrative stand-still. Vast deficits dating back at least two previous reigns had been growing at the rate of 100,000,000 pounds annually. Coupled with the economic crisis, several consecutive bad harvests caused food shortages and riots in the cities (known as the Flour Wars because the populace took to the streets to demand bread). Something had to be done. When the king could squeeze no more from the bourgeoisie he proposed the unheard-of – a land tax on the nobility and clergy. That was when Eugene de Mazenod's father, Charles-

Antoine de Mazenod, *Président a mortier* of the Court of Accounts in Aix, began his vigorous campaign of writing and pamphleteering in defence of the nobility's right to remain free of taxes. Exemption, he argued, was an ancestral privilege of the nobility. It was not a royal favour but a concession granted in recognition of the sacrifices made for the realm by those who had always defended it with their arms.

The king felt forced by circumstances to convoke an Assembly of Notables at Versailles on February 22, 1787. There, he hoped to persuade the nobles and high clergy to accept the land tax for the benefit of the country. The notables, however, were notably disinclined to altruism. At this point Eugene's father became an unwitting actor in the drama of the French Revolution. The Procurator-General of Aix, influenced by the senior de Mazenod's arguments, declared to the Assembly "Neither this assembly of notables, nor any other similar assembly, nor even the king . . . can impose land taxes. The only body with such a right is an assembly of the Estates General or a general parliament of the entire realm, elected by the people."[1] Thus Louis XVI had to convoke a general assembly of all the Estates – the first such assembly since 1614. It was scheduled to open May 5, 1789.

First, however, there had to be elections. Charles-Antoine de Mazenod objected vehemently to the royal decree making non-fiefed nobles eligible to represent the Second Estate to which he belonged. In the end, that eligibility kept him from participating, even though he went to Paris. In addition, Honoré-Gabriel Riqueti, Comte de Mirabeau, a black-sheep liberal nobleman, to the horror of the nobility of Aix, forsook his own class and was elected for the Third Estate. Physically grotesque, profligate and devious, he was a man of great eloquence and tremendous energy. He had tricked the most eligible girl of Aix into a disastrous marriage and had spent time in the daunting prison of the Château d'If for huge unpaid debts. By a *lettre de cachet*, or royal warrant, his furious mother-in-law had also had him locked in the Bastille for a time. Now he was on his way to Paris, proclaiming, "From tranquil chaos we go to troubled chaos. Creation has begun!"

May 5, 1789: The Assembly of the Estates General

We can say that the French Revolution began on May 5 with the convocation by Louis XVI of the Estates General. The nobility and clergy had seen the Assembly as a measure to maintain their tax-free privileges, but the Third Estate quickly took over. When the king closed the Hall of Debate to them, they went to the Jeu de Paume, a kind of royal gymnasium. There on

---

[1] Salvat, *Historia Universal*, vol. 10, p. 110.

June 17, led by Joseph Sieyès and Count Mirabeau, they swore themselves into office as the National Assembly in what came to be known as the Tennis-Court Oath. Ten days later they invited the nobles and clergy to join them in a unicameral National Constitutive Assembly and, indeed, many did go over, among them, Archbishop Boisgelin of Aix. When the king sent his master of ceremonies, Dreux-Brézé, to tell them to break up their assembly, Mirabeau stated boldly, "Tell your master that we are here by the will of the people. If you have orders to remove us from this hall, you must also get authority to use force, for we shall yield to nothing but bayonets."[2] The king relented. The revolution began with the high ideals of liberty, fraternity and equality, Later, many atrocities would be committed in the name of those same virtues. This was also the moment in history when "left" and "right" entered the political vocabulary.

July 14, 1789: The Storming of the Bastille

On July 12 Louis XVI dismissed Necker, his minister of state, who was in favour of the National Assembly's reforms. The move was seen as an "aristocratic plot," provoking unrest and protests throughout Paris. The crowds first sacked the armouries of Les Invalides, seizing 30,000 rifles with which they quickly wrested control of the city's districts from the army. Then on the afternoon of July 14, a massive and motley mob of carpenters, cabinet makers, tanners, cobblers, weavers, porters, servants, labourers, beggars, shop-keepers and salaried workers stormed the ancient fortress of the Bastille. The ill-equipped garrison of only 32 Swiss Guards and 82 invalided soldiers did not stand a chance against the attackers who ranged in age from 72 to less than 10. Although the Bastille had been used to hold prisoners indefinitely under the notorious *lettres de cachet*, abolished in 1784, at the time of its storming it held only seven prisoners – two demented paupers, four forgers and a young unruly aristocrat – all of whom were locked away again soon afterwards. The storming of the Bastille, however, must be seen in its wider context as the embodiment of all the chaos and injustice created by a despotic monarchy. The prison governor's head was victoriously paraded through the streets of Paris and the fortress itself was immediately demolished. Eighty-three of its stones, carved into replicas, were sent to the provinces as ominous reminders of despotism's consequences.

---

[2] Payard, *Histoire de France,* vol. 4, pp. 49-63.

July 12, 1790: The Civil Constitution of the Clergy

One of the aims of France's new constitution, which Mirabeau, Sieyès and Mounier had written for the Assembly, was to make the Church a French entity. In the name of liberty, all religious orders were suppressed because, it was reasoned, the vow of obedience went against an individual's freedom. Moreover, the Church's dependence on the pope and Rome had to be severed because allegiance to a foreign power was considered a breach of communal liberty. The Assembly promulgated the Civil Constitution of the Clergy, a measure meant to completely reorganize the French Church. The new constitution provided for the election of priests and bishops by local voters, state remuneration of the clergy which, de facto, would turn them into salaried government functionaries, a clerical oath of allegiance and renunciation of Roman primacy, and the dissolution of monastic orders. It was obvious that the pope could not accept such measures.

March 10 and April 13, 1791: Papal Condemnation of the Revolution

Worthy but unequal to the challenges of a new era, aged Pope Pius VI had long witnessed a rising tide of secularism and atheism, along with mounting claims by states to control the Church within their realms. But the French Civil Constitution of the Clergy raised the stakes much more ominously. The pope was cautious, at first taking no action. But when the oath of loyalty was demanded of the clergy, he denounced the constitution as schismatic, declared the ordination of the new state bishops sacrilegious, suspended priests and bishops who had taken the civil oath, and condemned the Declaration of the Rights of Man. Diplomatic relations broke off and the situation deteriorated even further when the pope gave his support to the First Coalition, a united effort of Europe's monarchies against the Revolution. The result was a complete split in the French Church. The oath to which the clergy were to submit read: I swear hatred of royalty and anarchy and I swear fidelity to the Republic and to the Constitutions of the Third Year.

All clergy, of whatever rank, were expected to put their names to the oath. Those who refused to sign were left with three options: exile, hiding or the guillotine. Almost all the bishops – even the Gallican bishops – and half of the clergy refused to submit on the grounds that the oath went counter to their faith. Thirty thousand of the richest bishops and priests, including the two uncles of Eugene, could afford to choose exile.

The poorer clergy had no escape and hence went into hiding, hunted down as *réfractaires* (insubordinates) but often protected by good Christian

6

families with whom they could celebrate the sacraments clandestinely. We know, for example, that at the age of 11 or 12 Henri Tempier sought out a *réfractaire* in Aix from whom he could receive his First Communion.

September 2-5, 1792: The September Massacres

Count Mirabeau was elected president of the National Assembly on January 30, 1791 and died soon afterwards. Although a radical in many ways, he had always remained basically a monarchist. On his deathbed he said, "I carry with me the ruin of the monarchy. After my death factions will dispute about the fragments."[3] His prediction very soon became reality. At the outset of September 1792, Georges-Jacques Danton was pressured by the Paris Commune, one of the radical Jacobins and the minister of justice, to set up an extraordinary tribunal to judge "the crimes of the counter-revolutionaries." Three thousand "suspects" were rounded up, and 1500 of them, including 318 priests imprisoned in the monastery of St-Germain-des-Prés, were summarily executed. It was the precedent for the bloody Reign of Terror.

1793-95: The Reign of Terror

Increasingly, the Revolution took a hard line against the Church. In the Movement of de-Christianization, Danton had priests hunted down with greater vigour. Pierre Gaspard Chaumetter, abetted by the ultra-radical Hébert, tried to substitute a new state cult of the Supreme Being along with the goddess Reason. Churches were vandalized then turned over to the cult of this new goddess. The Oblates' mission church in Aix, for example, which up until the Revolution had belonged to the Carmelite nuns, became a temple in Reason's honour. (Later it became an overnight stopping place for itinerant circus performers). Anti-clerical hatred found further expression in October, 1793, with the abolition of the Julian calendar, replaced by the Republican calendar.

On June 6, 1793, at Danton's instigation, in Paris especially but in the provinces as well, Committees of Public Safety began to proliferate. Their task was to process "suspects and traitors," but often they were little more than kangaroo courts bent more on mindless vengeance than on justice.

---

[3] *Encarta*, Microsoft Corp., 1993.

January 21, 1793: Louis XVI Goes to the Guillotine

When the Jacobins gained the upper hand in the Assembly, the king's fate was sealed. In a close vote – 387 to 334 – and against the concerted opposition of the Girondists, the Convention decreed his execution. The sovereign's death opened the way to extreme radicalism. In Paris, between March, 1793 and August, 1794, the guillotine's devastating blade accounted for the lives of 16,594 persons from all social classes, among them the unpopular queen, Marie-Antoinette, executed on October 16, 1793. There were atrocities in the provinces, as well, such as the drowning in the Loire River, near Nantes, of some 3,000 "priests, anti-revolutionaries, suspects, bandits and condemned persons by common right," placed in the hulls of barges that were then scuttled. Eight thousand more were guillotined in the same city during a three-month period. In all, approximately 42,000 persons were executed throughout France during this convulsive period of history: eight percent of the victims were nobles; six percent were clergy (proportionately, they were the group hardest hit by the Reign of Terror); fourteen percent were bourgeois; and seventy percent were workers and peasants charged with draft-dodging, hoarding, rebellion (especially in the Vendée) and various other crimes.[4]

In one form or another, the Reign of Terror lasted until 1795. By that time both Danton, the pillar of revolutionary thought, and Robespierre, rightly called the Father of the Terror, fell victims to their own creation. In *Robespierre, ou le délire décapité*,[5] historian Pierre-Alexandre Bourson states that the Terror uselessly prolonged both internal and external conflicts, did away with valuable thinkers needed by France, and retarded the birth of a modern republic by a century.

1795-99: The *Directoire*

Gradually, however, there was a softening of the Revolution as the nation grew tired of so much blood. A new form of government, in the hands of the moderate bourgeois (who had gotten even richer provisioning the victorious revolutionary armies) came out of the Constitution of Year III (1795). The new government, which came to power during the terrible winter food shortages of 1795-96, took the form of a Council of the 500, which proposed resolutions, and a Council of the Elders – 250 senators, which promulgated the resolutions into laws. Together they chose the *Directoire*, or Directory,

---

[4] *Encarta*, Microsoft Corp., 1993.
[5] Buchet-Chastel, 1993.

a five-member executive body, with one new member chosen each year. The result calmed spirits, but there were still periodic upheavals and serious threats to order. The *Directoire* proved to be unwieldy and weak; for the middle-class it was an era of "insolent opulence," but the majority experienced it as a further period of privation.

The failure of industry to recover and the spiralling devaluation of French currency made the lot of urban workers especially miserable. In 1797, when royalist deputies were at the point of gaining the majority in government, republican members of the *Directoire* invited a brilliant 28-year-old general to help them stage a coup so that the elections could be annulled. The general was Napoleon Bonaparte.

Two years earlier, at the behest of the *Directoire*, Napoleon had invaded the Papal States because Pope Pius VI refused to rescind his condemnation of the French Constitution. Nor did the pontiff's brief of July 5, 1796, *Pastoralis sollicitudo*, satisfy the *Directoire*. On February 15, the French army entered Rome and proclaimed a Roman Republic. The pope was deposed as head of state, separated from his advisors and sent into exile in Tuscany. The *Directoire* at first planned to banish him to Sardinia, but his precarious health ruled that out. However, when war broke out afresh and there was a danger that attempts would be made to rescue the pope, he was moved to Turin and thence over the Alps to Briançon and then to Valence, where he died as a prisoner in the citadel on July 13, 1799. Buried in the city cemetery of Valence, his remains were transferred to Rome in 1802. At his death, after one of the longest pontificates in history, it was assumed that the destruction of the Holy See had at last been accomplished. However, Pius VI had left instructions for the holding of the next conclave under emergency conditions.

December 9, 1799: *The Coup d'État* of 18 *Brumaire* and the Consulate

History proves that it is always dangerous to prop up a weak power-base by seeking support from the military. The result is that invariably the latter decides to do the governing itself. That is exactly what happened to the *Directoire*.

Surprisingly, while so much bloody revolutionary turmoil was taking place within the country during the 1790s, French armies abroad were winning resounding victories against neighbouring monarchies – which was why the de Mazenods had to keep moving. Through Napoleon's brilliant campaigns he had become an national idol. France saw him as "the man of destiny." Thus, two years after he helped the *Directoire* maintain power by staging a

9

coup for them, he staged an immensely popular one of his own on 18 *Brumaire* of the Republican calendar (December 9, 1799). First, he forced the Senate and the Council of the 500 to meet in session in St-Cloud, just outside Paris, where he forthwith stripped both of their powers. In their place he named three provisional consuls: himself, Sieyès and Ducos. The latter two, despite some initial reaction by Sieyès, were mere puppets – Napoleon was the true master of the situation. The country greeted the coup with joy, hoping for some peace and stability. With the Consulate a new period in French history began. A new form of government – the First Empire – would last 15 years, until Napoleon's abdication and exile to Elba in 1814. It would eventually be followed by the Bourbon Restoration.

Eugene's Father, Charles Antoine de Mazenod

Originally, the de Mazenods were highly successful bourgeois apothecary wholesalers in the port of Marseilles. By a royal patent of May, 1663, they entered the ranks of the nobility in the person of Charles de Mazenod, consul of Marseilles. From that time on, all de Mazenod men, including Eugene, took "Charles" as their first Christian name. Moving to Aix, the family became "nobility of the robe" – men in the judicial field – a step below the "nobility of the sword." All too often, however, the *noblesse oblige* of their rank and position forced them to live wildly beyond their means. Although they masked it expertly, the de Mazenods faced constant financial problems. Accumulated debts led to heavy borrowing. Their way out was through marriages to rich heiresses, putting financial considerations above sentiment.

Charles-Antoine, Eugene's father and of the fifth-generation of de Mazenod nobility, was educated by the Jesuits at the Collège Bourbon. He was a brilliant student, coming first in Christian doctrine, second in prose and in poetry and with an honourable mention in Latin. He graduated first in his class of philosophy, defending no less than 14 theses in such varied topics as universal philosophy, gnomonics (a branch of geometry), electricity and experimental physics. His studies would prepare him for the parliamentary jousts of future years when he would demonstrate his formidable logic. Charles-Antoine's father, Charles-Alexandre, had to obtain a special royal indult so his underage son could become a president of the Court of Accounts, Aids and Finances at the age of 26, in 1771.

In 1778, just after his 33rd birthday, Charles-Antoine married 18-year-old Marie-Rose Joannis. She was an Aix beauty and, while not of noble origin, came to the union with a considerable fortune – something the de Mazenods definitely needed. The marriage started out happily enough but gradually soured. The Revolution forced the de Mazenods into exile, from which Marie-Rose would return in 1795 by divorcing her husband and renouncing her title of nobility, thus reverting to the bourgeoisie. Charles Antoine, on the other hand, continued in exile, eventually returning to Marseilles, where he died at 75 on October 20, 1820, virtually penniless, cared for by his brother, Canon Fortuné and his son, Eugene. His divorced wife refused him any help, forcing Canon Fortuné to borrow 500 francs to defray final expenses.

While not particularly religious, Charles Antoine nonetheless would write to his son in 1816, a year after he returned to the practice of his faith, informing him about a serious illness he had just undergone: "I almost died, and if I am still alive it can be attributed to a special grace from the Lord, which, I am convinced, I owe to the Blessed Virgin, for whom, even in my worst escapades, I always maintained a special devotion, never letting a day pass without calling upon her many times."[6]

Eugene's Mother, Marie-Rose Joannis

Marie-Rose Joannis was the daughter of Joseph-Thomas Joannis, a Royal Professor at the Faculty of Medicine at the University of Aix. The bourgeois Joannis family had made its fortune in retail pharmacy and must certainly have recognized the economic inequality of a marriage agreement with the financially strapped de Mazenods. Yet they also recognized that this was an excellent opportunity for their daughter to quickly climb the social ladder as *Madame la Présidente*. Thus, the contract was drawn up between the families on February 2, 1778, and the couple was married the next day.

Personality differences often complement one another. That was not the case with Marie-Rose and Charles-Antoine. First, there was the 15-year age gap between them. Moreover, Marie-Rose's bourgeois convent education must have certainly clashed with the humanistic and classical formation of aristocratic Charles-Antoine. Also, while the de Mazenods, true to their class, were almost profligate in their spending, the Joannis clan, especially the women, were accustomed to acquisitiveness that bordered on avarice. Related to this was an even more serious problem: the constant interference and animosity of Marie-Rose's jealous mother who seemed determined to wreck the marriage.

Marie-Rose followed her husband and children into exile but returned to Aix with Ninette, Eugene's sister, in 1795. It marked the end of her

---

6 Bibliothèque Méjanes, Boisgelin archives, Aix.

11

marriage. Renouncing her nobility and divorcing her husband, she was successful in reclaiming not only her own family's property but most of her husband's as well. It was another instance of the Joannis cupidity, learned so well from her mother.

Eugene's mother was a complex person, almost manic-depressive in her mood swings. She was by turns compassionate and cruelly explosive, self-sacrificing and self-centred, understanding and disagreeable, firm and undecided, loving and spiteful. Her relationship to Eugene bore out those contradictions. She obviously loved her son, yet left him in exile in Venice when she returned to France with her daughter, referring to him as "your son" in letters to her husband.[7] And when Eugene could finally return to France, after not having seen his mother for seven years, she was not there to meet him. Instead, she and her cousin-companion, Rose-Joannis, were off on an excursion. Later, when Eugene decided to enter the seminary, she posed all sorts of obstacles. Ashamed of what people of her class might think of an only-son who was studying to become a priest, she found pretexts to prevent his coming home from the seminary during vacations. Yet when he was ordained, although she was not present (something not at all unusual in those days), she gave her wedding gown to be made into his ordination chasuble. Throughout these contradictions, one thing is certain and comes through repeatedly – Eugene de Mazenod genuinely loved his mother. Madame de Mazenod died at Aix in 1851 at the age of 91.

Vocation As History Of Grace

Life, especially when we consider the history of a vocation, is a history with God. The Lord is continuously present, even if at times he may seem silent and far away. Only after a period of faith-reflection is it possible to realize the providential hand in what one has lived and experienced. Thus, only gradually and after many years of faith-reflection could Eugene de Mazenod say, "He loved me and gave himself up for me" (Galatians, 12:20).

Childhood

The beginning of Eugene's life in Aix was a period of happiness. The family lived on the city's poshest avenue, the 17th-century tree-lined Cours. Surrounded by a dozen servants, the boy was coddled by his nanny, the doting Nanon, and enjoyed the warmth of family life in the happy times before marital bickering and hurtful in-fighting would lead to his parents'

---

[7] Leflon, vol. 1, p. 171.

divorce. He learned Provençal from Nanon and from his maternal grandfather Joannis. From the very outset they spoke to him in that patois, so it was probably the first language he learned. The boy's education was marked by the piety of his mother who, we know, daily prayed the little office of the Virgin Mary. Especially noteworthy, too, is the great popularity in Aix of the Immaculate Conception, of whom his mother was a devotee.

The Pitcho with Backbone

In the Oblate house in Aix, there is a portrait of Eugene de Mazenod, done in 1787, when he was five years old. The set of the boy's mouth in the painting already gives a hint of the strong will and headstrong nature that would characterize his life. Formed from birth to the aristocratic prejudices of his family and predisposed by his Provençal temperament, Eugene developed a fiery and impulsive personality at a very early age. It bothered his father because he saw too much of his own cutting disposition in his son, but the boy's maternal grandfather, a professor at the academy of medicine and counsellor to the king, defended him, saying, "This *pitcho* (little one) was born with backbone. Let him say 'I *want* it.' It's better than whining. He's got backbone. I like that."

An example of that backbone showed when he was only four years old:

> He had been taken to the theatre at Aix and, while he was there, a disturbance broke out down in the theatre pit. Indignantly drawing himself up to his full height and leaning over the edge of his box, he threatened the ringleader of the disturbance with, *"Vei! Tout aré se descendi!"* ("Just you wait! If I ever come down there . . .!") Completely taken by surprise at the youngster's challenge, the culprit sheepishly gave in to the peremptory threat.[8]

But the *pitcho* also had compassion and sensitivity. One day, seeing a little charcoal-hauler dressed in tattered rags, he exchanged his own clothes with the boy. Later, when scolded by his mother for conduct unbecoming to a noble child destined to follow his father as president of the Courts, he replied simply, "Very well, I shall be a charcoal-hauler president."

It was a carefree and easy life, but it was not to last.

Collège Bourbon

When Eugene was seven years old he was placed in the Collège Bourbon, where his father and uncles had been educated. But in their day the teachers were Jesuits who were strict and conservative. After the suppression of the

---

[8] Leflon, vol. 1, p. 36.

Society of Jesus by Clement XIV in 1773, their determined adversaries – a religious society, no longer existent, officially called the Priests of Christian Doctrine, but commonly known as the Doctrinaires – replaced them. In 1791, the year the de Mazenods went into political exile, the Doctrinaires would approve the anti-religious code of the Civil Constitution of the Clergy, which had been condemned by the pope.

> Their theological, political, social and pedagogical principles were totally different from those of the Jesuits and their triumph over the Jesuits was actually the triumph of the 18th century. Gallican, Jansenistic, enlightened, reformative and liberal, these educators personified the tendencies of that day. Their educational system modernized traditional methods of education by combining them with ideas in vogue at the time. Torn between the *Augustinus* and the *Émile*, between Bossuet and Rousseau, and between the *Ratio Studiorum* and Rollin and Condorcet, the Doctrinaires joined mild discipline with strict morality . . . . [They] did not succeed in winning the unanimous approval of Aix society by their modernism.[9]

At school the Doctrinaires were preparing the revolution in the minds of their young students. Indeed, the Collège became the meeting place for the city's lower-class liberal "patriots." While all this was going on in school, at home Eugene's aristocratic father kept turning out his learned treatises as the foremost defender in Aix of the nobility's prerogatives, even standing up to the king.

For Eugene it was a time of mixed loyalties. Children generally look at their teachers as heroes who are always right. Yet in this case, given the diametrically opposed views of his parents and teachers, and his own love for his father, he must surely have felt threatened at school.

Disturbances in Aix

More serious, however, were the dangers caused in Aix from the budding Revolution, especially in December, 1790. M. le Président Charles-Antoine de Mazenod, Eugene's father, was in grave danger because of his widely known views against the ideas of the Revolution. Indeed, he had even been cited in the parliamentary record as one of the best defenders of the aristocratic debates which had set the members of the Estates of Provence at odds with one another. The help of his pen was also sought repeatedly by the other nobles, and he wrote reams of protests, requests and memoranda that received wide distribution.

---

[9] Leflon, vol. 1, p. 55.

Nights of rioting and looting in March had already shown how precarious was the situation of the de Mazenods. Momentary calm was restored when city authorities abdicated, leaving it to Mirabeau to restore order – a move that made the fiery nobleman even more of a hero in the eyes of the populace. Surely Eugene must have overheard snatches of his parents' talk about the turncoat Mirabeau, and with the man's terribly pock-marked face, his grotesque, oversized head and wild oratory, he must have appeared like a monster to the small boy. In the countryside, meanwhile, peasants were attacking, pillaging and burning châteaux, manor houses, mills and monasteries.

The rest of the year passed in uneasy quiet until Sunday, December 12, when class troubles flared at the Café Guion, right beside the de Mazenod residence. That night, word spread that a mob was looking to arrest de la Roquette and Jean-Joseph-Pierre Pascalis a middle-class lawyer who had first sided with the "patriots" and later came over to the side of the nobility, reconciling himself openly with M. le Président de Mazenod. The latter saw the writing on the wall and took steps to protect himself.

On the following day, December 13, a man-hunt began for 11 "enemies of the Revolution," Charles Antoine de Mazenod among them. A summons to appear before the tribunal was served at the de Mazenod home, but by then Eugene's father had disappeared. Later, a witness at the tribunal hearing declared that on his return from the fair in St-Maxim he had seen M. le Président and another former high-court president in hunting clothes, each carrying a gun. Thus disguised, and armed to defend himself, Eugene's father made his way to safety in Nice. Pascalis and de la Roquette were not so fortunate. On Tuesday, December 14th, a lynch-mob forced its way into the prison, dragged the two hapless prisoners out and strung them up from a lamp post on the Cours, just outside the de Mazenod residence. It must have been traumatic for eight-year-old Eugene; surely he sensed the terror that gripped the household. Then to have stood at a window and to have looked down at the two corpses left dangling there at the end of their ropes, knowing that his father could just as easily have been there too. Why? Why was his world suddenly coming apart?

Exile

In April, 1791, the de Mazenod family went into exile. Eugene was just over eight years old at the time. He would not see France again until late October, 1802, when he was 20! – nearly 12 years of exile during an important period in a young man's life.

Nice

In January, 1791, M. le Président Charles-Antoine sent his brother, the naval commander Charles-Louis-Eugène, to Aix with orders to bring Eugene to Nice, which at that time did not belong to France but formed part of the Kingdom of Piedmont. The rest of the family followed in April and stayed for several months.

The de Mazenods, like most of the fleeing nobility, did not expect their hasty exit from France to last long. Surely, they thought, the very excesses of the revolutionaries would be their quick downfall. But it was not to be. The months dragged on and slowly reality began to sink in. At best, it would be a long haul – an exile, not a brief exit.

Turin

Turin was the next leg of Eugene's exile. The de Mazenods stayed there for two-and-a-half years, until April, 1794, and Eugene studied in the College of Nobles, a school that admitted only the sons of genuine nobility and only with the approval of the king himself. How did Charles-Antoine manage to put his son in such a prestigious school?: probably with the help of a strong French counter-revolutionary movement which had existed in Turin since 1791.[10] Eugene's father certainly must have had several friends in the movement, friends who would have known with what zeal and commitment he had defended the cause of the French nobility and crown. It was probably some of them who put in a good word.

Classes in the college were in Italian. Yet despite the language handicap, Eugene continually stood at the head of his class and was highly regarded by the Barnabite Fathers who directed the school. "Finding him more mature than his classmates, his superiors put him in charge of his dormitory. Father Rector and the other Fathers always presented him as a model because the child showed qualities rare for his age."[11]

Nonetheless, a letter Eugene wrote when 24 years old, to Alexandre d'Aubray, one of his Aix friends, and a classmate at the College of Nobles, shows him to have been a real boy, not a plaster saint or some pathetic introvert. He wrote: "I still have pleasurable memories of the punches that I rained on the fat cheeks of those Piedmontese classmates of ours, to protect you against their vexations."[12]

---

[10] Fayard, *Histoire de France,* vol. 4, p. 91.

[11] *Souvenirs de Famille,* from *Missions,* 1866, p. 116.

[12] Rey, vol. 1, p. 74.

Venice

The revolutionary armies kept advancing, so the de Mazenods were forced to move on to Venice This period – from April, 1794, to November, 1797 – deeply influenced Eugene's life. They were those crucial years between 12 and 16, "when the eyes open wide on life, and manhood begins its first stirrings in the boy." Initially, Eugene was left with nothing to do but while away the hours.

> (He was) tightly encompassed by a narrow circle of serious men-folk, all four of them equally worried-looking, and equally unoccupied: two former canons, one very old, the other rather stodgy; a naval officer no longer in the service of the king, and a president, stripped of his privileges and deprived of his position. The only ones who brought a youthful and refreshing touch to those dreary surroundings were Mme. de Mazenod (on her cheerful days), the ever-delightful and charming Ninette, or big Nanon, constantly bustling about and chattering in the typical fashion of the Midi . . . . His father and uncles had all the leisure time in the world to give him lessons, but the code of the aristocrats restricted this common employment to tutors. To make matters worse, there were no books in the house, and no money to buy any. Thus the young schoolboy found himself on an enforced vacation, and fell victim to boredom and day-dreaming.[13]

Then one day one of the greatest graces of his life came his way, in the person of a marvelous educator, Don Bartolo Zinelli.[14] Eugene served his great-uncle's Mass each morning in the church of San Silvestro. There, the kindly parish priest, Monsignor Milesi, took notice of the sad 12-year-old and discovered he was a French émigré. Accordingly, he contacted the gifted and devout Father Zinelli to check on the little boy's situation and see what could be done for him. The elderly pastor could not have entrusted Eugene to better hands.

Don Bartolo and his brother, also a priest, stayed with their parents, who were well-to-do trades people. As luck would have it, their home was directly opposite the de Mazenod's apartment, separated only by a narrow alley. Thus, one day as Eugene was at his window day-dreaming, Don Bartolo appeared at the opposite window. Bishop de Mazenod recalled years later:

> "M. Eugene! Aren't you afraid of wasting your time at the window like that?"

> "I regret to say I am, Monsieur," I answered, "but how can I help it? I am a foreigner, you know, and we don't have any books in the house." That was what the priest was waiting for.

---

[13] Leflon, vol. 1, pp. 101-102.

[14] Note that the name is pronounced *BAR'tolo.*

"That's no problem, my dear boy. The room I am in is my library, and I have all kinds of books here: Latin, Italian, even French, if you want any."

"There is nothing I want more," I answered him.

Immediately he unfastened the cross-bar which was used for holding the shutters in place and putting a book upon it, passed it over to me across the narrow street which separated our two houses. I finished the book in a matter of hours, for I was always an avid reader. The following day, my father suggested that I return it and thank Don Bartolo. Everything went according to plan.[15]

It was the beginning of a friendship. The next day Eugene returned the book and Don Bartolo put his entire library at the boy's disposal. Henceforth, he also had supper almost nightly with the Zinellis, and the young priest undertook to be Eugene's tutor and spiritual director.

For more than three years Eugene studied under the guidance of Don Bartolo and found him to be a wise spiritual guide. He provided Eugene with a firm and solid foundation in the Ignatian tradition, for the young priest was a great admirer of the suppressed Company of Jesus (later he would join the Society of the Faith of Jesus, whose purpose it was to restore the Jesuit Order). For Eugene, those four years were a decisive period, as he himself claimed: "It was during that time that a true man of God struck the foundations of faith and piety in my soul which he had prepared beforehand by his skillful direction, aided by the Holy Spirit whose instrument he was. And upon these same foundations did God, in his mercy, build the edifice of my spiritual life."[16]

Don Bartolo organized a very strict timetable for Eugene: study the entire morning (Latin, the Bible and some Church history). Eugene and Don Bartolo together recited the Little Office of the Blessed Virgin daily. There was also a special devotion to the Sacred Heart. "I went to Confession every Saturday and received Communion every Sunday. Prayer and the reading of good books were the only exceptions I made to my rigid schedule." Among the readings proposed by Don Bartolo for Eugene were "the edifying letters on the foreign missions written by the Missionaries of the Company of Jesus."[17] "I was only twelve years old when God planted in my heart the first real desires to devote my life to the missions."[18]

Years later, Eugene told his friend Jacques Jeancard that from that period onward he felt a great desire to devote his life to the conversion of non-

---

[15] *Mission,* March, 1866, pp. 126-127.
[16] Leflon, vol. 1, p. 106.
[17] To Father Tamburini, Oct.2, 1855; in *Oblate Writings,* vol. 11, p. 285, n. 1292.
[18] Ibid.

believers. The years in Venice were a time of true blessing. The boy found happiness in the Zinelli family and grew both humanly and spiritually. "My vocation to the priestly life," he was to say later, "dates back to those days." Moreover, an indication of how healthy was the education imparted by Don Bartolo Zinelli can be found in something Eugene wrote when he was only 12: "I shall fulfill those duties at fixed times, but with the freedom of God's Spirit which will allow me to respond to whatever the circumstances demand."[19]

"Freedom" is the key word, because it would be an important value throughout Eugene's life. We see this in an episode from his later life. The aftermath of the 1848 Revolution brought universal male suffrage – the first time that the right to vote was granted to the ordinary classes. However, a serious problem arose. To exercise this new right, voters had to go to the capital of the canton or to a major city. For those living in an urban centre there was no problem, but the majority of people lived in remote rural villages and hamlets where there was no voting. Thus, for a peasant, it meant walking all the way to the county seat to vote.

Eugene de Mazenod was then Bishop of Marseilles. He wrote a pastoral letter to all parish priests telling them to dispense from the obligation of Sunday Mass all persons for whom that obligation would pose a problem in the exercise of their franchise. It is worth noting that the French general elections of 1848 took place on EASTER SUNDAY!

Family Break-Up

The Reign of Terror had spent itself by 1795 when the Directoire took over. So, taking Eugene's sister Ninette with her, his mother left Venice for Aix to recover the family's properties. Her background was bourgeois, so by divorcing her aristocratic husband she stood in good stead to salvage some of them. Which is exactly what she did, eventually, changing from Mme. la Présidente de Mazenod to plain Mme. Joannis. Moreover, in the marriage contract the Joannis family had astutely stipulated that the dowry remain in Marie-Rose's name. Aided by the business acumen of her formidable mother, she was successful in not only recovering the Joannis properties but most of what had belonged to her aristocrat husband as well. Thus she could write to him, saying, "You now have nothing," and adding that if ever he returned to France he would find that he had all the debts while she had all the property. Where did that leave Eugene?: caught in the middle, between parents who had divorced over a question of money.

---

[19] Rey, vol. 1, p. 26.

The departure of Marie-Rose and Ninette left the young de Mazenod in Venice with his father, two uncles and a grand-uncle. Fortunately for Eugene, there was also the wholesome influence of the Zinelli family to fall back on. Signora Zinelli became his second mother.

The relationship of Eugene's parents leave us with questions. Were money and property the only reasons for the de Mazenod break-up? Probably not. We have already alluded to the 15-year age gap between husband and wife and to the differences in their education, but an even more serious problem was the constant interference and animosity of Charles-Antoine's jealous mother-in-law and neurotic sister-in-law. Years later, he would write to La Poire, an old friend, about the coming of his wife and the other two Joannis women into his exile with Eugene in Nice:

> I foresaw at the time everything I should have to suffer from this reunion, but was powerless to prevent it, and I cannot possibly tell you everything the poor *chevalier* and I had to put up with from that female triumvirate. We were compelled to share the same room and both of us were ignored as though we were lackeys. They took complete charge of everything, decided everything, gave all the orders. If by chance we wished to remonstrate with any one of them, we saw the three of them rise up against us like latter-day furies. Opposing them would have accomplished nothing but commotion. Thus, we took the only line of conduct available to wise and prudent people . . . retiring to our room.

After the mother-in-law was called back to Aix by her husband, Eugene's father wrote in the same letter: "My wife changed completely. She became sweet, obliging, pleasant, attentive; in a word, perfect!"[20]

What about the de Mazenod property in St-Laurent-du-Verdon? It must be recalled that the holdings of nobles had been confiscated and had become state property. So how was it possible that Eugene's mother managed to recover the de Mazenod country estate of St-Laurent-du-Verdon? The answer lies in the shrewd bourgeois business acumen of Eugene's maternal grandmother Joannis, aided by the enigmatic cousin-companion, Roze-Joannis. Somehow they were able to convince authorities to hand over the de Mazenod properties or at least delay the sale, so the divorced bourgeois wife of an exiled nobleman could acquire them. Prof. Jean Tulard of the Sorbonne says of that period: "Some indeed, by using the names of third parties, or through fictitious divorces or astute ruses, succeeded in recovering their noble property virtually intact."[21]

---

[20] Leflon, vol. 1, p. 80.
[21] Fayard, *Histoire de France,* vol.4, p. 171.

Is there anything suspicious in the relationship of Eugene's mother and her cousin, Roze-Joannis? Many say so. However, Eugene himself, who never took any pains to hide his dislike of his mother's cousin, wrote to his father: "He is so ugly that you have nothing to worry about." That reads like the reaction of a young man who deeply loves both his parents and doesn't want to see either of them get hurt. History shows that Roze-Joannis did not quite fit the righteous and holy Jansenist image he took pains to project. Although he had indeed been a seminarian with the Oratorian Fathers in his youth, he later fathered at least one illegitimate child in Grans.

The situation in Venice was becoming increasingly unsafe for French émigrés because the Republican armies were advancing against the city. It was time to move on – this time to Naples. The de Mazenods travelled by boat on the Adriatic, from Venice to Manfredonia, situated on the spur of the Italian boot. The distance is only about 600 kilometres, yet the voyage took a whole month at sea. From Manfredonia they went overland to Naples.

Naples

The Neapolitan exile lasted a year – from January 1, 1798, to January 3, 1799. Eugene was 16, an age that should have been carefree. But being surrounded by stodgy old uncles and a morose father in his 50s can mean "a year weighted down by dreary monotony," as he himself wrote. Again Eugene was at loose ends, greatly missing the warmth of the Zinelli home and Don Bartolo's guidance, even though the good priest sent him letters with precise counsel. Of this period in his life, Eugene later wrote: "I no longer had my good friends, the Zinellis, near me, nor did I have any daily occupation or association suited to my tastes and inclinations . . . . What a dreary existence for a youth of sixteen, with nothing to do, no way of using his time, no companionship, and no place to go except the church where I would serve my uncle's Mass."[22] Nor did it help his spirit when in his mother's letters to his father he read such cold words as: "I thank you, as well as *your son*, for your last note of October 9 . . . . Allow me to remind *your son* that merely because a person has a very strong and loud voice, it does not mean that he cannot have a sweet character and a very sweet disposition . . . ."[23]

To pass the time, Eugene studied German for three months and made remarkable progress. Then his teacher died. That basic knowledge of

---

[22] Leflon, vol. 1, p. 172.
[23] Ibid., p. 171.

German probably came in handy later, when, as a young priest in Aix, he would tend the Austrian prisoners in the Napoleonic wars.

Naples and Sicily formed a single realm known as the Kingdom of the Two Sicilies. With the French Republican Army approaching Naples and the lower classes, the *lazzaroni*, rioting in the streets, the king had forbidden émigrés to leave, fearing that there might be spies among them. But thanks to M. le Président's good relations with the crown and to the unpredictable and strange queen, Marie Caroline, the de Mazenods were not only granted permission to leave for Sicily but given a pension as well, along with an invitation to flee Naples in the company of the royal family on Admiral Nelson's flagship. Eugene's father gracefully declined the latter honour, preferring to go on a Portuguese ship commanded by an old family friend, the Comte de Puységur. Nelson's ship set sail first and almost foundered in a fearful storm that contributed to the death of one of the king's sons. The Portuguese flagship kept to port a full week longer, affording Eugene some harrowing experiences with the rioting populace as he tried to recover a few additional family belongings ashore. The storm was still blowing fiercely as the de Mazenods left the port of Naples. It was a dramatic end to yet another step in their long exile.[24]

Palermo

Eugene lived as an exile in Palermo roughly from his 17th to his 20th year – from January, 1799, to October, 1802. It was a complete about-face for the young man, definitely the worldly period in his life, and it continued for a while, even after he was finally permitted to return to Aix.

Palermo gave Eugene a second home but in a setting very different from the Zinellis in Venice. Here the Duke and Duchess of Cannizzaro accepted him as their own. With two younger sons, the Duchess was happy to have the 17-year-old émigré there as their friend. A saintly woman, she exerted a positive influence on Eugene. But at the same time, she was a lady of high society and brought the young man into a very exclusive circle of dukes, princes and all sorts of other nobility.

The changes in Eugene's life must have buffeted him about psychologically: Venice, a time of serious formation, prayer and study with the Zinellis and their two holy priest-sons, abandoned by his mother but virtually adopted by the Zinellis. Then there was Naples, with nothing to do and the divorce of his parents. And now, Palermo, with another mother and a whole new

---

[24] Leflon, vol. 1, p. 183.

glittering world of high society. Noteworthy here is the close friendship he struck up with the Duc de Berry, son of the future King Charles X of France.

Eugene frankly enjoyed this new life among the cream of Palermo society, having everything, including a valet, at his disposal. Indeed, the better to fit into the picture, he even gave himself the title of "Count" (in Italian he was referred to in the diminutive as *il contino*). The tutor of the Cannizzaros' sons was assigned to complete Eugene's piecemeal education. He studied history, literature, the handling of firearms, horsemanship, etc. Judging from his memoirs, he also appears to have been good at sports, a strong swimmer, and in good physical condition. He recounts how he badly dislocated his shoulder while diving from a boat, yet continued swimming a long distance.[25]

Eugene's Spiritual Life in Palermo

The young de Mazenod continued corresponding with Don Bartolo Zinelli who also wrote regularly to his former pupil, urging him to remain faithful to his principles. Thoughts of a vocation to the priesthood, however, seemed to have vanished for the moment, even though he continued faithful to the main duties of his Christian life. A new air of arrogance, extreme self-assurance, even conceit, was increasingly apparent in Eugene. In a telling letter, his sister Ninette chided:

> From what you and your friends write about the way you pass your time, it seems to me, my dear, that you have no lack of amusements . . . . Aren't you afraid of leading too frivolous a life? You used to be very pious once upon a time. Indeed, you would not even shake hands with ladies unless they were very old! If you have lost your high ideals, then I am afraid I shall have to give you advice, you who give so much of it to others, and God will bless me for it, too. Most likely it is not the only advice I shall ever give you, but even now, I can hear you sputtering at the liberty I have taken, so I won't say anything more except to assure you that nothing can ever change the affection we owe each other.[26]

Spiritual Groping

One of the difficulties in several of the early de Mazenod biographies is that they only mention sentences like the one where Ninette teases Eugene about only shaking hands with old ladies. Such editing takes him out of context and gives a false and plaster-saint image.

---

[25] Leflon, vol. 1, p. 198.

[26] Ibid., p. 219.

It is also apparent toward the end of Eugene's stay in Sicily that a kind of yearning emptiness began to pervade his spirit. He felt alone and lonely in the midst of that glittering life which had held such attraction in other moments. Years later in his memoirs he noted:

> I was far from taking part in these amusements; much to the contrary. It is a strange thing, but whenever I found myself in the midst of it, its noisy music and its completely worldly gaiety, I would feel my heart contract and sadness would take hold of me; whereupon I would slip off to some quiet spot and there, away from all those who seemed foolish to me, I gave myself over to serious and even melancholy thoughts, almost to the point of weeping. Several times acquaintances of mine came upon me unexpectedly while I was in that mood and, unable to understand, tried to draw me out of it. It was simply that I was out of my element.[27]

The last sentence is worth emphasizing: *"I was out of my element."* That feeling of emptiness was a grace of God. God allowed Eugene to feel out of his element in the social whirl of Palermo precisely because he was preparing him to discover his authentic vocation. When in Jewish rabbinical literature the rabbis comment on the psalms they speak of *the exile of the soul*. That is exactly the grace which young de Mazenod received toward the end of his Palermo exile: God made him feel exiled – out of his element – in order to invite him to look for his genuine homeland.

This is the beginning of a crisis which was to continue for several years more in Aix, a crisis accentuated by the death of the Duchess of Cannizzaro. He had been without his own mother for so long that the Duchess had taken her place. Deeply affected, Eugene wrote to his father: "This wound will never heal. I was awake all night. I shall never be able to shed enough tears for such a kind mother."[28]

Nonetheless, he did not turn to prayer or spiritual reading to get over his suffering. Instead, he buried himself in the long and mournful *Thoughts on Life, Death and Immortality* by Young, an obscure English romantic poet. Eugene describes the author and his poem as follows: "A wonderful man and, what is more important, the finest and most sympathetic friend I could possibly have at this moment. We both share the same feelings . . . . His writing is sublime and makes for reflective and satisfying reading." It is well to remember that Eugene was a product of the romantic age, a time when a new style of artistic thought began to replace Neo-classicism and Rococo. Moreover, like most young men at his age he was going through a romantic period. Nonetheless, his father rightly chided him: "You should discard this

---

[27] Leflon, vol. 1, p. 220.
[28] Ibid., p. 223.

reading which pleases you so much. In nourishing your grief it serves only to prevent the effect of the remedies which the doctors prescribe to relieve your sorrow."[29]

This, then, was Eugene de Mazenod at 20, tossed to and fro by circumstance during the most delicate years of his life.

Return to Aix-en-Provence

Eugene de Mazenod left France as a little boy of eight. He returned on October 24, 1802, as a young man of 20. Those years were a constant struggle between a worldly and shallow way of living, which obviously fascinated him, and the inner pull of deepening Christian life which eventually would bring him to the Good Friday experience. It is certainly safe to say that at this point that the priesthood was far from uppermost in his thoughts, yet, a fierce struggle was taking place in his heart. Without being fully aware of it, he was searching for God. He was back in France again, yet still in exile – an exile deep within him that yearned for home.

Coming Home

His arrival in Marseilles was a deep disappointment. There was no one there at the wharf to welcome him, not a single member of the Joannis family. It is hard to understand his mother's attitude: after all, she had not seen her son in seven years. One would think she would have rushed to meet him. Instead, she went off on an excursion with her companion-cousin, Roze-Joannis, and simply sent a cryptic and useless note of instruction to Marseilles. Eugene waited four days at the home of one of his father's friends in the port city and then finally set off on his own without any assurance that he would even find anyone home in Aix.

St-Laurent-du-Verdon

Eugene's stay in Aix was short-lived. Military service was compulsory in post-revolutionary France, but not every young man had to serve – only those were drafted whose names were pulled in a kind of national lottery. Even then, however, a man could escape the draft by paying a substitute to take one's place. Fearing that her son might be one of the unlucky ones to be called up and knowing that a substitute would be cheaper to hire among the peasants of the countryside than in the city – the matter of money again – Eugene's mother sent him off to live for five months in what had been his

---

[29] Leflon, vol. 1, p. 224.

father's country manor at St-Laurent-du-Verdon. There, on November 27, a month after he arrived in France, he was inscribed in the list of the commune under number 41 as Citizen Mazenod. He was able to return briefly to Aix, but political circumstances forced a rapid retreat to the run-down and all-but-empty country manor of St-Laurent by the beginning of June.

Even today, St-Laurent is a sleepy little hamlet – certainly a far cry from Palermo or Aix – and for five months Eugene again languished with nothing to do but count the days. On August 1, 1803, he wrote to his father: "At this moment I feel anything but young. Sagging beneath the weight of my twenty-one years, after camping here at St-Laurent for more than a month, I feel like a decrepit old man . . . . I am dying of boredom and loneliness."[30] A month later, he wrote to his mother: "Before returning to France, had I foreseen that I should have to dwell on the mountain apart, I would never have left . . . . My desire (was) to be near you and to live with you."[31]

At the manor, he must have been quite insufferable, strutting around like a proper martinet under his parasol, inspecting the work of the peasants in the fields and, as he himself wrote to his father, "acting like the lord of the manor." Certainly, he showed little grasp of the new order that had taken over in France. Nor did the peasant girls of St-Laurent hold much attraction for him. Later, writing to his father from Aix, he told him: "There was nothing of interest for me there, for the country nymphs smell like a dung-heap and their skin must be impregnated with a triple layer of the extracted essence."[32]

Finally in December he could go back to the city. He wrote his father, "I have left that hateful solitude after five months of exile. They seemed more like five centuries."[33]

Frivolous Life in Aix

Leaving St-Laurent was like a release from prison. Joining his aristocratic friends, Eugene threw himself into a dizzying whirl of social life. He wrote his father, "Lovely Aix has so many delights. Twice a week we get together at the Odeon for singing and dancing . . . . Very often, too, we attend musical comedies. Did I say musical comedies? They are more like bad operas . . . . I go to these things to have a good laugh."[34] Airs of superiority and

---

[30] Leflon, vol. 1, p. 244.

[31] Ibid.

[32] Ibid., p. 271.

[33] Ibid., p. 244.

[34] Ibid., p. 255.

insufferable conceit continually show through in letters of this period. At 23, to his father, Eugene stated:

> You would think that the 54 francs it cost to have my portrait engraved were well spent; but I am very sorry to have to tell you that it was money wasted. I am furious with this M. Chrétien who, after making a drawing that was perfectly life-like, made an engraving of it which was not. I was expecting that he would flatter me, but he had the talent to make me completely repugnant. From my nose to my mouth he established a monstrous distance; he obligingly provided me with a long, pointed chin and thought it good to place that chin on top of a second one. All these features give the lower part of my face an exaggerated length and leave it horribly out of proportion . . . . Since people claim to recognize me in this portrait, despite all its defects, I am sending you one of the engravings.[35]

Eugene's mother was shocked by her noble son's extravagance in his choice of costly clothing and jewellery and not infrequently voiced her displeasure. But as far as he was concerned, nothing was too fine or too expensive when it came to a de Mazenod keeping up with the latest fashions. Indeed, he must have been one of the dandies of the city, a regular *muscatin*.[36]

Two Marriage Proposals That Foundered

Twice Eugene almost married. Writing to his father, he stated, "I want a rich wife, *richissima e buona*" (rich and good). That certainly makes him sound venal and calculating, but in 1989, Oblate Father Kazimierz Lubowicki discovered a hitherto unpublished letter that Eugene wrote to his mother when he was already in the seminary of St-Sulpice. It presents a very different Eugene de Mazenod. He wrote: "You must have found on my desk a small book entitled *L'art d'aimer* (*The Art of Loving*). That book fell into my hands and I put it there to burn it . . . . It is poetry, well written, but bad. It could be dangerous for certain people."

His assessment of the book as bad poetry means that he had read it. In the same letter he mentions another book that should be gotten rid of, *L'ami des femmes* (*The Women's Friend*), that he likewise must have read. Thus we get an idea of some of his romantic reading matter at the time, which

---

[35] Roche, p. 18.

[36] When the Reign of Terror ended with Robespierre's fall, the 5-man Directoire took over. A sort of release-reaction set in among the young people, especially the rich, who had nothing to do but cause mischief and party the time away. They were the *jeunesse dorée* – the golden youth – the equivalent of the British dandies of the same period. They ran wild and dressed extravagantly and were heavily perfumed (their perfume was called *musque* in French, hence their name, *muscatins*). Most of the excesses and ugly scenes initially characterizing the group in Paris probably did not filter down to the provinces, but the materialist mentality certainly would have done so.

somewhat modifies the impression that Eugene only wanted to get married for the money involved. Still, money was definitely a consideration.

The first young woman, whom his mother had found for him while he was still in Sicily, was from a monied bourgeois family named Jauffret. She had "a lovely face and a fine figure," and "all the details were about to be settled," he wrote his father from Aix, when the girl died "of consumption." "The plan fell through. Let's drop the subject," he concluded tersely.

The second prospect, anonymous to history, was also found by Eugene's mother and by her cousin Roze-Joannis through an intermediary, but the dowry was a paltry 40,000 francs at marriage and another 20,000 at the death of her parents. He wrote indignantly to his father: "Can you imagine how interested I was in all this! Forty thousand francs when I want 150,000! And middle-class! How do you think that fits in with my plans? If they cannot do better than that, I'm afraid I shall die a virgin, if you'll pardon the expression."[37]

Disappointed by these failures, Eugene planned unrealistically to go back to Sicily where he hoped to find a well-connected noble friend who could put in a good word for him so that he might become an officer in the king's Palatine Guard. This is another sign of how dissatisfied he was with his life and how he was struggling to find his way. But to go to Sicily he needed a passport, which was flatly refused him in Paris. He had to stay on in Aix again.

Spiritual Stirrings

It seems almost incongruous that amidst all this shallowness, something was a stirring within Eugene – an urge to live a deeper Christian life. Indeed, in December, 1805, he was already on the path leading to his conversion. That was when he joined a confraternity at the service of prisoners. Typically, after only one week in the society, he was protesting against the baker who provided bad bread to the men behind bars. Eugene organized numerous collections to aid the poor but was too energetic and pushed too hard for the rest of the confraternity, who were considerably older than he. Frustrated by the group's plodding pace, he resigned after only nine months (although, apparently, he had already risen by then to the post of director of the confraternity). Here we already see a feature of his character: deep

---

[37] Leflon, vol. 1, p. 258. In the English version of Canon Leflon's biography of Eugene de Mazenod, Father Flanagan discreetly translated the expression that Eugene used in French as *virgin*. In reality, *puceau* is a disparaging way of referring to someone who is incapable of getting beyond puberty.

sensitivity that cannot tolerate injustice, especially towards the poor, even when they are convicted of crimes.

Vocation Amid Contrasts

Thus we see Eugene de Mazenod, in his twenties – a normal young man of his age, with all the struggles and contrast which that entailed. He was haughty (doesn't a man at 20 know everything?); he enjoyed the theatre and dancing. Yet he also thanked God for "not having sinned with 'the daughters of Babylon,'" indicating that even in his shallow world, he stayed true to his moral standards. Moreover, that old yearning reawakened within him, that dissatisfaction which made him strive to commit himself more generously as a Christian. Saying he had lost his priestly vocation would be simplistic. It may have been on the back-burner for a while, but during that time, deep down, he was always looking for a meaningful life, searching for God, without really knowing where to look. And yet God was present in Eugene's life. He loved him just as he was, but let his chosen one go through moments of darkness and trial. And from time to time he threw some light on the path, assuring him, "I love you, and never did I cease loving you."

Eugene de Mazenod's 1807 Good Friday Experience

Through letters that Eugene wrote we know that a progressive spiritual reawakening began gradually around 1806. He spoke of being "impelled more forcefully than ever by grace" and of "consecrating" himself "entirely to the Lord." In the second meditation of his 1814 retreat, he wrote of his profound Good Friday conversion experience that had taken place in 1807. In the first paragraph below, he recounts the wrenching encounter with Christ that took hold of him as he attended the Good Friday liturgy. The second paragraph is a meditative look back at the occurrence at a distance of seven years:

> I looked for happiness outside of God and, to my sorrow, looked there for too long a time. How many times, in my past life, did my heart, torn, tormented, throw itself in desperation at its God whom it had abandoned. Can I ever forget those bitter tears which the sight of the Cross caused to stream from my eyes one Good Friday? Ah! They welled up from the depths of my heart and nothing could stop them. They were too abundant to hide from the people who, like myself, were attending that moving service. I was in mortal sin, and it was this that caused my sorrow. It was a moment singularly different from what I had experienced in certain other instances. Never was my soul more relieved, and never did it feel happier. And it was simply because, during that torrent of tears, despite my grief, or better, by reason of it, my soul leapt toward its final end, toward God, its only good, whose loss it felt so keenly. Why say more? Could I ever do

justice describing what I felt at that moment? Just thinking about it fills my heart with sweet consolation.

Thus, I looked for happiness outside of God, and outside of him found only affliction and misfortune. But happily – happily a thousand times over – that good Father, despite my unworthiness, showered me with the riches of his mercy. The least I can do now is make up for lost time and redouble my love for him. Let all my actions, thoughts, etc., be directed toward that end. What more glorious occupation than, in all and for all, to act only for God, to love him above all, to love him all the more because I have come to love him so late. Ah! The happiness of heaven begins here below . . . . Let us choose now![38]

At the beginning of the preceding excerpt Eugene evoked the past *"I looked for happiness outside of God . . ."* – the internal struggle between the frivolities of Aix and his disillusionment in what he found. *"My torn and tormented heart turned back in desperation to its God . . . ."* makes that struggle evident. Eugene was never the easy-going type who could float along life's stream on whatever the current offered. Instead, he was the kind of person who had to give deep meaning to his life, even if it meant swimming against the current. And so, in answer to that struggle, God's grace touched his heart and even showed itself physically. In this, it is striking how closely Eugene's retreat notes parallel the conversion of St. Augustine. Indeed, one can find many similarities in the lives of the two.

"Those Bitter Tears . . ."

The *gift* of tears has little to do with sentimentality. It comes from the Holy Spirit. Indeed, it is a grace that makes one feel physically the immense gap between God's love and forgiveness and one's response to that love. In St. Luke's Gospel, for example, just after Peter had denied Jesus for the third time and was warming himself at the fire (Luke 22: 54-62) "the Lord turned and looked at Peter and Peter remembered the words of the Lord . . . . He went out and began to weep bitterly." That forgiving look told Peter how much the Lord loved him and how badly he had responded to that love. Hence the bitter tears. In the same way, at the realization of how very much God loved him – him, Eugene de Mazenod! – and of how he was ignoring that infinite love, Eugene's heart was smitten by that special grace of the Spirit, and he shed "those bitter tears." They were, in a way, his response to the anguish of the Church, reflected in the Lamentations of Good Friday, a Church weeping because her children do not respond to the love of God.

---

[38] Archives of the General Postulation, DM IV-2, OMI, Rome; also in Leflon, vol. 1, p. 279. (Note, however, that there is a typographical error in Leflon: "God, its only God" should read "God, its only *Good*.")

With this realization, his heart could sing along with Saint Paul the great hymn of Philippians 2:5-11:

> Jesus Christ, . . . though he was in the form of God, did not regard equality with God something to be hoarded. Rather, he emptied himself, taking the form of a slave, coming in human likeness; and found human in appearance, he humbled himself, becoming obedient to death, even death on a cross. Because of this, God greatly exalted him and bestowed on him the name that is above every name, that at the name of Jesus, every knee should bend, of those in heaven and on earth and under the earth, and every tongue confess that Jesus Christ is Lord, to the glory of God the Father.

"I Was in Mortal Sin . . ."

There have been all sorts of speculation about the nature of Eugene's mortal sin. Frankly, it strikes us as prurient meddling. The young man had mentioned to his sister on a number of occasions that he considered the theatre and the dances he had so often attended to have been mortal sins; nonetheless, he, like each of us, is entitled to the privacy of his conscience. He says that his soul was in mortal sin? So be it. What is important here is to realize that the greatest sin consists in knowingly ignoring the immensity of God's unconditional love, in turning one's back on the loving Christ who is always present within us. That is mortal sin. Certainly Eugene felt the weight of it on that fateful Good Friday in Aix.

"A Moment Singularly Different . . ."

This phrase clearly indicates that the grace of Good Friday was very special, yet it was not the only grace Eugene had experienced on the road along which God was leading him to an ever-deepening relationship. What made the Good Friday experience special, however, was that it was decisive. Henceforth Eugene de Mazenod's life would be unified – ever more consecrated to the love of God. Yet he had already been led to that moment by other experiences of God.

"Never Was My Soul More Relieved, Never Did It Feel Happier . . ."

He could never have said that were it not for the grace of God touching him so deeply.

"God Its Only Good . . ."

Eugene had discovered God's love, there before the crucifix. When he speaks of God, it is Christ to whom he refers as his only good. He had discovered that the loving God, the loving Lord, is the only one who meets all the desires of the heart. After that, he felt relief and blessed peace. He was happy, at last.

This was the special grace of Good Friday. It was not the final act, and he was still far from perfect, but that was the decisive moment: he had crossed over. Seven years later it remained so decisive that Eugene could recall every emotion, every feeling. And in retrospect he could clearly recognize the impact of the Good Friday experience on his life.

Like the eucharistic Christ, every person born to this earth is *chosen* from all eternity by the Father, blessed by him, broken, too, and meant thus to be given to humankind in service. Often we do not realize that we are the recipients of such wonderful grace, but when we do, it is the start of a journey to sainthood. For example, while Paul was persecuting the Church, he did not have the least idea that he had been chosen by God. It was only after he had become aware of his brokenness that he could see how the Lord had blessed him. Then he saw that God had been guiding him with the love that had been there even before his birth, so that he could be given to spreading the Good News among the gentiles. When he writes to the Ephesians he impresses on them that "before the world was made, he chose us in Christ" (Ephesians 1:4). And to the Galatians he says, "From my mother's womb he called me by his grace to reveal his Son in me so that I might preach the good news about him to the gentiles" (Galatians 1:15). Note that Paul says, "God chose to reveal his son *in* me," not "*to* me." This means that the grace received by Paul, just like the grace received by Eugene, is not mere intellectual knowledge of Jesus Christ. It is a spiritual gift that reaches the very depths of the heart, bringing about an unshakable conviction and a strong attachment to the person of Jesus.

Like Paul, Eugene de Mazenod was "grasped by Christ" (Phil. 3:12), who purchased the Church "at the cost of his own blood." The grace of the Good Friday experience would thereafter be the guiding force of his apostolate. Henceforth, Eugene's life would be more and more unified around Christ. Personal attachment to Jesus Christ the Saviour would become the prime characteristic of his charism.

Like Paul, too, Eugene de Mazenod could see that "God converts everything into good for those who love him" (Romans 8:28). He began to see that everything in his life – every success, every failure – somehow entered into his spiritual progress. Every failure can be an occasion for the Lord's grace, "even sins," St. Augustine adds. Eugene felt that very strongly, contrasting God's love to his "mortal sin."

Oblate spiritual theologian Kelly Nemeck says that in our spiritual journey God acts in us in two ways: by testing us in the obscure night and by transforming union. They are the two arms of God's all-embracing love. Rembrandt's striking painting of the Prodigal Son portrays the same idea by showing the Father with different hands: one larger and masculine, pushing against the son; the other, the delicate hand of a woman, a mother's loving hand. The painting helps us get a deeper insight into God's all-embracing love. That is the history of our own life as well.

In Eugene's life, the darkness that obscured God's love happened when, as a young man, he felt out of his element and grew conscious of his inner exile. God made him experience it deeply. The progressive transforming union was his Christian education, the influence of Don Bartolo, the searching for a more generous Christian life. There we can see Eugene in the two arms of God's all-embracing love.

Like Paul, Eugene de Mazenod was the object of compassionate love and would became the apostle of compassionate love against the severity and self-righteousness of Jansenism. Later, as he prepared for ordination, he would write:

> The different situations into which God has placed me . . . let me see clearly that his way of acting toward me is one of predilection . . . . I consider all those favours as a continuation of creation – as if God, after having formed me, took me by the hand, and placed me in those situations, telling me, "I created you so that you love and serve me." Lord, you have created me for yourself. All I want is to be yours – to work and to die for you.[39]

---

[39] *Selected Texts*, p. 256.

II

Evangelizing the Poor

Within months of the coup of 18 *Brumaire* that brought him to power, Napoleon indicated a desire to reconcile the French government with the Church. The reigning pope was Pius VII, a humble and holy Benedictine, more mystic than politician. Elected to the papacy just a year earlier, the pontiff was obviously overjoyed at the prospect of a rapprochement and acceded to Napoleon's wishes to the extent he deemed possible without compromising the papacy. Article 3 of the Concordat is proof of that. But it quickly became evident that what the emperor really wanted was to control and to use the Church for his own ends, even in lands he conquered. For him, the pope was a pawn on his chessboard – a pawn he was determined to convert into a rubber stamp. Thus began the power struggle between an imperious emperor who could brook no opposition and a pope whose meekness he had misjudged for weakness.

The Concordat of 1801

The Concordat of 1801 restored Catholicism in France, recognizing it as "the religion of the French majority" – very different from its position as "the religion of France" in the *ancien régime*. Although it was a hard bargain, the new arrangements, hammered out through eight complicated drafts, brought distinct advantages to the Church. They were reduced, however, by the Organic Articles which Napoleon unilaterally appended nine months later in 1802, tightening the state's hold over the Church and restricting papal intervention in France.

Considering its content, the Concordat was remarkably short: a preamble and 17 articles. However, it is Article 3 which interests us. It reads in part, "To the titulars of French episcopal sees, His Holiness declares that he expects of them . . . every kind of sacrifice, even that of their sees . . . for the good of the Church." Thus, Article 3 compelled all the *ancien régime* bishops (all who were bishops before the Revolution and who had thus been nominated by the king) to resign. On that measure, the pope went the limit, but his intention was to create an atmosphere of peace and harmony in France by putting all bishops on the same footing.

The prelates affected by this measure, having suffered the brunt of the Revolution and having held fast, felt deeply hurt and betrayed by the decision, as though their fidelity despite so many trials had been inconsequential. Canon Fortuné de Mazenod wrote ruefully, "Article 3 seems frightful to me and I am dismayed by the consequences it will bring about. Such an agreement is entirely without precedent and is contrary to all principles."[1] Nineteen-year-old Eugene, still in Sicily, had a far more intense reaction He violently disagreed with the papacy and could not accept the universal pardon and the indulgence for all who submitted to the Republic. Writing to his father, he railed:

> I send you the news sheets, my dear papa. They contain the Legate's brief for granting a plenary indulgence to all Frenchmen. If that is the only thing needed to wash them of their crimes, then I can only say that there must be no end to apostolic powers.... I question the validity of such a pardon and I demand unconditionally the complete restitution of everything they have stolen. No restitution, no pardon. . . . A worthy canon of the Bishop's palace . . . was enthusiastic in praising the pope's handling of this matter, and called the concordat a masterpiece of politics in which the pope showed superlative ingenuity.... I considered his opinion too outlandish to let pass, but I had no desire to argue with him because he is one of those creatures who, for no other reason than ignorance, think they know everything. "Monsieur l'Abbé," I said to him, "no matter what you say, on this occasion the pope has sullied himself."[2]

Eugene used the Italian words, *il papa si ha sporcificato*, which meant that he had dishonoured himself by stooping to base means. This reaction is important in tracing Eugene's adherence to the pope. At 19 he was headstrong and French, putting the king before the Revolution. Over the years we will see how a change took place.

Absolutist Rule

Napoleon was a superb organizer. Indeed, he brought about reforms that France still enjoys today, including the establishment of the Bank of France, the centralization of tax collection, the codification of law along classic Roman models, and the reform and extension of secondary and university education. But as emperor he suffered from a messianic flaw – he was absolutely absolutist. Everything had to depend directly on him and he had to be in complete control of the last detail. Hence he viewed any kind of

---

[1] Leflon, vol. 1, p. 233.

[2] Ibid., p. 233.

society, including religious, as dangerous or subversive. His solution: ban them all.

Napoleon sought to exercise control in every area of life, with the feared secret police under Fouché watching all. The press was gagged and the minutest aspects of education strictly monitored – even down to what could and could not be taught in catechism. Indeed, there was a chapter on obedience to the emperor. Soon Pius VII found himself opposing Napoleon in all his decisions. Renewed war between France and her neighbours worsened their relations even more, especially when the emperor expected the pope's cooperation and the pope felt obliged to stay neutral. When Pius VII refused to support the Continental Blockade, a measure meant to isolate England, Napoleon forthwith annexed the Papal States. Rome was occupied on May 18, 1809, for which the pope excommunicated the emperor and his invading army. That was when he was taken prisoner.

The Pope, a Prisoner

It seems, initially at least, that making the pope a prisoner may have been a comedy of errors. In Vienna, on May 17, 1809, Napoleon had annexed the Papal States to France with the stroke of a pen and had declared Rome a free imperial city. To the accompaniment of artillery salvoes, General Miollis, whose troops had occupied the Eternal City three months earlier, ran the French flag up the staff atop ancient Castel Sant'Angelo. The pope's answer was ready. By next morning Rome's walls were plastered with the text of a papal bull excommunicating "the usurpers of Peter's patrimony, the agitators, advisors, adherents and executors" of that violation. The emperor's name was not mentioned, but obviously he fell under the excommunication.

Nobody could ever accuse Napoleon of having religious scruples, so personally he could not have cared less about being excommunicated. But what about his image? What would be the reaction of the people whom he was trying to persuade that he governed as "the anointed of the Lord"? That is what infuriated him. His pique was obvious in a letter he wrote to his brother-in-law, Murat, in Naples: "I received word that the pope has excommunicated me. He is a mad fool who should be locked up." The emperor's subordinates in Rome took him at his word. The next day the pope was arrested and taken under escort from the Quirinal Palace. All he took with him was his breviary.[3]

---

[3] *Nouvelle Histoire de l'Église,* vol. 4, pp. 276-294.

The pope was now in Napoleon's hands, but like a hot potato. The emperor did not know what to do with so meek yet so recalcitrant a prisoner. He had Pius VII transferred to Savona on the Ligurian coast, trying to make it appear that the pope was his guest and hoping at the same time to soften up the old man so he could eventually take him in triumph as a puppet to Paris. Indeed, to facilitate the softening-up, he had rounded up 28 cardinals, including the papal secretary of state, Cardinal Pacca, all of whom had refused to recognize the emperor's actions. They were stripped of their scarlet and sent to Paris – Pacca to prison, the rest to house arrest where they could not influence the pope. Henceforth, because of the simple black cassocks they were forced to wear, they were known as the Black Cardinals.

The problem remained, however, that Pius VII would not cooperate. Instead, he chose purposely to continue living as a prisoner rather than as a "guest," refusing among other things to confirm the investiture of bishops nominated by the emperor. Soon there were vacant sees all over France, even Paris. One thing led to another, and in 1812 Napoleon could take no more. He moved the pope to Fontainebleau, just outside Paris, but not in glory with cheering crowds, as had been the case when the pontiff went to preside at the coronation of the emperor. This time it was a gruelling trip in a closed carriage under military escort, which left the pope near death by the time he arrived in the City of Light.

In Paris, exhausted and ill, he was forced to sign a draft convention in which he made far-reaching concessions (which concessions he repudiated soon after by withdrawing his signature). Before long, military reverses forced Napoleon to return the pope to Savona in January, 1814. Pius VII re-entered Rome in triumph on March 10 of the same year, just as Napoleon abdicated and went into exile on Elba. After Waterloo and the emperor's final exile to St. Helena, all members of the Bonaparte family found themselves proscribed throughout Europe and several had to seek refuge in Rome from the same Pope Pius VII.

Evangelizing the Poor

Eugene Opts for the Priesthood

A little over a year after his Good Friday conversion, and despite grave misgivings on the part of his parents, Eugene entered the seminary of Saint-Sulpice in Paris, in the autumn of 1808. He was 26 years old. His father, still

---

[4] *Oblate Writings,* vol. 14, p. 126 ff., n. 56.

in Palermo, only learned of his son's decision, and then only by accident, when the son had already been in the seminary for almost a year and was already tonsured and in minor orders.[4] Nor was it easy to convince his mother. Just before entering, he had written her from St-Julien on June 29, to allay some of her doubts and anxiety over his decision:

> As the Lord is my witness, what he wants from me is that I renounce the world . . . that I devote myself especially to his service and try to reawaken the faith that is becoming extinct amongst the poor. In a word, that I make myself available to carry out any orders he may wish to give me for his glory and the salvation of the souls he has redeemed by his precious blood.
> . . . If I stayed in the world and established myself therein, taking a wife, setting up my own home and having children, all these things, far from knitting together the bonds that bind us, would be capable of weakening them. . . .
>
> I do not believe that it means a lot to you to see my name perpetuated in this vale of tears. Such vanity did once steal its way into my heart and would have led to my losing all the graces the Lord was reserving for me. Now I do not see, and no doubt you are of the same mind, that there is any other necessity than to see them – our names – written in the book of life.[5]

His mother's misgivings did not die easily. Several times during his seminary days he had to assure her and even plead with her not to interfere with his vocation. Writing her at length on February 28, 1809, he stressed:

> What, then, would you have me doing in the world with all its vanities? ... When the divine Master calls me to Him to serve his Church, at a time when she is abandoned by everyone, am I to resist his voice? . . . Believe me, dear mother, the worry you give yourself over this is a veritable temptation of the devil. You can be sure of this, I know in my heart that I am destined to do some good. The graces that God gave me in the past, those he gives me each day, are a warrant of the even greater ones he is keeping for when I shall be in the ministry. This being so, should one be surprised if the demon does everything in his power to put obstacles in the way of carrying out a project that must be harmful to him? But do we have to listen? I put that question to you. When all is said and done, we are upsetting ourselves in a struggle with phantoms of our own creation . . . .
>
> There are some people who cannot conceive how I could come to a decision to see my name come to an end with me in the obscurity of the sanctuary. My reaction today is one of pity, and I am now ashamed that I lingered for so long over such futile vanity. Now is the time to apply something I said when I was 14 years old and that you reminded me of one day. What family, even of royal blood, would not feel itself honoured to become extinct in the person of a priest, invested with all the powers of Jesus Christ? . . .[6]

---

[5] *Oblate Writings*, vol. 14, p. 55 ff., n. 27.

[6] Ibid., p. 102 ff., n. 46.

A Self-Portrait of Eugene de Mazenod

In October, 1808, upon entering the seminary of St-Sulpice, Eugene was asked by his spiritual director there, the Abbé Antoine du Puget Duclaux, to sketch out a self-portrait of his character. He did so, candidly showing all its flaws and shortcomings: he admitted being self-willed, obstinate, proud, severe, overbearing and unbending; he found correction difficult and had little patience with anyone opposing him. On the other hand, the fine and noble aspects of his character also came out: he was a man of desire – he *wanted* to be holy, a condition absolutely necessary to attain the fullness of Christ. He was warm and generous, almost to a fault, and obviously a man of duty and of charity Above all, he was all heart. His flaws and shortcomings would be the subject of a lifelong struggle, making the beauty and generosity of his character shine through more and more. Even as the aged bishop of Marseilles, he could point to this character portrait if anyone wanted to know who Eugene de Mazenod really was. Over the years his character would be tempered by trials and maturity, but he would always be himself. In reading this summary it is surprising to find how well he knew himself, even at this early juncture in his life.

> You will know my interior life better from the few lines I am about to put down on paper than from any number of my spoken words.

> By character I am lively and impetuous. My desires are impassioned, making me impatient with the least hindrance so that I find delays unbearable. Firm in my resolve, I chafe at anything getting in the way of what I want, and do whatever it takes to overcome even the greatest of obstacles. Solid in my wishes and feelings, I rebel at the mere hint of opposition; if it persists, and unless I am really sure that I am being opposed for a higher good, I become fiery and my spirit seems to acquire new and hitherto unknown resources. What I mean is that I immediately become uncommonly voluble in expressing my ideas, that come tumbling forth in a rush, when I would normally have to drag them out and express them tediously. I manifest the same ease of expression when deeply moved by something and really want others to share my feelings.

> In sharp contrast, if someone gives in instead of opposing me, I am completely disarmed, and if I note embarrassment in a person who tried to defend an untenable position against me, far from gloating and pressing home my arguments, I go out of my way to give him excuses. In either case, if I let slip an ungracious word, I am as upset as if I had committed some serious crime.

> From all this you can see that I have a generous character – you might even call it just, though it is excessively so, at times, for I am naturally inclined to humble anyone who is too forward, yet I leave nothing undone to extol the merits of the humble.

If I am wrong and someone puts me down with a supercilious or triumphalist air, I find it hard to give in and can come up with specious reasons to cover my mistake. But if I am corrected in a spirit of good will and friendship, I will not utter a single word in my defence, and will frankly admit I could have done better, been more thoughtful or expressed myself better.

I am naturally inclined to severity, very determined never to allow myself the least degree of self-indulgence, nor can I tolerate it in others. Moreover, I cannot accept the least compromise in anything to do with duty. Death – and I mean this literally – death seems preferable to transgressing an essential duty.

I hate jealously and regard it as a vice unworthy of a generous heart. Thus, I am delighted when others display worth, even extraordinary worth. If they shine in some area that is foreign to me I will prod myself on to imitate them. And if I foresee that it would be futile to make the effort, I feel chagrined for having wasted my time when young, and frustrated at being stupidly limited to only certain kinds of knowledge.

I have always been exceptionally frank, which causes me to distance myself from giving any sort of flattering compliment that would bring my sincerity into question. In the world, people have come to accept me as I am.

Experience having shown me that my judgments are rarely wide of the mark, I must be careful not to dispense them freely when there is really no need to do so.

I have never been able to content myself by explaining the actions of others on the basis of their apparent intentions. Experience has convinced me that a sure way to make mistakes is to presume good intentions where someone's actions are bad. I prefer to suspend judgment, that is, not to act on conclusions I am tempted to draw from appearances. Moreover, from my infancy it has been noted that I readily pick up nuances that escape the majority of those who see without truly observing; it has helped me almost unerringly to discern the character, tastes, dispositions, and sincerity of the persons with whom I live.

Nature is best observed during early age while it is still evolving with candour. Thus, the attributes of my character, peremptory, steadfast and wilful as it is, can be judged from the following. When I wanted something, I did not beg for it, or wheedle or cajole. Instead, I demanded it in an overbearing tone as though it were my due. If it was refused, I would not cry – with me, crying was as rare as laughter – but would try to take by force what was not given me by consent.

When I was four, one of my uncles took me to the theatre. The noise they were making down on the parterre annoyed me and I am told that, standing on tip-toe to discover who was causing it, I sharply berated the entire ground level with these words which made everyone in our box burst into laughter, *"tout are se descendi!"* – "Just watch out, if I ever come down there!"

41

It was no use trying to get anything out of me by punishment; the only way to do so was to play up to my self-admiration or to get through to my heart.

Given the self-portrait I have just painted, it is hard to understand what a sensitive heart I have – too much so, in fact. It would take too long to enumerate all the stories related to me of my childhood temperament, stories which are truly astounding, all things considered. It was quite normal for me to give away my breakfast, even when I was very hungry, to satisfy the hunger of the poor; I would take firewood to people who complained of the cold and of not being able to afford buying it; on one occasion I went so far as to give away the clothes off my back to clothe a poor person – and many, many other incidents in the same vein.

When I had offended someone, even a servant, I never had a moment's peace until I could repair the damage done with a gift or a gesture of friendship or even a hug for the person who had reason to complain about me.

My heart has not changed over the years. I adore my family and would allow myself to be cut to pieces for some of its members; that covers a lot of ground, for I would unhesitatingly give up my life for my father, mother, grandmother, my sister and my father's two brothers. Generally speaking, I love with a passion everyone whom I believe loves me – but their love for me must be passionate as well. Thus, gratitude is the final element in the electricity of my heart.

This feeling is so intense in me that it has never wavered. I have always longed for a friend but have never found one, at least, not one such as I look for. True, I am hard to please, for it is my nature to give generously and expect the same in return.

Even so, I do not spurn friendships of an ordinary, less exalted nature, though they are hardly to my taste. In such cases I give in proportion to what I think I can get. Saint Augustine is a man (here I do not consider him in his capacity of saint and doctor of the Church) whom I love best because he had a heart like my own. He understood what it means to love; when I read his *Confessions,* where he speaks of his friendship with Saint Lipius, it was as if he were writing in my name. Saint Basil and Saint Gregory captivate me. All such stories from history which recount similar examples of heroic friendship enthrall me. At moments like that, my heart longs to meet such a treasure. In a word, my heart needs to love and since, deep down, it knows what perfect love should be, it will never be satisfied with the sort of ordinary friendship that gratifies the majority of people. My heart aims at a friendship which, put briefly, from two beings would make but one.

Yet there is nothing carnal mixed with such desires coming from the noblest part of my heart. This is so true that I have always spurned relationships with women, since such relationships between the sexes deal more with the senses than with the heart. Nor does a person's rank in society at all enter as a factor into the feeling to love someone who truly loves me. Proof of this lies in the incredible affection in which I hold servants who are truly fond of me. I find it hard, even wrenching, to leave them; I take an interest in their welfare and overlook nothing to secure it. Moreover I do so, not out of magnanimity of spirit – such motivations influence me only when dealing with people who are cold – but out of feelings of tenderness, in a word, out of friendship. You must not, however, think that I feel called to do something only for those who love me. Quite the contrary: whoever suffers or needs me can count on my help.

For me, gratitude, far from being a nagging burden, as it is for many people, is one of the things I like best. It calls me to love the person to whom I am indebted, so I am happy to have incurred an obligation to someone who acted out of affection for me. If it is an affection that singles me out and is partial toward me, there is nothing I would not do in gratitude for such friendship rather than for the service.

If someone with only common or everyday feelings for me does me the kind of favour they might do for anyone, I still feel obliged to respond as any gentleman would under the circumstances, that is, with an external show of gratitude, one that does not really come from the heart. It is a disposition to be of service to pay a debt, while in the other case I truly enjoy being indebted to the person. Thus, I appreciate a trivial service that comes from someone's heart infinitely more than a much greater one from a person who simply obliges me.[7]

A Man of Heart

It is worthwhile noting how many times in his character sketch Eugene made reference to the heart. But what did he mean by "heart"? Oblate canon lawyer and spiritual theologian Father Francis Demers observes that there are many shadows between our consciousness and the depths of the heart; far from simply denoting feelings, emotions or sentiment, *heart* in the affective theological sense encompasses the deepest recesses of a person's being. The great Saint Augustine referred to it as *ubi quicumque sum* – where I am whatever I truly am. Accordingly, when he says, "I love you, Lord, with my heart," it takes on profound meaning. This is also the sense in which Eugene used the word.

"A Sensitive Heart – Too Much So, In Fact . . ."

Eugene, as we will see later, had to struggle to come to terms with his emotions and it would only be in later life that he fully understood how his affectionate nature was truly a unique gift from God that had to be lovingly and constantly returned to the Lord. At this early point in his life, however, he wrote that he always "spurned relationships with women" so as to avoid the "carnal" element entering into a friendship. It sounds very much as

---

[7] Manuscript in the General Archives of the Postulation, DM IV-4. O.M.I., Rome; also in *Oblate Writings,* vol. 14, p. 65, n. 30.

though, with his fiery and impassioned temperament, he was not at all confident that he could keep a handle on his emotions in such relationships, so he chose to flee them. Yet, with time and maturity he would see that all friendships are a gift from God and, as the 63-year-old bishop of Marseilles, he could write the following without hesitation and with perfect equanimity to Madame the Comtesse de Damas on August 25, 1845, "Dare I tell you that I too love you very much. I know that expressing it so openly is not the generally accepted thing to do, but that is the way my heart is made; your virtues arouse my admiration and my respect."[8]

Friends: Two Beings with One Spirit

As a boy fleeing the Revolution, Eugene was surrounded by older people in a dysfunctional family and singularly bereft of friends his own age. By the time he reached his late teens in Palermo and his early twenties back in Aix, he had certainly had acquaintances his age, but everything then had been light and superficial. The character sketch betrays how he longed in vain to experience true and profound friendship. His models, he stated, were the friendships of St. Augustine and St. Lipius, and of the great Saints Basil and Gregory, making it obvious that he already had had some exposure to the writings of the early Fathers of the Church. To give an idea of the kind of relationship Eugene sought, here is an excerpt from Gregory's eulogy at Basil's funeral in the year 379. Both saints were 49 when Basil died. Eugene's words, "My heart aims at a friendship which, put briefly, from two beings would make but one," is a clear reference to the eulogy:

> Basil and I were both in Athens. We had come, like streams of a river, from the same source in our native land, had separated in pursuit of learning, and were now reunited as if by plan, for God had so arranged it. . . . Such was the prelude to our friendship, the kindling of that flame that was to bind us together. In this way we began to feel affection for one another. When, in the course of time, we acknowledged our friendship and recognized that our ambition was a life of true wisdom, we became everything to each other: we shared the same lodging, the same table, the same desires, the same goal. Our love for each other grew daily warmer and deeper.

> The same hope inspired us: the pursuit of learning. This is an ambition especially subject to envy. Yet, between us there was no envy. On the contrary, we made capital of our rivalry. Our rivalry consisted, not in seeking the first place for oneself but in yielding it to the other, for we each looked on the other's success as his own.

> We seemed to be two bodies with a single spirit. . . . Our single object and ambition was virtue, and a life of hope in the blessings that are to come; we

---

[8] Émilien Lamirande, *Le Coeur de Mgr. de Mazenod,* in *Mission,* 1954, p. 263.

wanted to withdraw from the world before we departed from it. With this end in view we ordered our lives and all our actions. We followed the guidance of God's law and spurred each other on to virtue. If it is not too boastful to say so, we found in each other a standard and rule for discerning right from wrong.

Different men have different names which they owe to their parents or to themselves, that is, to their own pursuits and achievements. But our great pursuit, the great name we wanted, was to be Christians, to be called Christians . . . .[9]

Less than eight years after penning his character portrait, Eugene would finally find such a friend in the person of Henri Tempier, a priest so different from, yet so like, de Mazenod in the pursuit of Christ's fullness. For the next 45 years, until Eugene's death, Tempier would be his brother, his confidant, his soul companion, his friend.

The Black Cardinals – Eugene's Involvement in Subversive Activity against Napoleon

At St-Sulpice, the seminary director M. Jacques-André Émery accepted Eugene like a son, calling him "Mazenod," rather than the more usual "Monsieur" Mazenod. After the arrival of the Black Cardinals the following year, the kindly but demanding superior organized clandestine support for them through a secret organization inside the seminary known as the *Association apostolique,* the Apostolic Association. M. Émery's underground network managed to keep the pope in Savona and the cardinals in Paris in touch with one another. To that end, Eugene's 12 years of Italian exile and his fluency in the language served the operation well. He entered the *Association apostolique* in 1810 and was given the task of copying Italian texts and translating French texts into Italian and vice versa. Avoiding Fouché's secret police, he would then surreptitiously deliver the information to the Black Cardinals. Some of those cardinals, such as Bartolomeo Pacca, would remember him later in Rome in 1825. Others, for political reasons, would prefer to forget what he had done to help them. At any rate, this was a forceful experience in the young man's life. He came out of it certainly a far cry from the Eugene de Mazenod of Sicily who considered that "the pope had sullied himself."

Eugene de Mazenod did not wish to become a priest at the hands of the Gallican archbishop of Paris, so he went to Amiens. There, he was ordained by Bishop de Mandolx on December 21, 1811, but returned to St-Sulpice which had fallen into a crisis. After M. Émery stood up to Napoleon, toe-to-

---

[9] Oratio 43, *In laudem Basilii Magni,* 15, 16-17, 19-21.

toe in defence of the Church, the emperor angrily dispersed the seminary's entire staff of directors, suspecting that they like their superior were involved in aiding and abetting the Black Cardinals. About the same time the exhausted M. Émery died. The institution was truncated. For that reason Eugene stayed on as a spiritual director, accepting as well the responsibility of the liturgy. He continued in that capacity until October, 1812, when he went back to Aix to begin his apostolic work there.

Eugene's Situation upon His Return to Aix

It is striking to see how sure Eugene de Mazenod was that his vocation was to dedicate himself as a priest to serve the poor. He would progressively discover many of the other aspects of his vocation, but his option to serve the poor was a strong, deeply-felt and abiding conviction from the beginning. St. Ignatius refers to situations wherein the Holy Spirit's grace is so all-pervading that the person is absolutely sure of his or her choice. Something similar took place in Eugene's life. In one of his early sermons at the Madeleine he said, "Feeling as I do, that I have been called to be the servant and priest of the poor, and hoping to devote my life to their service . . . ."[10]

For the same reason he gracefully declined the invitation of the bishop of Amiens to become his vicar-general, "so that I would not be swerved from the vocation which urged me to devote myself to the service and welfare of souls towards whom I felt a love akin to the love Christ felt for all men."[11] Likewise, when in Paris in 1817 to try to get royal approval for his new society, Eugene did not visit his friend, the Duc de Berry, lest he be asked to remain on as chaplain in the royal palace. Not seeing the close acquaintance with whom he had shared exile in Sicily was certainly a sacrifice, yet he made it to remain faithful to his vocation as a priest to the poor.

In 1812, upon his return to Aix as a young priest, he already had his sights set upon serving the poor. In his journal he would later write:[12]

> When I returned to Aix, the Bishop of Metz, who was then the administrator of the diocese, asked me what I wanted to do. There was not the slightest thought in my mind of capitalizing on my social standing by hinting that I would like what everyone else found reasonable at the time. . . . I therefore told the Bishop of Metz that my only ambition was to consecrate myself to the service of the poor and to the children. Thus, my

---

[10] Leflon, vol. 1, p. 412.

[11] Ibid., p. 480, n. 9.

[12] *Missions,* March 31, 1839.

first struggle was my work in the prisons and my apprenticeship consisted in gathering the children around me so that I might instruct them.[13]

Discovering God's Call Through the Events in His Life

Eugene de Mazenod did not start out with some grand preconceived strategy. Instead, he let God speak to him through the concrete events of his life and in the process discovered his calling step by step. Let us first examine a preliminary stage of his discernment and its importance as a grace of the Holy Spirit.

Preliminary Stage: The End of October, 1812 to March 7, 1813

The first months of Eugene's priesthood in Aix were a time of preparation, of intense prayer. He was with Brother Maur, a Trappist who was awaiting the re-opening of his monastery. They had met at the Seminary of St-Sulpice, whence the brother accompanied the young priest to Aix as his domestic. Very soon, however, the two became friends and companions in a strictly regimented life. It was Eugene's first experience of religious living with a brother and would come back to him later when brothers became part of the congregation. The two lived with Eugene's grandmother and his mother on the rue Papassaudi, but also spent time at the Enclos de Mazenod, a property situated on the outskirts of Aix which Eugene's mother had recovered after the Revolution. Life was lived strictly according to a severe monastic timetable which the young priest had drawn up:

4:30   Rising.

5:00   Vocal prayer, followed by meditation (generally from the works of Father Olier) and a short reading of Scripture.

6:00   Mass, followed by thanksgiving, then, recitation of Prime from the Divine Office.

        Reading of the martyrology and a half-hour of Scripture.

        Study during the entire morning.

        Recitation of Terce before lunch.

---

[13] Leflon, vol. 1, p. 482, n. 27.

Lunch

   Recitation of Sexte and study of theology.

2:00 Recitation of Nones.

4:30 Vespers and Particular Examen,

5:00 Dinner.

7:00 Compline and a visit to the Blessed Sacrament.

   Diverting but instructive reading.

9:00 Matins and Lauds.

   Half-hour of spiritual reading with the family.

10:00 Night prayers and retire for the night.

Eugene's only diversion during this period appears to have been to go to the seminary to give spiritual direction or to meet with a group of priests to discuss pastoral and spiritual matters.

Principles Which Guided Eugene's Choice

Listening to God Calling Through Events

Leflon quotes Bishop Jeancard as writing:

> The Founder of the Oblates was far from knowing the whole extent of his mission. By no means did he draw up a vast plan *a priori,* complete in all its parts. . . . The plan was inspired in him and, in a way, revealed to him progressively as circumstances opened up new horizons to his zeal. The Lord who was guiding him, allowed him to see only what had to be done in the immediate situation and rewarded his fervent love for the Church and his zeal for souls by allowing him to see the exact distance he had to cover in each new advance toward the completion of the work which devolved upon him.[14]

Here we begin to understand the value of the long period devoted to prayer in order to have the freedom needed to discover how God was calling him. When Canon Leflon finished his monumental work on the life of Eugene de Mazenod he declared that the Oblates were true improvisers. It was real

---

[14] *Jeancard,* quoted in Leflon, vol. 2, p. 41. Jacques Jeancard originally joined the Founder but left during the vow crisis. He later returned but Eugene told him that his place was in the ranks of the diocesan clergy. They remained close friends and later, in Marseilles, Bishop de Mazenod requested that he be his auxiliary bishop.

fidelity to the Lord to be deeply and internally free. This leads us to the second principle.

Being Free in Order to Meet the Needs of the Most Abandoned

While studying at St-Sulpice, Eugene was assigned as a form of pastoral work to teach catechism to the poorest children in the local parish. Of them the zealous seminarian wrote to his mother: "They are the poorest of the parish, children of tavern-keepers and crawling with lice. The seminary authorities feel that perhaps I shall be able to put new life into this failing body, and so they have chosen me as its head. . . . I shall make every effort to bring them back to God."[15]

By way of apology, the superior promised him that after a while he would have a better choice. Eugene, however, was very happy working with those abandoned children, and although he could have changed to "better" groups, he stayed willingly with the poor throughout his seminary years.

Eugene became a priest with his mind made up to dedicate himself in the most absolute way to the service of the Church. Upon his return to Aix he saw that the parochial institutions of the Church were not responding to the needs of the poor. Indeed, he felt strongly that the Church, with its aged priests in a pre-Revolution mind-set, had actually abandoned the poor. He clearly and astutely saw that the Church was not sufficiently addressing the concrete needs of a post-Revolutionary era. Instead, it appeared to be in a holding pattern, managing little more than to reach practising Catholics. For that reason he had no intention of taking part in diocesan administration, nor did he intend to limit his activities to those of a Concordat parish. He felt the need to be free to respond to the most urgent actual needs.

That thought was expressed in his memoirs in 1845:

> So I entered the Seminary of St-Sulpice with the desire, or rather, with the firm determination, to devote myself in the most complete way to serving the Church by exercising a ministry that would be most useful to souls for whose salvation I was on fire to consecrate myself. . . .
>
> During my seminary days, I entertained the thought of making myself as useful as possible to the Church, our Mother, for whom the Lord had given me the grace always to have a filial love. The destitution in which I saw her had been one of the motivating factors that prompted me to embrace the ecclesiastical state. I had recognized that vocation from my adolescence, but could not follow it then, due to the events of the dreadful Revolution. . . . After I returned to France I was pained to the depths of my soul at

---

[15] Letter to his mother, Feb. 4, 1809, St-Martin.

seeing the service of the altar despised, because the Church could no longer offer rich benefices to the sacrilegious greed of families that were more or less world-famous.[16]

It was that desire to be free that prompted the Abbé de Mazenod when, at the start of his priestly ministry, he presented himself to the vicar-general of Aix. Instead of asking what he might do in the local Church, he insisted on being given a free hand. Everything he did as a young priest seemed to cry out, "Give me elbow room to take care of needs which you are not addressing. There are poor people out there whom you have abandoned." "Abandoned" keeps coming up, time after time.

Being free also meant not being tied down to mundane obligations. On April 22, 1812, he wrote to his mother:

> I have already acquainted you with my plans. . . . No one must imagine that when I come back to Aix my time will be taken up with visiting, entertaining or taking part in the activities of what is called polite society. . . . I want none of that. . . . People can call me rude if they wish, even uncivilized; it will not bother me, just as long as I am a good priest. And if they try to bolster their argument by citing the conduct of other priests, far from weakening my resolve, they will only strengthen it further. My conscience and my God, these will be my judges and my rule of conduct.[17]

For Eugene, freedom was a grace – one for which he prayed during his first Mass. Among the intentions of that Mass were "to obtain pardon for my sins, the love of God above all things and the most complete charity for my neighbour, *a holy freedom of spirit in the service of God*, and in my actions, great purity of heart and spirit . . . ."[18]

A Basic Conviction – The Value of Every Soul

Eugene considered every soul, even the poorest, to be an infinite prize because it had been redeemed by the Blood of the Son of God. He wrote: "If only we could appraise the true worth of a single human soul, a soul ransomed by God made man, who shed his blood to the last drop . . . then, perchance, we might rouse ourselves out of our lethargy, summon all our strength and be ready, if need be, to lay down our lives."[19]

---

[16] Rambert, vol. 1, p. 161; also in *Selected Texts*, p. 72, n. 50.

[17] Leflon, vol. 1, p. 405.

[18] Rambert, vol. 1, p. 95.

[19] *Our Founder's Love for the Church*, in *Vie Oblate Life 36*, p. 98, English.

How Eugene Progressively Answered God's Call

From what we have just seen, it is evident that Eugene de Mazenod clearly saw the urgent necessity of dedicating himself to everyone, especially to those who were most neglected. There were three steps in his progressive realization of his call:

> **I. Through the Most Abandoned.**
>
> **II. Through Community.**
>
> **III. Through Religious Life.**

Let us now take a closer look at each step in order to recognize how the hand of God led him, often without his realizing it, to the eventual founding of the Missionary Oblates of Mary Immaculate.

I. Through the Most Abandoned

For Eugene de Mazenod, who were the most abandoned?: artisans, servants, and the poor. His first public pastoral action that we know about was his famous instruction in the Church of the Madeleine, early on the first Sunday of Lent, 1813.

> When it was announced that at six o'clock each Sunday morning during Lent, the Abbé de Mazenod would deliver informal instructions to artisans, servants and paupers at the Church of the Madeleine – and in Provençal – the city's high society made no secret of its astonishment, disappointment and even indignation. To catechize the lower classes, and in *patois*, was that not an outright renunciation of nobility on the part of the gentleman priest?[20]

What that "gentleman priest" said in his first sermon tells us much about him as well:

> During this holy season, a good number of conferences will be provided for the rich and the educated. Will there be none for the poor and the unlearned? . . . Well, here the pastor's love and concern has taken care of that. What a pity it would be if we did not now profit from such an opportunity! . . . The Gospel must be taught to all, and in an understandable way. The poor, that precious portion of the Christian family, cannot be left in ignorance.
>
> Our divine Saviour considered the poor so important that he took it upon himself to personally instruct them. The proof he offered to show that his mission was divine was the fact that the poor were being instructed: *Pauperes evangelizantur.*

---

[20] Leflon, vol. 1, p. 409.

51

Now, since knowledge of the truth he came to bring to mankind is necessary to attain everlasting life and be saved, it follows that it must be accessible to all. This makes it quite different from what the ancient philosophers held. They limited their teaching to only a small number of devotees and excluded the multitude. Thus, their teaching bore the mark of error, for truth must be known by all, since all have an equal right to possess it.

We shall speak in such a way that everyone, even the most unlettered, may comprehend. Like the father of a family, we shall gather together our children and reveal a treasure to them. But courage and perseverance are needed to acquire it. . . .

Come therefore, whoever you may be, come diligently to the instructions which seek to deliver you from so many fatal errors and enlighten you on your own true interests. Come, especially you, the poor of Jesus Christ! Please God I could make my voice heard to the four corners of the world to awaken all the many people lulled by fatal sloth that leads them to perdition.

We shall begin by teaching you who you are, what your noble origins are, the rights you derive therefrom, and the obligations they entail.

So, let us put the world to the test. It will react in accord with the laws of prejudiced men, in accord with the foolish code that is the rule of their life and the yardstick by which they judge others.

Artisans, who are you in the eyes of the world? A class of people destined to toil laboriously all your lives in some obscure occupation that makes you dependent and subjects you to the whims of those from whom you must beg employment.

Servants, what are you in the eyes of the world? A class of slaves to those who pay you; exposed to the contempt, injustice and often even to the abusive treatment of demanding and even barbarous masters – masters who believe that they have bought the right to treat you unjustly for the pittance they pay you.

And what about you, farmers and peasants, what are you in the eyes of the world? However useful your labours, you are judged only by the strength of your arms, and if, indeed, with distaste they take your sweat into account, it is only appreciated in so far as it makes the earth bountiful by watering it.

What about you, the poor and the needy, who are obliged by man's injustice or the harshness of fate to beg for your pitiful subsistence, to make a nuisance of yourself pleading for the bread you need to stay alive? The world considers you the scum of society. It cannot bear to look at you, so it turns its back, lest it be moved to pity by your condition which it has no intention of changing.

That is what the world thinks. That is what you are in its eyes. But that is the chosen master to whom you have hitherto paid your homage. And what can you expect from such a master? Insults and contempt – that is the reward the world gives you. And it will never give you anything better. . . .

Come now, and learn from us what you are in the eyes of faith.

You, the poor of Jesus Christ, the afflicted and the wretched, the sick and suffering, those covered with sores – all of you whom misery overwhelms, my brethren, my dear brethren, my respectable brethren, listen to me.

You are the children of God, the brothers and sisters of Jesus Christ, the co-heirs of his eternal Kingdom, the cherished portion of his inheritance; you are, in the words of Saint Peter, the holy nation, you are kings, you are priests, you are, yes, in a certain way, gods. . . .

So, lift up your heads! Let your dejected spirit rise! Stop grovelling on the ground and raise yourselves toward heaven where you were meant to attain what should be your most normal relationship. . . . For once, let your eyes look inward and see through the rags you wear. There, within you, is an immortal soul, created to the image of God whom it is destined one day to possess – a soul redeemed at the cost of the blood of Jesus Christ, more precious before God than all the riches of the world, than all the kingdoms of the earth, a soul about which he is more concerned than about all the governments of the entire world . . . Therefore, O Christians, recognize your dignity . . . .[21]

The people of his social class may not have appreciated this type of preaching, but the poor were delighted. On the Fourth Sunday of Lent, Eugene felt obligated to thank his "reverend brothers, the poor" who had flocked to the church in such great numbers to hear him:

We placed the success of this Lenten Course in the hands of God and our hopes were not deceived, since we have seen with our own eyes that the sacred message which was brought to you through our ministry has been received with enthusiasm. God be praised for it, my brothers! I feel so overjoyed that I cannot refrain from mentioning it. Feeling as I do, that I have been called to be the servant and priest of the poor, and hoping to devote my life to their service, I cannot help but be touched by their eagerness to hear my voice.[22]

"Will There Be None for the Poor and Unlearned?"

The domestics and artisans could not go to church during the day because they had to work. Moreover, most of them did not understand French. It was enough to convince Eugene that there must be some instruction tailored particularly to them. In this attitude we see how necessary it is for the missionary to adapt himself to the poor: *"The Gospel must be taught to all in a way it can be understood."*

---

[21] *Manuscript in the Postulation,* Rome, DM V 3.
[22] Leflon, vol. 1, p. 412.

"Pauperes Evangelizantur" – The Poor Are Evangelized

It is important always to remember that Jesus was the unifying force in Eugene's life. In his Lenten instruction he stressed that as a sign that his mission was divine, Jesus showed that the poor had the gospel preached to them. So, what did that mean to de Mazenod and what should it mean to his missionary sons? It should mean that Oblates, like their Founder, must preach the gospel to the poor if the Oblates want to follow Christ. But the gospel must be preached in a way that it can be understood – *"We shall speak in a way that even the least educated may comprehend."* This latter point is repeatedly stressed in Eugene's letters: the missionaries' way of speaking must be direct and uncomplicated. Moreover, he insisted on the necessity of speaking in the language of the poor. In Provence, the language was Provençal; thus it was in Provençal that he proclaimed the Word. Later, in overseas missions, he would insist that his missionaries speak the local language of the indigenous people.

Eugene's Analysis of the Situation

Eugene de Mazenod had a special quality that we should never lose sight of: he was able to see! Keenness of vision is requisite if one is to be attentive to the call of God. The Oblate Founder's heightened sensitivity made him spontaneously attentive, attuned to the needs of others, especially the poor and the most abandoned. But he was also able to see those needs because he was a man of prayer. It is thanks to the freedom acquired in prayer that he could launch out into new ventures which responded to the real needs of the times.

Eugene de Mazenod's analysis was certainly not scientific, but the poor embraced it because in it they could recognize their own real needs. His way of examining the situation from the springboard of economics put him close to the Marxist analysis of production. According to Marx, the wage is not a labourer's equitable return for work done. Instead, it is merely the minimum necessary to maintain the worker's strength at a level that permits continued labour. Compare that to Eugene's words: "And what about you, farmers and peasants? . . . However useful your labours, you are judged only by the strength of your arms, and if, indeed, with distaste, they take your sweat into account, it is only in so far as it makes the earth bountiful by watering it."

Moreover, Eugene de Mazenod's analysis of the situation was in direct contrast to the view generally held in the 19th century, even in Catholic circles. Compare Eugene's assessment of the condition of the poor with that of a celebrated Catholic layman of the era, Louis Veuillot. Writing in *l'Univers*, the outspoken newspaper he edited, Veuillot stated: "Misery is the lot which fate apportions to a segment of society. It is a law of God to which one must comply."[23] On another occasion he wrote: "Society needs slaves. It is the price it must pay to keep going. There must be persons who work a great deal and live poorly."[24]

When one realizes that in many ways Louis Veuillot was considered an advanced thinker in Catholic circles, it shows just how far in the forefront was the Founder of the Oblates!

Abandoned: Young People

Another group which Eugene considered abandoned was the youth of the nation. We have already seen how Napoleon reneged on the Concordat of 1801 by unilaterally appending modifications that were more acceptable to the Gallicans and republicans. In addition to forbidding the publication of any papal bull in France or the convocation of any episcopal council without the emperor's approval, the changes limited the number of dioceses to around 60 and included such details as the manner of conducting religious processions and even the way church bells could be rung.

Education was strictly controlled by the state: priests were allowed to teach only catechism, and even there, all subject matter had to be approved by the government and included, as we saw, a lesson on obedience to the emperor. Nor was it permitted to organize youth movements of any kind. Such groups, the emperor suspected, might support the Roman resistance at a moment when his relations with the pope were extremely thorny. The result was that young people were left abandoned. The Abbé de Mazenod was conscious of the void which the situation was creating and wrote:

> It is not difficult to see that the plan of the impious Bonaparte and of his irreverent government is to wipe out the Catholic religion in the entire country he usurped. Since the oppressed people's attachment to the faith of their fathers prevents him from rapidly executing the detestable strategy that is essential to his diabolic plans, it now appears that he is satisfied to let time and the means he has taken achieve the desired results. What he counts on most is the destruction of the moral fibre of the youth. The success of the measures he has taken is frightening.
>
> Should I be persecuted and should I fail . . . I shall not have to reproach myself for not having tried. What means shall I employ in order to succeed in such a great undertaking? None other than what the seducer himself has used. He believes that only by perverting the youth will he succeed in corrupting France. And so it is toward the youth that he directs all his

---

[23] *L'Univers*, July 7, 1848.
[24] *L'Univers*, February 12, 1849.

efforts. Very well! I, too, will concentrate on the adolescent. I will make every effort to preserve the youth from the evils that threaten them, some of which have already affected them. And I will do it by inspiring them early in life with a love of virtue, respect for religion, a taste of piety and a horror of vice.[25]

To heed God's call through the most abandoned Eugene, decided to form a sodality through which young people could deepen their faith and live it. Forming the sodality was dangerous, because it meant he was going counter to the law, a law he considered unjust, but a law nevertheless. He wrote:

> It is a difficult undertaking and I fully realize what it entails. It is actually dangerous since what I plan to do amounts to opposing with all my might the insidious policies of a suspicious government which persecutes and destroys anything that does not support it. However, I have no fear because I am putting my trust in God and am seeking his glory and the salvation of souls redeemed by his Son, our Lord Jesus Christ, to whom be honour, glory and power for endless ages.[26]

Although Eugene named the group the Holy Association of Christian Youth, it was never called that in public and he took the precaution of making it appear that it was simply a spontaneous and casual get-together of adolescents. Six youngsters and the Abbé de Mazenod attended the initial meeting, held on the Sunday after Easter, 1813. Their charter, which put the group under the patronage of the Immaculate Conception, read in part:

> We, the undersigned members of the Congregation of Christian Youth, founded in Aix under the patronage of the Immaculate Conception of the Most Holy Virgin Mary, testify by those here present, as members of the said Sodality, pledge to consecrate ourselves perpetually to the Most Holy Trinity . . . to whom we offer this gift of our entire being through the hands of the Most Holy and Immaculate Virgin Mary, our Mother and Patroness, to whose service, at the same time, we devote ourselves with all our heart.[27]

Of the six charter members who signed the document, two would become Oblates: Jacques-Joseph Marcoux and Hippolyte Courtès, whom the Founder later said was "pivotal" in the congregation. By year's end there were 23 members in the sodality. At the end of 1814 the number reached 60. The roster increased steadily: 1815 – 120, 1816 – 200, 1817 – 300. Meetings consisted of games and sports outdoors, along with prayer and Christian teaching. The sodality was characterized by strong Marian devotion, with each member offering himself to Christ through the Virgin Mary. At the end

---

[25] Leflon, vol. 1, p. 415.

[26] Ibid., p. 414.

[27] Charbonneau, *My Name is Eugene,* pp. 51-52.

[28] Praised eternally be Jesus Christ and praised also be Mary, ever Immaculate.

of each celebration, once the group had permanently moved into the old Carmelite chapel on the Cours Mirabeau, they heartily sang in Provençal:

Que Jesus-Christ siègué laoza eternelament,

et què Mario tougeou immaculado, émé suon divin fiou

siègué tanben laouzado.[28]

At first the group got together in the Pavillon d'Enfant, a hunting lodge outside the city. But it soon proved to be too far from the centre, so Eugene began to look for other places. For a long time they used the Enclos, a property of the Joannis family. After October, 1815, when Napoleon had been defeated, the sodality began to use the chapel on the Cours Mirabeau. It was with their help that this desecrated Carmelite church was restored, even before the Oblate Congregation, as such, got its start.

What strikes one at first glance is the incredible number of regulations governing the sodality and the lives of its members – over 500! However, all of this must be understood in the context of the times. One thing is certain: such an apparent surfeit of rules did not hamper the *joie de vivre* of the boys, nor the popularity of the director in their eyes. "As soon as he appeared they all rushed upon him; one would take hold of his neck, the other his cincture; this one would kiss his hand, and that one his cassock. As for the Abbé himself, he showed them the love and affection of a real father. . . . He treated a cobbler's son as cordially and affectionately as he did the son of a high court official."[29]

That last sentence is important because it shows he considered all youth to be among the most abandoned, whether rich or poor. In the sodality there were a number of members who could never have been called economically poor, but they were as welcome as the others.

Abandoned: Criminals and Prisoners of War

We have already seen that after his return from exile Eugene joined a charitable association working to alleviate the plight of prisoners, so he obviously had some first-hand experience of conditions in the prison. He also knew that the prisoners were bereft of any religious aid. In a word, they were *abandoned*. Thus, when he returned to Aix as a priest he volunteered his services as a prison chaplain.[30] Eugene visited the prisoners almost every day, striving to instruct, encourage and convert them.

---

[29] Leflon, vol. 1, p. 416.
[30] The central prison was restored in 1820. It has again been partially demolished in 1995.

What is remarkable is that his actions ran so completely counter to the severe Jansenist mentality so prevalent among the clergy of Aix. For example, the rule in France at the time, and very much so in Aix, was to refuse the eucharist to prisoners condemned to death because they were judged unworthy. The young Abbé de Mazenod turned that way of thinking on its head. Not only did he give Communion to the condemned prisoner, he celebrated the Mass especially for him or her, right in the prison cell. And after giving Holy Communion he accompanied the prisoner all the way to the scaffold, staying alongside right through the final moments. We have eyewitness testimony of this in the case of La Germaine, a notorious Aixoise who "had drawn the horror and indignation of the people upon herself because of the enormity of her crimes." It appears that from the scaffold, before she was executed, she spoke of her conversion and gave a talk on Jesus Christ. Father Joseph-Alphonse Martin, in his memoirs, relates:

> So moved was she by the Abbé de Mazenod's exhortations that she made a complete conversion and showed such an excellent disposition that, contrary to what was usually done at that time, the Abbé de Mazenod permitted her to receive Communion. The people's attitude toward her changed when they saw her advance toward the scaffold giving the most touching proofs of her repentance. The exhortations which her deeply moved confessor addressed to her as he walked by her side, sustained her courage, and more than one voice in the crowd was heard blessing the charitable apostle who had been such an efficacious instrument in this miracle of grace.[31]

The Oblates remained as prison chaplains in Aix, faithful to Eugene's practices, until the expulsion of all religious from France in 1903.

Napoleon's far-ranging wars brought captured soldiers to France from all parts of Europe. Aix, for example, received about 2,000 Austrian prisoners of war who were confined in a camp that is now the army barracks at the beginning of the present-day rue Gambetta. Shortly after their arrival a typhus epidemic ran through the overcrowded camp. Many died, among them the chaplain, and Eugene volunteered to take his place. Again, he saw those prisoners as the most abandoned. It was not long, however, before he himself contracted typhus and for a long time hovered near death. On March 14, 1814, he received Viaticum while the members of the youth sodality organized a chain of prayer at the foot of the statue of Notre-Dame de la Grâce in the Church of the Madeleine. Thanks to their prayers, his health was restored, and on May 3, almost two months after he had received

---

[31] Leflon, vol. 1, p. 417.

Viaticum, he and the sodality celebrated a Mass of thanksgiving in the Madeleine. The interval between those dates give us an idea of how prolonged was his illness.

Eugene de Mazenod's Illness Leads to a Momentous Decision

The typhus, however, had a salutary effect: *It helped show Eugene that it was not possible for him to work alone.* Listening to God through the concrete events in life showed him that to serve the most abandoned, he needed a group of companions – a community of persons who thought as he did. *That would be the second stage in following God's invitation to dedicate himself to the most abandoned.*

II. Through Community

It is enlightening to follow the evolution of Eugene de Mazenod's thought on the necessity of community through his letters. It is worth highlighting one of them, written to his friend, the Abbé Charles de Forbin-Janson. Here is an excerpt:

> Now I ask you and I ask myself how I, who hitherto could not make up my mind in this matter, suddenly find myself setting wheels in motion, renouncing comfort and risking my fortune by launching an enterprise of which I know the worth but for which I only have a liking negated by other diametrically opposed views! This is a riddle to me and it is *the second time in my* life that I see myself moved to resolve something of the utmost seriousness as if by *a strong impulse from without.* When I reflect on it, I am convinced that it so pleases God to put an end to my wavering. And in such a way that I am committed to the hilt! I assure you that in such circumstances I am quite another man. . . . You would no longer call me a lazy rump if you saw how I am struggling.[32]

The Founder of the Oblates referred to that moment as the *second* time in his life that he had been moved to take a decision "by a strong impulse from without." The first such special grace was surely the Good Friday experience in 1807.

Needed: A Few Good Men

To get his society of priests off the ground, Father de Mazenod wrote to a humble young country curate in Arles, Father Henri Tempier, urgently inviting him to join in the project of evangelizing the Provençal countryside. The letter is reproduced, along with Father Tempier's reply, at the end of this chapter. In it he tells Tempier, "You are necessary for the work which

---

[32] *Oblate Writings,* vol. 6, 1815, p. 8, n. 5.

the Lord inspires us to undertake," and assures him that "happiness awaits us in the holy society which will have but one heart and one soul . . . ." He concludes the letter with a plea:

> Dear friend, I conjure you, do not let yourself say no to the greatest good that may possibly be done to the Church. Vicars can easily be found to replace you, but it would not be as easy to come across dedicated men who wish to devote themselves to the glory of God and the salvation of souls with no more reward on earth than much sorrow and all else that the Saviour announced to his true disciples.

In the emotion of the moment Father de Mazenod forgot to sign his name. At first Father Tempier thought it was a joke of some sort, and it took him some time to find out who the sender was, but when he discovered its author and the seriousness of the request, he replied simply: "I share your views completely, and far from needing your urging to enter this holy Society, which satisfies my own desires so completely, I assure you that had I known of your plans before, I would have been the first to speak of joining your society. . . . You can, therefore, count entirely on me."

With Tempier's entry, the nascent community counted five members: Eugene de Mazenod, aged 33, Henri Tempier, 26, Jean François Deblieu, 26, Auguste Icard, 25, and Pierre Nolasque Mie, 47.

Finding a Home

Father de Mazenod was acutely aware that an apostolic community such as he envisioned needed a home where it could regenerate its forces and recharge its spiritual batteries. To that end he sought to purchase the former monastery of the Minim Friars on the outskirts of Aix. However, that was not to be. Somewhat chagrined, he wrote to his friend, Forbin Janson, "The nuns of the Blessed Sacrament, by some kind of skullduggery, tricked me out of it."[33]

His next choice was to buy a major portion of the former Carmelite nuns' convent, built between 1695 and 1701, and situated at the head of the Cours Mirabeau, a stone's throw from the palatial house where he was born. It came with the nuns' choir chapel adjoining a public church, the latter not included in the purchase price. The public church, moreover, was so dilapidated that Father de Mazenod commented, "It rains as much inside the building as it does out in the street." It had been turned into a shrine of the goddess Reason during the Revolution and later served as a stopover for itinerant circus performers and vagrants. After its eventual purchase by the

---

[33] Leflon, vol. 2, p. 36.

Abbé de Mazenod, it became known as the Church of the Mission, a title it holds to this day. Following the fall of Napoleon, the youth sodality became the first group to use the newly acquired premises. On November 21, 1815, the Feast of the Presentation, the boys met in the choir chapel. The sodality would eventually help restore both the choir chapel and the church, making the latter again a place of public worship. It was inaugurated on Palm Sunday, 1816.

Although the part of the convent that Eugene de Mazenod acquired came at an excellent price, it had strings attached. It belonged to a Mme. Gontier who had established there a girls' academy of remarkable mediocrity. The academy was in financial difficulty, so in the purchase agreement she astutely stipulated that it be allowed to continue on the premises for some time. Accordingly, when Father de Maze-nod's little group of priests went there to take up residence, they discovered to their chagrin that Mme. Gontier's academy continued to occupy all but the choir chapel and two small upper rooms, along with a narrow stairway that led out to the street. For the first five months, Father de Mazenod's room was a narrow passageway which he referred to as a *boyau,* a tube or passageway in polite terms, but in more common parlance, a "gut."

Beyond the "gut" and up a couple of rickety steps was a doorway that led to the small common room. There the tiny community met and cooked its meals in the smoky fireplace, using a plank over two barrels as a table. Fathers Tempier and Icard also utilized the room as their dormitory (Fathers Deblieu and Mie came to live only after more space became available). At bedtime the priests placed a lamp on the floor in the doorway to give light to both rooms. The community was in the honeymoon of its beginnings, in the first fervour of the common life. Hardships could be laughed off. Later, the Oblate Founder would write, "I can assure you that we lost none of our cheerfulness; on the contrary, since that new way of living was in striking contrast with what we had left behind, we often had a hearty laugh over it. . . . How happy I would be to continue living it with you."[34]

The days of crisis were still in the future.

The Missionaries of Provence

On January 25, 1816, the Feast of St. Paul's Conversion, the five young priests gathered in the common room to sign a formal petition asking the

---

[34] *Selected Texts*, p. 255, n. 221.

archdiocese to authorize their budding society, to be known as the Missionaries of Provence. Their purpose was twofold:

1.   To preach missions for the re-Christianization "of the small towns and villages in Provence, which have almost entirely lost the faith, since the ordinary means furnished by the parochial ministry are not effective enough . . . ."

2.   To "form a community of missionaries governed by a rule, so that they might serve the diocese and, at the same time, strive to sanctify themselves in accordance with this particular vocation."

The document was signed by Fathers de Mazenod, Tempier, Icard, Deblieu and Mie. Immediately afterwards the group began a ten-day retreat to prepare themselves for their first parochial mission preached in Grans.

The Characteristics of the First Community in the Founder's Own Words

Poverty

> Never, since we took the vow, have we again had the good fortune of being as poor as we were then. Even without suspecting it, we were taking the first steps to the perfect state we now live so imperfectly. But I purposely underline the completely voluntary nature of our privation – for it would have been easy to get whatever I needed, transported over from my mother's place – in order to conclude therefrom that God was already there, guiding us, even without our realizing it at the time, towards the evangelical counsels we were to profess later on. It was in observing them that we came to appreciate their value.[35]

Unity

> Between us missionaries . . . we are what we ought to be, that is to say, we have but one heart, one soul, one thought. It is admirable! Our consolations, like our hardships, are unequalled.[36]

Charity

> It is God's custom to reward his generous apostles who have left everything to serve him. He filled their souls with a superabundance of spiritual joy, along with that peace which surpasses all human understanding.[37]

---

[35] *Selected Texts*, pp. 254-255, n. 222.

[36] *Oblate Writings*, vol. 6, 1816, p. 18, n. 5, from Grans.

[37] Rambert, vol. 1, p. 176.

Happiness and Joy

> Happiness awaits us in the holy society which will have but one heart and soul .... It suffices to give some intimation of the spiritual delights we will taste together.[38]

Prayer

> Thus assembled in the name of Jesus Christ,[39] and forming a single regular community, the members of this new little religious family went into retreat in order to prepare themselves through prayer and meditation for the work of the Missions of Provence.[40]

III. Through Religious Life

In what light did the Oblate Founder consider religious consecration, which he called "oblation"? In his memoirs, written around 1845, he said that it was his intention in dedicating himself to the ministry of the missions to work especially for the instruction and conversion of the most abandoned souls and to follow the example of the apostles in their life of *devotion* and *self-denial*: He wrote:

> My intention in dedicating myself to the ministry of the missions, working especially for the instruction and conversion of the most abandoned souls, was to follow the example of the apostles in their life of *devotedness* and *self-denial.* I became convinced that, in order to obtain the same results from our preaching, we would have to walk in their footsteps and, as far as we could, practise the same virtues as they. Hence I considered it indispensable that we opt for the evangelical counsels, to which they had been so faithful, lest our words be no more than . . . sounding brass and tinkling cymbals. I always thought that our little family should consecrate itself to God and to the service of the Church through the vows of religion.[41]

The foregoing selection from the Oblate Founder's memoirs is worth analyzing. His aim was to convert the most abandoned. That was a basic decision. How? By imitating the *devotedness* and *self-denial* of the apostles, *devotedness* in the sense of Mark's Gospel, to "be one with Christ," *self-denial* in emptying oneself totally to Christ so that, filled with Christ's inspiration, the Oblate can be sent as a missionary.

De Mazenod saw the evangelical counsels as a prerequisite if his society were to follow in the apostles' footsteps. In other words, all members must dedicate themselves totally to God through their vows in order to be faithful

---

[38] First letter from Father Tempier, *Oblate Writings,* vol. 6, p. 7.

[39] After electing Eugene the superior of the initial community in Aix.

[40] Rambert, vol. 1, p. 177.

[41] Ibid., p. 187; *Selected Texts,* p. 39, n. 16.

in proclaiming the Good News which, in turn, is God's total dedication to them.

His memoirs continue with an account of the first vows on Holy Thursday of the previous year, 1816:

> Father Tempier and I felt that we should delay no longer. Thus, on Holy Thursday, when both of us had taken our place under the structure of the beautiful repository we had put up over the main altar of the Mission church, we pronounced our vows with an indescribable joy in the night of that holy day . . . and we prayed to the Divine Master that if it was his holy will to bless our undertaking, we would *lead our present companions as well as those who would be associated with us in the future* to appreciate the full value of the *oblation* of one's entire self to God, wanting to serve him unreservedly and consecrate one's life to the spread of his holy Gospel and the conversion of souls. Our petitions were answered.[42]

Note de Mazenod's use of the word *oblation* It was a term he employed long before the congregation received the name "Oblates of Mary Immaculate." And from the 1818 Rule onward, he referred to those who had taken vows as Oblates. *Oblate* means a total dedication to God, like the apostles, like Jesus and with Jesus.

We get a deeper understanding of what the Founder of the Oblates meant when he spoke of the apostles as "our first fathers." The vocation of an apostle is Jesus' grace calling someone to be with him and to be sent by him. It was the beginning of a history of grace which continues unbroken among Oblates even today. So deep was that intuition that the apostles can indeed be said to be the congregation's first fathers.

Needed: A Rule

Bishop Miollis of Digne had asked the Founder to establish a community at Notre-Dame de Laus. After discernment, all six members of the community agreed on acceptance. However, such an undertaking had its implications. For the first time some members of the society would no longer be living under the roof of the original community. Thus, for the unity of the group, they felt the necessity of a Rule.

At the very outset, Eugene had asked Father Tempier to prepare some notes for a kind of rule of life. He now took those to the manor house at St-Laurent-du-Verdon and for 13 days in the peace and solitude of the Provençal countryside that he had so abhorred upon his return from exile, he wrote the first Rule. The Oblate Founder based himself largely on the rule of St.

---

[42] Rambert, vol. 1, p. 187; *Selected Texts*, p. 39, n. 16.

Alphonsus Liguori, with some modifications and additions, yet his forcefulness and charism gives the Oblate rule its distinctive imprint. Although both congregations observe a rule with certain similar traits, no one today would mistake an Oblate for a Redemptorist.

For almost two weeks in St-Laurent de Mazenod wrote feverishly as the Spirit inspired him. The original text of that rule, written with extra-wide margins, is still in the Oblate general archives in Rome. After that he returned to Aix, spending most of October calmly and prayerfully completing and polishing up his text, adding sentences and phrases in the margins, preparing the rule for presentation to the community at the end of the month. True, he had at first copied his rule's practical directives from St. Alphonsus – very often word-for-word – but then he added his own spiritual considerations. In the 1982 Oblate Constitutions and Rules the texts in italics which appear on the left-hand pages are Father de Mazenod's originals. There is nothing "copied" about them: they come from the very heart. So too, all the strong and forceful sentences in the present Oblate Rule come from the Founder's heart.

October 24, 1818: The First Rule

Eugene presented the Rule to his companions at the beginning of the retreat on October 24, 1818. The six priests readily accepted the first part, but some balked at the second section on religious life. In a spirited session Fathers Tempier and Moreau, with the Founder, voted in favour; Fathers Mie, Deblieu, Maunier and Aubert, against. Thus the vote stood at four in favour to three against. Eugene then called the three scholastics, Joseph-Hippolyte Courtès, Marius Suzanne and a Brother Dupuy, stating that they had most of a stake in the society because they were its future. Another vote was taken and the scholastics carried the day. The final result was six to four in favour of religious life and vows! It was the only general chapter in the congregation's history wherein scholastics actively participated with voice and vote. Immediately afterwards, the participants unanimously confirmed Eugene de Mazenod as superior of the group – proof that despite momentary dissensions, unity and charity still prevailed. In his memoirs Father François Moreau recalled:

> (Acting as) a constituted society gathered in General Chapter according to the terms of the Rule which had just been accepted, the assembly unanimously requested Father de Mazenod to continue in his position as superior general. Then, as proof of the affection which everyone felt toward Father Deblieu, despite his refusal to bind himself by vows, the assembly almost unanimously elected him first assistant-general and admonitor to the superior general. . . . Father Maunier was chosen second

assistant and secretary general, Father Tempier third assistant, and Father Mie, fourth. Brother Courtès was elected bursar general.[43]

That means there were six executive positions in a congregation where only ten men were in vows. Why was it so top-heavy? Leflon observes: "This clever apportioning of positions meant at one and the same time approving Eugene de Mazenod's firm determination to make his plan for the religious life prevail and proving to those who opposed it that they still enjoyed everyone's esteem. Certainly they must have been deeply affected by such thoughtfulness."[44]

All the necessary authorizations were made with Msgr. Guigou, the vicar-general of Aix, de Mazenod's staunch ally. At the end of the week-long retreat in which the general chapter took place, the newly constituted religious congregation took first vows on November 1, 1818. "[The Founder] pronounced his vows of chastity, obedience and perseverance in the presence of Fortuné; during the Mass which followed, he accepted the vows of Fathers Maunier, Mie, Tempier and Moreau, and of the scholastic brothers Dupuy, Courtès and Suzanne.[45] . . . Thus, the Society of the Missionaries of Provence was permanently founded."[46]

What is Perfection?

What was the significance of the vow of obedience exchanged between Fathers Tempier and de Mazenod on that Holy Thursday night? For the unflappable Tempier it was a sanctifying vow that he fully intended to fulfil, nothing more complicated. For de Mazenod, the vow was also a curb. Tying his will to Tempier kept him from being too authoritarian, too impulsive, too imprudent – defects to which he was all to prone. In matters of health, too, Father Tempier could forbid the Founder to preach, and he obeyed!

But despite their vow, Tempier often had to face, not "the slings and arrows of outrageous fortune," but the slings and arrows of an outraged Founder's hair-trigger temper. There is an unrecorded story, handed down from the old Oblates of France, from the time when de Mazenod was already bishop of Marseilles and Father Tempier his vicar-general. It seems that during a Mass the two of them were kneeling next to one another and Tempier was reciting his office. In a whispered aside, de Mazenod told him to close his

---

[43] Leflon, vol. 2, p. 168.
[44] Ibid., p. 268.
[45] Deblieu had requested a year's grace before committing himself; Aubert requested temporary vows.
[46] Leflon, vol. 2, p. 169.

breviary. When there was no reaction from Tempier, he repeated the order. Still there was no reaction, as Father Tempier kept reciting his office. Whereupon the furious bishop exploded: "Tempier, what do you take me for, a piece of dog-shit?" With that, he knocked the breviary from the priest's hands and it went skittering across the sanctuary floor.

That incident, taken from Oblate oral tradition, shows the impetuous temperament of the man. To the Founder's credit, he always felt bad after such an outburst and sought to apologize as soon as possible. Moreover, the incident is yet another example of how providential it was that he had at his side someone as even-keeled as Tempier, who understood him perfectly, shared his decisions and curbed his temper. Indeed, Henri Tempier's equanimity was a perfect foil to Eugene de Mazenod's tempestuous character and constantly served as a calming influence. Leflon relates:

> As much a victim as anyone to those outbursts, good Father Tempier had his own method of calming the "mistral" immediately. Without saying a word, he allowed the prelate to blow off steam, and when everything became quiet simply asked, "What then? . . ." Nothing further was needed to restore calm immediately. To those who overlooked such outbursts and accepted him as he was, Bishop de Mazenod was deeply grateful, for never would he have deliberately or needlessly hurt anyone. In fact, whenever the responsibility of his office obliged him to give a reprimand or a just punishment, it actually pained him to do so. But once his duty as superior was fulfilled, he made every effort to encourage and console.[47]

All of which leads to the question: what is perfection? In the Greek sense of the word *perfect*, Eugene de Mazenod certainly died imperfect, as all of us will some day. But it is worth remembering that Scripture does not consider perfection in the Greek sense. Biblical perfection has to do with the quality of our relationship to God our Father. De Mazenod was deeply related to God, despite the human deficiencies which dogged him to the end of his days. Hopefully, we can say the same at the end of ours.

---

[47] Leflon, vol. 4, p. 311.

October 15, 1815

My dear friend, read this letter at the foot of your crucifix with a mind to heed only God and what is demanded of a priest like yourself in the interests of God's glory and the salvation of souls. Stifle any voice of cupidity or love of comfort and convenience; dwell deeply on the plight of our country people, on their religious situation and on the apostasy that daily spreads wider with dreadfully ravaging effects. Look at how feeble are the means employed up to now to oppose this flood of evil; ask your heart what it would do to counter such disasters and then reply to my letter.

Well, dear man, without going into details, I want to tell you that you are necessary for the work which the Lord inspires us to undertake. The head of the Church is convinced that, given the wretched state in which France finds herself, only missions can bring people back to the Faith which they have practically abandoned. Hence, good men of the Church from different dioceses are banding together in response to the views of our Supreme Pastor. We also feel that it is utterly necessary to employ the same remedy here in our region and, full of confidence in the goodness of Providence, we have laid down the foundations of an establishment which will steadily furnish our countryside with fervent missionaries. They will ceaselessly engage in destroying the demon's empire, at the same time providing the example of a life worthy of the Church in the community which they will form. Indeed, we will live together in one house, the one I bought, under a Rule we shall adopt with common accord and for which we will draw the elements from the statutes of St. Ignatius, of St. Charles for his Oblates, of St. Philip Neri, of St. Vincent de Paul, and of Blessed Liguori.

Happiness awaits us in the holy society which will have but one heart and one soul. One part of the year will be devoted to the conversion of souls, the other to seclusion, study and our individual sanctification. I will say no more for the moment; suffice it to give you some intimation of the spiritual delights we will taste together.

Should you wish, as I hope, to be one of us, you will not find yourself in unknown terrain; you will have four companions. If presently we are not more numerous, it means we wish to choose men with the will and the courage to walk in the footsteps of the apostles. It is important to lay solid foundations. The greatest regularity must be planned and introduced in the house the very moment we enter it. And it is precisely for that reason that you are necessary to me because I know you to be capable of embracing an exemplary rule and persevering in it.

Once I have your reply, I will give you all the details you could wish for. But, dear friend, I conjure you, do not let yourself say no to the greatest good that may possibly be done to the Church. Vicars can easily be found to replace you, but it would not be as easy to come across dedicated men who wish to devote themselves to the glory of God and the salvation of souls with no more reward on earth than much sorrow and all else that the Saviour announced to his true disciples. The harm your refusal would do to our new-born enterprise would be incalculable. I speak sincerely and with reflection. Your modesty may suffer, but no matter. I do not hesitate to add that if I believed it necessary to make the journey to Arles to convince you, I would wing my way there. Everything depends on how we begin. We need perfect unanimity of sentiments, the same good will, the same disinterestedness, the same devotion. That sums it up.

I share your views completely, my dear confrère, and far from needing your urging to enter this holy Society which satisfies my own desires so completely, I assure you that had I known of your plans before you mentioned them to me, I would have been the first to speak of my joining your Society. Thus, I feel that I owe you a debt of gratitude for judging me worthy to work with you for the glory of God and the salvation of souls.

True, I can make no claim to any talent for preaching, which is so essential in a missionary, but *alius sic, alius autem sic*. What I cannot do in eloquent sermons, I shall do in catechism classes and instructions. . . . I find nothing lowly or inferior in that.

Besides, what you want most in someone you choose as your collaborator is a priest who will not get into a rut, and, as Father Charles' predecessor used to say, plod along day after day without accomplishing anything; you want priests who will be ready to follow in the footsteps of the apostles and work for the salvation of souls with no other reward here on earth but hardship and fatigue. I think that God's grace has given me that desire. If not, then with all my heart I want it, and working with you will make it all the easier to attain. You can, therefore, count entirely on me.

François de Paule-Henri Tempier

III

Parochial Missions

The Restoration

With the initial abdication of Napoleon in 1814 and his subsequent exile to Elba, the First Republic floundered to an end and a new political era dawned in France. To general shouts of "Long live the King!" the Bourbon monarchy returned. When Louis de Bourbon, Count of Provence, landed from his exile in England, the Marquis de Maisonfort told him, "Sire, you are now the king." To which the monarch replied, "Have I ever been otherwise?"[1] Thus the period got its name – the Restoration – because the monarchy was restored, not newly invented. Louis XVIII's reign, however, would be a new type of monarchy, for he committed himself to a constitutional government. Still, the nobility was elated by the change, as was the Church. With Napoleon gone, apostolic works could leave the underground and come into the open.

But the first period of the Restoration was short-lived. Indeed, almost before the king took the throne, he was forced to flee the Tuilleries, taking refuge in the provinces because, less than a year after the start of Napoleon's exile on Elba, he escaped and landed near Cannes on March 1, 1815. Thus began the epic Hundred Days that would end with his defeat at Waterloo in Belgium on June 18, 1815. At that point, rather than continue a hopeless war, the emperor submitted his final abdication and soon afterwards was exiled to St. Helena in the south Atlantic. There he died under questionable circumstances on May 5, 1821.[2]

In Provence, the Abbé de Mazenod had to interrupt his plans to preach a mission in Grans, near Aix, where his mother's Jansenist cousin-confidant (and his own opponent in religious clashes) Roze-Joannis was mayor. More indignant than surprised at Napoleon's return, de Mazenod wrote, "What a nation we are. When we lost the faith we lost all sense of honour and

---

[1] Fayard, *Histoire de France,* vol. 4, p. 307.
[2] Officially, Napoleon died of a perforated ulcer, but tests have since shown that it was probably from accumulated doses of arsenic.

credibility as well." No one, not even an intimidating mob of volunteers and regular soldiers could wring a "Long live the Emperor," from Eugene's lips, and he continued to say the prayer for the king in a loud voice at Mass. On July 19, 1815, Eugene wrote to his father that he had to face three drawn swords in order to save a hapless man from being run through. Generally speaking, however, Provence was strongly royalist, so there was little sympathy for Napoleon's return. Despite some run-ins with rag-tag local republican volunteers, Aix remained royalist. The "infamous marshal" Brune threatened to punish the city and an attack appeared imminent. *La Quotidienne* of Aix reported on July 28, 1815, that everyone, even the peasants from the neighbouring towns, came with their pitchforks, bayonets, guns and whatever else they had to defend the city. Eugene described the scene thus to his father:

> Disillusioned after twenty-five years of revolution, the people, more royalist than ourselves, if that were possible, were the first to appear; they came with such fearlessness and such nobility of soul that they would have wrung tears from anyone. At the first sound of the alarm, everyone from Milles, Bouc, Gardanne, etc. set out for Aix, ignoring the harvests they were leaving behind with selflessness, the likes of which had never before been seen. The king's name was on every tongue.[3]

Luckily, Marshal Brune was kept busy by the English at Toulon and Antibes, so the attack never materialized.

The White Terror

The 15 years of Napoleon's Empire, with its wars and blockades, left Provence in economic shambles. In Marseilles between 1799 and 1814 the population shrank from 111,000 to 96,000.[4] Obviously the situation created great dissatisfaction. When Napoleon's efforts to re-establish the Republic failed at Waterloo, the king returned to Paris and in Provence the royalists sharpened their knives. They were not going to let something like the Hundred Days happen again. The king promised to mete out justice to "the instigators and authors of that horrible plot," but when instead he proclaimed a general amnesty the royalists took matters into their own hands. Sparing the Jacobins and Napoleon's followers in 1814 had been the cause of all their problems. They were determined that history would not repeat itself. Thus, in the fiery days of July they began the White Terror, three months of anarchy that released bitter passions. There is no record of how many republicans were killed, but the number, although frequently exaggerated,

---

[3] Letter to his father, July 7, 1815, Bibliothèque Méjanes, Aix, B69.

[4] Fayard, *Histoire de France,* vol. 4, p. 238.

must have been significant. The Founder certainly did not take part, yet it is obvious from his letters that he thought the revolutionaries were getting what they deserved. In the letter quoted above, Eugene told his father: "I always felt the king pardoned villains to whom no one but God has the right to show mercy."[5]

A month later, on August 8, he again wrote his father to tell him of the fate of Brune at the hands of the mob in Avignon: "The people . . . literally tore him to shreds. If you want to know what sort he was, it was he who waved the head of the Princesse de Lamballe beneath the window of the Knights Templar church. He was once a marshal; now he is with the devil."[6]

The Social Classes During the Restoration

The nobles were as conservative as ever and saw the Church as the protector of the old moral order. Upon their return, they looked for a restoration that would be something akin to the *ancien régime,* a restoration that would allow them to recover their belongings and positions of privilege.

The bourgeoisie was the big winner in the Revolution and stood to be the big loser if ever the nobles and the Church recouped the power they once had. For the most part the members of the bourgeoisie were Voltairian free-thinkers and deeply anti-clerical. Although they believed in a God, they believed even more firmly in getting rid of the Church. The practising Catholics among them were not immune to this influence and Father de Mazenod always had problems with the bourgeois wherever his community preached missions.

France had just come through a quarter-century of continuous warfare on a score of fronts – 25 years during which the ordinary people served as cannon-fodder for the armies. Now they were fed up with all the carnage of revolt and war and longed for peace, searching for constancy in their constantly changing world. The religion of Reason, imposed by the state during the Revolution, had failed, for it did not correspond to their deep religious feelings. They were ripe for a religious reawakening. This explains, in part, the great success of Father de Mazenod and his little band of missionaries.

Politically, the Restoration was characterized by the monarchy's struggle against the bourgeoisie, which had grown fat and powerful during the Revolution at the expense of the poor, the nobles and the Church.

---

5 Letter to his father, July 7, 1815, Bibliothèque Méjanes, Aix, B69.
6 Letter to his father, August 8, 1815, Bibliothèque Méjanes, Aix, B69.

Understandably, the middle class had no intention of losing ground to the royalists who now sought to reclaim a*ncien régime* prerogatives.

The Catholic Restoration

Until 1870, the universal Catholic Church continued to be a temporal power ruled by an absolute monarch, the pope. Thus the Church had a difficult time dealing with a secular democracy which, by very definition, separated itself from religious obedience. It was obvious that in France the Church felt much more at home when the monarchy was restored. Moreover, the lines between the restoration of the monarchy and the restoration of the Church frequently became blurred. In the hymns of the period, for example, it is striking how frequently praise for the king appears in divine worship. Yet the Restoration was also a time of spiritual renewal and the parochial mission seemed the proper vehicle to carry that renewal. In his first letter to the Abbé Tempier, Father de Mazenod said: "The Head of the Church is persuaded that, given the wretched state in which France finds herself, only missions can bring the people back to the Faith which they have practically abandoned. Hence, good men of the Church from different dioceses are banding together in response to the views of our Supreme Pastor."[7]

The Duc de Berry Assassinated

The severest test of the Restoration came five years later when Father de Mazenod's friend from the days of exile in Palermo, the Duc de Berry, was ambushed and assassinated on the night of February 14, 1820, by a disgruntled veteran of Napoleon's army. The sharp knives came out again with shouts for general reprisals against revolutionaries and the liberal bourgeois. This time Father de Mazenod, who was preaching a mission in Marseilles at the time, used his influence to avoid bloodshed. Gone were the feelings of "just desserts for the guilty." Later, Bishop Jeancard would write:

> Fortunately, the old districts where these reprisals were on the point of being carried out were being evangelized at that moment by the Missionaries of Provence; religion was the only force powerful enough to restrain arms poised to strike, and it was stronger than ever in those districts. Consequently, by intervening and appealing to the people in the name of religion, Father de Mazenod warded off the danger. Although he abhorred the crime which plunged France into mourning, he spoke only in the peaceful and gentle language of the gospel when he spoke from the pulpit of St-Laurent church and he used the same language in the Carmelite

---

[7] *Selected Texts*, p. 17, n. 2.

church. After the evening service he went out into the street and talked with the different groups which had formed there. Everyone listened to him with pious respect and he succeeded thereby in allaying the violent passions which had been seething within the masses and which were about to erupt upon the city with all their fury. Some days later, the men of the two parishes said it was only because of him that they had held back.[8]

At the death of Louis XVIII in 1824, Charles X came to the throne, and one crisis succeeded another in government. Finally, the Restoration ground to a halt with the July Revolt in 1830, whereupon the king abdicated and went into exile. Louis-Philippe took over and inaugurated a new period in French history, known as the July Monarchy.

In 1832, the Duc de Berry's widow, Marie-Christine, went secretly to Marseilles to seek support for a legitimist coup against Louis-Philippe, in favour of her son the Duc de Bordeaux. By that time Eugene was already his uncle's vicar-general in Marseilles. Despite the fact that he knew the Duchess well from the court of her father, the king of the Sicilies, and especially from the days of their exile in Palermo, he made absolutely no effort to see her. Indeed, it would appear that he avoided any contact with her at all. Louis-Philippe discovered the plot and the Duchess was imprisoned in the Castle of Blaye for a while before returning to Palermo. In this episode we can see how a political change had taken place in Eugene de Mazenod: from sympathy with the sharp knives of the White Terror in 1815, to peace-making in 1820, to non-involvement in the political cause of the legitimists in 1832.

The First Parochial Missions

Grans (March, 1816)

Situated some 30 kilometres outside of Aix, Grans was the site of the group's first parochial mission. We have no reports about it, just a couple of references. During the mission, Father de Mazenod jotted off a quick note to Father Tempier: "It is absolutely impossible for me to write to you, my good brother and friend. We have no time to eat or even to sleep . . . . Were I to enter into details, you would be moved to tears . . . . Religion would be lost in this country without the mission. It is a triumph. Though it be the death of us I shall not complain. Our work is indispensable and only if we are twelve shall it be able to continue. Plead for recruits in your prayers . . . ."[9]

---

[8] Leflon, vol. 2, p. 112.
[9] *Oblate Writings,* vol. 6, 1816, p. 18, n. 10.

About the mission in Grans, Rambert later wrote:

> We will always regret that a detailed report of that mission was never made. It was the first that our Fathers gave and they often spoke to us about it with the greatest enthusiasm. How many miracles of grace and blessings from God! What devotion, austerity, pious daring, yes, and holy folly, too, on the part of the ardent missionaries, devoured as they were by zeal! . . . Father de Mazenod always deplored the fact that no report was ever made of that mission. Years later, he tried to make one, but it was too late.[10]

In his journal, the Founder of the Oblates described an incident that happened during the Grans mission. It shows how distant his way of thinking was from Jansenism:

> A man who had gone to confession and, like the rest, promised to stop blaspheming, came back in a state of utter confusion to look for me. "What can be troubling you, my friend, to make you so sad?" I asked.
>
> "Alas, Father," he replied in Provençal, *"M'en a esquia un"*, which meant that a blasphemy had escaped him, despite his best intentions. "But," he added, "I gave myself a good licking."
>
> Here is what happened. The good man was on the way to his field, walking behind his donkey cart loaded with barnyard manure. All of a sudden, the donkey balked, kicking over the malodorous load. Taken unprepared, in that first instant of anger the poor man let slip one of those salty words with which he had regularly laced his conversation. Instantly he realized what he had just said, and considered it a serious moral breach. He immediately grabbed his whip, and after giving a few good licks to the donkey, the cause of all his woes, he turned it on himself and administered a self-thrashing worthy of someone who had learned what it truly meant to apply the discipline. "That was for punishment," he told me, "and so I'll remember, the next time when something happens."
>
> I reassured the good man and sent him on his way, happy. As for me, I was both dumb-founded and deeply edified.[11]

Today, that incident may not seem very significant, but in the 19th-century Jansenist context it was far from usual. Had the man gone to a Jansenist priest, he would have been told, "You are a hopeless sinner lost in mortal sin. You must confess again." Perhaps he would not even have received absolution at that time but would have had to go back to the confessional repeatedly before the sin was finally absolved. Father de Mazenod in no way condemned the hapless peasant. Instead, he "reassured the good man and sent him on his way." Nor did he see him as a terrible sinner. On the contrary, he was "dumfounded and deeply edified" by the man's basic goodness.

---

[10] Rambert, vol. 1, p. 179.

[11] Ibid., p. 183.

Fuveau (September, 1816)

So great was the success of this epic and heroic mission that the ceremonies had to take place in the square outside the church, for want of space within. The missionaries worked day and night to accommodate all the people, not only from Fuveau itself but from the neighbouring towns and from the mines of Gardanne, 8 kilometres away. Surprisingly for those times, as many men as women crowded into the ceremonies.

That the missionaries put themselves completely at the disposal of the populace was an important aspect of the mission and warrants notice. Two missions ran concurrently – one for the people of Fuveau and the surrounding district, during the day, and another at night for the miners of Gardanne, who daily walked the 16 kilometres to and from Fuveau to attend the mission after their long hours of work in the mines.

Late at night, after an exhausting day of ministering, the missionaries would sit down to their frugal evening meal, with a watch placed on the table so as not to eat beyond midnight. (Remember, those were still the days of eucharistic fast from midnight on.) They would then go off to bed, but rise again at 3:30 A.M. for their religious exercises and to get the mission ceremonies of the day underway. That was the "holy folly" of which Rambert spoke in the reference cited. The missionaries were in the honeymoon of their beginnings, when no sacrifice was too great and when everything, no matter how difficult, was a joy.

The Rule of 1818

The Rule of 1818 had an entire chapter on preaching missions and, in addition, some particular regulations for their execution. Missions was the only topic meriting such regulations in the whole rule. Thus, it is important to examine some of the articles, especially the first two.

> *Article 1.* The end of the Institute of the said Missionaries of Provence is, first of all, to form a group of secular priests who live together and strive to imitate the virtues and example of our Saviour Jesus Christ, mainly by dedicating themselves to preaching the Divine Word to the poor.

> *Article 2.* (They) will dedicate themselves . . . to bringing spiritual assistance to the poor scattered throughout the countryside, as well as to the inhabitants of small rural settlements deprived of such spiritual assistance. They will take care of such needs through missions, sessions of catechism, retreats or other spiritual exercises.

From Articles 1 and 2 it is clear that Father de Mazenod meant to address the needs of the poor by various means. The Society of Missionaries of Provence was not founded simply to preach parochial missions.

Article 6 indicated that each mission was to be given by at least two Oblates, never by one alone. In this we see the importance of community as a gospel witness.

Another article, included in later editions of the rule but never put into practice, stated that the mission should be given at the expense of the society. To that end the Founder proposed setting up a foundation fund that would afford the Oblates freedom in the exercise of their ministry. It was a beautiful idea, but probably too idealistic; thus it was never realized.

Article 7 dealt with apostolic poverty. One application of this rule was that when going to give a mission, the missionaries were to do so on foot, if possible, or failing that, on horseback. Only when their destination was distant would they use public transportation. For example, the missionaries walked from Aix to Grans to give their first mission, a distance of 30 kilometres. Again we must recall that they were in the honeymoon of their beginnings.

Article 10 stated, "In order to confirm the good done during a mission, it would be desirable that the missionaries return within a year to the same places. . . ." In practice, on the return visit the missionaries spent a few days giving a mini-mission, with spiritual exercises and exhortations. It was a sort of booster-shot.

Articles 15-17 forbade the members of the society from getting involved in occupations which would be foreign to their work. In practice, they would not take part in grandiose processions (outside of their own mission ceremonies), nor were they to be ordinary confessors of nuns, etc. They were to keep foremost the principal aim of the congregation – to labour for the most abandoned. This rule was doubly important in the beginning when there were so few members. It reminds one of Luke 10: "Greet no one along the way. . . ."

Particular Regulations for the Missions

The Rule of 1818 contained a set of precise regulations that formed a sort of directory to be strictly adhered to and used in all missions. Here are its features:

Common Preparation

The work was organized by the superior. He was to appoint a mission director who would confer in good time with those who were to share the work. The director need not necessarily be the oldest Oblate of the mission group; what was important was his fitness for the job. Father Mie, for example, was the oldest and had a great deal of experience, yet was never a director of mission.

Mission team members were to prepare themselves by personal and community prayer. There was also to be a one-day retreat for the group before every mission.

In the ceremony of departure the entire community assembled and the superior blessed the mission team. Particular prayers were used which became the basis of the prayers now used in the departure ceremony for missionaries going to foreign lands.

Christ walked from place to place throughout the countryside of Galilee. As far as feasible, the missionaries were to imitate him in that. They were to arrive at their destination late on Sunday afternoon; this would accommodate the farmers who had work to do in the afternoon.

The people, along with their parish priest (who carried a cross), awaited the arrival of the missionaries at the entrance to the village. When they got there, the cross was passed to the director of the group and the procession into town began. Once in the church, the parish priest blessed the missionaries and the first ceremony of the mission got underway. The place of the parish priest was never usurped: the missionaries came to second his efforts and make his ministry more effective; they were there at the service of the Christian community.

Visiting the People

The first two days of the mission were set aside to make visits to the homes of the people. Except in overly-populated areas, it meant visiting every home without exception, even if an unfriendly reception was foreseen. The idea was to meet the people on their own ground to get to know their concrete problems and needs. Thus the missionaries would be preaching from life rather than from some lofty theory. According to several historians this was an innovation introduced by the Abbé de Mazenod; nothing similar can be found in other groups that gave parochial missions in France. Cardinal Poupard wrote: "If we take into account the searching study by Canon Severin on the missions at the time of the Restoration, it appears obvious that those house visits constitute a fortunate initiative taken by Father de Mazenod, without equal among other groups of missionaries."[12]

---

[12] *XIX° siècle, siècle de grâces*, p. 81.

Father de Mazenod himself wrote in his journal:

> Those visits are not very enjoyable, but they are very important because they bring the missionaries closer to the people they have come to evangelize. With true graciousness they will display a charity which is all things to all men, thereby winning the hearts of the most indifferent. Thus, they will be enabled to encourage and to urge the people, and to cope with certain resistance; and, as they proceed with those visits, they will frequently discover and begin to remedy disorders which very often would escape the notice of even a zealous pastor.[13]

The Missionaries' Schedule

4:00 a.m.	Rising, followed by a half-hour of meditation
Mass	(Concelebration was not permitted in those days; priests celebrated Mass two-by-two, with one celebrating while the other served, then the reverse.)
Morning	In the church and at the disposal of anyone who wanted to talk with a priest.
Noon	Lunch in community; on certain days, the priests went two-by-two to visit the sick.
Evening	The main exercises of the mission, with all missionaries participating.
10:00 p.m.	Supper in common.
11:00 p.m.	Lights out so as to have at least six hours of rest. This regulation was added after the missionaries almost worked themselves to death without sleep in Fuveau. There was also a one-hour siesta.

Mission Team Meeting

The regulations insisted that there be a meeting of the missionaries in the director's room on Saturday afternoons. This was a kind of *culpe* wherein the missionaries asked pardon for their shortcomings. Then followed a discussion on various points regarding the mission, especially on the *casus conscientiae* – difficult cases that had come up in the confessional in the course of the mission. It is well to note that the youngest Oblates were traditionally the first to speak, a precaution meant to keep them from being overawed in their opinions by what the veterans had to say.

---

13 Leflon, vol. 2, p. 91.

Closure

The ending of a mission, highlighted by setting up a mission cross, was a special ceremony. The cross was meant to be a reminder to the people of their commitment.

Announcements

The regulations contain a paragraph on announcements, saying that they should not be given as any kind of reproach, but in a way that puts the congregation at ease.

Preaching the Word of God

The Rule of 1818 insisted that if the missionaries were to have any impact in preaching the gospel, they had to be, above all, men of prayer, living the Word of God themselves. The virtues take on special importance as a foundation for everything. A quotation from the early rule, reproduced on page 16 of the present Oblate Constitutions and Rules, states: "Like the Apostles, to preach "Jesus Christ, and him crucified . . . not in loftiness of speech, but in the showing of the Spirit," that is to say, by making manifest that we have pondered in our hearts the words which we proclaim, and *that we began to practice before setting out to teach.*"

The meaning of the paragraph is its call to an authentic spiritual life. First, the missionary is called to virtue, prayer, generosity and simplicity, then to the humility that makes grace work.

In a letter to Father Tempier, dated March 30, 1826, Father de Mazenod enlarged upon the virtues he expected of his missionaries in order to fructify the preaching of the Word:

> My only wish is that we preach in a beneficial manner, putting aside all self-interest. Unless we do that, not much good can be achieved. I hope that our Fathers are also firmly determined to act with great prudence, since they have to deal with such ill-disposed persons. Advise them to behave like saints, true apostles, adding exterior modesty and a great love for sinners to their preaching. It should be evident from their behaviour that they are not just ordinary preachers, but men animated by zeal proper to their holy vocation. Let them not neglect themselves if they wish to be useful to others. Consequently, they should pray much. Then the good Lord will come to their aid and everything will go well.[14]

---

[14] *Selected Texts*, p. 38, n. 15.

With good reason the introductory paragraph in the Oblate rule on preaching the Word concludes with a call for humility. For Eugene de Mazenod, the way to win "souls for the Glory of God" was not through eloquence but through simple, faith-filled preaching, letting the very power of God work conversion and change. His missionaries, he insisted, must never forget that the marvels of the apostolate are the result of God's grace, not of their doing. That is why he referred at times to preaching as a "perilous ministry." By this Father de Mazenod meant that the ministry was so marvelous that there was a danger that some priests could get caught up in themselves, thinking that they were responsible for the great results of their preaching and forgetting that the Spirit, not they, worked the miracles of grace. It was never perilous for them to "empty themselves," putting everything they have into preaching for the glory of God. Indeed, Father de Mazenod himself rejoiced unreservedly at the marvels accomplished by the missionaries. In his journal of March 13, 1842, he wrote:

> Father Vincens sent me Father Burfin's letter telling of the blessings showered on the mission he just preached with Father Lavigne in the diocese of Grenoble. Once again our Fathers have been *the instruments of God's mercy* in those areas. Should we not be grateful for having been *chosen* to accomplish so much good in God's Church? Why not make a brief of this synthesis? We would be amazed; it is an achievement of which our Congregation can rightly be proud.[15]

Penance and the Ministry of Reconciliation

In *The Call of the Congregation,* Father Robert Eimer wrote:

> As a missionary, as a priest in the confessional or a preacher in the pulpit who made sinners weep, as a man who preached the boundless love of Jesus on the cross, de Mazenod was a merciful, kind, gentle man. He had a passion to reconcile all peoples with the Lord of the cross. In regard to confession, he wrote to Father Courtès in 1827, "I have made it a rule, my dear friend, never to refuse to hear anyone's confession." He and his small band of Oblates were called laxists in the confessional . . . .[16]

Hoarse and exhausted from so much preaching, Father de Mazenod wrote a letter to Father Tempier in Aix during the Barjols mission in 1818 that gives an idea of the missionaries' daunting task in instructing and bringing back to Christian practice people who had been bereft of the sacraments for more than a generation:

> The men came flocking at the first announcement and God knows they needed to do so! What we have here, for them and for the women alike, are

---

[15] *Selected Texts*, p. 169, n. 141.
[16] "The Call of the Congregation", in *Vie Oblate Life,* April, 1991, p. 93.

lapses of thirty, forty, even fifty years. People are astonished at the success of the mission . . . . They are so attentive, the silence they keep is so great, that they hear me everywhere, although I speak in a low voice. Also I am better; I gulp down goat's milk, donkey's milk and fresh eggs. That does me good.[17]

The original rule referred to the sacrament in the traditional way of the time, as *penance*, not as *reconciliation*, the title by which we know it today. It stated that this sacrament completes what has been begun in preaching – hearts moved by the Word are sanctified by the action of grace in the sacrament of reconciliation – and when necessary, the hearing of confessions was to be preferred over preaching.

Father de Mazenod gave several other directives. There should be a *healthy balance* between severity and indulgence. The *problems of life* which the people carry as their cross must be taken into account, an approach far more beneficial than invoking probabilism, equi-probabilism, or any of the other "isms" associated with the theoretic cases studied in moral theology at the seminary. A missionary must "be ready to receive sinners with *inexhaustible charity*; giving courage to the faint-hearted."

In the *Directory of Missions*, Father de Mazenod said, "Give a light penance. For example, for sins against purity, a few *Ave Marias*." And during his famous Lenten instructions of 1813, in the Church of the Madeleine, he told the congregation: "My brethren, we appear threatening only in the pulpit. But, really, in the sacred tribunal we change our way of speaking and then, perhaps, we are even too indulgent. Yes, my brethren, come and you will see with what joy we will help you carry your burden."[18] Compare that to a terror-of-hell-fire approach from a non-Oblate in Dijon:

O, how the soul of the sinner suffers to find itself transfixed by God's fierce glare during Judgment. Suddenly there are no friends. The soul leaps to the right, only to fall onto the teeth of a tiger. Then to the left – onto a bear's paw. And behind, there are only serpents. "O, my God, what can I do?" cries the anguished soul, too late. Below, the gaping jaws of hell open wide. O, how the soul suffers at that moment! So much so, that the sinner would almost prefer to plunge into that terrible abyss immediately . . . .

Jesus is seated on his throne before the sinner: on his right, the guardian angel; on his left, Satan. Then the interrogation begins, and in vain the sinner tries to stutter some poor excuse. God is unrelenting. Satan opens his book – he has not forgotten a thing. Indeed, the least fault is written there. "Master," he screams, "this soul is mine! I was its tireless enemy; I wanted only its downfall and it always obeyed me and outraged you. Yes,

---

[17] *Oblate Writings,* vol. 6, p. 51, n. 34.
[18] *Écrits spirituels: 1812-1856,* p. 61.

it mocked you, its very God, you who died on the Cross to save it." And Satan continues, "Master, this soul is worthy of death."

Jesus shouts, "Then let it die" and turning to the sinner he says, "Away from my sight, damned soul, for you are horrible to look at. Disappear forever from my eyes. All of you, friends and relatives of this sinner, come and curse him as well." They all come to condemn the poor person whom Satan drags to hell. All of what we have just recounted, in reality, takes but an instant. The body of the dead person is still warm when his soul already roars and blasphemes in its infernal habitation.[19]

It was Father de Mazenod who introduced the theology of St. Alphonsus into Southern France. In 1980 a group of eight French historians – all lay persons – collaborated in the publication of a book on French Church history entitled *Histoire des catholiques en France du XV ͤ siècle á nos jours (The History of Catholics in France from the 15th Century to Our Day)*. One of the authors, Claude Langlois, writing about religious renewal during the Restoration, stated:

> Perhaps the introduction of St. Alphonsus Liguori's moral theology was the strongest element modifying religious sensitivity in France. It was a major event in pastoral practice, for the aim of this new theology was to pull down "the barriers between Christians and the normal frequenting of the sacraments." In reality, it countered the moral rigorism of confessors and did away with results flowing naturally from their closed mentality – such as the refusal to give absolution. That new theology only took hold gradually. It came into France through the *Midi* (the South), *where Mazenod and his Oblates were its propagators.*[20]

The compassion and the inexhaustible charity that Father de Mazenod asked of his missionaries can be seen in his reply to Father Eugene Guigues during the mission in Theys in 1837. There "certain bourgeois families gave scandal," Guigues informed him, "by taking part in a sort of crude, provocative and mocking musical parody. A number of young people who had let themselves be carried away by this later came to make their confession. Should Communion be refused to them?" The Jansenist reply would have been obvious. De Mazenod, however, wrote in his journal: "God grant that such an unfortunate idea, born of inexperience, did not lead the missionaries to receive such sinners coldly: they should have been welcomed with the warmest kindness." And in his reply to Father Guigues, he stated:

> Remember that you are sent to sinners . . . . We are ministers of mercy, so let us always show a father's tenderness toward everyone. Let us also

---

[19] *Élisabeth de la Trinité*, vol. 2, n. 51.
[20] *Histoire des catholiques en France – du XV ͤ siècle á nos jours*, p. 340.

easily forget the insults sometimes heaped on us in the exercise of our ministry, just as the good Lord chooses to forget the offences continually committed against him. The prodigal son's father was not content with just putting the best robe on his son and a ring on his finger – he also had the fatted calf killed. In like manner, we must not only reconcile sinners, but admit them to the Sacred Banquet, giving them the Bread of Life in view of all the graces granted them during the mission . . . .[21]

Father de Mazenod made it very clear that the sacrament of reconciliation should be well-prepared. Writing from Marseilles to Father Jean Viala in Gréasque in 1849, he stated:

I congratulate you for the good which, by the grace of God, you have already achieved and for all that you still have to do. I recommend that you insist a good deal on the degree of instruction and the state of mind necessary for the sacrament of Penance. . . . Insist on making Jesus Christ known and loved. Speak often of this divine Saviour and of all he has done to save mankind. Make people resolve never to spend a day without praying.[22]

Values and Characteristics of the First Parochial Missions

What values do we find upon examining the parochial missions preached by those early Missionaries of Provence?

The Mission – A Time of Renewal

Father de Mazenod had great confidence in parochial missions because they provided an excellent opportunity for Christians to take time to reflect on and change their lives. That is also why times of renewal appear so frequently in his first rule – retreat days, personal prayer, particular examen, community meetings, etc. He felt strongly that we all need to have some time dedicated to personal renewal, to take stock of where we stand in our relationship with Jesus. And as for his missionaries, he firmly believed that they could not give to others what they themselves did not have.

A Deep Respect for the People

Remember the 1813 sermon in La Madeleine: "Come now, and learn from us what you are in the eyes of faith. You are the children of God, the brothers and sisters of Jesus Christ, the co-heirs of his eternal Kingdom, the cherished portion of his inheritance; you are, in the words of Saint Peter, a holy nation, you are kings, you are priests, you are, in a certain way, gods. . . ." Article 5

---

[21] *Selected Texts*, pp. 167 ff., n. 140.
[22] *Oblate Writings*, vol. 4, 1849, p. 166, n. 4.

of the present Oblate Constitutions and Rules echoes Father de Mazenod's firm respect for the people to be evangelized: "We preach the Gospel among people who have not yet received it and *help them see their own values in its light*. Where the Church is already established, our commitment is to those groups it least touches." His attitude is also reflected strongly in Article 4 of the same Constitutions and Rules: "Through the eyes of the crucified Saviour we see the world which he redeemed with his blood, desiring that those in whom he continues to suffer will know also the power of his resurrection (Philippians 3:10)."

Always Close to the People

When we examine the methods practised by the first missionaries, we find that they visited everyone without distinction, that they spent their mornings in church *making themselves available* to anyone who wanted to discuss their problems or seek counsel, that they spoke Provençal, the language of the common people. In his journal of February 2, 1837, the Founder of the Oblates recorded:

> Father Honorat tells me that the parish priest was delighted because the Oblates gave the instructions in Provençal. Yet, with the consent of the same parish priest, and to cater to the desire of five or six bourgeois who had demanded that the talks be given in French, he gave way to preaching alternatively in the two languages. I cannot sufficiently remonstrate against such weakness! Never did I accept, when giving missions, to satisfy the stupid vanity of a few bourgeois. That goes against the goal of our Institute.

And to Father Honorat himself he wrote:

> I worry little about the infinitely small number of bourgeois who have not shown any sign of good will. . . . In any case, their souls are worth neither more nor less than those of the poorest peasants, if we consider them in terms of the price the Lord paid. Indeed, all things considered, they may even be worth less. Thus, it is foolish to be more concerned about those gentlemen than about the common people of the area. It is bad, perhaps even sinful, to sacrifice the common good to their caprice and vanity. Therefore you have succumbed to weakness in giving in to their request for instructions in French.[23]

Applying the Gospel to Concrete Life

Provence was rife with serious difficulties and messy situations at the time. It was the Restoration in France, after 10 years of Revolution, followed by 15 years of Napoleon. Properties had been confiscated, then resold,

---

[23] *Oblate Writings*, vol. 9, pp. 15 ff., n. 606.

generally to the bourgeois and often at ridiculously low prices on the basis of promissory notes whose declining value made the purchase even cheaper. When the former owners returned from exile, it is understandable that they wanted justice done and their belongings returned. There were litigations and bad feelings everywhere.

In their parochial missions Father de Mazenod and his men always set up a mediation board to arbitrate such problems. It must have been an even-handed way of trying to find a solution because, had it not been, the bourgeois – always against mission activity – would certainly have brought the issue to the attention of the prefecture. Yet it comes up very seldom in official reports: a few times at the outset, and nothing afterwards. Leflon writes in his biography:

> (At first) the Missionaries of Provence were accused of excessive severity in their solution of problems created by the sale of property and the payment of extended debts through promissory notes whose value decreased during the Revolution . . . After 1820 Father de Mazenod appears to have become less rigorous in the matter, at least if official reports are any indication. . . . It must be admitted to the credit of the Founder that in this delicate matter he practised prudent reserve. There is no document showing that the superior ever treated the problem with fire and brimstone. . . . As little inclined to benevolence as such reports may have been, they contain no reproaches against him. Given a chance they would certainly have jumped at it, since they would have been only too happy to denounce any provocation. Instead, public officials paid homage to his moderation and tact.[24]

Father de Mazenod's mediation boards had no legal standing. They were unofficial offices set up to reconcile enemies and to put an end to dissension between groups and rivalries between families. A board consisted of lay persons and one or two missionaries. In all this, the message is clear: de Mazenod was convinced that the gospel had to exercise its influence every day in all areas of life. It had to tackle current problems, thorny as they might be. And thorny they were: problems of reconciling royalists and republicans, problems of money borrowed under the *ancien régime*, and repaid in inflated post-Revolutionary currency that had little worth. Problems, problems, problems . . . . The missionaries could not simply preach a gospel of beautiful platitudes. Describing a case of such reconciliation, Canon Leflon quotes the Founder: "(At Barjols) the mayor, his deputies, judges, notaries, lawyers, merchants, manufacturers, bourgeois – all came forward and vied with one another in making amends.

---

[24] Leflon, vol. 2, p. 131.

Reconciliations were made publicly and voluntarily at the foot of the Cross. What a thrilling experience this has been! Pray both for us and for them."[25]

Adaptation to Real-Life Situations

Being close to the people and applying the gospel to real life also led de Mazenod to address the particular circumstances of each group in any given parish. Men, women, youth, children – all had their own talks and ceremonies.

An example of this concerns the innkeepers of Remollon. During a parish mission there, they signed a pledge (a facsimile appears on the next page). Quite probably they soon succumbed again to the lure of profit, but the incident shows the effort of the missionaries to apply the gospel to real life situations.

Moreover, the missionaries' humanity and compassion come through especially in the fact that they not only organized groups for Catholic action, but provided opportunities for people to get together in a healthy atmosphere. "At Marignane it was announced that the sodality would have a *chambrée* (a kind of club-room) where the members could get together to socialize and for wholesome amusement. The idea appealed to our men very much; we put it into effect in all the missions."[26]

This would have been unusual among any other religious groups of parochial mission preachers, but it was characteristic of the Missionaries of Provence. Indeed, the Oblate community in Aix continued to work that way long after de Mazenod's time. The city used to be full of young soldiers with off-duty time on their hands on Sunday afternoons. The house provided a billiard table, along with a chance to socialize or talk with a priest. And the young soldiers took ample advantage of the Oblate welcome.

---

[25] Leflon, vol. 2, p. 149.
[26] Ibid., p. 96.

REGULATIONS

FOR THE

INNS, PUBS AND CABARETS

OF THE

PARISH OF REMOLLON

Deeply convinced of their duties as Christians, the innkeepers, pub-owners and cabaret-owners have unanimously decided that henceforth they will carry on their work in a way that does not compromise their conscience.

Accordingly they bind themselves before God:

1. Never to serve meat on days when the Holy Church prescribes abstinence.

2. To forbid any person from singing obscene or lewd songs in their cabarets, inns or pubs respectively.

3. Never to allow on their premises people who utter blasphemies against God, impieties or use bad language.

4. Never to allow the playing of forbidden games.

5. To tenaciously refuse wine to those who want to drink to excess.

6. To punctually close the inns, pubs or cabarets during divine celebrations, and during hours prescribed by the civil administration, and not to admit anyone during those hours. An exception is made for the inns which may receive passing foreigners.

The articles cited above will be placed in

the Sanctuary of Our Lady of Laus

as an everlasting memorial to the sincere, effective and unchanging will of the innkeepers, pub-owners and cabaret-owners of

Remollon who keep the Holy Laws of God and of the Church.

Given at Remollon during the Mission, on the second day of February, in the year 1819.

Simplicity

Father de Mazenod's Rule of 1818 stated:

> To aim at elegance of style rather than solidity of doctrine would go counter to the spirit of our Rule. . . . Our one and only aim should be to instruct the people . . . not only to break the bread of the Word for them but to chew it for them, as well; in a word, to insure that when our discourses are over they are not tempted to heap foolish praise on what they have not understood but, instead, that they go home edified, touched, instructed, able to repeat in their own family circle what they have learned form our mouth.

The Gospel Addressed to Peoples' Sensitivity

Too often the gospel is presented in a coldly intellectual way. The Missionaries of Provence always tried to involve the heart. Their Founder was very much aware of that need and carefully selected hymns that would touch the heart yet not be syrupy. To Father Mille he wrote in 1837:

> In the missions I recommend that you use hymns with a refrain the congregation can repeat. I insist that there be refrains which the whole congregation can sing. Nothing more. I do not find anything more wearisome than listening to a few isolated voices which annoy one by their unison without ever letting one understand a word they utter. That is the very opposite of devotion. In that case, music, far from sending souls to God, turns them away from him. Instead of praying at such precious moments, people languish. People prefer to pray fervently without being distracted by the singing. And so, in our missions I would like to suppress any song of adoration, any hymn, in which the refrain could not be repeated by the entire congregation. Hence I insist on hymns with a refrain because during the mission all must sing. We must remove from our hymnals any ridiculous expressions of love that are out of place. Verses that are significant and inspiring of piety are what are needed.[27]

Ceremonies in the First Parochial Missions

The parochial missions of Father de Mazenod's little band of preachers were characterized by some deeply emotional ceremonies. Among them, the following always had their place:

Feast of the Children

This was a good way to also involve parents.

---

[27] *Oblate Writings*, vol. 9, p. 24, n. 611.

Procession and Consecration to the Blessed Virgin

Memorial of the Dead

This was celebrated before an open and empty tomb. This gave rise, a number of times, to the accusation that Father de Mazenod had removed a body from its grave. The anti-clerical government authorities of the day, who would have been more than happy to prosecute if there were cause, paid no attention because the charges were too ridiculous.

Feast in Honour of the Law

This was one of the more important ceremonies of the mission and performed with special ostentation because it was meant to counteract the liberal and agnostic mentality which the Revolution had planted in the people. Indeed, just beyond the cathedral in Aix, there is the Monument to the Law, erected by Joseph Sec in 1792. On it are inscribed the words:

> Sorti d'un cruel esclavage, je n'ai d'autre maître que moi, mais ma liberté je ne veux faire usage que pour obéir a la Loi.[28]

With all suitable pomp, and in the presence of as many priests as possible, all vested in surplice and cape, the ceremony opened with the solemn adoration of the Blessed Sacrament. A deacon then read each commandment of the law – the law of God – and the congregation repeated it. Then one of the missionaries gave a commentary, after which the deacon proclaimed the next commandment, and so on. When all ten had been reviewed, the congregation pledged its fidelity and the ceremony ended. All of this spoke clearly to the people of the true law which sets us free in Jesus Christ. This was proclaiming the Good News to the whole person: heart, body and mind.

Celebration of Penance

This was probably the most impressive and emotion-filled of all the mission ceremonies. We have the account of the one that took place in Marignane: "Now that he represented sinners, Father de Mazenod took off his surplice, the symbol of innocence, and came down from the pulpit. Kneeling at the foot of the altar, he received from the pastor a thick rope which he tied in a noose and placed it around his neck. Next, he removed his shoes and stockings, took the penitential cross, and in that condition, went to the head of the procession."[29]

---

[28] Translation: Freed from cruel slavery, I have no other master but myself, but I wish to use my liberty only to obey the Law.

[29] *Oblate Writings*, vol. 2, p. 93.

Such processions were generally long and impressed the people deeply. They could see in them a symbol of God's mercy. One priest, usually the director of the group, took upon himself all the sins of the people in the village, symbolically freeing them by the sacrifice of that one priest. The meaning of Christ's sacrifice became obvious. Indeed, in the mission in Barjols, the people were so struck by the procession and its meaning that for many years afterwards they kept as a reminder in the church the hangman's rope that Father de Mazenod had worn around his neck as he led the procession. Later, even after he had become bishop, the Founder wrote several letters insisting that the missionaries "must keep the Ceremony of Penance. The only change that I will accept is that you keep your shoes on."

Everything Done in Community

Community was required for the mission group. We have already dealt with the Saturday afternoon meetings meant to review the missionaries' work and community life. The Founder of the Oblates was very insistent that no one be absent from those meetings. Prayer, religious exercises, meals – all was done in community.

IV

Roman Approval

The French Revolution had tried to de-Christianize France and had ended in anarchy. Then Napoleon's Empire had tried to put religion at the service of the State and had ended in tyranny. With the Restoration, a king would try to put the State at the service of the Church through a union of Throne and Altar. At least, that was how the ultra-royalists and the Gallicans saw the agenda and, indeed, the lines between the two powers were frequently blurred.

Almost from the inception of his reign, Louis XVIII wanted to do away with the Concordat of 1801-1802, wrung from Pius VII by Napoleon. But the pope could not just cancel it without appearing to have been wrong in submitting to Napoleon. Negotiations began over changes to the notorious Organic Articles, arbitrarily added by Napoleon. Finally in June of 1817, a new Concordat was signed by the King's ambassador and Cardinal Consalvi, the papal secretary of state. That was when Fortuné de Mazenod, believing he had been nominated bishop, returned to France from his exile in Sicily. The Marseilles press reported:

> M. de Mazenod, whose nomination to the see of Marseilles was announced in the newspapers, arrived here from Palermo a few days ago. From here he will go to Aix and then to Paris. The vicar-general and the pastors went in a body to visit him; and on New Year's day he said Mass in Holy Trinity church. The prelate has edified everyone by his gentle, modest and pious manner. The re-establishment of the see of Marseilles and the choice of M. de Mazenod for that see are a matter of great joy for the faithful. It is a two-fold boon from the King.[1]

The announcement was premature because the Concordat of 1817 touched too close to home in a chamber leaning ever more toward the liberal side with a strong dose of Gallicanism thrown in. In mid-1822, after a five-year hiatus in which nothing was done to change the ecclesiastic map of France, the nation in practice went back to the Concordat of 1801-1802, with some

---

[1] Leflon, vol. 2, p. 85.

modifications to the Organic Articles. These modifications included an end to discrimination against *ancien régime* appointments. Further, the king, with the consent of the Holy See, would augment the number of dioceses in France to around 80 (one diocese, more or less, for every Department of the country). This explains why Fortuné's future hung in limbo for almost six years, while he lived a kind of retreat with the Oblates in Aix. The new agreement with the Holy See took effect in August, 1822. Fortuné's nomination to Marseilles was officially promulgated the same month.

Pope Leo XII

Despite the heavy-handed machinations of Metternich to have a conciliatory candidate favourable to Austria chosen pope, 63-year-old Annibale Cardinal Sermattei della Genga, an independent with conservative views, was elected in 1823 and ruled the Church for six years, until his death in 1829. His tenure was expected to be short because it was rumoured that he had already received the last sacraments at least 17 times prior to his election. Before becoming pope he had enjoyed a successful diplomatic career in various German states, but then Napoleon removed him in public disgrace. When Pius VII returned to Rome later, he was fully reinstated. Indeed, the aged pontiff sent him to the court of Louis XVIII to look after papal interests in France. In 1816 he became cardinal and was named to several sacred congregations of the curia.

The new pope was a saintly man, tall and impressive, yet of fragile health and quite worn out. Chateaubriand described him as "both serene and sad." As pope he seemed to fit the Roman proverb: *"La regola di ogni Papa è il rovescio di quella del suo predecessore."*[2] He moved from the Quirinal to the Vatican, and from the previous pope's middle course, to the right. As secretary of state, in place of the brilliant and progressive Consalvi, he named 80-year-old Giulio-Maria della Somaglia, a conservative, long-winded and indecisive cardinal whose chief qualification for the job appears to have been that he waited a long time to get it. He had been one of the Black Cardinals whom Eugene helped in Paris, yet he failed to remember Eugene in Rome. The pope soon realized, however, that if he wanted to get

---

[2] Translation: The rule of every pope is to upend the rule of his predecessor.

96

anything done, he had to do it himself. That may explain, in part, why he took such a direct hand in the approbation of the Oblate Congregation.

To his credit, Pope Leo XII came to appreciate the worth of Cardinal Consalvi, whom he had sacked, and soon sought his advice frequently, especially on international affairs. He also appointed him to head the Congregation of the Propagation of the Faith. When della Somaglia had to be replaced because of senility in 1828, the pope named one of Consalvi's co-workers, Tommaso Bernetti, to take his place and relations with the states of Europe immediately improved.

With the spectre of death almost constantly upon him, Pope Leo XII issued a veritable flood of reformatory decrees, among them, on May 5, 1824, an encyclical stating that what the Church needed more than material restoration was a spiritual renewal with pastors leading the way. We can see how the Oblate Congregation fit in with his way of thinking. As a springboard for spiritual renewal, and despite much opposition from the cardinals, the pope announced a Jubilee Year for 1825. The city of Rome, instead of giving scandal, was to provide the example and truly become the Holy City. Unfortunately, being Rome, it kept giving scandal as it always has, but the Jubilee Year was a success, with hundreds of thousands of pilgrims coming to the city to pray. On December 9, 1825, Father de Mazenod, in a letter to Father Tempier told him, "Please God, I gained my Jubilee today."[3] The pope, too, in a ceremony reminiscent of the Founder's processions of penance in parochial missions, and despite his ill-health, walked barefoot in procession to visit the major basilicas. Despite the best of intentions, his efforts at reform were often hampered by a narrow clerical outlook that failed to understand the world developing around him. He became profoundly unpopular with the largely anti-clerical people of Rome, and when he died in 1829, an irreverent *pasquinade* appeared, tacked to the famous statue of Pasquino just off the Piazza Navona:

Qui Della Genga giace, per la sua e nostra pace.

(Here lies Della Genga in peace – his and ours.)

---

[3] *Oblate Writings,* vol. 6, p. 208, n. 211.

De Mazenod's Work and the Society Endangered

We have seen how, on October 24, 1818, with the help of the scholastics in vows, the Founder of the Oblates carried the vote six to four, in favour of religious vows in the budding society. The first vows in the newly constituted religious congregation took place on November 1, 1818. Leflon describes the scene: "The Founder) pronounced his vows of chastity, obedience and perseverance in the presence of Fortuné. During the Mass which followed, he accepted the vows of Fathers Maunier, Mie, Tempier and Moreau, and of the scholastic brothers Dupuy, Courtès and Suzanne. . .

Thus, the Society of the Missionaries of Provence was permanently founded."[4]

"Permanently," however, was a very tenuous state for the new society. Indeed, the group was still at the whim of the bishops who had "lent" their subjects to de Mazenod's apostolate. Moreover, a year before the community took vows, the clash he had with some of the parish priests of Aix over the privileged place given to his sodality boys in confirmations at the cathedral and, even more, the trouble with the pastors because he had given First Communion to "their" children in the Mission chapel, showed Father de Mazenod that, as things were going, the future did not look bright. He became increasingly convinced, especially as new members arrived, that the society needed a protector. To that end, even before the group took vows, he had begun to promote Fortuné as bishop for the newly reorganized see of Marseilles.

At first things seemed hopeless; then, inexplicably, the situation changed overnight. On a trip to Paris, Father de Mazenod was warmly recommended to the royal chaplain by Mme. de Verac, a family friend from his days in Sicily. There is nothing written about the meeting of the two men beyond a cryptic comment by Eugene: "Mention was made of my uncle. I put a half-sheet of paper listing his qualifications on the bishop's desk. The next day he is named Bishop of Marseilles."[5] To Tempier, Eugene then wrote ecstatically: "What enormous good we are going to do! Provence will be regenerated. All the bishops of the province will be of one mind; I know them all. The Society which the good God has confided to me has been made astonishingly strong; I am preparing choice troops for the Bishop of Marseilles. There are beautiful days ahead for the Church. . . ."[6]

---

4 Leflon, vol. 2, p. 169.
5 Ibid., p. 74.
6 Ibid., p. 75.

His rejoicing was premature. Rather than help the congregation, Fortuné's appointment to the see of Marseilles almost destroyed it.

Rebellion in the Ranks

Fortuné de Mazenod took possession of his see on August 10, 1823, when the Missionaries of Provence had already been in vows for almost five years. He had accepted the position only on condition that Eugene and Tempier be his vicars-general. To Eugene, it seemed like a good way to protect the society from the vicissitudes that constantly buffeted it. After deliberating with one another, the two priests left Aix and the Oblate community to go to Marseilles to live with Fortuné.

With that move, the crisis began. At the Chapter of 1818, Deblieu and Maunier had vigorously opposed taking vows. Indeed, the brilliant preacher Deblieu, whose pride made obedience to a superior burdensome, had held off until 1820 before consenting to vows. Now he rebelled and, along with Maunier, accused de Mazenod and Tempier of abandoning their brothers and jeopardizing the future of the congregation for the interests of a single diocese or, worse, for their personal ambitions.

The two protesting priests had originally been incardinated to Bishop de Richery of Fréjus. In 1823, after consulting with his council, the bishop declared null and void the vows his priests had taken with the Missionaries of Provence. On that topic Father Maunier wrote to Father Tempier and not to de Mazenod. In a smooth and sanctimonious letter, dated October 21, 1823, he stated:

> My very dear Father: I learned that the Bishop of Fréjus was forced to recall those priests who originally belonged to his diocese and also that the vows taken at our mission house cannot strip bishops of the right to recall us. Realizing that it was close to the date for renewing our vows, I wanted to know what the bishop intended doing in this regard, since I could not renew my vows if I were not sure that they could be observed. He replied that he needed me and was releasing me from all the vows I had made as a missionary. Meanwhile, to set my mind and heart at ease, he has written to Rome for confirmation. He invited me to return to him without delay, stating that all the theologians agree that a vow cannot be made to the prejudice of a third party.[7]

The letter reeks of duplicity and makes one suspect that it was the dissatisfied priest, not the bishop, who initiated the crisis. Father Deblieu, who was probably the originator of the entire controversy, was more direct and to the point. In the letter he wrote to the Founder he stated:

---

[7] Leflon, vol. 2, p. 244.

It is only fitting that I inform you of the reasons, as they were presented to me, why the vows made in your community are null. The following is what the vicar-general wrote to me:

> The Council has unanimously decided that your supposed vows are null:
> 1) through lack of power on the part of your superior who cannot, without authorization from the Holy See, impose any obligation upon those belonging to his worthy society; 2) because the vow of stability in the Mission Society makes illusory the obedience promised to one's bishop at ordination, and a vow can never be made to the prejudice of a third party. The Council has likewise decided that even were that vow of stability valid, your superior still could not reserve to the pope the right to dispense you from it if it prejudiced your bishop's rights. We know that the only vows reserved to the Head of the Church are the vow of perpetual chastity, the vow to enter a religious order and the vow of the three pilgrimages. That being so, there should be no need to caution you against renewing your vows this coming All Saints Day if, at that time, you are still with your confrères.[8]

Fighting to Save the Little Congregation

That flag of rebellion signalled that the little congregation was under siege. Father de Mazenod angrily referred to the two dissenting priests as "apostates" and their attitude as "Iscariotism." Yet Bishop de Richery did have a point, though his arguments were heavily coloured by Gallicanism, and he lacked courtesy in presenting so grave a question through third parties and not directly to the superior. Worse still, it appeared that Archbishop de Bausset of Aix, who could hardly boast of ever having had an opinion of his own, was about to follow de Richery's lead and withdraw his men from the society too. At that point it would appear that Father de Mazenod did not trust himself to hold back his feelings, because he sent a cooler head, Father Joseph Hippolyte Courtès, to plead the group's cause with the Archbishop of Aix. To Father Courtès he wrote:

> The promise of obedience to a bishop does not prevent anyone from aspiring to perfection; the paths are open to priest and layman alike . . . . Far from preventing religious vocations, bishops have an obligation to favour and encourage them by counsel and exhortation. Finally, reserving the dispensation from the vow of perseverance to the Sovereign Pontiff in no way prejudices episcopal jurisdiction: the subject himself willingly and freely contracts not to have recourse to his bishop for such a dispensation.[9]

Courtès may have been a calmer person, but the two-and-a-half-hour meeting with the archbishop on October 24, 1823, apparently was quite stormy and augured poorly. The prelate insisted in the strongest terms that his

---

[8] Leflon, vol. 2, pp. 245-246.
[9] Ibid., p. 248.

priests were not to renew vows. Worse still, dissension kept growing in the Oblate camp. De Mazenod was frankly at a loss about what to do. On the first Friday of November he felt it necessary to go to the Oblate community in Aix where he ordered a strict fast of bread and water all day. Oblate historian Father Ortolan described it:

> In the evening, with the community assembled in the oratory, and after delivering a stirring conference on the perils threatening the Society, "born of my heart," he offered himself as he had often done during missions, as a "victim of appeasement to the anger of God". Thereupon he ordered all the lights extinguished and began scourging himself to the point of blood, drawing tears and sobs from all the members. The scene, reminiscent of the most stirring incidents in the lives of the holy founders of religious orders, re-strengthened any vocations that had been weakened by the defection of a few older members. Everyone felt a resurgence of affection for the Founder and, to console him for the betrayal of his false brethren, they promised their unbound devotion. Fervour would make up for the lack of numbers.[10]

Ortolan's assessment of the effect of that *culpe* in the motherhouse in Aix hardly stands up to the facts. It may have had a momentary emotional effect, but the truth was that the tiny congregation was bleeding profusely from what looked to be a fatal haemorrhage. Father de Maze-nod managed to stem the flow somewhat by two meetings with the archbishop of Aix, one in November, the second in December. The first was polite and positive. In the second, the Archbishop, whose decisions seemed forever to swing with the tide, had a complete and unexplainable change of heart. He treated the Founder with every courtesy, asked him to forget the past, and even requested that the missionaries provide a chaplain at the Aix hospital.

Nonetheless, the bleeding continued; before long, the society had lost over half its members!

Oblates who left	*Oblates who stayed*
3 priests	11 priests
1 deacib	2 priest novices
12 scholastic novices	6 Oblates in temporary vows
2 novices for Brothers	(scholastics or brothers)
6 aspirants	2 novices
24 departed	*21 remained*

---

[10] Ortolan, vol. 1, pp. 175-175.

The Founder could say that such losses "separated the straw from the good grain." The fact was, however, that he was at a loss for a genuine solution, so he temporized.

> Like any true Provençal, the Founder knew that the fury of the *mistral* had to blow itself out before the return of the warm sunshine could be expected. After such a violent upheaval, wisdom advised leaving to time, God's providential helper, the task of slowly settling things back into place. An indiscreet uproar, far from re-establishing order, would have had the opposite effect of throwing everything into confusion.[11]

He was certainly aware that the heart of the problem was that, without consulting the community, he and Tempier had agreed to be Bishop Fortuné's vicars-general and to live in Marseilles. But that had been the condition *sine qua non* to Fortuné's acceptance of the diocese. By taking the posts in Marseilles, and thus having a Provençal bishop and staunch ally on the see, they hoped to assure the protection that the beleaguered missionary society so badly needed. Their absence from Aix, however, left a vacuum.

A Decisive General Chapter in Aix

On September 30, 1824 – almost a year after the crisis over vows exploded – the Founder convened a general chapter at the motherhouse in Aix.

> After a day of penance and prayer, he asked the chapter to decide the following: is it, or is it not, in the best interests of the Society that the superior general and Father Tempier continue as vicars-general to Msgr. Fortuné de Mazenod, the Bishop of Marseilles? By secret ballot, each one was to decide freely and as his conscience dictated. The result of the balloting proved that unanimity, fortunately, had been restored.[12]

Father Rey adds that, without a single exception, "(The capitulants) spontaneously and unanimously approved what the Founder had done, thereby confirming the harmony of mind and heart that reigned between the father of the family and his sons."[13]

The Congregation Changes Its Name

The crisis was over, but the problem was far from solved. The solution would have to come from beyond any one diocese, because the tiny congregation was expanding, even beyond Provence. "Missionaries of Provence" had become a misnomer. In October, 1825, the society's name

---

[11] Leflon, vol. 2, p. 252.
[12] Ibid., p. 253.
[13] *Registre des délibérations des chapitres généraux*, p. 339

was officially changed to "Oblates of St. Charles" in honour of St. Charles Borromeo, the patron saint of the de Mazenod family.

Roman Approval

Impending danger continued to hang over the congregation and the whim of a bishop could again bring it crashing down at any time. Fortuné's support was not enough. Besides, he was an old man and would not be Bishop of Marseilles forever.

Father de Mazenod was fully aware that a lasting solution to the problem had to be more universal. Earlier he had gone to Paris to seek government approval for his little group. While only partially successful, the move had put some distance between him and the hounds snapping at his heels. He had even considered joining his group to the Oblates of the Virgin Mary and to that end he had spoken in Turin with their founder, Father Lanteri, on November 16, 1825.[14] The Founder thought it might help to spread beyond the borders of France and to open his missionaries to ministry in Italy. Father Lanteri was amenable, but his companions told him to "be careful with those Frenchmen. If we join them we are lost." The project was eventually dropped in May of 1826.

All along, however, he knew that the real solution was in papal approval of the congregation. Yet he hesitated to take any steps in that direction because the path was so strewn with pitfalls. The society was far too small – only 25 members – and, since 1800 Rome had not approved a single religious institute. Nor did Eugene de Mazenod consider himself a founder in the same league with the other great founders of religious institutes. He felt it would be presumptuous on his part to present himself as such in Rome with so small a group of followers. Moreover, if he initiated proceedings with the Holy See and failed to obtain approval, the discredit would probably bury the congregation. Not even official "praise and encouragement" (a *laudanda*) would be enough, for that would signal that the society was not worthy to become a truly universal religious congregation. The Founder was fully aware that there is nothing deadlier than faint praise.

The Wheels Begin to Turn

Just when Father de Mazenod was at a complete loss about what to do, a providential sign came. Father Charles Albini was as quiet and self-effacing as de Mazenod was explosive and extroverted. Yet during a community

---

[14] Cf. *Oblate Writings,* vol. 6, p. 196, n. 207 and vol. 7, p. 99, n. 242, and p. 104, n. 245.

meeting in which every detail of the question was discussed, Albini, the saintly little priest from Menton who would become the apostle of Corsica, did something unprecedented. Standing up, he faced the Founder resolutely. Then taking him firmly by the shoulders and squeezing hard with both hands he begged earnestly, "Go to Rome, Father, go!" The Oblate Founder was impressed. There and then it was decided. He would go to Rome to seek approval from the pope.

Eugene de Mazenod arrived in Rome on November 26, 1825, and took up residence with the Lazarist Fathers at San Silvestro, near the Quirinal. He did not waste time before beginning to make the rounds of prelates whom he hoped could help his cause. Unfortunately, most of the Black Cardinals whom Eugene had helped in Paris while at St-Sulpice had already died. However, one who still remembered seeing him in those days was Cardinal di Gregorio. The Founder wrote to Father Tempier on December 9, 1825:

> They give me little hope. Cardinal di Gregorio, to whom I had been warmly recommended from Turin and who has treated me with much friendship, already hosting me to a dinner and a thousand courtesies, has positively told me that he does not believe the pope would give his formal approbation; he could, however, by graces and indulgences, recognize and be presumed to approve indirectly . . . . I begged the cardinal to speak to the pope beforehand in my favour; he will not fail. Previous to that, it appears that the cardinal-vicar (Zurla) will have spoken to him of me. If the audience is delayed a little, other cardinals will be able to render me the same service. In the meantime, I have not wasted my time; and since, in the absence of all else, grace should signify something, I have asked for some of it which will carry weight. For this I have gone to see the prelate who is Secretary of the Propaganda (Archbishop Caprano) and who is disposed not to refuse me anything.[15]

A Black Cardinal who, to Eugene de Mazenod's disappointment, did not remember him or the services he had rendered in Paris, was the pope's secretary of state, 82-year-old Cardinal della Somaglia. Was it a convenient lapse of memory or was it old age? At any rate, he treated the Founder with "friendly courtesy" but with reserve. To Father Tempier, on December 10, 1825, the Founder observed:

> He has completely forgotten me and the services I had performed for the cardinals during their exile in Paris. I had to refresh his memory by recalling that I had frequently gone to his residence, that I had dined with him on occasion, and that I had presented him with *The Life of the Venerable Agnes* (bound at my expense). . . . It was I who served him when he came to say Mass at the German chapel; it was I who was appointed to ask this same Cardinal della Somaglia what the cardinals needed during

---

[15] *Oblate Writings,* vol. 6, p. 209, n. 211.

that fateful period when they were in complete disfavour with Napoleon. . . . So many thing have happened since then, that events of long ago could easily have been forgotten. The cardinal remained as courteous as ever but the thought occurred to me that it would be folly to do good solely for the purpose of self-advancement; only God keeps an account of favours rendered.[16]

December 20, 1825: Eugene de Mazenod Puts His Case Before the Pope

A second visit with the aged cardinal went far better. Father de Mazenod was received courteously and told the Holy Father would soon see him. Nevertheless, nothing seemed to happen and with each day de Mazenod grew more impatient. A letter posted to Father Tempier on Christmas Day shows us how insistent the Founder was:

> You know that the Holy Father had been informed by the Cardinal Secretary of State and by several others that I wished to have the honour of presenting myself to him. Those who were good enough to speak to him about me had been so conscientious in doing so that the pope had indicated he would see me with the greatest pleasure. If the dean of the Rota had not requested Msgr. Barberini, the Master Chamberlain, to arrange the day for me to present myself for the audience, I would have gone the next day; but waiting for the convenience of that *Monsignorino* obliged me to put it off from one day to another. Such delay was insupportable, for I feared that the pope, whose attention has been drawn to me by all that people kindly said to him, might find it strange and out of place that I showed so little haste to present myself before him, after he had given his permission with such good will.
>
> Thus, one fine morning I made my decision. It was the 20th . . . and having obtained the loan of a carriage from Msgr. the Dean, I arrived in full dress at the Vatican. The first person I met at the papal apartments was a certain prelate, one of those they call here *de mantellone*, that is to say, of inferior rank but always near the pope to serve him as private secretary. This good man, a little awkward at his trade, advised me to retrace my steps because it would not be possible to see His Holiness that day; that I could not have chosen a worse day, that it was the last of the audiences of the year, that cardinals were coming in crowds, along with ministers and goodness knows who else, hence I must put off my visit until the first days of the new year. I mollified him a little and to be accommodating, he told me to come back on the second day of Christmastide, then on the Eve and, finally, the day following that at which we were. That did not suit me at all. I have since concluded that, thinking I wished to get in to see the pope by his mediation, he saw no way of introducing me that day. He was wrong. I had not the slightest wish to enter by the back door.

---

[16] Leflon, vol. 2, p. 260.

The moment the good man disappeared, Msgr. Barberini arrived; I went to him and explained my situation, reproaching him somewhat for having grieved me by his forgetfulness. A little embarrassed by my gentle reprimand, of which he acknowledged the justice, he prayed me enter the salon and, in my quality of prelate or gentleman, I went without ado into the apartment which is next to the pope's study, where cardinals, bishops and other prelates, as well as ministers, wait their turn to enter the presence of the Holy Father.[17]

The Audience with Pope Leo XII

In the salon the Founder encountered a number of papal ministers, including Cardinal Bartolomeo Pacca, another Black Cardinal whom he had known in Paris. They all preceded him into the papal chambers to take care of the day's work. When their audiences came to an end, some two-and-a-half hours later, who, he wondered, would be next? "The General of the Dominicans, whose stomach noised its hunger, would have wagered that it would be he; not at all, it was I! I arrived at the door with the dignity you know me to have, but left it there to pick up again on coming out."[18]

The Founder of the Oblates was very well received and the audience lasted more than half an hour, with the pope speaking amiably and listening well to what he had to say. The pontiff's manner was encouraging, especially when he told de Mazenod not to change his methods. But, at that point there was no indication that the pope intended to approve the congregation.

It would be impossible for me to relate to you all that was said, and still less to describe the goodness, the pleasant manner and courtesy of the Sovereign Pontiff. I explained the principal purpose of my journey, but many were the episodes that entered into this narration. . . . I took care not to forget to tell him what you had just written to me: "At this moment the two youngest missionaries of the Society are working marvels, etc. One of them (Father Guibert), Most Holy Father, is not yet old enough to become a priest; he was ordained in August with the dispensation of 16 months that your Holiness deigned to grant us. And yet the good God has used them to convert Protestants, etc." You would have been touched, my dear friend, to see, while I spoke, how this holy Pontiff raised his eyes towards heaven, then joined his hands and bowed his head on them clasped together, glowing with gratitude and thanking God with all his heart. It seemed to me that this invocation alone would draw new graces on our ministry.[19]

That was the very moment the Oblate Congregation was approved. Up to that point it was clear the pope had meant only to bless the Founder's work,

---

[17] *Oblate Writings,* vol. 6, pp. 216-217, n. 212.

[18] Ibid, p. 218, n. 212.

[19] Ibid.

but when he heard of the missionaries' deeds, his mind changed in the instant. From then on, too, Father de Mazenod began to speak of papal approbation in positive terms.

As the audience came to an end, he asked the pontiff if the name of the society could be changed from Oblates of St. Charles to Oblates of Mary Immaculate. The pope did not give him an immediate answer, preferring to wait for the outcome of the approbation process. He then sent him to the archpriest Adinolfi, a kind of executive secretary whose task it would be to study the text of the rule and present a brief to the pope.

"This Society Pleases Me"

The following day, Thursday, December 21, the anniversary of his own ordination as a priest, Eugene celebrated the eucharist at St. Peter's, laying the rule on the altar of the Apostle and asking for his blessing. Afterwards, he went to see the archpriest, who unfortunately would not arrive home until a couple of hours later. When he did finally get there, he put himself completely at the disposal of the Founder, even foregoing dinner. It was their first meeting and Father de Mazenod had immediate confidence in his competence and skill. The archpriest told him frankly that the most he could expect to get from the pope was a *laudanda*. He would go over the text that night, he said, and prepare a report for his Friday morning audience with the pope. The Founder was to come back Saturday morning for news of any progress.

Saturday morning saw Father de Mazenod at the archpriest's house at the appointed time; he described the scene thus:

> He first read to me the succinct report that he had made to the Holy Father which, it must be said, basically contained my memoir and the essential points which ought to stand out but, as he had given me to understand the day before yesterday, he concluded in favour of the *laudanda* after the text had been examined to see if there was anything to change. But give praise to God's goodness and unite yourselves, all of you, to me to thank him! Such was not the mind of the Holy Father: "No," said the Pontiff, "This Society pleases me; I know the good it does, etc., etc." And he entered into a number of details which completely surprised the archpriest. "I wish to favour it. Choose a cardinal, one of the mildest of the Congregation, to be *ponent* of his cause; go to him on my behalf and tell him my intention is not merely that these Rules be praised but that they be *approved*." O Leo XII*!* Even were the Congregation to reject our Rules, you would nonetheless be forever considered among us as the benefactor and father of our Society.[20]

---

[20] *Oblate Writings*, vol. 6, pp. 222-223, n. 212.

Father de Mazenod wept for pure joy as he ran from the archpriest's house to the church of St. Joseph Calasanctius nearby, where he sang a glorious *Te Deum*. Despite the good news, however, formal approbation would still prove a long way off. There was still the Holy See's complex procedure to contend with. The text of the rule had to be gone over carefully by seven cardinals, one after the other. Imagine the impetuous Founder of the Oblates waiting around Rome for months and months, his goal always just out of reach, while seven cardinals consecutively studied and discussed the text slowly and painstakingly, word for word! He wrote to Father Tempier:

> It will have to be passed on to Cardinal Fesch, and then to Cardinal Haeffelin: from him it will go to Cardinal Bertazzoli; from Bertazzoli to Cardinal Pallotta, then to Cardinal Turiossi and from him to Cardinal Pacca who will finally send it back to Cardinal Pedicini. Pedicini will discuss it with the pope, and after that the Congregation will meet and give their decision. How do you like that for procedure? A quicker way could be devised, but that is the way it is done.[21]

Father de Mazenod's impatience emboldened him to ask the pope to make an exception and lower the number of cardinals on the board of examiners from seven to three. Amazingly, the pope agreed! As chairman of the panel he appointed Cardinal Pacca, the Black Cardinal who as Pius VII's secretary of state had been imprisoned by Napoleon, and who remembered Father de Mazenod well from Paris. The *ponent* (the equivalent of an advocate who presents the case) was Cardinal Pedicini, known as one of the mildest cardinals in the College, while the third on the board was the latter's friend, Cardinal Pallotta.

At this juncture, on January 2, the Founder was surprised to find opposition from someone whom, he had hoped, would lend support –Cardinal Castiglioni who, as Pius VIII, would become the next pope three years later. The cardinal had nothing to do with the process, but now that approbation was so close, Eugene feared that a wrong word from him to the pope might nullify everything. However, the cardinal was simply testing Father de Mazenod to see his reactions. The following day he warmly encouraged him to go ahead with his work.

The Oblate Passport: Missionaries to the Poor

What prompted the pope's change of heart? In the audience he had stated, "Today the Holy See still proceeds as it did a hundred years ago," and went on to explain in detail the drawn-out process. Moreover, he pointedly told Father de Mazenod that the number of requests for approbation had been so

---

[21] Leflon, vol. 2, p. 266.

great – especially from France – that the Sacred Congregation had made it a policy to give a *laudanda*, that is, praise and encouragement without formally approval. Yet when the archpriest Adinolfi presented his report and advised a *laudanda* for the Oblates, the pope's answer was, "This society pleases me . . . . I want to favour it."

What transpired to change the pope's mind so completely? Certainly, there was the letter to the pope against approbation, written by three Gallican bishops – de Bausset of Aix, Arbaud of Gap and Miollis of Digne. True Gallicans, they indirectly questioned the pope's right to interfere in what they considered a French matter. Their letter backfired, however, strengthening de Mazenod's position and showing clearly how un-Gallican he was. Their objections were termed "nonsense," and Father de Mazenod's cause now became the cause of papal rights. However, when the letter from the bishops arrived, the pope had already made up his mind, so it could hardly have influenced the pope's change of heart.

Something else must have prompted the decision. That "something" was Father de Mazenod's account of the marvels being worked by Oblate missionaries.

The pope was moved to approve the Oblate Congregation because of its witness as missionaries dedicated to the poor. That is where divine providence had led them and keeps leading them. Remaining faithful to that impulse is the challenge of every Missionary Oblate of Mary Immaculate today and for as long as the Lord sees fit to preserve the congregation.

Throughout the episode of the congregation's approbation, the Founder's fidelity to the Spirit was exemplary. Writing to Father Tempier on January 10, 1826, he underlined why he felt that approbation was of utmost importance: *"For the building of the Church, the glorifying of God and the sanctifying of souls."* Such an endeavour can only succeed, he stated, "thanks to very special protection from God to whom alone belongs the power to touch the hearts and guide the wills of men." Then he added: "Of necessity, I have had to convince myself that it is my duty to do all in my power to live in the most intimate state of union with God that I possibly can and be resolved in consequence to *be faithful to his grace and not give cause for grief to his Spirit.*"[22]

Tempier was his confidant. Thus what he shared with him on January 20, at such a key moment in the life of the congregation, takes on special significance: "I must admit that never in my life have I understood as well as

---

[22] *Oblate Writings,* vol. 7, p. 10, n. 217.

now the value of self-surrender to God, never have I felt more disposed to put virtue – for such it is – into practice as in the present circumstances."[23]

And on February 16, the eve of approbation, he wrote again:

> Hush, dear Tempier! I speak to you softly, yet loud enough for you to hear. Yesterday, the 15th of the month of February of the year of grace 1826, the Congregation of Cardinals assembled under the presidency of the prefect, Cardinal Pacca, and unanimously approved the Rules, except with slight modifications proposed by the Cardinal ponent, the judgment of the Congregation being that our Holy Father the Pope grant the brief of approbation in good and due form . . . . Let us acknowledge that the conduct of Divine Providence in this matter has been admirable and that *none of us should ever become oblivious of how evident his protection has been.*
>
> It is true that *I have always put all my confidence in the goodness of God.* As I have told you, I offered the holy Sacrifice every day for this intention: I constantly invoked the holy Virgin and all the saints, but especially the sovereign Mediator, to whose glory all our intentions are directed. And I ought to avow, if ever I prayed as much, never have I prayed with so much consolation (effect of an absolute and filial confidence) to the point of speaking to our Lord as I dare believe I would have done had I had the happiness of living when he moved about this earth to spread his goodness and grant to each what he asked.
>
> It was especially at Communion, when our Divine Saviour is on the point of giving us the utmost proof of his love, that I was prompted to abandon myself to all the sentiments that his divine presence and the immensity of his mercy toward a sinner like me, inspired in my miserable soul at that precious moment. Those same sentiments were renewed when I presented myself before him to adore him, whether at my hour of adoration, or appearing before him as I entered the house, or still again, on visits I tried to make often . . . where the Holy Sacrament was exposed. But I ought to let you know that such confidence and feelings were all due, after the grace which inspired them, to the thought that *I was asking something in keeping with the will of God, something apt to procure his glory: the salvation of souls and the good of the Church,* and also because I regarded myself as the interpreter of all of you and because *I felt, so to speak, borne along by the prayers, merits and works of the whole Society.*[24]

Approval At Last!

> Finally, on Thursday, February 15, after thoroughly studying the Oblate Rule, the three cardinals Pedicini, Pallotta and Pacca met in the residence of the latter. Father de Mazenod had asked a servant there to let him know when they had finished their deliberations – he would be praying, he told him, in the church of Santa Maria in Campitelli, directly across from the

---

[23] *Oblate Writings,* vol. 7, p. 15, n. 219.
[24] Ibid., pp. 30-31, n. 224.

palazzo where the cardinals were meeting. The Founder prayed long and fervently for a favourable outcome. Finally, after assisting at nine consecutive Masses, his empty stomach growling complaints at his prolonged fast, he crossed over to find out what was taking so long. There he discovered that the session had long ended, but the servant had forgotten to call. The Founder left, but returned to see Cardinal Pacca that same evening.

The prelate could tell Father de Mazenod that all had gone very well and that with but a few minor changes the cardinals had unanimously approved the rule. It was now up to the Founder to get together with Msgr. Marchetti for the final touches. Father de Mazenod, working alone long into the night and then the following day with Marchetti, put the final touches on the rule so that by Friday, February 16, everything was completed.

The following day, Saturday, February 17, 1826, Pope Leo XII formally approved and confirmed the decision of the Sacred Congregation. The Founder wrote ecstatically to Father Tempier and the community on Sunday, February 18, the day after the approbation. The letter starts out giving glory, praise and thanks to God for such a signal favour:

> Te Deum laudamus, te Dominum confitemur. Te per orben terrarum sancta confitetur ecclesia. Per singulos dies benedicimus te et laudamus nomen tuum in saeculum et in saeculum seculi!

> My dear friend, my dear brothers, on February 17, 1826, yesterday evening, the Sovereign Pontiff Leo XII confirmed the decision of the Congregation of Cardinals and specifically approved the Institute, the Rules and Constitutions of the Missionary Oblates of the most Holy and Immaculate Virgin Mary, and accompanied this solemn act of his pontifical power with the most admiring words for those who happily form this Society from which the head of the Church indeed expects the greatest good.[25]

The Significance of the Rule to the Founder

Father de Mazenod saw the approbation of the congregation and its rules as an extraordinary grace. The letter, quoted above, continued:

> Everyone is stupefied at this. Even those called upon to contribute with their votes to the execution of the very emphatic will of the pope, are surprised by the unanimous agreement of views and especially the imperturbable resolution of the Holy Father, whom nothing could deter from the first thought with which the Holy Spirit inspired him on that first day when I knelt at his feet and presented him with the plan of this enterprise which now we can call *divine*. The pope knew everything and weighed everything in his profound wisdom. . . . I need not tell you that he

---

[25] *Oblate Writings*, vol. 7, p. 39, n. 226.

was not delayed for an instant by the fine protestations brought to his attention. They will have left him with no great opinion of the one whose sorry idea it was to make them, for they impugned his sovereign jurisdiction, as he well remarked, since the logical conclusion to their way of thinking would be that no pope could ever have been right in approving in the Church religious Orders or regular Congregations, all of which are exempt from ordinary jurisdiction, in their interior rule as well as in their membership.[26]

. . .

We must attach ourselves heart and soul to our Rules and practice more exactly what they prescribe to us. . . They are not a *bagatelle*, they are no longer simple regulations, merely pious directions; they are *Rules approved by the Church* after most minute examination. They have been judged holy and eminently suited to lead those who have embraced them to their goal. They have become *the property of the Church* that has adopted them. *The pope*, by approving them, has become *their guarantor.* He whom God used to draw them up disappears; it is certain today that he was merely the *mechanical instrument which the Spirit of God put into play in order to show the path he wanted to be followed* by those whom he had predestined and preordained for the work of his mercy, in calling them to form and maintain our poor, little and modest Society. Puny as we are, weak and few in number, nonetheless, *we have an existence in the Church*, no less than that of the most celebrated bodies, the most holy societies.

. . .

Know your dignity, take care never to dishonour your Mother who has just been enthroned and recognized as Queen in the household of the Spouse, whose grace will make her fecund enough to engender a great number of children, if we are faithful and do not draw upon us a shameful sterility by our prevarications. *In the name of God, let us be saints.*[27]

The emphasized phrases show that the Oblate Founder saw approbation as an extraordinary grace, one of tremendous importance for the life of the Oblate Congregation and for its members. The rule, henceforth *property of the Church*, provides the Oblates of Mary Immaculate with their *own existence in the Church*, to be at the service of the Church. This throws the doors of the Oblate apostolate wide open to the world and with greater reason *it impels Oblates to be ever more faithful to the Spirit* – in a word, *to be saints.*

---

[26] This was an obvious reference to Bishops de Bausset of Aix, Arbaud of Gap and de Miollis of Digne, Gallican bishops who had sent a letter to the pope asking him not to approve the Oblates because such approbation would encroach on their ordinary jurisdiction.

[27] *Oblate Writings*, vol. 7, p. 40, n. 229.

L. J. C. & M. I.

The process was almost, but not quite over. Before the promulgation of the official brief of approbation, there was the matter of recopying the 200 hand-written pages of the rule to include the cardinals' amendments. At first, Father de Mazenod was going to hire a scribe to do the work, but when he found out how much scribes charged, how long they took and how poorly they wrote, he decided to do it himself. Working day and night, he recopied the entire rule in three days, suffering from writer's cramp when it was all over. Despite his efforts, the process would drag out another month, with briefs to be prepared, a decree of the Congregation of Bishops and Regulars, etc. But Eugene was no longer the impatient supplicant, frustrated by the slow turning of the bureaucratic wheels of the Curia. The end was already in sight, and at times he could still not believe the good fortune of such a signal grace. On March 9, 1826, he wrote Father Tempier:

> Cardinal Pedicini was only too right; if the good God had not intervened, we would have had enough to take up more than a year. It is amusing to see the surprise of the archpriest Adinolfi who is, as I have told you, the key worker in the secretariat. He cannot believe the way this matter has gone since the beginning. *Non si è visto mai!* – never have we seen the pope, he said, take it upon himself in a matter of this kind, to personally smooth out everything, cut through all difficulties, prescribe in detail, stipulate even the wording of a brief!

> These gentlemen of ours, do they at least realize this? If they knew what all this means they would jump for joy or be overcome with admiration. Here, people sometimes wait six months for a *yes* or a *no*, scrutinize a sign, try to divine the meaning of some thought of the Pontiff who for us has done everything. What right did we have to merit this? Who is it who gave me, in a single audience, the wherewithal to inspire in him an interest so strong, so real, so constant? From now on, how can we not be overwhelmed with gratitude towards God and, looking seriously at ourselves, not attach ourselves still more to the Society which has obtained such convincing proofs of the protection of the Lord?. . . Now is the time to adopt an *esprit de corps* which drives us to not be surpassed in regularity, etc., by any other community.[28]

On March 16, even as the official approbation document lay languishing on the desk of Msgr. Capaccini, the Founder sent Father Tempier a copy of the Latin text. Until then, the Founder had always penned the initials *L. J. C.* – *Laudetur Jesus Christus* (Praised be Jesus Christ) – in the upper corner of his letters. On March 20, 1816, in a letter to Father Tempier, for the first time he wrote what henceforth would become a tradition in the Oblate Congregation: *L. J. C. et M. I.* – Praised be Jesus Christ and Mary

---

[28] *Oblate Writings*, vol. 7, pp. 52-53, n. 229.

Immaculate. In the letter he again commented on the tremendous grace bestowed upon the congregation:

> O yes, we must needs tell ourselves that we have received a great grace! The more closely I consider it in all its aspects, the more I see the worth of this gift. We can never properly respond to it other than by unwavering fidelity and by redoubled zeal and devotedness for the glory of God, the service of the Church and the salvation of souls, especially the most abandoned, as is called for by our vocation. For the rest, what I ask of God is that he choose for us and send us the people we need to do this work.[29]

Mary Immaculate

For de Mazenod, Oblates were consecrated to God under the patronage of Mary. For that reason, it is worthwhile noting the full title the pope gave the congregation in the Apostolic Brief of approbation: "We hereby, with ready and willing mind, establish (the Congregation) and wish it to be known by the name of *the Congregation of the Missionary Oblates of the Most Holy Virgin Mary, conceived without sin.*"

The title is not just Oblates of Mary Immaculate, but *Missionary* Oblates of Mary Immaculate. The congregation was neither founded nor approved simply to proclaim the glories of Mary but to be missionary – to be sent to the most abandoned, to see them through the eyes of the crucified Christ – *under the patronage of Mary.* The essential element in the spirituality of the original rule is *attachment to the person of Jesus Christ.* Therefore de Mazenod insisted that his Oblates always wear the cross, even against the wishes of the often troublesome coadjutor of Colombo, Bishop Bravi. To Father Semaria, head of the Ceylon mission, de Mazenod wrote on July 2, 1852: "We do not wear a hood or a rosary hanging from our belts, but the cross, given to us on the day of our profession as a distinctive sign of our ministry. Therefore, we do not wear it *ad libitum,* as other missionaries might."[30]

That Oblates are primarily missionaries to the poor in no way lessens what Father de Mazenod had to say about Mary. In a letter to Father Tempier, already quoted, he asserted:

> Does it not seem to you that it is a sign of predestination to bear the name of Oblates of Mary, that is, men consecrated to God under the patronage of Mary – the name the Congregation bears as its family name held in common with the most holy and immaculate Mother of God? It is enough to make others jealous. But it is the Church who has given us that beautiful

---

[29] *Oblate Writings,* vol. 7, p. 63, n. 231.
[30] Ibid., vol. 4, p. 102, n. 30.

name; we receive it with respect, love and gratitude, proud of our dignity and of the rights it gives us to the protection of her who is All Powerful in God's presence. Let us delay no longer in taking upon ourselves that beautiful name whenever prudence permits.[31]

Attachment to the Person of Jesus Christ

Time and again the Founder's writings show how clearly he saw *a vital link between being missionary and loving Christ.* In his commentary of 1831 he insisted on that attachment to the person of Jesus. "Could anyone think that the Rule has already insisted sufficiently on the indispensable need to imitate Jesus Christ? No, it further represents the Saviour to us as the real Founder of the Congregation."[32] Earlier, in the rule of 1818, he had written: "Their founder is Jesus Christ, the very Son of God; their first fathers are the Apostles. They are called to be the Saviour's co-workers, the co-redeemers of mankind . . . ." This echoes what Paul says in I Corinthians 3:9 and I Thessalonians 3:2 of those who are "labourers together with God." For Eugene it meant that Oblates are so highly esteemed by Christ as to be *chosen.* And hearkening back to his Good Friday experience of 1807, the fidelity of his life would be his response to the love of Christ. The vital link between loving Christ and being a missionary is obvious.

The Wondrous Grace of Approbation and Its Implications

Over and over again in his correspondence the Founder of the Oblates repeated his awe at how evident the hand of God was in the approbation and at the signal grace bestowed upon the congregation:

> The more I think of our situation, the more I see therein the hand of God and his doings. Those who have been instruments of his mercies toward us have all perceived it, too. . . . The pope not only approves the Congregation, he founds it: *Constituimus.* They first thought that we were only asking for France and so the Cardinal Ponent said to me, "Take that for now; the rest will come later." I did not agree and the matter was subsequently resolved as we wanted. I must mention that what made them accede to my views was my observation that the Congregation would not limit its charity to a small corner of the earth and that all abandoned souls, wherever they were, would always be the object of its zeal and would have the right to its services. . . . Is there not something supernatural here? When have popes ever taken such matters upon themselves? Usually petitions are presented to them that they do not even read; these are then sent to the Congregation and the Secretary makes a report; the Congregation decides and the pope approves what has been done, for or

---

[31] *Oblate Writings*, vol. 7, p. 63, n. 231.
[32] *Selected Texts*, p. 32, n. 9.

against. . . . (But in this instance) it was the pope himself who said more in favour of our case than I could have done.[33]

Five days later, on March 25, the Founder wrote a joyous letter to the entire congregation:

> Rejoice with me and congratulate yourselves, my beloved, for it has pleased the Lord to grant us great favours; our Holy Father, Pope Leo XII, gloriously reigning from the chair of Peter, has sanctioned with his apostolic approbation, on March 21 of this current year, our Institute, our Constitutions and our Rules. . . .
>
> What prayers of thanksgiving, in keeping with such a favour, can we possibly offer to God who is so great and good? Is it not by being consumed with burning piety and by eagerly performing the duties of our holy vocation with more joy than ever? Even while happy over the grace obtained, there is no one among you who cannot understand at the same time how strict an account we must render for it. The Church has the right to expect work which is commensurate with the benefit bestowed.[34]

It was over. Approbation was a fact. Eugene de Mazenod could return to his tiny congregation, now with its own niche in the Church, and get down to the everyday work of the apostolate. A dozen years later, in the notes of his 1837 retreat, he wrote:

> In the course of my meditations, the thought occurred that we shall never be able to sufficiently thank the good God for having given us the Rules, for God is indeed and beyond all dispute their author. He who wrote them does not recognize in them anything that came from himself, so he can judge impartially, as if he had never seen them before. But why should I speak of judging them when the Head of the Church has already spoken?[35]

We recall how, after his Good Friday experience in 1807, Eugene followed the Spirit in fidelity and how he constantly sought to grow in his attachment to the person of Jesus Christ. We would do well to meditate upon a prayer which he composed during the retreat before his ordination to the priesthood in 1811.

---

[33] *Oblate Writings,* vol. 7, pp. 65-66.
[34] Ibid., p. 68, n. 232.
[35] *Missions 1950,* p. 362.

Prayer to Jesus to Grow in Love

O Jesus, look with compassion
upon your poor servant.
It seems to me that I do love you,
but I am afraid of deceiving myself.

I feel that, were you to question me
as you once questioned the Prince of the Apostles . . .
I would answer "Yes, Lord, I love you,"
but you would not have to ask me three times
to make me uneasy about the love I pledged to you.
I repeat, I am afraid of deceiving myself.

I do indeed believe that I love you,
but you, the uncreated Light,
you penetrate the hidden recesses of my heart,
you can read all its secrets;
you sound the depths of every human heart,
and perhaps you see that I do not really love you.

O, my Saviour, my Father, my Love,
make me love you
– I do not ask for any other thing –
because to love you is everything.

Grant that I may love you.

V

Trials of an Apostolic Man

An Absolutist Backlash to Republican Principles

After the collapse of Napoleon's Empire in 1814, Austrian chancellor Count von Metternich called Europe's heads of state together for a meeting meant to put an end forever to the "dangerous republican ideals" of the French Revolution. The Congress of Vienna set about re-establishing once and for all that the various kingdoms of Europe were meant by God to be governed by traditional monarchs within traditional historic territories. It was a moment of euphoric expectations – even Beethoven, who had at first embraced the French Revolution only to be disillusioned by its excesses, put the services of his musical genius at the disposition of the Congress. His opera, *Fidelio*, debuted in Vienna in the greatest possible royal splendour.[1]

Politically, despite lofty words about the sacredness of historic territories, each of the great powers took advantage of the opportunity to expand its empire. Great Britain strengthened its hegemony over the seas by acquiring such strategic points as Malta and some Ionic islands in the Mediterranean, Heligoland in the North Sea, the Cape in South Africa, Ceylon (Sri Lanka) in the Indian Ocean, and some of the Antilles islands in the Caribbean.

What is more important for an understanding of the historic context of Eugene de Mazenod, however, is the birth of the tiny Kingdom of Sardinia-Piedmont and Austria's annexation of the Kingdom of Lombardy-Venice along with several smaller northern Italian territories. In a convoluted turn of events, that combination would in 1860 cost the Founder of the Oblates the cardinalate he had been promised by Pope Pius IX. France, the loser after Napoleon's defeat, was obliged to pay heavy indemnities to the Allies of Waterloo and was virtually forced back into the monarchy.

With the Bourbon restoration in 1814, France was once again, at least officially, "the first-born daughter of the Church," and the "divine right" of the monarch was again expounded by such ultra-conservative philosophers as Count Joseph de Maistre. Perhaps a hymn sung in the churches

---

[1] Javier Paniagua, *La Europa revolucionaria*, Anaya, Madrid, p. 30.

throughout the country best exemplifies what was taking place. In the couplet of the hymn, Faith comes in last place after France, the king and the Bourbons:

> Vive la France, vive le Roi,
> Toujours en France les Bourbons et la Foi.

King Louis XVIII

We have seen how, after Napoleon, the Restoration in France sought to bring about a union of Throne and Altar. The Church was more than willing to cooperate with the restored Bourbon king, Louis XVIII, to renew the nation morally along traditional lines. Yet despite the suppression of the tricolor of the Revolution in favour of the *cocarde blanche* – the Bourbon white banner with blue fleurs-de-lys – Louis XVIII did not govern in the style of the *ancien régime*: he kept Napoleon's administrative apparatus along with his civil and penal codes. Further, the king promulgated an electoral law in 1817, and a year later, a decree giving some freedom to the press, a measure opening the door to expressions of divergent and often critical opinion. He became more intransigent and absolutist only after his nephew, the Duc de Berry, Eugene de Mazenod's friend from his exile in Palermo, was assassinated by a disgruntled old veteran of Napoleon's army who wanted to do away with all Bourbons.

The Monarchy Takes a More Conservative Turn

When Louis XVIII died in 1824 at the age of 77, his brother succeeded him to the throne as Charles X. The new king greatly favoured the Church, having been converted from a life of amiable frivolity to fervent religion by the death of his mistress, Mme de Polastron, in 1804. In him, the ultra-conservatives felt they had finally won their battle against the liberals. The monarch was consecrated in the cathedral of Reims where all the kings of France traditionally had been crowned, thus evoking the splendours of the *ancien régime* with its divine right. Indeed, he was anointed with what was purported to be some of the chrism used by St. Rémy to anoint Clovis and which served throughout history in the coronation of the kings of France. (The genuine vial of oil was destroyed in the Revolution.) During the ceremony the sword and sceptre of the Holy Roman Emperor, Charlemagne, were brought out and revered by the public. And from the moment of his coronation, the new king showed political intransigence which often put him at odds with his more liberal subjects. At the very outset of his reign he promulgated a law against sacrilege and made the profanation of the eucharist a capital offence. He also began indemnifying the aristocracy for possessions lost during the Revolution. That drained 600 million francs from the national treasury, but still led to frequent litigations and bad feelings.

The liberal opposition had no trouble seeing worrisome similarities between the reign of Charles X and the absolutist monarchy of the *ancien régime*. Thus there were clandestine republican groups, much subversive pamphleteering and several attempts on the monarch's life. The situation took an even grimmer turn for the king after 1827, with a constant shortage of bread and widespread unemployment in the principal cities. Street protests became increasingly frequent, along with shouts of "Down with the ministers, down with the Jesuits!"

The national elections in November of 1827 brought moderate monarchists into power – people who were fearful that the dispositions which the "ultras" sought would bring about a bloody repetition of the Revolution. The unyielding prime minister, Villèle, dissolved the recalcitrant National Guard but was himself forced to resign almost immediately afterwards. His successor, Martignac, tried to put through a number of compromises and was sacked by the king without the consent or knowledge of the Chamber of Deputies.

The July Revolution of 1830

A protest spread across the nation and a number of newspapers such as *La Nation* openly advocated deposing the king. The crisis came to a head between July 26 and August 6, 1830, after Charles X, by the ordinances of St-Cloud, abrogated the law of freedom of the press, dissolved the Chamber of Deputies, changed the electoral laws and tried to convoke new counsellors. In the famous Three Days of July the people of Paris took to the streets, throwing up barricades from which they challenged the army in a popular rising reminiscent of the demonstrations heralding the 1789 Revolution. Again the populace invaded and sacked the royal residence of the Tuilleries. And again the disturbances were orchestrated by the bourgeoisie which had much to lose from a union of Throne and Altar.

Charles X was forced to abdicate; as his successor he chose his grandson, Henry V, son of the assassinated Duc de Berry. His abdication, however, came too late, and Henry V never reached the throne. As a result, the young prince would be backed for years to come by the legitimists (also known as the Carlists) – those who saw him as the legitimate Bourbon successor to Charles X. In actuality, the white flag with the blue fleurs-de-lys of the Bourbons was suppressed and the tricolor of the Revolution was brought out again. Yet it was not a return to a republican form of government. Moderate liberals, among them Lafayette, now an old man, along with Thiers, Lafitte and others, remembered all too well the bloody episodes of the 1789 Revolution, and preferred to change the sovereign and not the system. Acting quickly, before the radical republicans could get organized, the Chamber of Deputies on August 7, 1830 proclaimed Louis-Philippe of Orleans the new king of France. The July monarchy had begun. It would last eighteen years.

The July Monarchy

Louis-Philippe, the "Citizen King," ascended the throne on July 9, 1830. He styled himself not King of France, but King of the French, a very different and wide-ranging concept. He represented the interests of the monied bourgeoisie and was the defender of moderate liberalism. In outward appearance nothing much seemed to have changed in the way of governing the country. Yet a basic concept had died with the July Revolution. Gone was the divine right of French kings, supplanted by a monarchy that ruled by popular will.

The new ruler was the son of Louis-Philippe-Joseph d'Orléans, cousin of King Louis XVI. Influenced by the liberal thought of Voltaire, the father had shared the ideals of the Revolution and even changed his name to Philippe Égalité. He was among the first nobles to go over to the Third Estate in the first Constitutive National Assembly and even signed the death warrant that sent his cousin, Louis XVI, to the guillotine. All that, however, did not save his own neck. Despite having fought for the Republic, Égalité himself was condemned and guillotined soon afterwards by the Revolutionary Tribunal. Louis Philippe, the son, had joined the Jacobins in 1790; at the age of eighteen, he was given a command in the Revolutionary Army and fought as a colonel in the battles of Valmy and Jemappes. Eventually, however, he was implicated in a plot against the Republic and had to flee into exile. He went to Palermo at the invitation of King Ferdinand I of the Two Sicilies. His stay there coincided with that of Eugene de Mazenod. In 1809 Louis Philippe married the king's daughter, Marie-Amélie de Bourbon. She and the young de Mazenod knew one another socially at the royal court.

Under the regime of Charles X, the interests of Church and State had been so intertwined that the July Revolution affected the Church almost as much as it did the dynasty. Popular violence exploded in the cities against seminaries, churches, mission crosses, etc. Parochial missions such as those the Oblates preached were banned and for a while, in Paris especially, priests dared not show themselves in cassock in the street. The anti-clerical republican press spewed a constant torrent of hate literature. Pius VIII was pope at the time – the same man who, as Cardinal Castiglione, had tested the Founder by pretending to oppose approval of the Oblate Congregation in 1826. Against the advice of the Curia and of his own nuncio, the pontiff quickly accepted the July Revolution. When some legitimist bishops and priests fled from France, he showed his disapproval by refusing them admission to the Papal States. In view of the new regime's promise to respect the Concordat of 1801, he invited the French clergy to rally to it and insisted on bestowing on Louis-Philippe the traditional title of "Most Christian King." That did not sit well in Marseilles.

Catholicism, however, was no longer the official state religion. As in Napoleon's time, it was the "religion of the majority of the French." With the beginning of Louis-Philippe's reign there was also a return to Napoleon's concept of the Church at the service of the State. Catholicism lost its privileges with the July Revolution, yet the monarch did not touch the Concordat of 1801. That sat well with the Gallicans, but it was to be a major cause of Eugene de Mazenod's great trials and troubles.

In truth, however, Louis-Philippe was conservative at heart and wanted to be seen as such, both by the other rulers of Europe and by the monied classes of France. The policy of Voltairian anti-clericalism espoused by the republicans who had put him on the throne was unbecoming to his prudence as well as to his moderate character. Beginning in 1833, he sought to re-establish normal relations with the Holy See. The new pope, Gregory XVI, a timid conservative, was only too happy to comply by not roiling the royal waters. At the French court, Cardinal Garibaldi, his representative, quietly went about smoothing the way to a satisfactory solution for choosing French bishops. This is the historical context into which Eugene de Mazenod's grave episcopal problems were to fit.

Pope Gregory XVI

In Rome, in a difficult fifty-day-long conclave in 1830, Bartolomeo Cappellari was elected pope following the brief eighteen-month papacy of Pius VIII. An austere, learned, but obtuse Camaldolese monk (Benedictine of the strict observance), with little comprehension of the contemporary world, he took the name Gregory XVI. His hostility to modern trends (he banned railways in the Papal States, calling them *chemins d'enfer*[2]) put him

---

[2] A play on words. In French railways are *chemins de fer*. The pope refers to them as *chemins d'enfer* – "roads of hell."

in almost immediate opposition with virtually everyone. There were uprisings throughout his domains – even in Rome itself – requiring that Austria be brought in the quell the fires.

Sooner or later, however, favours must be repaid, and so Austria demanded that Rome gag Felicité Robert de Lamennais. De Lamennais was a brilliant thinker and the champion of Catholic liberalism in the first half of the 19th century. The papal nuncio to France used to say of him that he was highly intelligent, but unfortunately knew it. A priest and the brother of Father Jean-Marie de Lamennais, founder of the Brothers of Christian Instruction, Felicité Robert had new ideas on how the Church should influence society. Seeing the tremendous ravages of the Revolution around him and the injustices of the new industrial era, he proposed that there was only one solution – that the Church use its influence to change the world. But, he added, to exert that sort of influence on the life of a society, the Church must free itself by separating itself from every state and every government.

The European governments, especially Austria under Chancellor Prince von Metternich, saw such ideas as extremely dangerous to continental stability. Reminding the pope that Austria had gone to his aid during the serious uprisings in Rome and the Papal States, Metternich now pressured him to return the favour by stifling the "subversive" ideas of de Lamennais on freedom of conscience and of the press and on church-state separation. Weak, ultra-conservative, and anxious to keep Austria's support, Gregory XVI capitulated. Although the pontiff had received de Lamennais kindly in Rome in November of 1831, acquiescing to the Austrian chancellor, he denounced de Lamennais' ideas less than a year later in the papal bull, *Mirari vos*. Unfortunately, de Lamennais' pride did not let him bow to the authority of the pope. In his newspaper, *l'Avenir*, he wrote a scathing reply to the papal bull, for which both he and the newspaper were subsequently condemned. Though considered by many today to have been a prophet, he died excommunicated in 1854.

During the time of the Founder's episcopal trials, there were also other examples of the pope sacrificing one cause for what he saw as the good of another. Poland had been wiped from the map (and would remain thus until 1919), gobbled up in 1795 by Catherine the Great of Russia with the help of Frederick II of Prussia and Maria Theresa of Austria. Gregory showed himself sympathetic to the plight of the Poles, yet when they revolted against Tsar Nicholas, he addressed an encyclical to the bishops of Poland on June 9, 1832, sharply condemning all revolutionary movements. It came at a moment when the pope was negotiating to secure better conditions from the tsar for Catholics in Russia.

To Gregory XVI's credit, he reorganized the hierarchy, reformed existing orders and founded new congregations. Doctrinally he promoted the Immaculate Conception, without, however defining it as dogma. More noteworthy were his efforts devoted to the Church outside Europe. The 19th-century revival of missions dates from his reign. He established over 70 dioceses and vicariates apostolic, several of which were eventually confided to the Oblates. In addition, he named Father Guibert a bishop in 1842. Gregory XVI died in 1846, leaving his successor a grievous legacy, both in the Church and in the Papal States.

Eugene de Mazenod: The Trials of an Apostolic Man

This chapter might just as well be titled "Desolation in the Dark Night of an Apostolic Man." Reading the mystics gives one the impression that the dark night of the soul is a totally interior phenomenon. For mystics, that may be true. The apostolic person has to go through trials and spiritual desolation just as painful as anything experienced by the contemplative, but such trials are affected by the active life one leads. For the apostolic person, just as for the mystic, although such trials are a source of great suffering, they are at the same time a grace whereby the apostle is purified and emptied of self. That allows the Lord to invest the person totally with his love.

For de Mazenod, the painful crisis he experienced from 1826 to 1836 was what Oblate Father Kelly Nemeck refers to as a *critical threshold:*

> The term *critical* derives from *krino* (krino), meaning to separate, to make a distinction between, to exercise judgement upon. . . . *Critical thresholds* designate those which are more fundamental: those which really separate one stage from another, those which delineate basic qualitative distinctions in progress upon which solid judgements are made. Three qualities characterize critical thresholds: (1) They are radical. (2) They are irreversible. (3) They are successive.[3]

Particular note should be taken of the fact that *peace* is a fruit of purification. It can be compared with what Nemeck calls *stabilization:*

> Gradually we become at home in the mystery of our new life in God. We are content to have let go the past and are well immersed in the challenges of the present. Even as we grow accustomed to this new stage of transformed life, however, the Spirit is already leading us toward a progressively deeper quality of life in Christ and thus, eventually to a more

---

[3] Nemeck, *The Spiritual Journey,* p. 33.

advanced threshold of spiritualization. Greater incorporation in Christ always lies further on ahead.[4]

Great Projects, Great Successes . . .

It is common for the apostolic person that trials come along at a time of great projects. Let us look at Eugene de Mazenod as we know him after the approval of the congregation. We can readily see how successful he had been thus far. First, he founded a new society of priests, destined to address itself to the needs of the poor and the most abandoned. Then there was the outstanding success enjoyed by his little group in preaching parochial missions. Afterwards, as vicar-general in Marseilles, he enjoyed continued success in thoroughly restoring and renewing the diocese, starting new parishes and initiating many works. Roman approval of the tiny society came against all odds and despite the fact that it had only 25 members. When Father de Mazenod returned from Rome and convoked a general chapter of the little group in 1826 to announce the approval of the congregation and the Constitution, he told the Oblates that they were on the threshold of

> the happy beginning of a new era for our Society. God has ratified the projects we planned for his glory and blessed the bonds uniting us; henceforth we will fight the enemies of heaven under our own standard given us by the Church. From this standard shines forth the glorious name of the most holy Virgin Mary Immaculate.[5]

. . . And Special Graces

Despite some often avoidable frictions and arbitrary actions, the Founder's successes were accompanied – and even preceded – by outstanding graces. There was first the special grace of Good Friday, 1807. Christ gave him to understand *the meaning of his life*, which could be described as *love for love*, response to the inestimable love of Jesus, and *the meaning of his ministry*. In that grace-filled experience he discovered the value of every soul redeemed by the blood of Jesus and the value of the Church to which he dedicated himself.

Another outstanding grace was the founding of the congregation. We can recall what he wrote to Charles de Forbin-Janson:

> This is . . . *the second time in my life* that I see myself moved to resolve something of the utmost seriousness as if by *a strong impulse from without*. When I reflect on it, I am convinced that it so pleases God to put

---

4 Ibid., p. 36.
5 *Oblate Writings*, vol. 7, p. xxvii.

an end to my wavering. And in such a way that I am engaged to the hilt! I
assure you that in such circumstances I am quite another man . . . .[6]

That "strong impulse from without" was true mystical grace which he
received to found the congregation.

A further mystical grace inspiring the Founder's confidence was one he
received almost three years before the Oblates' papal approbation. It
happened at the feet to the statue of the Immaculate Conception, known as
the "Oblate Madonna" that is now in the chapel of the Oblate General House
in Rome. Writing from Aix to Father Tempier at Notre-Dame de Laus on
August 15, 1822, the day the statue was enthroned, Eugene said:

> Would that I could share with you all that I experienced in the way of
> consolation on this beautiful day devoted to Mary our Queen! . . . I would
> like to think that I was understood and can well believe that all the faithful
> who came to our church this evening also shared the fervour that inspired
> me at the sight of the image of the Holy Virgin, and greater still, shared the
> graces which, I dare to say, she obtained from her divine Son while we
> were calling upon her with such affection because she is our Mother. I
> believe I also owe to her a special experience that I felt today; I will not go
> so far as to say more than ever, but certainly more than usual. I cannot
> describe it too well because it comprised several things but all are related
> to a single object, our dear Society.[7]

What the Blessed Virgin Mary revealed to Eugene was the value of his
congregation for the ministry to the poor and for the sanctification of its own
members – another mystical grace. A tradition grew in some parts of the
congregation that the statue of the Virgin inclined her head toward the
Founder. He himself never made such a claim, nor did any of the first fathers
of the congregation ever speak of a miracle. But that moment before the
statue of the Virgin in the chapel at Aix was one of great mystic grace.[8]

The grace of approbation he received through Pope Leo XII, while not
specifically a mystical or spiritual grace, was certainly a grace nonetheless –
especially considering the decision of the Holy Father to have the society
formally approved and not just given a *laudanda* to encourage its works. To
that grace is added the agreement on the part of the pope to allow a shorter
procedure in order to hasten the congregation's approbation.

To complete the picture, it is well to recall how the Founder returned from
Rome in excellent health and in better form than ever. He was enthusiastic
and eager to push ahead against any odds with the work of the new

---

6 *Oblate Writings,* vol. 6, 1815, p. 8, n. 5.

7 Ibid., 1822, pp. 92-93, n. 86.

8 See also Chapter 9.

congregation – to conquer the world: "This is the happy beginning of a new era for our the Society."[9]

This period of his life was indeed one of great projects and great successes. Probably, like Eugene, all of us have experienced the success of important projects. And probably, like Eugene, in the middle of those projects all of us have suddenly found ourselves a captive of divine providence.

Trials

In the very midst of all Eugene's successes came his trials. God touched him in the very things he had set his heart upon. In his introduction to Volume 8 of *Oblate Writings,* Yvon Beaudoin wrote: "The period from 1826 to 1831 was as drab as any that the Congregation has seen, while the Founder himself went through a dark night both of the senses and of the soul which lasted for ten years."[10]

Ten years! A long period – from the congregation's approval in July 1826 until 1836. Father Beaudoin lists the difficulties encountered by de Mazenod; here we will simply enlarge on a few of them

The congregation numbered 15 priests and 15 novices or scholastics in 1826, while in 1831 there were 22 priests, 18 scholastic brothers, 2 lay brothers and 5 or 6 novices. Behind that apparently solid facade, there were fissures in the edifice.

To begin with, there was a serious problem of perseverance. The Oblates received a good number of candidates to the noviciate, but most of them left. From 1815 to 1836, 205 young men entered noviciate – an average of nine per year. Yet in the same period there were only about two new professed Oblates each year, giving a dropout rate of seventy five percent! Serious difficulties arose because it was customary to take one's perpetual vows immediately after the noviciate. Those who were already priests and mature adults would have been making a knowledgeable decision, but those who went directly from secondary school to the novitiate were really too young to undertake such a momentous commitment. How painful it must have been for the Founder to lose so many candidates.

Another problem related to the novitiate was that the novices were not getting the solid training the Founder wanted. Father Guibert had asked to be relieved as novice master and those who followed him were not up to the job. The result was an erratic and constantly improvised formation. While

---

[9] *Oblate Writings*, vol. 7, p. xxvii.
[10] Ibid.

visiting religious houses in Italy from 1825 to 1826, the Founder was struck by the perfect regularity which reigned everywhere. On March 16, 1826, he wrote:

> Here I am, visiting the most reputed religious houses. I interview the most experienced men. In a word, I try as hard as I can to render my journey useful to our Society. From all I have seen and heard I can only conclude that from the very beginning we have sinned regarding the noviciate and that it is not yet what it should be.[11]

Aside from some notable exceptions, such as Courtès, Suzanne, Marcoux and, of course, Guibert, recruitment was not very discerning and frankly rather poor. Thus Father de Mazenod wrote to Father Tempier about other congregations, very obviously disappointed at the lack of quality he saw among the young men recruited to be Oblates:

> Can we look around us and see anything similar? We work laboriously at training a few children, most of whom cannot grasp the high ideals that would raise them above their surroundings. Not one of them has anything of his own to give – a stone to bring to the edifice that, together, we are to build. How wretched the times and how detestable the influence of this age on minds! If any of them can produce anything, it is in the contrary sense; instead of soaring achievements gained by wills acting together to attain the same goal, we are left to watch the dampening and deadening of all the impulses of our souls by the care, caution and scheming we must use toward them so that they can at least be useful in some average sphere where such cold and flabby souls prefer to be.[12]

Then too, there was the constant fighting with the clergy of Aix. As the budding congregation struggled to survive, we see the Founder engaged in a series of running battles with the local clergy. Often the fault was not his, but many unfortunate incidents could have been avoided with a little flexibility, tact and accommodation on his part. Leflon states:

> There was a sharp contrast between Father de Mazenod and the local clergy. First of all, his noble birth set him in a class above the others; unquestionably, no one could justly accuse him of having taken advantage of it to gain major benefices and to further his career, as was the custom of clerics of the nobility before 1789. In fact, his voluntary self-effacement did him credit, particularly at a time when the Restoration government was striving to counteract the democratization of the Gallican Church, brought about by the 1801 concordat and was "removing the slag from the episcopate," by replacing Napoleonic prelates with bishops boasting of titles and coats of arms. Even his chosen ministry to the humble brought this gentleman-priest no closer to the rank and file of the diocesan clergy since it, too, set him apart from the others and, in a certain sense, made him

---

[11] *Oblate Writings*, vol. 7, p. xxviii.

[12] Ibid., p. xxxi.

a privileged member of the diocese. It appeared to be simply another way of remaining aloof from all the rest. To make matters worse, his aristocracy asserted itself through his distinguished appearance, a certain consciousness of superiority, a somewhat high-handed way of acting and an easy nonchalance. His forceful personality, stubborn temperament and uncompromising attitude widened the breach even further. Finally, he belonged to a new generation of priests who had been stiffened by a long resistance to the Revolution and Napoleon and were impatient to start a religious restoration through energetic action. Thus, he was all too prone to be severe with old priests almost all of whom belonged to the concordat ecclesiastical corps and who still bore the mark of the eighteenth century. . . . It was not that the superior of the Missionaries was lacking in virtue, but to soften all those contrasts, he needed a more enlightened understanding, complemented by diplomacy, experience, psychology and an appreciation of his milieu. These were gifts that Father de Mazenod possessed to a far lesser degree than his virtues. Consequently, there were frequent petty conflicts which inevitably provoked mutual misunderstanding and aroused an all-too-human irascibility.[13]

Marseilles had been without a bishop from the Revolution until 1823 – 34 years. Both the Founder and Bishop Fortuné often had to act with firmness towards diocesan priests long accustomed to running their lives their own way. Outsiders telling the priests what they were to do or which direction they were to take did not always sit well. Frequently, they made life very difficult for the vicar-general. The Founder never concealed that the problems of the diocese weighed heavily upon him. "The reports of the prefect Thomas, the articles that appeared in the liberal press and the memoranda that were drawn up against the bishop's administration always distinguished between the meek executant and his adviser who led him about and controlled him. They extolled the uncle only the better to downgrade the nephew."[14]

Eugene de Mazenod was far more open and far-sighted than the Jansenist and Gallican bishops of Provence and it often led to problems. An example is to be found in Bishop Arbaud of Gap, a dyed-in-the-wool Gallican and severe Jansenist. His predecessor had invited the Oblates into Notre-Dame de Laus with open arms. Arbaud, however, threw them out. He entrusted the Oblates with the occasional parochial mission in his diocese but then always found their ministry and preaching too lax. It was especially so in the case of Father Guibert.

During one mission when Guibert directed the Oblate team, the pastor presented the group with a list of sins whose confession would be reserved

---

[13] Leflon, vol. 2, pp. 45-46.
[14] Ibid., p. 525.

for the hearing of the bishop alone during the mission: drunkenness, dancing by either sex, habitual sins, usury, pawn-broking, failure to complete one's Easter duty, etc. Guibert exploded and told the other priest, "If you think we came here just to hear the confessions of pious old ladies, think again, because in that case we are leaving immediately." The pastor quickly sent a message to the bishop, who rushed his vicar-general to cancel the list of reserved sins. Later, Bishop Arbaud would convince Bishops Miollis of Digne and de Bausset of Aix to join him in writing a letter to the pope against the approbation of the Oblates.

There was also the Oblate Founder's excessive sensitivity. Later we will see how he eventually learned to channel his feelings, but in his early days they often presented a stumbling block. His overwhelming sensitivity is apparent especially in his dealings with Father Suzanne, who was Eugene's son of special predilection and who, of all the candidates, offered the greatest promise for the congregation. Suzanne first felt the stirring of his religious vocation as a young seminarian in the great mission that the Missionaries of Provence preached in Fuveau, where he helped the preachers with the catechetics and liturgy. Leflon states: "Undoubtedly, grace was operating during that apostolic collaboration, but a mutual affection also played a role in drawing this unspoiled and gently fervent soul to the superior-general; none of his sons loved him more and none was loved more by him."[15]

When we read the Oblate Founder's letters to Father Suzanne we have to keep reminding ourselves that Eugene de Mazenod was not only from Provence, with all the effusiveness of expression so typical of that region, he was also a product of the Romantic Age. Even so, our reaction is that no one today would speak that way.

> I had resolved, my dear friend, not to write to you because your letters and the sentiments they express gave me too much pleasure. My heart is so responsive, so loving, that I need to be careful when it meets in those it loves certain tenderness which reveals a reciprocity too close to its liking. I love you extremely and my affection is so lively that I am always fearful of taking from God something which he ought to reserve to himself.[16]

But despite such great affection for his sons, Eugene de Mazenod could at times ride roughshod over them. Nowhere is that more blatantly apparent than in his treatment of Suzanne when he publicly berated and deposed him as superior of the community at Les Accoules in Marseilles.

> Following the proofs of confidence which prematurely put this favoured Benjamin in positions of authority, was his most spectacular fall from

---

[15] Leflon, vol. 2, p. 586.
[16] *Oblate Writings*, vol. 6, p. 65, n. 50.

favour. . . . At the age of 27 he was appointed superior of the Calvaire community in Marseilles; there, in the church he succeeded in building next to the Fathers' residence, for the purpose of reviving the name *Notre-Dame de Bon Secours*, formerly used by the Accoules, Suzanne attracted a large number of the faithful from all parts of the city, through his preaching, zeal, winning manner and precocious wisdom. Then, one day, without any sign of an impending storm, lightning suddenly struck.

It may have been because his religious life had seriously suffered from his increased occupations or because the Founder wanted to provide his favourite son with a "counterpoise" he felt was necessary for his humility; whatever the case, without giving any advance notification, the superior-general came to preside over the ceremony of the *culpe*, and at the very beginning of it, spent a long time heaping the strongest and most bitter reproaches upon the head of the poor stricken superior, deposed him without any further ado, and announced that henceforth he himself would fulfil the functions of local superior in order to remedy the disorder. The condemnation, which was as unexpected as it was ruthless, deeply wounded the model religious and became all the more painful because he felt he had lost his superior's affection.[17]

This incident shows how harsh de Mazenod could be and how he wanted to be everywhere and supervise everything. By way of extenuating circumstances for such unreasonable behaviour, it should be noted that at that point he was in a serious state of exhaustion. Even so, it was certainly not one of his finest hours. As for Father Suzanne, he returned to mission preaching and literally worked himself to death. After a drawn-out and painful illness the young priest died in 1829. The Founder was profoundly grief-stricken.

Difficulties did not normally lay the Oblate Founder low; indeed, in the past they had always had the opposite effect, making him more energetic and more determined. However, during the period 1826-1831 his resilience was gone. In that time five of his best Oblates died: Father J. Marcoux in 1826, Father V. Arnoux and Brother P. Dumolard in 1828, Father M. Suzanne in 1829, and Father J. Capmas in 1831. In addition, illness hampered some of the senior and more active members: Dupuy in 1826, Reynier, Albini and Guibert in 1827, Mie, Courtès and the Founder himself in 1829-1830.

The sorrow caused by the death of persons dear to him drained the Founder physically and morally. His discouragement is evident in a letter he wrote to Father Courtès on January 2, 1828, to wish him a happy new year. After doing so, he added:

My desk is so cluttered that I cannot even find room on it for a lamp, yet it is as though there were nothing here for me to do. I do not feel I have the

---

[17] Leflon, vol. 2, p. 587 ff.

strength to continue in this office. If my conscience did not hold me back I would have left, but my responsibility makes me a little apprehensive to do so, or rather, causes me a great deal of apprehension . . . . Every day I can witness the results of the good I have done here, but I have not taken my own interests sufficiently into account: my rest, my existence that is completely sacrificed, tied down by a surfeit of annoyances and by my position which is essentially one of dependence that keeps me from doing half the good I would like to – and even the good I am happy enough to do, I cannot do the way I think it ought to be done.[18]

The way the Founder handled the loss of his Oblates underscores his extreme sensitivity. In Chapter 7 we will see how his feelings were eventually channelled into the Oblates' mission. But it was not so in the beginning. That is obvious in what he wrote to Father Courtès after the latter had failed to inform him immediately that Father Arnoux of the Aix community had died after an illness:

I preferred to remain silent but I deeply felt the deprivation you imposed on me by neglecting to inform me of our saintly sufferer's health. Do you not know that I consider it a principal duty to assist all our brothers within reach of me who are in danger? Are we then so far from Aix that in several hours I could not have come to the bedside of the sick man? . . . I need not tell you how avidly we read the details you gave of his last moments and his burial: I have watered your letters with tears each time I have read them.[19]

What the Oblate Founder said about watering the letters with his tears was no exaggeration. He himself referred to "the susceptibility of my excessive tenderness" at the illness and death of Father Suzanne.[20] His excessive sensitivity comes across very strongly. Writing to Father Courtès about the young priest's death, he said:

As for me . . . the sorrow I have felt these past two days has been so acute and so constant that I consider it a kind of miracle not to have succumbed to it. Happily, I could shed tears in great abundance and this, I believe, saved me. I remain, however, extremely fatigued. It will cost my life to love you in the manner I do. Yet I cannot either regret or complain about it. Adieu.[21]

"It will cost me my life to love you in the manner that I do" sounds exaggerated today. But the Founder *was* devastated by Father Suzanne's death – all the more so, since, in addition to feeling the loss to the congregation's of one of its most promising young priest, he believed himself to be responsible. Indeed, soon after Suzanne's death the Founder

---

[18] *Oblate Writings*, vol. 7, p. 148, n. 289.

[19] Ibid., vol. 7, p. xxxiv.

[20] Letter to Father Suzanne, March 19, 1828.

[21] *Oblate Writings*, vol. 7, p. xxxv.

fell ill and had to rest for a few months in 1829. His excessive depth of feeling was, without a doubt, a weakness, but later we will see how that weakness purified him. Especially noteworthy is the letter he sent to Father Courtès: "If I showed outwardly all the anguish I am going through, they would take me for a madman when, in truth, I am simply a man."[22]

There is a beautiful letter written to Father Tempier on January 11, 1831, when Eugene did not yet know that Father Capmas had died the previous day. It clearly reveals the principles that inspired his affection and shows that the trials he endured helped him to better dominate his heart. In his letter the Oblate Founder spoke of submitting to God's will, but said that, even while doing so, he suffered greatly from such trials of the Lord. He was convinced that Christianity is not lived in a glorious vacuum where one is supposed to isolate one's feelings from anything transitory. He knew he did not have to stifle his feelings since they, too, are a gift from God. Because of the example of Jesus, who shed tears before the tomb of Lazarus, he did not feel that he had to mutilate a part of his personality to be faithful to the Lord.

> One must confess that sickness and death are finding their mark among us in an uncanny way; men less submissive to God's will than ourselves would be dismayed. The thought does not daunt me – I think it is because I am sufficiently accustomed to bending to the impenetrable designs of divine Providence, although I make no claim to be insensitive to the blows that seem at times about to crush us. I would not want that kind of perfection, even were it offered to me. Indeed, I will go further and say that I am, in a way, scandalized to see insensitivity lauded in some biographies and attributed (no doubt, without foundation) to men who are thereby, in my opinion, dehumanized and calumniated in a cruel way at the expense of truth. Jesus Christ is our only model and he did not set us an example of that kind. I adore him as he weeps and sighs outside Lazarus' tomb as much as I disdain and abhor the stoicism, the insensitivity and the egoism of all those who would apparently seek to outdo the one who is our prototype of all perfection, who so wanted to sanctify every aspect of our sad pilgrimage. Thus, I tremble as I await the news that you will give me on Thursday. On this occasion my thoughts are all for the common welfare of the family, more than of any personal consideration or affection. I prepare myself for whatever may happen by prayer and by the most absolute surrender to the will of the Master of our destinies, for whom we have been placed on this earth.[23]

---

[22] *Oblate Writings*, vol. 7, p. 171, n. 318.

[23] Ibid., vol. 8, p. 5, n. 380.

The Icosia Incident

The Situation in Marseilles

Eugene's major trial, long and serious, came while he was vicar-general of Marseilles. It arose from the fact that the pope named him bishop *in partibus* of Icosia without the consulting, or receiving the consent of, the French government.

During the early part of Louis-Philippe's reign, there was an anti-clerical liberal-masonic backlash against the privileged position the Church had held prior to the July Revolution of 1830. In Marseilles it made itself apparent at first in lesser measures – the banning of parochial missions, the enforced removal of the fleurs-de-lys from crosses and churches, the reduction of stipends for the bishop and vicars-general, constant spying, and other minor curbs of all kinds. Father de Mazenod, who had just returned to his post of vicar-general after several months of rest in Switzerland, wrote dejectedly to Father Mille on May 7, 1831: "It is a long, endless paper war against the powers of the world, big and small, far and near."

But the attrition and nit-picking by the authorities was only a prelude to something far more serious, a plan to do away with the see of Marseilles altogether. The official reason was that the Revolution of 1789 and the Concordat of 1801 allowed only one diocese in each of the country's jurisdictional departments. The basis of such logic lay in the three main tenets of the French Revolution: liberty, fraternity and equality. In the name of equality France had been divided into some eighty departments, all of more or less the same size. Neither variations in population density nor the regional mentality of the people were taken into account, and such age-old province names as Provence, Brittany, Normandy, Flanders, etc., had been suppressed, along with the use of any regional languages (one nation, one language). Each department, moreover, was to have one government prefect and one church bishop – no more. But in Bouches-du-Rhône there were two bishoprics: the archdiocese of Aix and the diocese of Marseilles. The liberal republicans were out to have the see of Marseilles suppressed at the death of Bishop Fortuné de Mazenod.

Bishop Fortuné Fights Back

Bishop Fortuné, then eighty-three, knew that he had little time left for counter-measures. His first step was to mount a campaign of letters, written by the clergy and laity of the diocese. He realized, however, that something more effective was needed, so he hatched a plan known only to Eugene,

135

Tempier and Courtès. His idea was to have Eugene consecrated a bishop *in partibus*, without consigning him to any real see and without informing the French government. Once consecrated, Eugene would return to Marseilles to continue his duties as vicar-general. Upon Fortuné's death, however, with another bishop already in place, it would be much more difficult for the French government to suppress the see. Accordingly, on March 11, 1832, he wrote to Pope Gregory XVI:

> I am now exceedingly old, Holy Father and I do not entertain the vain hope that God will keep me alive much longer. . . . It is not the closeness of death, however, that causes me pain – my pilgrimage has lasted long enough. What troubles me is the thought of what will become of my poor diocese. As I mulled over the impending situation, God gave me this inspiration: that Your Holiness might grant me, not a coadjutor (that is impossible and, besides, I do not want the Government to get involved in this matter in any way) but a bishop *in partibus*, someone who would enjoy not only my confidence, but that of the clergy and people, as well. For the little time left to me, such a bishop would be the guardian of my flock, the hope of my clergy and the mainstay of all my institutions.[24]

Eugene de Mazenod Becomes a Bishop

In great secrecy Bishop Fortuné sent Father Tempier to Rome to personally deliver the letter to Gregory XVI and to give him an verbal report of the machinations taking place in France at all levels of government to suppress the diocese of Marseilles. The pontiff did not consult the French authorities and was probably pleased to put one over on the Freemasons who seemed to have such a free hand. After careful consideration, he acceded to Bishop Fortuné's request. Eugene de Mazenod was quietly called to Rome, and on October 14, 1832, the cardinal prefect of the Sacred Congregation of Bishops and Regular Clergy, at the pope's command, ordained him a bishop at the Church of San Silvestro, near the Quirinal palace – the church where his mentor in Venice, Don Bartolo Zinelli is buried. Officially, his title was Bishop of Icosia *in partibus infidelium* (Icosia was a defunct Church see in Algeria). Additionally, the Sacred Congregation for the Propagation of the Faith named him apostolic visitor to Tunis and Tripoli. That was a mere juridical fiction to cover the presence of another bishop in Marseilles. Eugene had absolutely nothing to do in either Tunis or Tripoli.

Three months later we find the Oblate Founder back in Marseilles, carrying out his usual duties as vicar-general and occasionally taking his uncle's place in confirmations and pastoral visits. All seemed to be going without a

---

[24] *Oblate Writings*, vol. 8, p. xxiv.

hitch. Even the new bishop's relations with the prefect and the city authorities – testy even at the best of times – seemed to run smoothly.

The Calvary of Icosia Begins

Suddenly, and without explanation, two letters from the curia arrived in Marseilles at the end of July, 1833, telling Bishop de Mazenod to appear immediately before the pope in Rome. Not knowing what to expect from the ominous message, he wrote to Father Courtès on July 31:

> The pope has just put my obedience to this test. Do not tell anyone about this journey before it has been made public and do not even say that I am going at the pope's command. My sense of foreboding in view of the trust that the Head of the Church is showing me is more than I can say. He wants me to leave without the least delay for an important message that he wishes to communicate to me personally; to induce me to respond promptly to his invitation, he appeals to my well-known sense of devotion to our holy faith. Not content with communicating with me through the Cardinal Prefect of the Propaganda, he also commissioned another prelate who is accustomed to handling very sensitive matters and whose friendship with me he well knew, to urge me on his part, in the pope's sovereign name, to hasten my departure. I do not hesitate for a moment to obey, but I have a presentiment that I am going to be entrusted with some troublesome mission in some region of America. Colleagues who have been brought in on the matter are carried away by other kinds of conjectures. For myself, I see no other possibility. When the pope speaks to a bishop for the good of the Church, he must be obeyed, whatever the cost. Redouble your prayers on my behalf . . . .[25]

We can see that Eugene had absolutely no idea what awaited him – even guessing apprehensively that he might be sent to America! To add to his consternation, upon his arrival in Rome, nothing happened. He was not received by the pope. The curial cardinals who met him instead spoke in vague terms. None told him the truth of the situation. Only gradually did he begin to realize the motive behind getting him out of France.

During the previous year, while he thought his uncle's stratagem was working and everything was going smoothly, a veritable storm had been churning furiously below the calm surface waters of Marseilles. The prefect, the mayor, the civil and military authorities, all had been keeping him under constant surveillance, twisting his words and misinterpreting his actions in their frequent reports to Paris. As a result, the French government refused to recognize him as bishop and accused him of being a Carlist working against King Louis-Philippe. Gregory XVI was pressured to recall the Bishop of Icosia to Rome or send him to Africa, where he supposedly belonged

---

[25] *Oblate Writings*, vol. 8, pp. 85-86, n. 448.

anyway as apostolic visitor. He was no longer recognized as vicar-general of Marseilles, thus leaving him without a stipend. It was not until September – two months after his arrival in Rome – when Cardinal Bernetti, the secretary of state, gave him a copy of the French allegations, that Bishop de Mazenod finally knew clearly what he was up against. To Father Tempier he wrote: "I now know explicitly what charges the French government has made against me."[26]

A Bishop with His Hands Tied

Eugene de Mazenod was able to return to Marseilles in December, 1833. In January, 1834, he set about defending himself in the courts. The accusations were patently unfounded and he wanted to defend his honour against a Voltairian and masonic government that did not have the well-being of the Church at heart. At the same time, Bishop Fortuné mounted a concerted campaign on his behalf among the bishops of France. The court case and the campaign came to an abrupt halt when Cardinal Bernetti, in an unofficial letter written through a third party, strongly suggested that it was the pontiff's own will that Eugene not go ahead with the court case and that he live as far as possible in the shadow of retirement and away from the public eye.

The message was clear: Bishop de Mazenod, "the most Roman of the French bishops," was dropped by the pope to unruffle French feathers. He must have suffered deeply, yet he obeyed. To be sure, the unofficial letter, a perfect model of unctuous political expediency that left no doubt about what was at the heart of the matter, did pour some balm on the wound which it had itself inflicted:

> The line of conduct called for here is quite unconnected with the personal opinion held of you. You are esteemed as a bishop who has every quality needed to make the Church loved in time of peace and feared in time of war, conferring honour on the Church in both cases, even to the point of martyrdom. However, you are not considered sufficiently flexible or easy enough to deal with when it is a question of neither peace nor war.[27]

The letter, although "unofficial," showed that the pope was not prepared to stand up for principles. It must have hurt deeply, yet, obedient to the wishes of the pontiff, Eugene renounced his attempt to seek justice in the courts and maintained a low profile, taking care of his congregation, visiting the various houses, and so forth. However, the French government was still not satisfied. Before long, further steps were taken to force him out of the

---

[26] *Oblate Writings*, vol. 8, p. 101, n. 463.
[27] Ibid., p. xxvi.

country by striking his name from the electoral list. Eugene de Mazenod became an alien in his own land, liable to exile by force. When he informed Rome that he wanted to defend himself, the immediate reply let him know sharply that the pope was displeased and did not want him to go ahead with any legal action. To allay the papal displeasure he wrote a letter to Bishop Capaccini stating:

> The distress with which the Holy Father views the continuance of the legal proceeding which have been instituted against me and my desire to abstain from anything that might displease him, determine me to withdraw my appeal. Whatever the result, may the will of God be done All the legal advisors I consulted assured me of complete success. By withdrawing my appeal I am submitting to an iniquitous decision made against me and to the evil consequences which could flow from it; but neither the advantages of which I was assured nor the disadvantages which I now must fear, could make me hesitate where the will, or even a simple desire, of the Head of the Church is concerned.[28]

This was the lowest point of all. The pope had tied his hands, while his enemies were free to do as they pleased. To Bishop Frezza he wrote: "I leave everything up to Divine Providence and throw myself upon it; I should like to add, and on the benevolence of the Holy Father, but I hope for little from that direction."[29]

The Icosia Problem Resolved

Bishop de Mazenod's predicament was finally solved thanks largely to Fathers Joseph-Henri Guibert and Tempier. Like de Mazenod, Guibert was born in Aix, but the similarity ended there. The one came from the city's aristocracy; the other was a son of the working class. The former was impetuous and fiery, the latter, deliberate and calmly persistent, his decisions tactfully flowing from mature reflection. Yet both were by nature warm-hearted sons of the South.

Father Guibert, after having been named superior of Ajaccio's major seminary in Corsica, had gone to Paris to seek government subsidies for the seminary, available under the Concordat of 1801. Consummate diplomat that he was, he soon managed to obtain private audiences with the king and the queen and with key ministers, for reasons that went far beyond mere seminary subsidies. In those meetings he dispelled the misunderstandings of the crown and the government and showed them that their grievances against Bishop de Mazenod were founded on lies fed to them from

---

[28] Leflon, vol. 2, p. 483.
[29] Ibid., vol. 2, p. 484.

Marseilles, principally from Thomas, the prefect. Louis-Philippe agreed to withdraw the condemnation but in return, Bishop de Mazenod would have to take an oath of allegiance.

It would appear that the problem had finally ended. Not quite. The oath of allegiance posed a sticky problem. Eugene could find it in himself to yield unconditionally to God and the pope, but he had much more difficulty bowing to an earthly king. The matter dragged on for a half-year, until late in the-summer of 1835, with the king increasingly seeing the bishop as "an obstinate man who does not want to make the necessary overtures." Defending himself in a letter to Father Tempier, Eugene wrote: "By no means am I being obstinate in all this. All I want is to reconcile honour, conscience and my tranquillity with the requirements of the government and the desires of my friends."[30]

His view of himself was not universally shared, however. Indeed, his obstinacy exasperated those who were trying to help him. Father Tempier, always the calmest and most unflappable of men, must have been at the very end of his patience to have written the Founder the following letter:

> Do you or do you not want to get out of the frightful situation in which you find yourself? If you say no, very well! But then we should not have had to bear all the burden of the steps taken solely on your behalf. From the outset, Guibert should have been forbidden to say a single word on your behalf and you should have had to endure all the terrible things they said about you. Henceforth you should be prepared to say *amen* to all past, present and future vexations from disobedient members of the community or from the government. If that makes you happy, I have nothing more to say. On the other hand, if you wish to get out of this situation, which I consider miserable, you will have to give in a little to the way your friends feel. They, too, are at least a little interested in your honour. Up to now they have done nothing unworthy of you, and not for anything would they want to advise you to take a debasing or improper step.
>
> It is absolutely indispensable that you approve the measures taken on your behalf. So indispensable do we judge them to be that, in order not to lose another week in negotiating by letter, we have decided to send Jeancard to you. Everything he will tell you has been thoroughly discussed in committee with Bishop Fortuné. . . . I think this is the last time I will speak to you of this entire matter, for I am tired of it. I assure you that if tranquillity is what you want, I pray for it myself and want it just as much as you do. Why should I be here, sweating blood for twelve years, always hitched to the plough under the most trying difficulties! Divine Providence has disposed things in such a way that there has never been a troublesome crisis of any kind when I did not find myself alone to savour its charms. All the bad moments which it was my lot to experience on behalf of the

---

[30] Letter to Father Tempier, Aug. 31, 1835.

diocese and, in particular, for you, on a thousand occasions, have worn me down. They have wearied me to the point where matters of concern bore me – today, especially. I am tired of them. Why should I not enjoy a little tranquillity, as well? That seems to be asking no more than what is just.[31]

Bishop Eugene finally sat down and wrote the required letter of allegiance, a letter so overtly understated and unenthusiastic that it provoked yet another hurried flurry of correspondence between Guibert and Tempier to head off a break-down of the delicate negotiations they had so painstakingly worked out. The Founder had to be convinced immediately to write a second letter in more amenable terms. But even before his first letter reached Paris, Louis-Philippe, on August 25, restored his rights of citizenship. For his part, as though oblivious of the negative impact of his letter and of the lengths to which his colleagues had gone for him, he wrote to Father Tempier:

> One cannot deny that the king has acted with good grace, for he did not wait for my letter, of which they must have informed him. I feel that it would be only proper for me to thank the king. However, that puts the writer at a loss for, after all, it was no more than the justice they owed me and the reparation it was up to them to make. Is that any reason for me to get enthused?[32]

The Queen's Role in the Solution of the Problem

Father Guibert's diplomatic shrewdness finally prevailed, thanks also to the discreet influence of the queen, Marie-Amélie de Bourbon, with whom Guibert had spoken on Eugene's behalf. Did she remember having met Eugene de Mazenod in 1800 at Monreale during a pageant she attended with her father, King Ferdinand I of the Two Sicilies? Eugene certainly did. In his memoirs, years later, he wrote:

> I shall terminate this long recital, made possible by my notes, and which I have had the whimsy of wanting to write, hasty as it is, by describing the tableau of the century at Monreale. That remarkable feast took place in 1800 . . . . The king had been invited and was there with the three princesses, his daughters, then as young as I. Two of them are now dead: Marie-Antoinette, the youngest, who became Queen of Spain, and the other, Marie-Christine, who was destined for the Duc de Berry, as Queen of Sardinia. The only surviving one, Marie-Amélie, is the wife of Louis-Philippe, King of the French. She was exactly my age – of the same year as I. We were very close when we saw the famous procession go by.[33]

---

[31] Letter to the Founder, Aug. 24, 1835.

[32] Rey, vol.1, p. 657.

[33] *Missions, 1866*, pp. 209-301; a partial account appears in Leflon, vol. 1, p. 209.

The Duc de Berry had been Eugene's close friend during their Sicilian exile. Thus he most certainly would have known the Duc's fiancée, Marie-Christine – which meant that he surely would have known her younger sister, Marie Amélie. Indeed, that he kept his notes on the Monreale festival all those years and that he knew the young princess's age with such precision strongly indicate that he had spoken with her, possibly on a number of occasions – or done some very thorough investigating. In any case, she had obviously attracted his attention. Had he attracted hers? And did she, 35 years later, remember the young émigré in Sicily during the Revolution? One thing is certain – she influenced her husband's recognition and restoration of the Bishop of Icosia.

When Eugene was later Bishop of Marseilles, he was host to the son of Louis-Philippe and Marie-Amélie on a visit to Marseilles. Rey tells us that some of the bishop's conversation on that occasion was praise for the prince's mother, showing his esteem for her. Moreover, after the Icosia incident, whenever Eugene visited the king he also paid his respects to the queen and they spoke about their days in Sicily. An ageing bishop reminiscing with a friend of times long past – here is a man who is simple, straightforward and eminently human.

Finally, in 1836, four years after the beginning of the Bishop of Icosia's long and painful dark night, the French government entered into its registers the papal bull that had raised him to the episcopacy in 1832. It was official. He could now get on with his life and his work. After taking the oath he continued to help his uncle as honorary vicar-general until his nomination to the see of Marseilles a year later, in 1837.

Eugene de Mazenod's Attitude During the Period of Crisis

The Oblate Founder's faith told him that divine providence is always present, and therefore that he could face whatever came along with confidence and serenity. His submission to the will of God and his longing for peace are evident in his correspondence with Father Tempier. On October 24, 1833, he wrote him from Rome, saying,

> There is no need for regrets when one has done one's best. God makes use even of human mistakes to achieve his purpose. I do not know what he expects of me; all I know is that in his wisdom he governs those whose sole purpose is to work for his glory. The thought of peace and quiet attracts me. I have good reason to be weary of human injustice. And so I act in view of my soul's good, even though peace be obtained for a time only. If God has decided differently, he will direct events and bend the will of his creatures in such a way that he achieves his ends.

For my own part, I will gladly retire to the seminary of Marseilles where I can be of some use to the young ecclesiastics who must be formed in the knowledge and practice of the virtues of their state; I will keep up my ministry to the sick, with its consolations, and I will live in obscurity, as is my deepest wish . . . .[34]

Four days later, on October 28, he again wrote to Tempier, stating: "My dear friend, I am trying to ground myself ever more securely in the principles I unfolded in my last letter, namely, that one must discern within the course of events and even within the course set by man's deliberate choice, of a higher course set by Providence which governs all by its wisdom."[35]

His obedience to the pope is an extension of his submission to divine providence and comes through strongly in a letter written from Rome on September 13, 1833, to Father Tempier and quoted above: "If a man does not steep himself in obedience, he is good for nothing, whatever be his virtues."[36] And in the letter he wrote to Father Courtès immediately after receiving the call to Rome, he wrote: "When the pope speaks to a bishop for the good of the Church, he must be obeyed, whatever the cost. Redouble your prayers on my behalf . . . ."[37]

Recall, too, that after initiating a defence of his honour before the High Court of France, when he was told, unofficially, that the Holy Father did not wish him to continue with it, he unhesitatingly withdrew his case. Time and again obedience was his response to the call of God, having discovered that call through the authority of the pope. It was already reflected in the Oblate Constitutions and Rules when he wrote: "In following the directives of superiors, let our members keep before their eyes God himself, for it is out of love for him that they obey and to him alone that they submit in the person of their superiors."[38]

Consider the similarities and differences between de Lamennais' situation and response, described above, and those of Eugene de Mazenod. Received kindly in Rome and consecrated Bishop of Icosia *in partibus*, he fell victim to the bull *Sollicitudo ecclesiarum* which made it the clear policy of the Holy See to negotiate episcopal investitures with the new French regime. Thus, the Founder was sacrificed to French-Vatican détente the same year that de Lamennais was cut down by *Mirari vos*. Yet there is a distinct difference. Whereas de Lamennais' pride would not let him bow, de

---

[34] *Oblate Writings*, vol. 8, p. 108, n. 469.

[35] Ibid., p. 109, n. 470.

[36] Ibid., p. 101, n. 462.

[37] Ibid., p. 86, n. 448.

[38] *Constitutions and Rules*, p. 36 (English).

Mazenod submitted to the pope and suffered in silence, thus arriving at final vindication. "If a man does not steep himself in obedience," he wrote to Father Tempier from Rome on September 13, 1833, "he is good for nothing, whatever be his virtues."[39]

Obedience Without Servility

Throughout the Icosia crisis Eugene de Mazenod practised obedience without servility. He did not bow his head, not even before the king of France. To the pope, Christ's vicar, it was different. He surrendered his judgment to the pontiff, but that does not mean he had no judgment. When he acceded to the pope, it was with the full knowledge that Gregory XVI was not a man to stand up to the King of France and fight. But he was the pope, nonetheless. To Father Tempier the bishop confided: *"Le Saint-Père se penche toujours vers ce qui est bénin."* The word *bénin*, which means *benign* in English, also has the nuance in French of lenient or of having little resistance. The closest translation of Eugene's observation to Tempier would be: "The Holy Father is always inclined toward the easy way out."[40]

To Bishop Frezza, a secretary in the Roman Curia, he wrote a letter in November, 1834, that showed his deep internal freedom:

> It is not I who began proceedings against the French government, as Bishop Cappacini wrongly asserts . . . . The French government itself brought the case before the tribunals. Peacefully ensconced in the Quirinal, Bishop Cappacini need not trouble himself – he has no worries about the nature and importance of the sacrifice imposed on a bishop who must relinquish his rights and surrender before a wily and powerful enemy. . . . I leave everything and commit myself to Divine Providence. I would like to add: and to the Holy Father's benevolence, but I expect very little from that source.[41]

Loyal dissent is positive and healthy. It criticizes the bad by practising the better and characterizes those who serve the Kingdom unconditionally. It allows them to bow their will yet remain free and at peace. Eugene de Mazenod was such a loyal dissenter. Despite his turmoil, he displayed the deep inner peace and dignity that comes from true freedom. He obeyed the Holy Father unreservedly because, despite everything, he was the pope. He clearly recognized the weak side of the pontiff's character, yet could live with it because he himself was free.

---

[39] *Oblate Writings*, vol. 8, p. 101, n. 462.

[40] Ibid., vol. 7, p. 101, n. 463.

[41] Rey, vol.1, p. 603 ff.

Repeatedly we are given signs of Eugene's great internal freedom even in the face of papal decisions. In 1830, two years before his episcopal ordination, he expressed his freedom when Pope Pius VIII allowed the clergy to take an oath of allegiance to King Louis-Philippe under the traditional title of "Most Christian King," and to say the *Domine, salvum fac regem* at the end of Mass. Having seen his work suffer from the anti-Church attitude that initially characterized the sovereign, Eugene's position was that if the pope says something *may* be done, one is free to do it or not to do it. After friction with the government over the Marseilles diocesan administration's decision not to take the political oath it demanded, and after Pope Pius VIII expressed himself as favouring the government, the Founder wrote on October 18, 1830, to Father Tempier from Billens in Switzerland, where he was recuperating:

> Do not further compromise yourself with the authorities of your country. If the pope states that you can do something, you remain free to do it or not to do it, but a bishop cannot forbid it. It is no dishonour to modify your opinion when the head of the Church gives his instructions. If the decision of the pope is what they have told me, my opinion is that no one should give an order but instead, simply let this decision be known and abstain from forbidding what it authorizes. One must be consistent in one's positions. The pope, doctor of the Church, has pronounced himself; let that suffice for our consciences. The truth is, it is not a point of dogma and, therefore, not a question of infallibility. Thus, each is free not to do it. But also, it is permitted to each to conform to the decision of the prime authority on this earth! According to the charter, the oath can no longer be considered as something sacred; it is a formality that is required, a transitory promise meant to last only as long as this temporary state of affairs persists.[42]

That letter presented a problem in the Founder's beatification process because some regarded it as disobedience to the pope. In the *Inquisitio Historica*,[43] Father Mitri, the postulator-general, had to explain it expressly in the light of Eugene's inner freedom and his freedom of conscience – that same freedom of conscience that is the right of every person.

Later, in 1860, Bishop de Mazenod would be caught in the crossfire when relations between Pope Pius IX and the Emperor Napoleon III reached the breaking point. The Oblate Founder confided his criticisms and observations either to his journal or to his closest friends, Tempier and Guibert – never to others. On this particular occasion he wrote to Archbishop Guibert in Tours[44] that Pius IX did not make him a cardinal because of politics. The

---

[42] *Oblate Writings*, vol. 8, pp. 220-221, n. 562.

[43] *Inquisitio historica*, p. 236, n. 15.

[44] December 10, 1860.

pope was not happy that the French emperor had gone to war against Austria, the papacy's staunchest ally, and let his displeasure be noted by failing to make any church appointments in France. There had been a letter in Latin from the pope to Bishop de Mazenod unofficially informing him that he would receive the red hat, but with the change in the political climate it never happened. Eugene's comment on French-Vatican relations in the letter to Guibert, was another example of the great internal freedom that allowed him to practice obedience without servility. He wrote: "All the reflections regarding my case are absolutely right, but in Rome they are formalists and sometimes too political."[45]

Continued Work for the Congregation's Welfare

With the Icosia crisis hanging over him, Eugene de Mazenod had to leave Marseilles and work in Aix for a while. Although he could do nothing as bishop, he remained very much the superior general and animator of the Oblates. Despite his own crisis and dark trials, he continued to work at reviving the spirit of the flagging congregation which, like its Founder, was going through its own crisis at the time. We find Eugene spending long periods in the communities, not only for canonical visitations but also to be with the Oblates, to animate and encourage them.

At first the Oblates' situation did not change very much: almost the same number of deaths and departures between 1831 and 1836 as before. However the number for priests did increase from 34 to 39, thanks to the entry to the noviciate each year of several diocesan priests, about half of whom remained.

With the anti-clerical attitude prevalent at the beginning of the July Monarchy, parochial missions had been banned in the autumn of 1830, leaving the missionaries chafing for something to do. Only in Switzerland, whence the Founder deemed it wise to move the house of formation, was continued preaching possible. The rest had to content themselves, for the moment, with parish ministry. To Father Tempier he wrote on January 14, 1831: "I am in complete agreement with you concerning the disadvantages of parochial ministry. The state of necessity to which we are reduced is a heavy cross for me and I would wish more than anything not to be reduced to this extremity."[46]

How concerned Bishop de Mazenod continued to be for the life of the congregation is evident in two letters he wrote in 1833 to the *Propaganda*

---

[45] *Oblate Writings,* vol. 12, Circular Letter, p. 153, n. 1.
[46] *Oblate Writings,* vol. 8, p. xxxi.

Fide in Rome, requesting that Oblates be sent to Algeria and presenting Father Guibert as a possible bishop for the mission.[47] In retrospect it was a grace for the Oblates that *Propaganda Fide* did not accept the proposal. To have followed in the wake of the French army would have involved them in ambiguities and left them open to charges of complicity in French colonialism. Both the Holy Spirit Fathers and the Society of African Missions of Lyon were tinged by such accusations. In 1848 the Oblates did have a mission in Algeria, but it lasted only a year.

In the midst of his difficulties, it is quite natural that many of Bishop de Mazenod's letters concerned the problems with the French government over his episcopacy. What is surprising, however, is that most of his correspondence highlights his concern for the Oblates. Indeed, it would be worthwhile to read all his letters of 1833-1834. Eugene made several proposals to the authorities in Rome. Among them were a projected international seminary in Rome, conducted by Oblates[48] and, again, the question of Algeria.[49]

Things finally began to look up in 1834. The government relaxed its anti-clerical posture and parochial missions could begin again.

> Rey writes that it was a year of agony for the Founder, but the cross is a source of life: *1834 witnessed an exceptional fecundity in the congregation.* The preaching of missions begins again in all the dioceses; in addition, two important works are offered and accepted: the major seminary of Ajaccio and the sanctuary of N.-D. de l'Osier. Father Guibert is named superior of the Ajaccio seminary and Father Guigues, superior of l'Osier. It is there that these two Fathers will in the course of a few years display the whole range of their talents and zeal before becoming bishops. ... These foundations and the revival of the parochial missions are a new lease on life and the Founder judges the moment ripe to set the Congregation once again on a fair course. He insists on two points: a) an almost exclusive application to the principal end of the Institute, and b) renewal of religious life in complete fidelity to the Rule.[50]

There is a beautiful letter from the Founder to Father Guibert on October 18, 1834. No one reading it would suspect how Eugene was suffering at the moment he wrote it. Here are some excerpts:

> My dear friend, today is not the first time I have bewailed the necessity of being separated from the men Providence has given me as councillors in the administration of the family. I would not want to arrive at any decision without hearing all of them; I feel a need to supplement my own judgement

---

[47] *Oblate Writings,* vol. 5, p. 7, n. 2.

[48] Ibid., vol. 8, p. 100, n. 462 and p. 112, n. 472.

[49] Ibid., p. 117, n. 477.

[50] Rey, vol. 1, p. 608, quoted in *Oblate Writings,* vol. 8, p. xxxii.

with their ideas and helpful advice, inspired, as they are, with zeal for the family's prosperity and the Church's good in the exercise of the ministry that it embraces.

At this particular moment, more than ever, I would have liked to dialogue with you, especially before taking a decision which must have very great consequences. . . . A vast horizon opens up before us: we are perhaps called to the work of regenerating the clergy and the entire people of Corsica. The bishop calls us to direct the seminary and is ready to confide the missions of the diocese to us. We must take it or leave it, but the latter choice would be unworthy . . . . It would be disheartening if we should find ourselves unable to respond to the pressing invitation which offers us everything we hope for. . . . I shall never manage to explain it all in a letter. . . . I have put all the objections to myself, I have considered all the disadvantages and the inescapable conclusion is that we must be prepared for any sacrifice at all if we are not going to reproach ourselves for closing the door that Providence is opening for us. . . .[51]

In 1835 a cholera epidemic raged throughout Provence, and both Aix and Marseilles were particularly hard hit. In Aix, Father Daniel André of the Oblate community coordinated aid to victims, using a local bistro as his centre. There he spent exhausting nights on a bench, organizing the city's relief operations. No less noteworthy, however, were the efforts of Eugene de Mazenod in Marseilles. Forgotten for the moment were his personal troubles as he gave himself over wholeheartedly to the victims of the epidemic. He was still under legal interdict and the work he was doing in the diocese of Marseilles was, in theory at least, against the law. When Father Casimir Aubert asked him to come to Aix he had to beg off with the following letter, written on March 10, 1835:

My dear Son, the demands on us increase daily. It was two hours past midnight before I got to bed yesterday. We are in a state of maximum effort because of the reappearance of the horrid disease afflicting our city. We have had to bring immediate relief to the most urgent cases. In some parishes, such as *La Major*[52] and Saint-Laurent, the clergy had reached the limit of their endurance. I have given two missionaries to Saint-Laurent. The *Calvaire* is doing more in the line of service than a parish should have to; the people like to go to the missionaries when in need. I myself am on call in every district for the administration of the sacrament of confirmation to the large number of those who have neglected to receive it; I am just back from the hospital, and on my return there was a host of matters from all over to be taken care of. At this very moment I received a call to go to a poor woman who will not be in this world tomorrow.

---

[51] *Oblate Writings*, vol. 8, p. 134 ff., n. 493.

[52] The old Cathedral of Marseilles. Bishop de Mazenod would begin the construction of the present cathedral in 1852, but its consecration would take place in 1897, long after his death.

I take up my pen again to express my regret that I cannot respond to your request that I would like to satisfy, but you must understand that my place is here and that I must give an example of holy courage. . . . Please pass on my news to my mother. I do not have the time to write her. But do not tell her what I am up to, for it would only cause her needless worry. Pray for us.[53]

And even amidst the anguishing trials of his own dark night and the cholera epidemic raging around him, Eugene still had time to concern himself for each individual Oblate. The letter quoted above concludes: "Please take special care of Brother Kotterer. Take advantage of his retreat to instil in him the great principles of religious life: detachment, especially, death to self, cheerful obedience, total dedication to the Church and to the family, support of his brothers, etc. I hold you close to my heart and wish you every blessing."[54] Reading between the lines, we note that the "great principles of religious life" he enumerates are precisely those he had to practice in the long, agonizing trials in his dark night.

What Eugene de Mazenod Gained
from the Calvary of Icosia

The troubles surrounding Eugene de Mazenod's episcopal appointment had a profound and positive effect on his life. It had been a bitter and painful experience, and yet it had been beneficial too. Indeed, he came out of it profoundly changed in mind and spirit. In the retreat he made in 1837, before taking possession of the see of Marseilles, Eugene de Mazenod wrote the following in his journal.

The episcopacy, which heretofore I could only consider as the fullness of the priesthood with which I had been favoured, and as the complement of all the graces the Lord had deigned to grant me in the course of my life, now appears to me as it was meant to be by the constitution of the Church – a relationship to the flock. In other words, it is the heaviest burden with which a weak mortal can be charged.

I have always singularly dreaded that kind of responsibility, even in the lower order of the priesthood. That is why, upon entering the ecclesiastical state, I undertook to be a missionary; nothing could have made me decide to become a parish priest. In agreeing to be a bishop I remained consistent, since I wished to be a bishop *in partibus*, which gave me the double advantage of not having any responsibility or care for a diocese and, at the same time, being in a position to do greater good for the Church in virtue of the consecrated character with which I had been invested. . . .

---

[53] *Oblate Writings*, vol. 8, pp. 150-151, n. 508.
[54] Ibid., p. 151.

Such beautiful dreams, however, have vanished. Here I am, in very fact, a pastor – indeed, the foremost pastor of a diocese which, regardless of what they say, is not peopled solely by saints. It has been given to me; I did not choose it.

Now, I shall have to become attached to those people as a father to his children. My existence, my life, my whole being, must be consecrated to them. May I have no thought but for their welfare, no fear but that of not doing enough for their happiness and sanctification, no solicitude but that of embracing all their spiritual interests, and even in a certain way, their temporal well being. In a word, I will have to spend myself completely for them; for them I must be prepared to sacrifice comfort, inclinations, rest, even life itself . . .

Above all, I must humble myself profoundly before God for having become, by his grace, so different from the person I once was; even though, while I should, in fact, be at the height of my perfection, I am overwhelmed by my need for further renewal – the edifice must be overhauled from the very foundations upward. I should be able to say: ecce adsum, ecce ego mitte me. But if my strength is weakened, if the salt has lost its savour, if the light no longer shines, how can I respond with confidence to the Master's call? Lord, help me; come – you yourself – to my assistance: Deus in adjutorium meum intende; Domine, ad adjuvandum me festina.

You alone can give strength to my soul; only you can renew in me the sacred fire of your love, which must first embrace my heart and then, through my ministry, spread to the souls you would confide to me. I want to be a good bishop; from the very outset of my episcopate, I want to discharge all my duties worthily. In a word, I want to work effectively for the sanctification of my flock and, by so doing, I want to sanctify myself to the high degree of perfection which the sublime and eminent dignity of my consecrated character demands. . . .

To do that I must go down into the very depths of my inner self, purifying it of all imperfection, uprooting all that could be an obstacle to the working of the Holy Spirit. Henceforth, that Divine Spirit must be the absolute Master of my soul, the sole motor of my thoughts, desires, affections and entire will. I must be attentive to all the Spirit's inspirations, listening to them, first of all, in the silence of prayer, then following and obeying them in my actions while carefully avoiding all that could jeopardize or weaken the influence of the Spirit's power within me. . . .[55]

We see here the depth to which his dark night transformed his convictions and perspectives. For the Oblate Founder the dawn after his long dark night brought dedication to the people, utter dependence on the Lord, absolute fidelity to the Spirit, and deep inner peace.

We see how the episcopacy took on new meaning for Eugene. No longer did he see himself as the freelance bishop carrying "the fullness of the

---

[55] Rambert, vol. 1, pp. 746-749.

priesthood with which I had been favoured," enjoying the "advantage of not having any responsibility or care for a diocese." "Now," he wrote, "the episcopacy appears to me as it should be . . . a relationship to the flock. . . . I shall have to become attached to those people as a father to his children. My existence, my life, my whole being, must be consecrated to them." As a consequence, he realized that his normal way of sanctification would have to be with and through the people he was sent to serve.

Eugene realized that the Lord had already done great things in him, transforming him from the person he had been. Yet he also humbly acknowledged that the task was far from done and that the Lord was the only source of his strength – that without the Lord's continued help he could not effectively carry out his obligations as pastor of the flock.

Theologian René Laurentin has said that the 19th century forgot the Holy Spirit and applied to Mary attributes that should have been applied to the Spirit. That certainly was not Eugene de Mazenod's case; he always gave the Holy Spirit its due. The last paragraph of the journal passage is an eloquent and clear testimony of his absolute fidelity to the Spirit.

Eugene de Mazenod was ground in the mortar of obedience and refined in the crucible of faith. The result was a new era of inner peace in his life. If at times in his correspondence he comes across as arrogant and overly self-assured, one would do well to check the date of the letter in question, for in later life we find an emptying of that arrogance, its place taken by great serenity. The change is especially noteworthy in Volume 12 of his letters,[56] all of which warrant a careful reading. Among them is one to Father Charles Bellon, dated March 19, 1856.

> We are poor, so it does not suit us to pretend we are rich. We have to know how to be satisfied with the little we can do, with the small number of members we have, and to spare ourselves useless lamentations and unjust recriminations. What good is there in wanting to go faster than time allows? Let us be patient; all our hope is that at the end of the year we shall have some new priests. Yet, when we have to apportion them among so many needs, we will have to concede that we are still not sufficiently provided for. Should we be upset by that? Is it our role to revolt against Providence? God knows our needs; he is master of hearts. If he does not move a greater number and direct them to us, what can we say? We must do the best with the means we have, we must not become upset nor weary our superiors with untimely impositions. That is what both common sense and religion tell us.[57]

---

[56] *Oblate Writings.*
[57] *Oblate Writings*, vol. 12, p. 8, n. 1309.

And to Father Jean-François de l'Hermite he wrote on October 5, 1858:

> In the whirlwind all around me, I am happy, my dear son, whenever an urgent reason pushes me to do what I have been long thinking of doing and from which I am hindered and side-tracked by incessant business matters. So, today I shall leave aside everything else and go to you, first of all, to thank you for the lovely little gift you gave me from the shrine of Cléry. . . .[58]

For the Founder of the Oblates, inner peace meant accepting certain situations, knowing that Providence never abandons anyone, even during great periods of anguish and divine silence, and that he would come out of the crucible refined, with serene inner growth and greater human understanding.

The Vèze Incident

Perhaps Eugene de Mazenod's inner peace shines forth most strongly in the Vèze incident. François Vèze was a querulous and violent valet in the service of the episcopal residence; Bishop de Mazenod dismissed him for dishonesty and for flirting with a chambermaid. When the bishop went to Roquevaire on March 31, 1838, to re-bless a church that had been desecrated, Vèze came to his carriage and begged to be rehired. The bishop's negative reply prompted Vèze to seek revenge by causing a scandalous public stir. From the midst of the congregation during the ceremony in the church Vèze threw a key into the holy water font, loudly accusing Bishop de Mazenod of homosexuality and stating that the key was the one he used to let himself into the bishop's bedroom. (It must be remembered that as the bishop's valet it was only natural that he should have a key to the bedroom.)

While an indignant crowd dragged Vèze out of the church and took him to jail, Bishop de Mazenod calmly finished the ceremony and Mass in complete self-control. The following day he wrote something that shows the depth of his inner peace: "Evidently God's grace was with me at that moment. I felt neither any hatred nor any desire for vengeance, however justified it might have been. I sincerely felt I should pray for the wicked man. . . . I myself was amazed by my absolute calm. God grant that I remain inwardly resigned to this new kind of humiliation."[59]

The bishop was at first adverse to taking Vèze to court for calumny, not wanting to cause an even greater public stir, for even the anti-clerical press had been discreet about the incident. Indeed, the only one who tried to stir things up was a certain M. Massy, who wanted to take revenge for having

---

[58] *Oblate Writings*, vol. 12, p. 109, n. 1389.
[59] Leflon, vol. 3, p. 41.

lost the bishop's printing business. But the police seized Massy's pamphlet before it reached the press. Friends and even the court prevailed on Bishop de Mazenod to sue Vèze. The former servant's testimony was full of holes and his charges easily refuted. He was convicted and sentenced to five years in prison. There, despite several exorcisms, he spent his days in turmoil, madly screaming blasphemies at the world.

François Vèze died in prison at the age of 38. Before his death, however, having found peace and serenity at last, he sent the bishop the following witnessed letter from Embrun on April 26, 1843:

> It is from the bed of my suffering and agony, prepared to render an account to my Creator of the existence he gave me, that I send you this letter. I wanted to write you, Monseigneur, because I am not unaware of the calumnies that perfidious and evil-intentioned persons have spread in Marseilles. With this letter I wish to testify against those falsehoods and calumnies. I know your heart and your virtues too well not to suffer and feel indignation for all the harm caused to your character. Monseigneur, I always looked upon you as a father: I bear in my heart the recognition and gratitude for all the goodness you showed me.
>
> I ask of you, Monseigneur, that you pardon all my offences against you, for which I have the deepest repentance. I plead that you do not forget me in your prayers and that, each day, you say a prayer for the repose of my soul. Fully confident in advance that you have pardoned all the wrong I have done you, and that you will not forget to pray for a dying man, I have the honour to be.
>
> Your respectful servant in Our Lord.
>
> (for Vèze François who could not sign).[60]

Vèze's falsehoods and calumnies had indeed deeply wounded Bishop de Mazenod and had added one more trial to the many that came his way. His serenity and inner peace throughout this whole painful incident are an inspiration.

Conclusion

If trials in the dark night of the spirit can lead the contemplative to new insights into the knowledge of God, for the active apostolic person they it surely lead to a new attitude to his or her apostolic commitment, and just as certainly, to a deep sense of inner peace and serenity. That was obviously the case with Eugene de Mazenod.

Inner peace, however, does not mean that he had lost the explosiveness of his volatile Provençal character. In some ways he remained the person he

---

[60] Rambert, vol. 2, p. 10.

was since the beginning of his life. An illustration of this is found in the incident of the hapless press office functionary in the Marseilles Prefecture in 1859, when Bishop de Mazenod was just two years away from death. Napoleon III had just bested the Austrian armies in a resounding victory at Magenta. Knowing that the bishop was on cordial terms with the emperor and thinking that it would please him to be the first to get the news, he came to announce, "I have wonderful news, Your Excellency: our army has defeated the Emperor of Austria." It was anything but wonderful news to the aged bishop. What it meant, in addition to a great loss of life, was that Napoleon III had gone back on his word and was prejudicing the temporal power of the pope.

Bishop de Mazenod was furious and dressed the man down so loudly that the priests rushed to the ground floor to see what was happening. They got there in time to see the poor man from the prefecture almost running for his life. That was de Mazenod at 77: strong, indomitable, with a stentorian voice and a temper he still had trouble controlling.

According to the Greek concept of perfection, Eugene de Mazenod died quite imperfect. But we must keep remembering that biblical perfection is quite another concept and has to do with our relationship to God our Father. It is the only way we can make sense of Jesus' admonition, "You must be perfect, just as your heavenly Father is perfect" (Matthew 5: 48). Eugene de Mazenod was deeply related to God, and despite the storms provoked by the human deficiencies which dogged him to the end of his days, he was gifted by the Spirit with a deep inner peace. Hopefully, the same can be said of us some day.

Pope Paul VI once posed the question that could well be applied to St. Eugene de Mazenod:

> What do we want to know about a saint? . . . we prefer to know his human side rather than his mystical or ascetic traits. We want to discover in the saints whatever brings them closer to us, rather than whatever sets them apart; we want to put them on our level as human beings, plunged into the sometimes unedifying experiences of this world, and to find in them sharers of our labour and, perhaps also, of our misery, so that we might have confidence in them and share with them the common and burdensome state of our earthly existence. . . .[61]

---

[61] Quoted in Leflon, vol. 4, p. 339.

VI

Bishop of Marseilles

A New Social Order

Between 1789 and 1848 Europe underwent an upheaval that completely transformed its absolutist character. The French Revolution and subsequent periods (Napoleon's Empire, the Restoration and the revolutionary cycles of 1820, 1830 and especially 1848), accompanied by profound economic and social changes, left a European society based largely on liberal principles and constitutions. Romanticism, the birth of socialism and the rise of nationalist movements all sought idealistically to do away with the feudal structures of the ancien régime in order to create a new world where all citizens lived in freedom, equality and fraternity. The major problem was, however, that one segment of the citizenry, the bourgeoisie, came out of the process more free, more equal, and decidedly less fraternal, than the poor.

Thus the nobility were not the only losers in the French Revolution. Those who fared worst were the poor, especially the working classes. Prior to 1790 they had their guilds and associations which guaranteed them at least a modicum of security. When the Revolution destroyed the French economy, it also did away with the system of apprentices and master tradesmen, virtually eliminating the artisan class. Furthermore, the Constitutive Assembly in 1791 passed the Chapelier Law which reaffirmed the freedom of owners to fix salaries as they saw fit and forbade workers any right of assembly in groups of more than 20 persons. During the Restoration, fierce industrial competition with England forced export prices down, while poor crops from 1827 to 1830 pushed the cost of food up. It was possibly the first instance of *stagflation* – a combination of economic stagnation and monetary inflation – in an industrializing world. Men, women and children had to work up to 18 hours a day merely to subsist.

The Rise of Social Doctrines

The July Revolution of 1830 had shown workers that there was strength in unity, yet their condition did not improve under the new bourgeois-oriented monarchy. After the Lyon workers' riot in December, 1831, the editor of the bourgeois *Journal des débats* wrote in alarm: "The sedition in Lyon revealed a grave secret: that there is a class struggle between the *haves* and the *have-nots*. The barbarians who threaten society are no longer in the Caucuses or on the Tartar steppes. They are in the suburbs of our manufacturing cities. This is not a question of the Republic or of a monarchy, but of the well-being of society itself."[1] Men worked up to 18 interminable hours daily for only 2 francs; women, for 15 sous, children, for 10 sous. A loaf of bread cost a fifth of a franc, a pair of shoes, 20 francs. For their part, the bourgeoisie saw nothing inherently wrong with a situation that forced workers into destitution. In 1845, in an article entitled *De la liberté du travail* (*The Freedom of Work*), Dunoyer, after arguing that the State had no right to interfere in favour of the poor, added:

> Of course, misery exists, but like inequality, it is inevitable and necessary. Society needs lower echelons into which badly managed families can fall. Misery is a redoubtable hell. . . . It offers a salutary spectacle to those sectors of the less endowed classes which have remained healthy, filling them with wholesome fear and exhorting them to practice the difficult virtues they need in order to get ahead.[2]

Such conditions brought a new word into the universal vocabulary: *proletariat.* Latin in origin, it refers to urban workers, without capital or the means of production, whose sole resource for the future – their *proles* – is a capacity to work, which, like a birthright, is sold to the captains of industry.

Socialism Appeals to the Poor

The Restoration, and even more, the July Monarchy, were marked by a development of a wide spectrum of socialist doctrines. The Comte de St-Simon was an early proponent of utopian socialism. His theory of technocracy virtually became a religion. Charles Fourier, an isolated and self-taught socialist ideologue who lived for a while in Marseilles during the Oblate Founder's episcopate, made a stir by advocating the elimination of middle-men through the creation of producer-consumer co-operatives. He held that social harmony could be achieved in a society based on the *phalanx*, an economic unit of 1,620 people sharing a communal dwelling and dividing work according to their natural inclination. Louis Blanc was for an all-embracing state socialism that would put an end to unhealthy competition. In *The Organization of Work* (1840) he presented the principle of his ideal social order: "From each according to his abilities, to each according to his needs."

---

[1] Fayard, *Histoire de France,* vol. 4, p. 419.

[2] Ibid., p. 422.

Social theorist Pierre Proudhon, on the other hand, totally discounted the utility of any governmental intervention in the lives of workers. His pamphlet *What is Property?* led to an anarchist model of socialism. Whatever model French socialists espoused, however, they were an elitist group imbued with the desire for equality and social justice, questioning the very right to private property and the legitimacy of a free market economy. Victor Prosper Considérant, a disciple of Fourier, and later his successor, wrote in 1847: "Generations which are born in penury, poverty and misery spend their existence in penury, poverty and misery, and then pass that terrible inheritance on to their descendants."[3]

The Church and the Proletariat

With their concern for such burning questions, the socialists theorists, all intellectuals from the bourgeois class, created workers' movements that won the proletariat from the very outset of the industrial revolution. Observers have said that in the mid-19th century the Church lost the urban worker. The Church certainly had the opportunity at that historic moment to win the worker, but failed to recognize the signs of the times. Thus, it cannot be said that the Church lost the urban worker – the fact is that the Church never had the worker in the first place. At the outset of the Europe's new industrial civilization, the Church saw political economy as lying outside its domain and failed to recognize the birth of a new social order. Only a few Catholics denounced the misery in which the working class was forced to live. The chief Catholic liberal, Félicité de Lamennais fiercely condemned the exploitation of the proletariat from 1823 onward, and even after his excommunication: "Modern politics only sees the poor person as a work machine from which one has to get the most possible effort within a given time. . . . Are such men free? Let us not fool ourselves, they are not free . . . . Their needs put them at our mercy; necessity makes slaves of them."[4]

Philippe Buchez, a converted socialist, ex-Carbonaro and former disciple of St-Simon, called upon all Christians to promote structural reforms that would do away with private property and return society to the spirit of the early Church. His dream inspired some clerics to work alongside the poor in a foretaste of the worker-priest movement of the 1950s. In 1834 Alban de Villeneuve-Barge-mont, shocked by the conditions in the textile factories of Lille, wrote the treatise *Christian Political Economy*, wherein he decried the moral degradation resulting from the industrial culture and called for justice, rather than charity.

---

[3] Javier Paniagua, *La Europa revolucionaria – 1789-1848,* Madrid, p. 53.

[4] *L'Avenir,* Paris.

More Charity Than Justice

With few exceptions, the Church dealt with the plight of destitute workers and the unemployed, by opting for traditional charity rather than by attacking the root of the problem: social injustice, greed and exploitation. That attack, unfortunately, was left to the "enemies of the Church," the socialists. By the time Pope Leo XIII issued the landmark encyclical *Rerum Novarum* – a half-century after Engels and Marx came out with the *Communist Manifesto* – Europe's proletariat had long since opted for socialism.

In Bishop de Mazenod's time only a few prelates in France – all of them bishops in industrial centres – thought of seriously questioning the basis for the social order created by the liberal regime's runaway capitalism. They can be counted on one hand: Belmas and Giraud of Cambrai, Fayet of Rouen, Bonald of Lyon, and Affre of Paris.[5] The failure of most to see the problem can be partially explained by the fact that the majority of bishops in France came, as did Bishop de Mazenod, from the aristocracy of the *ancien régime,* in which almsgiving and charity formed part of the traditional obligations. What is noteworthy, however, is that while de Mazenod did indeed practice traditional charity and almsgiving to the destitute, the acute sense of justice which had led him to minister to the prisoners of Aix even before he was ordained, and then as a young priest to protest against the inhuman conditions in which prisoners lived, also impelled him as bishop to promote works and services in the social order whereby the poor could attain a more decent life.

Marseilles

When Bishop de Mazenod took over the see of Marseilles in 1837, that port was the second most populous city in all of France (Paris – 713,000 inhabitants, Marseilles – 116,000, Lyon – 115,000, Bordeaux – 90,000, Rouen – 87,500, Nantes – 74,100). Thanks largely to the campaign in Algeria, Marseilles had become the country's busiest port, with 3,360 ships docking that year. Goods worth 564 million francs were imported, while exports amounted to 629 million. Six years later, in 1843, the port became linked by rail to Lyon and Paris, and in 1845, despite the intervening cholera epidemics of 1835 and 1837, the number of ships visiting Marseilles had risen to 4,153, forcing the construction of new docks to the north of the

---

[5] Denis Auguste Affre had been Eugene de Mazenod's classmate at the seminary of St-Sulpice. Though somewhat younger than the 26-year-old de Mazenod, Affre received the tonsure with him on December 7, 1808.

cathedral. By then, annual imports had reached 956 million francs, considerably outdistancing exports which amounted to 720 million. Heavy industry with large factories had not yet moved into the South. Few establishments, apart from the port itself, boasted more than 25 workers.[6]

Despite a population explosion, unemployment in Marseilles did not reach the forty per cent figure of Paris, and the port's social evolution was not as critical as in cities with large industrial concentrations, such as Lyon. Yet living conditions for the poor were hardly less abominable. Reading Guepin's first-hand description of conditions in the port city of Nantes, we can perhaps get a better picture of what de Mazenod saw when, as an aged bishop, he continued visiting the people in Marseilles's back-streets such as the rue de l'Échelle, near the harbour, where he entered hovels to minister to the sick and the dying:

> If you want to know where and how the poor live, go to the *rue des Fumiers* which is almost exclusively peopled by that class. You have to go down a dark, dank alley where the air is humid and chilled, as in a cave. To get an idea of how it feels to enter such miserable lodgings, you should experience the sensation of your foot slipping on the filthy street, and the fear of falling in the mud. . . . On each side of the alley the walls ooze rivulets of dirty water. Enter one of the doors, if the fetid odour you breathe does not throw you back. Note that the uneven floor is not paved, even though the cracks are filled with such a coating of crud that you can hardly tell the difference. A sack of straw, a covering of tattered rags, rarely washed because it is the only one there is, occasionally sheets or a pillow – there you have what passes for the bed. No need for clothes closets or dressers in such a dwelling. . . . As for the man of the house, he looks for nothing and hopes for nothing beyond the daily bread to feed his family, beyond the bottle of wine to momentarily blank his consciousness of the pain. For him, living means not dying.[7]

1848 – Year of the Revolutions

At the beginning of 1848 the liberal French thinker and social philosopher, Alexis de Tocqueville, declared prophetically in the Chamber of Deputies, "We are asleep on a volcano. Do you not feel the earth tremble anew? A revolutionary wind is blowing and already on the horizon one can see the oncoming storm." When the volcano erupted at the start of 1848, it shook all of Europe and set it aflame. Within a short time, fierce riots broke out in Paris, Rome, Milan, Turin, Venice, Naples, Prague, Vienna, Berlin, Warsaw and Budapest. The year of revolutions had begun.

---

[6] Fayard, *Histoire de France*, vol. 4, pp. 389-410.

[7] Ibid., p. 426.

In France, the Revolution of 1848 took most people by surprise, perhaps Louis-Philippe, "the bourgeois king," most of all. It exploded almost innocently – like a firecracker that turns out to be a stick of dynamite. On February 22 there were riots to protest the forced cancellation of one of several political banquets in Paris, sponsored by the radical left to promote changes in the electoral laws. The protesting crowd, shouting *"Vive la République!"* and singing the *Marseillaise,* converged on the Place de la Madeleine.

The following day, the army moved in, shooting indiscriminately; barricades went up, and fierce fighting then raged for three days throughout the city. Louis-Philippe abdicated, stating "I will not be party to the shedding of more French blood." France had a new revolution.

But if the outbreak of the revolution was a surprise, there had been clear danger signals for anyone to recognize. Indeed, many of the elements that triggered the Revolution of 1789 were to be seen in 1848. Louis-Philippe, who had come to power as the "republican monarch", failed to realize that he was supposed to be "a king who reigns but does not govern." His regime, led by an authoritarian conservative prime-minister, Guizot, seemed to grow more unpopular by the day. Moreover, the country was in the worst economic crisis of the century. It began with an extreme drought in 1846 which completely destroyed the country's crops.

Things Get Worse

With no grain reserves on hand, the price of a hectolitre of wheat shot up from 17 francs in 1845, to 39, then to 43 francs by the end of the year. The worker's loaf of daily bread went from 20 centimes to 70, while his salary – if he still had a salary – went down. Then came a chain of calamities, precipitated by excessive borrowing and greedy commodity and money speculation during 1842 – 1846 by industrialist and banking elements of the bourgeoisie. The result was a severe bank crash that, in turn, created an industrial recession that produced massive unemployment.[8] The cancellation of the political banquet was simply a spark that fell into the tinder-box.

The Secondary School Question

Napoleon had deprived France's Catholics of their freedom of religious education when he took power. During the Restoration that followed,

---

[8]   Fayard, *Histoire de France,* vol. 4, pp. 426-460.

tensions eased, but the Napoleonic laws were never taken off the books. Then, at the inception of the Revolution of 1830 and the July Monarchy, Louis Philippe reluctantly reinvoked the Napoleonic education laws to appease the liberal Voltairians who had brought him to power, again denying Catholics the right to a religious education. Still, he sought to ease up on these strictures as soon as he could. Indeed he undertook a definite policy of détente with the Church in 1836 – the year Bishop de Mazenod's Icosia situation was regularized. However, it did not take long for the cordiality to cool, undermined by a failure to resolve the ten-year-old school question which had simply been swept under the carpet time and again.

Nor did it help when, on August 17, 1838, the Royal Council of Public Education decided that to obtain a bachelor's diploma students must have taken their courses of rhetoric and philosophy in a state-run secondary school under university auspices. To get a Catholic education many young laymen had been taking their classical studies in seminaries. The government's move would automatically have denied them graduate or post-graduate degrees. Moreover, a student for the priesthood who decided to leave the seminary would be effectively barred from any professional career because his classical studies in the seminary would not be recognized. Protesting in a private letter to the Minister of Worship, Bishop de Mazenod wrote: "What a curse for Church and society! What tyranny against those hapless young men! No father in any family would want his son to run a risk like that, and the springs of recruitment for the clergy would run dry."[9]

The debate exploded in public in 1841 with two seemingly innocuous draft bills which would have given a stranglehold on education, especially at the secondary school level, to the secular and anti-clerical universities. The heated debate would carry on even beyond the country's next revolution in 1848, until a favourable settlement was reached with the Falloux Law of 1850. Very often in the thick of the battle, the Bishop of Marseilles came on as a fighter with renewed vigour. Indeed, de Mazenod's letter to the Minister of Worship on March 23 was a salvo fired across the bow of the French ship of state. And to alert the public to the danger inherent in the draft laws, he had the letter published in two prestigious religious newspapers, *l'Ami de la Religion* and *l'Univers*. "Newspapers," he believed, "are today's means of making oneself heard." Unfortunately, *l'Univers* and its editor, Louis Veillot, would eventually grow fanatically ultra-conservative and in 1852 turn on Bishop de Mazenod in an endless diatribe of false accusations of heterodoxy that would force the bishop to have recourse directly to Pius IX.

---

9   Marseilles diocesan archives, reg. IV, p. 6.

Among the country's hierarchy, opposition at this point to the government's move had become quite general – even extreme at times. But when some of the bishops were frightened off by the prospect of an all-out public show-down in the press and, instead, proposed that the question be resolved directly with the authorities, thus avoiding publicity, Bishop de Mazenod turned his pen on them. To Archbishop Affre, he wrote: "Seeing how important the issue has been from the very onset, I believe we have much more to fear from silence than from firm and frank speech. People should not be left to think that there is a conflict of opinion among us. After we have been so badly insulted and affronted no one can complain because we have resorted to the press."[10]

Affre was persuaded to enter the debate. Despite the moderate tone of his letter in the Parisian press, his great influence and the prestige of his person had a salutary and conciliatory effect on the government. The worst parts of the draft bills were removed. De Mazenod, however, felt it was still not enough. He sought nothing less than "true freedom" and believed the mitigations in the draft bills would only end, as he wrote Affre, "in stripping the episcopate of its rights over the education of clerics and laymen." The battle continued and finally the bills were withdrawn for further study.

When "further study" appeared to last indefinitely, the battle was again taken up. Smarting from one of the attacks, Minister of Worship Martin du Nord sent the bishop of Marseilles a private warning and demanded a copy of a pastoral letter in which the bishop had referred to a number of unnamed university figures as "chairs of pestilence." In reply, de Mazenod wrote: "A bishop is not an underling of the Administration of Worship. Being a minister of God and shepherd of the Church, he is answerable to higher authority and is not permitted to ever forget it."[11]

The Jesuits in France Threatened

The "further study" finally came to an end on February 2, 1844, with the proposal of a new draft bill which hardly pleased Bishop de Mazenod any more than the previous measures had. Despite his best efforts, however, he failed to rally the French hierarchy to a unified stand. Nonetheless, his and other Bishops' efforts (notably those of Affre and the Paris region) did arouse public opinion, along with a fierce backlash from the beleaguered university and their anti-clerical supporters. The government used the polarization to try to convince Rome to silence the bishops, threatening at

---

[10] Letter to Archbishop Denis Affre, April 2, 1841.
[11] Leflon, vol. 3, p. 195.

the same time to proscribe the Jesuits, believing them to be the only credible body capable of competing with the state universities. In the universities as well as in the Chamber the big guns were suddenly trained on the Company of Jesus, as had been the case in 1828, making them out to be power-hungry ogres and subversives who were the manipulators behind the episcopate's opposition.

The government knew full well that the outright expulsion of the Jesuits would provoke riots throughout the country, so it decided to have Rome do the job for them through the papal dissolution of the communities in France. Bishop de Mazenod had himself introduced the Company of Jesus to Marseilles and knew all too well from the Icosia crisis just how prone was the weak Gregory XVI to caving in under political pressure. On July 8, 1845, he felt obliged to go over the head Vatican officials in Paris, sending the pope his own report on the Church in France and the real reasons behind the attacks on the Jesuits. A week later he was in Rome for an audience with Gregory XVI that lasted an hour and a half. In it the pontiff assured him that under no circumstances would he agree to expel the Jesuits from France.

That may have been what the pope told Bishop de Mazenod, but in an action reminiscent of his treatment of de Mazenod in the Icosia crisis he sent two cardinals, Patrizi and Acton, as emissaries on an "unofficial" visit to the Jesuit superior general to say that while he did not wish in any way to give the head of the Company of Jesus any command or imposition in this matter, it would be wise for the head of so powerful an order to reflect on the consequences to the French Church should there be no gesture of concilia-tion. The message, though unofficial, was clear: something had to be done, but Gregory XVI was again avoiding any personal decision-making. Furthermore, he expected a reply by ten o'clock that night, giving the hapless superior general no opportunity to consult with Jesuits in France. Out of respect for the pontiff and feeling the only option was to conform, no matter what his personal views, the Jesuit general consented to divide the houses of Paris, Lyon and Avignon and to limit the number of Jesuit novices in France. In France this was falsely heralded as the closing of Jesuit churches. The pope became resentful that French diplomatic circles praised him for precisely what he had not wanted to do, but he really had no one to blame but himself and his lack of commitment.[12]

Even before this turn of events, however, relations between de Mazenod and Louis Philippe had been cooling, indeed, turning frigid. It did not help that

---

[12] A detailed account of Bishop de Mazenod's papal audience along with the machinations that took place behind the scenes is to be found in his personal journal of August-September, 1845.

a protest the bishop had written to the king was published in the press precisely at the moment that Berryer, a legitimist politician fiercely opposed to the king, won a landslide victory in the 1844 Marseilles election to the National Chamber. The bishop had kept completely aloof from the turmoil of political electioneering, but it was not seen thus in Paris. In his journal he wrote:

> The bishop of Orleans informed me that when the king complained to him about the opposition of certain bishops, he was not afraid to say to His Majesty, "Name just one." "Very well," said Louis Philippe, "The bishop of Marseilles showed that he favoured Berryer's candidacy; he even forbade the *Domine salvum fac* to be sung." The bishop of Orleans did not hesitate to tell him that this was not true. . . . Although I am little concerned by what one may think of me and although I need only the approval of my conscience for my piece of mind, I still do not like to be blamed for what I do not do. The government should know that I have the courage of my convictions and my actions and that I am not afraid of admitting them or of upholding them, because, thank God, they are always prompted by a sense of duty. I therefore felt it à propos to write a firm and dignified letter to the king denying these false charges.[13]

Bishop de Mazenod felt obliged to write a letter directly to the king to refute the accusations, a letter to which the king did not reply. Indeed, their relations continued to sour as Louis Philippe became increasingly authoritarian and intolerant. This was not simply an attitude toward the bishop of Marseilles, but one against the Church in general.

The Church Rides Out the New Revolution

The July Revolution of 1830 had been promoted by the largely anti-clerical and opulent bourgeoisie – the same class that gave the Founder and the first Oblates so much trouble in their parochial missions. It is understandable why the upheaval at that time hit almost as hard against the Church as it did against the deposed Restoration monarchy. After 1830 Louis Philippe had tried to smooth out relations with the Church, but his conciliation was short-lived and it soon soured – to the degree that by 1848 religion had become openly divorced from the political regime. Thus, when the Revolution of 1848 came, it was not anti-clerical as its predecessor had been and the Church rode out the storm with relative calm. Indeed, with Louis Philippe's overthrow, a large segment of the Church entered into an exciting era of liberal Catholicism highlighted by de Lamennais, Lacordaire and Montalambert. Even Bishop de Mazenod was caught up by the writings of Lamennais, but like Lacordaire and Montalambert, he was offended by the

---

[13] Leflon, vol. 3, p. 213.

man's refusal to submit to Rome. The Oblate Founder would go on to eventually forbid any Oblate to read de Lamennais' works.

Initially, the Church even joined in what appeared to be a springtime of the French people – a meeting of the gospel spirit with the spirit of revolution. For several weeks at the outset, Jesus Christ and his gospel were the driving force for most of the ideologies involved. Priests and bishops happily blessed the trees of liberty which euphoric citizens planted and Lacordaire proclaimed the triumph of Christian socialism in *l'Ere nouvelle*, the newspaper he published:

> Amid the moral misery and material suffering that press upon us, we joyously greet the definitive arrival of modern democracy and the accomplishment of its destinies. Such democracy is the work of God, of the times and of man's genius. Let the clergy enter fully onto this new path which the finger of God is tracing. Let them commit themselves to the triumph and social realization of equality, liberty and fraternity . . . .[14]

In Marseilles the Revolution itself raised hardly a ripple. In his journal the bishop noted: "I went around the city visiting the sick today. Everything appeared perfectly normal. People are reading the posted proclamations with indifference."

A couple of months later, on May 10, 1848, he informed Father Henri Faraud in Canada's Arctic, of the revolution that had taken place. The letter shows that it had caught him by surprise: "You will have learned that an unexpected revolution has saddled us with a republic which, up to now, has done us no good and much harm. . . Now for lack of resources . . . I find myself forced to postpone the sending of new missionaries to the beautiful island of Ceylon. . . ."[15]

High Ideals That Mostly Fell Flat

With the King's abdication, the provisional government of the Second Republic immediately attacked the country's most serious problem – the plight of the worker. They shortened the work-day in Paris to ten hours (to eleven hours in the provinces), abolished debtors' prisons, and did away with such degrading physical punishments as the pillory. They also granted universal male suffrage for the first time in France and abolished slavery in the colonies. In Marseilles, Émile Olivier set up a government arbitration board to settle workers' complaints, the first of its kind in France. Perhaps the most daring measure of the new government, however, was the

---

[14] P. Pierrard, *L'Église de France face aux crises révolutionnaires*, ed. du Chalet, 1974.

[15] *Oblate Writings*, vol. 1, n. 95 p. 192.

subsidized *ateliers nationaux* – socialized national workshops meant to allay the hunger of the poor in Paris. The brain-child of socialist Louis Blanc, the idea was meant to give work to some fifty or sixty thousand unemployed men and women in a wide range of worker-run industries, all at two francs daily. Unfortunately, lack of preparation, planning and technical know-how, combined with outright bourgeois sabotage, damned the project to failure almost from the beginning.

By the end of May the workers had grown increasingly frustrated. They had given the government three months during which they were prepared to tighten their belts more, but they wanted to see results. When their lot became even worse because of panic in the economic and industrial sectors, the mood became ugly. The closing of the ateliers on June 22 sparked massive riots. Known as the June Days, they raged for three days in Paris and spread to many other parts of the country. The army suffered a thousand fatalities, while several thousand workers died in the clashes. In Marseilles, where the riots flared fiercely, Bishop de Mazenod cancelled the Corpus Christi procession, stating that "French blood which ran in the streets of our city has covered it with a funeral veil."[16]

Cardinal Denis Auguste Affre, the Archbishop of Paris, tried to make peace between the army and the workers behind the barricades in the Faubourg St-Antoine and fell victim himself to the carnage. If anyone among the hierarchy of France understood the emerging social order, if anyone saw that the problem was *unjustifiable* destitution and not simply destitution, it was Affre. While still just a priest he had already written prophetic articles about justice that made clear distinctions about the root causes of poverty. As the Cardinal Archbishop of Paris, he, more than any of his episcopal colleagues, could verify that his perspectives were true.

With the quelling of the workers riots, the press was muzzled and liberties were curtailed. As a result, there was no national outcry when 11,000 workers were transported to Algeria, condemned to a life of hard labour in the fierce North African sun. In the face of such oppression, the Church remained silent – even liberal Catholics like Lacordaire and Montalambert. Victor Hugo cried out in anguish:

> But you – Catholics, priests, bishops, men of religion, you who sit in this assembly and whom I see in the midst of us – why do you not rise up? It is your duty! What are you doing sitting there on those benches? Go up to the podium with the authority of your holy traditions; go up there and say to those who inspire cruel measures and to those who applaud barbarous

---

[16] Rey, vol. 2, pp. 278 ff.

laws and to those who push the majority onto a disastrous path – go up there and say to them that what they are doing is bad, that what they are doing is detestable, that what they are doing is impious. Why do you just sit there and say nothing?[17]

France Looks for Change

The mood of the ruling classes took a distinct swing to the right. With the sympathy of most churchmen on its side, the conservative Party of Order gained the upper hand. Elections were called for Easter Sunday – the first time France had universal male suffrage, for which Bishop de Mazenod dispensed the faithful from their duty of Sunday Mass attendance if it precluded voting. Louis Bonaparte, nephew of Napoleon I, was elected president of the Second Republic by a crushing majority, much to the chagrin of the Republican party. He received 5,400,000 votes against the Socialists' 370,000 and the Liberal Republicans' (freemasons) 1,400,000.[18] After a coup in 1851, the "prince-president" would become the Emperor Napoleon III. Meanwhile, in Marseilles the fishwives feared post-election reprisals by the republicans against their beloved Bishop de Mazenod and vowed to protect him.

As for the proletariat, it went the way of secular socialism. On July 1, 1848, Bishop Guibert wrote to Bishop de Mazenod, telling him that "the sect of socialists and communists is perhaps feeble numerically, but it is forever feeding upon perverse men and upon *those who have nothing* – and this latter group is very numerous."[19] Exactly six months before Bishop Guibert wrote that letter, an obscure and morose member of the "sect of socialists and communists," Karl Marx, just before he fled Paris, launched the *Communist Manifesto,* which he and Engels had authored, with the words, "Workers of the world, unite!"

Napoleon III Comes to Power

When Pius IX was beleaguered by revolution in Rome in 1848, Bishop de Mazenod wrote inviting him in the warmest of terms to take refuge in Marseilles. And, indeed, rumours were rife that the pontiff had already left Rome for that port. As things turned out, he did flee the Eternal City, but to Gaeta in the Kingdom of Naples, not to Marseilles. Upon hearing this, the bishop of Marseilles rushed a letter off to Gaeta again putting his residence in Marseilles at the pontiff's complete disposal should Gaeta become

---

[17] P. Pierrard, *L'Église de France face aux crises révolutionnaires.* Ed. du Chalet.

[18] *Historia Universal,* vol. 11, Salvat, p. 51.

[19] Rey, vol. 11, p. 279.

endangered. In the letter he assured the pope that the house in Marseilles was spacious and functional and that "filial devotion will make up for anything found unworthy of the great Pontiff who is to grace it with his presence." Nothing came of it, but the pope did not forget.

Elected on a ticket of law and order, Louis Napoleon had become president of the Second Republic on December 10, 1848. One of his first acts was to send French troops to rescue Pius IX from his refuge in Gaeta. The pope was triumphantly reinstalled in Rome on December 2, 1851, after the French overthrew the Republic of Rome, set up by Mazzini and Garibaldi. That same year the French president had all his republican and royalist adversaries arrested, dissolved the Assembly and held a plebiscite which approved him as Consul for ten years. A year later, on December 2, 1852, after another plebiscite, the prince-president was proclaimed Emperor of the French – Napoleon III – thus inaugurating France's Second Empire.

Bishop de Mazenod actively and unequivocally promoted "the re-establishment of imperial dignity in the person of Louis Napoleon." Deep down, he must still have felt inclined to see a Bourbon on the throne, but his choice was governed by a desire to have stability come to the nation after so many years of turmoil. He had come to the point of accepting any form of government on its merits. As far as he was concerned, Louis Napoleon had proved himself: he had come out in favour of the Falloux Law which provided religious freedom of education, and his armies had reinstated the pope on his throne in Rome. A friendship between the emperor and the bishop grew and resulted in Eugene de Mazenod being named senator of the nation on June 24, 1856, when he and a large number of other prelates were on hand in Paris for the baptism of the emperor's son. He also received the cross of an Officer of the Legion of Honour which he had been awarded a year earlier. Surprised by this latest honour, the bishop wrote in his journal on June 25, 1856: "Lo and behold, I am embarked on a new career, apparently by the will of God; certainly, it is one at which I was not aiming. . . ."[20] Two days later Bishop de Mazenod was received into the senate with prescribed ceremony. He took this new post seriously. Senate sessions lasted from January to June each year. De Mazenod would attend from the opening until Holy Week, and then return for the closing.

---

[20] Leflon, vol. 11, p. 371.

The Rise of Nationalism in Europe

When the Revolution was crushed and the high hopes of 1848 faded into grim reality, another movement, newly born and difficult to define, began to gather momentum – nationalism. It would eventually erode the relations between Napoleon III and Pius IX, and relieve them of their temporal kingdoms. It would also keep Bishop de Mazenod from becoming a cardinal.

In Italy, the growing feeling of *nazione* coincided with the *Resorgimento*, a political movement of national identity and cultural affirmation. Immediately after 1848 some foresaw the possibility of an Italian federation presided over by the pope himself. But it would have meant countering Catholic Austria which held a large northern portion of the peninsula. Such intellectuals as Cesare Balbo and Massimo d'Azeglio concluded that the unity of Italy would have to come about through a kingdom or a state with tenacious politicians. The logical choice was the Kingdom of Sardinia-Piedmont under King Victor Emmanuel II; the tenacious politician needed to bring it about was his sly and calculating minister of state, Count Camillo Cavour.

Astutely, Cavour had plunged the tiny kingdom into the Crimean War, sending a token force to fight alongside France and Britain against Russia. This garnered him France's support when, in 1859, the Austrian Emperor, Franz Josef, demanded that Sardinia-Piedmont stop its rearmament which threatened the balance of power in the region. Cavour not only rejected the demand, he declared war against Austria. It may have sounded like the mouse that roared, but Cavour was confident that Napoleon III, despite his promises to protect the Papal States, would be cornered into having to make good his promise to protect Piedmont. Napoleon III maintained an ambiguous attitude: he declared himself in favour of the pope's authority, yet reluctantly joined battle against the pope's ally, Austria, which by then was an old and feeble giant. The result was a resounding Austrian defeat in two battles – Magenta on June 4 and Solferino on June 24. Bishop de Mazenod, a staunch ultramontanist, felt strongly that Napoleon III had gone back on his word to defend the pope – which was why he stormed at the news of the victory of Magenta, seeing it as a betrayal of the pontiff.

French-Vatican Relations Eroded

Napoleon III wanted to get out of his commitments with Cavour as soon as possible because the war was not at all popular in France. Moreover, matters had gone far beyond what he expected – and exactly the way Cavour had calculated. By the time a peace treaty was signed with Austria on November 10, 1859, the papacy had virtually lost its temporal power. With the defeat of Austria in Italy all the Papal States, with the exception of Rome itself, were wrested from the pontiff. At that point relations between pope and emperor had all but broken down and Pius IX pointedly refused to grant any papal favours or privileges to France or to the French.

It was in this context that Bishop de Mazenod was denied the red cardinal's hat he was promised. That he did not become cardinal – as Pius IX had promised him in a letter – was a barb aimed at the emperor of France, not at the bishop of Marseilles, who had always been his staunch supporter. The Founder would write ruefully, "All the reflections on my case are absolutely right, but in Rome they are formalists and sometimes too political."[21] Napoleon III and Pius IX eventually reached an understanding, but by then it was too late. Bishop de Mazenod had died, and the pontiff went on to lose his last vestiges of temporal power in 1870 when Napoleon III, because of a disastrous war being waged against Prussia, was forced to withdraw his garrison from Rome (which by coincidence had been billeted on the grounds of the present Oblate general house). With the French gone, Garibaldi's volunteers breached the ancient walls at the Porta Pia, captured the Eternal City and ended the pope's monarchy. Henceforth, Pius IX considered himself a prisoner and never again set foot outside the Vatican. The victory marked the complete unification of Italy and happened only two months after Napoleon III's own ignominious defeat and capture by the Prussians, thus terminating France's Second Empire and leading to its Third Republic.

Pope Pius IX

Reputed to be a liberal because he advocated administrative changes in the Papal States and sympathized with Italian national aspirations, Giovanni Maria Mastai-Ferretti was named cardinal in 1840, and at a two-day conclave in 1846 was elected pope as a moderate progressive against the reactionary Cardinal Lambruschini. He immediately declared a political amnesty, granted practical reforms in the Papal States and set up city and state councils. In addition, he made a few gestures of support toward Italian nationalism. His overwhelming popularity ebbed somewhat, however, when he made it clear in 1848 that he had no intentions of relinquishing any temporal power over the Papal States. An ensuing revolution forced him to flee in disguise to Gaeta. When he returned to Rome with French help any

---

[21] *Oblate Writings,* vol. 12, p. 153, n. 1420.

trace of liberal sentiment in him had disappeared, and its place had been taken by a reactionary attitude that was to cover most aspects of his papacy.

Seen politically, Pius IX's pontificate, the longest in history, may have been a disaster. Seen ecclesiastically, however, it was full of achievements. He eliminated the last vestiges of Gallicanism in France and identified himself wholeheartedly with ultramontanism, that is, a Rome-centred Church government. He re-established the English hierarchy and throughout the world created over 200 new dioceses and vicariates apostolic, a good number of them confided to the Oblates. Pius IX, however, is generally best remembered for three events which stand out with special significance. First, he defined the dogma of the Immaculate Conception of the Virgin Mary on December 8, 1854, thus giving a powerful stimulus to Marian devotion and opening fresh possibilities for theological development. (The Founder was in Rome from October 27 to December 30 to participate in the proclamation.) Secondly, he published the encyclical *Quanta cura* with the *Syllabus of Errors* denouncing "the principal errors of our time." Condemned among them was the view that "the pope can or should reconcile himself to, or agree with, progress, liberalism and modern civilization" – which dealt a death blow to liberal Catholicism. Thirdly he summoned the First Vatican Council, which issued a constitution basing positive Catholic doctrine firmly on revelation, while defining the spheres of reason and faith and deploring contemporary pantheism, materialism and atheism.

Pius IX's closed attitude may have left the Church ill-equipped to respond to modern challenges, but he also left it profoundly changed and strengthened in its inner life. Whether at the level of the clergy or the great body of faithful, his long reign witnessed a vigorous spiritual regeneration. Affectionately known as *Pio Nono* and loved by the *popolini*, the common people, his winning personality, kindly wit and patience in adversity also won the respect of his enemies – all except, perhaps, the anti-clerical Roman mob which, on July 13, 1881 halted the procession transporting his remains between St. Peter's and San Lorenzo fuori le Mura and tried unsuccessfully to fling his coffin into the Tiber. His canonization cause was introduced in Rome in 1954, and his heroic virtues were recognized in 1985.

Eugene de Mazenod – Bishop of Marseilles

Missionary to the Poor

"A bishop is a missionary par excellence. I know my duty; it only remains for me to accomplish it as I ought."[22] Even as bishop, Eugene de Mazenod was an authentic missionary Oblate. His love and dedication to the people are obvious. Let us now look at some of the characteristics of his lengthy episcopacy.

He Welcomed Everyone and Knew His People

The bishop's residence was open daily from 10:00 A.M. to 2:00 P.M. – and not just for "important" people. There were no limitations on who could come to see the bishop, whether they were poor or rich. And by far, most who came were poor. According to Father Timon-David, Bishop de Mazenod had his room and his office on the ground floor to be more accessible to the people. It was only during the last years of his life that he moved upstairs. In 1985, at the time of his beatification, Professor Bernard Couzin of the University of Aix-en-Provence stated in a conference that the people who came to see Bishop de Mazenod often brought their lunch along to avoid losing their place in line. Father Rambert recounts:

> He admitted everyone, without distinction. One simply had to present oneself at the bishop's residence to be admitted. In a port like Marseilles, with its constant ebb and flow of people, where all sorts of miseries seemed to come together, it is not difficult to surmise who the persons were that showed up most often in the crowds at the episcopal palace, knowing that they need not even give their name. There, in a very modestly furnished salon, the bishop of Marseilles received and welcomed with tender compassion all those unfortunate beings who sought his help.[23]

The strict poverty which Bishop de Mazenod practised in his own life made him all the more compassionate and responsive to the needs of the poor. The conservative bourgeois and masonic liberal republicans were as uncomfortable with him as he was with them, and frequently it showed. To them he appeared cold and unapproachable. But the poor who came to seek his help and to whom he threw opened his doors, his heart and his purse, knew better. In his journal he wrote: "What a trying day! Such a stream of

---

[22] Letter to Father Courtès, May 4, 1833, *Oblate Writings,* vol. 8, p. 83, n. 445. Also in *Ecrits oblats,* vol. 15.

[23] Rambert, vol. 2, p. 17.

unfortunate persons whose miseries, much to my regret, I was able to relieve only slightly, despite giving out a large sum of money."[24]

There is a telling entry on September 5, 1838, in which he wrote:

> If mornings such as today come back-to-back too often I do not know how I will keep up. It is no great matter to give away money – it is being face to face with such terribly unfortunate beings and seeing oneself in the impossible situation, despite efforts to do more than one can, of still not being able to satisfy their needs. It goes beyond my strength.[25]

Then he noted three dramatic cases he had encountered that day:

> A widow who lost her husband in Cayenne, has not got a *sou* to her name, making it impossible for her to either live here or return to home.

> A young Belgian, just out of hospital where he spent all his money; exhausted by sickness and misfortune, he only had the 10 francs the consul gave him which are supposed to get him all the way to Belgium.

> An old woman, the sister of a long-deceased diocesan priest, has all her things in hock at a pawn shop and hasn't a farthing left to get her to the home of another of her brothers, where she would at least have a bowl of soup to keep her from dying of hunger. And how many more persons in misery! Truly, I can do no more.

> Aside from what I could do personally, I wrote a letter recommending the widow to a lawyer who, upon my letter will prepare for her a kind of petition that will be presented to all the doctors – that was her husband's profession before he died of sunstroke. For the young Belgian I wrote to the *Miséricorde*. After all that, sit down to the table and eat, if you can.

> But even if my heart was already full, my day was not yet over. I just learned that d'Herbes, the pastor of St-Julien, has been vomiting blood for the past three days. Despite the rain, I hurried to him; my unexpected visit made him very happy. It was my duty since I am the father of all the diocese, but I have a special love for my priests who are the first-born of my spiritual family. I pray that the Lord spare me this son.[26]

The passage shows how he gave of himself in *practical* charity. In other words, he *did* something.

The reference to Cayenne in his journal is also interesting. Better known in the English world as Devil's Island, it was a notoriously brutal French penal colony in the Antilles for prisoners condemned to a life of hard labour. The widow's husband, a doctor, died there of sunstroke,[27] leaving her without

---

[24] Rambert, vol. 2, p. 18, and Leflon, vol. 2, p. 320.

[25] Rambert, vol. 2, p. 17.

[26] Ibid., pp. 17-18; also partially quoted in Leflon, vol. 4, p. 320.

[27] Note that death by sunstroke in a penal colony appears to indicate that the man was a convict and not a prison doctor.

any means of support. For that reason Bishop de Mazenod enlisted the doctors of Marseilles to help her. Reading such a litany of misfortune we begin to understand why he wrote, "After all that, sit down to the table and eat, if you can."

For Eugene de Mazenod, being accessible to anyone who wanted to see him was part of his missionary vocation as their bishop: "The daily audiences take up all my time, yet they are necessary. It is the duty of a bishop to be accessible to each one of his flock."[28] Father Marius Nogaret, in an article entitled "Monseigneur de Mazenod, l'Évèque" ("Msgr. de Mazenod, the Bishop") continues the above chronicle where Rey and Leflon leave off: "Everyone has the right to be listened to by his pastor. Granted, one could use one's time more agreeably, but what does it matter, as long as one does his duty! Let us not lose sight of St. Paul's beautiful words, *"nos autem servos vestros per Jesum."* With that, one can support all the worry and grief that comes one's way.[29]

As was to be expected, not all who came for help were truly needy. So sometimes situations not only called for an open heart but a discerning spirit. It was not surprising to find the occasional "con artists" out for some easy money. Once, a presentable young man introduced himself as the nephew of a certain bishop. It turned out that Bishop de Mazenod knew the other prelate well, so they talked about him for a while before the true motive of the visit eventually came to the fore: in the name of Christian charity, could the kind bishop please provide the poor young man the money needed for a trip to visit his uncle? "You want to visit with your uncle? Nothing easier, my dear young man," Bishop de Mazenod told him with an affable smile. "You are truly in luck, for it so happens that your uncle is here in this house at this very minute." The youthful con artist performed a quick disappearing act.

The Hidden Poor

But there were also the desperately poor who were too ashamed to come to the *éveché* to seek charity. An account by Father A. Mouchette gives another insight into the bishop's compassionate care for the poor: "There was a lady, I think she was called *la Grande Marie*, whom he delegated to distribute his alms secretly to the poor who were too ashamed to ask for help. That woman sought them out diligently, then reported back to the

---

[28] Rey, vol. 2, p. 18, and Leflon, vol. 2, p. 320.
[29] *Vie Oblate Life*, 1982, p. 72.

bishop, informing him of her discoveries, and went off again, bringing them his help."[30]

The Abbé Brandouin, a diocesan priest of Marseilles, related the following incident, not widely known, that reminds us of the little boy in Aix, son of the president of the Court of Accounts, who traded clothes with a poor charcoal-hauler:

> I heard this from a priest who is thoroughly trustworthy; he related the incident at my table in the presence of several other priests when I was pastor of l'Éstaque: with his own eyes he saw Bishop de Mazenod, dressed as a simple priest and divested of all the insignia of his dignity, remove his shoes in the very middle of the street – this, in the dead of winter, mind you – and after making a pauper put them on, he went in his stocking feet to buy a new pair at a nearby shoemaker's.[31]

He Visited the Poor

When we read the Founder's journal it is obvious that he let himself be evangelized by the poor. He was deeply impressed by their neighbourly solidarity, which led them to present a common front in the face of adversity and to help one another in times of distress: "For the *third time this week*, I went to administer Confirmation in our worst quarters. I always come away edified from those poor dwellings where abject misery is addressed by such genuine charity. It is truly admirable to see so many good people hastening to the bedside of the sick in their neighbourhood to lavish their care on them."[32]

During the Revolution – from 1789 to 1801 – there was no catechism and no Christian teaching in France. Then came 14 years when Napoleon closely controlled everything. Thus, after a quarter-century without instruction – one entire generation – knowledge of the Faith was very limited or completely non-existent for the vast majority of the poor. We have already touched upon St. Eugene's absolute fidelity to the Holy Spirit; accordingly, he felt driven to help as many people as possible receive the Holy Spirit in Confirmation so that through the Spirit, they would be protected from Satan. It explains the constancy of his tireless confirmation visits throughout the city, even at an advanced age. There is also this entry in his journal, dated January 13, 1856:

---

[30] Leflon, vol. 4, p. 321, quoted from Rambert, vol. 2, pp. 680-681.

[31] Leflon, vol. 4, p. 322.

[32] *Selected Texts*, p. 64, n. 40.

It would be interesting to calculate the number of times in a year I have been called to make partial confirmations (apart from general confirmations), whether in the chapel, in the hospitals, or in the homes of the sick who call upon me constantly. I confess that, personally, this ministry, so truly pastoral, fills my soul with holy joy. That is especially so when, as happened today, I am called to go to the home of a poor person. Often I must climb up to just under the roof, by way of impractical stairs. Well, those stairs, which are almost always dark and more like a ladder than a staircase, are lit up by a great number of lamps placed at short distances from one another on each step, where one sometimes has to hoist oneself by grabbing hold of the rope that serves as a hand-rail.[33]

In the back streets near the port, the rue de l'Échelle (Street of the Ladder) was where the poorest of the poor lived. Imagine, for a moment, the aged bishop, in cassock, surplice and stole, threading his way along dark streets, to bring consolation to the sick and dying. On January 8, 1859 – *two years before his death, when he was already 77 years old* – Bishop de Mazenod penned the following in his journal:

I have just returned after confirming a sick person in the rue de l'Échelle. Though accustomed to the warm welcome I receive everywhere when I go to minister among the poor, this time the expression of gratitude from the people of the section was so touching and so wide-spread that I cannot help but mention it here. They vied with one another to see who could best keep me from slipping. They appeared at doorways to receive my blessing. They were astonished and loudly expressed their satisfaction and gratitude at seeing me visit their poor neighbourhood. In the house of the sick woman, the closest neighbours were gathered to receive me, and the sick person herself was in ecstasy to see that the bishop had not been deterred by her miserable hovel, but had come to see her. What the good lady did not know was that I considered myself just as blessed as she to be able to approach the poorest of my children in this way and fulfil the duties of my ministry towards that unfortunate class of people who claim my interest more than the world's richest and most powerful could.[34]

On March 22, 1838, there is a lengthy entry in his journal that gives us another vivid insight into what life was like for many of the poor and exploited of Marseilles – those who scraped a living doing piece-work in sweat-shop conditions in their homes. Bishop de Mazenod wrote:

Today I witnessed a miracle, a miracle that showed me the extent of the help which God accords to his prime shepherd in the exercise of his charitable charge.

I was called to the bedside of a poor woman, the most unfortunate creature in the world. Bereft of mobility in half her body from infancy, she only had

---

[33] Nogaret, *Monseigneur de Mazenod, l'Évêque,* in *Vie Oblate Life,* 1982, p. 73.

[34] Rambert, vol. 2, p. 514; also *Selected Texts,* p. 65 ff., n. 42.

the use of her hands, and since she was alone in the world, she has not left her room during the past 40 years. At the age of 20, complete deafness added itself to the list of her woes, so that she could not understand anything. And despite her deplorable state she had to provide for an aged father who could do nothing. Tireless application to her job had made her a worker of the most extraordinary ability, but her employers exploited her situation and underpaid her work. In the midst of all her sufferings, she had no one to turn to. Left to herself and to the temptations of the demon – and, moreover, without any religious instruction, – she gave in to despair. She had a reasoned hate of God, seeing him as unjust for having created her to drag herself through a life of misery. Evil neighbours provided her with bad books and thus, this poor creature lost her faith completely.

To make matters worse, the house in which she lived was devoured by a fire not long ago. She was saved by pure luck and carried out through the flames. A good woman then took her in and gave her all the care that Christian charity can inspire. The poor recluse was grateful, but the charitable lady who had taken her in could never bring her thoughts around to resignation and faith. All she did was confide her grief to the woman, a confidence full of resentment against God who, as she saw things, had made her so unfortunate.

"If God existed," she would say, "he would have treated me like a father. He would have sent an angel to comfort me in this excess of evil."

Well, would you believe it! God sent her help in the person of Mme. Liautard and Mme. Martin who are always looking for ways to ease any misfortune. I have no idea how those terrestrial angels found her but they began what would be left to my sublime ministry to complete. The presence of those charitable visitors sweetened the bitterness of a wounded heart and, to the pious lady of the house, the two women provided strong arguments with which to counter her guest's despair.

The ways of Providence have dealt extraordinarily with that poor girl. The day before yesterday, the lady of the house came to present to me a little *mousse* — her godson – for confirmation, before I set sail. During the Mass she had been inspired to speak to me about the sick woman in her home and did so before I left the chapel. I sent a blessing and a few words of consolation to the poor woman. Mme Éron – that is the name of the lady of the house – had managed to make herself understood by lip-reading and I knew she would carry out my commission. However she was totally surprised when the poor girl began to cry.

"The bishop wants to see *me?*"

"Yes, of course," replied Mme Éron.

"Oh, but that can't be!"

"You'll see," replied Mme Éron.

She came to see me this morning to kindly ask of me that act of charity. Of course! I was happy to oblige because I consider it a duty with which justice charges me. We agreed on the time and place and I went to visit the sick girl. There I found Mme Éron and Mme Liautard who told me that they thought she was about to die a few minutes earlier. My presence reanimated her. I tried to make her understand; she looked at me with a gracious smile, but despite repeated efforts on my part, she gave no reply that expressed confidence in God or repentance.

I was taken aback by that lack of feeling; she kept speaking of the evils that had befallen her and of her misfortunes. I set about writing what I wanted to make her understand; she read it with difficulty, without appearing to be touched by it. I insisted; I prayed over her, imposed my hands on her head. To the great astonishment of the charitable persons who had showered their care on her, for the first time since they had begun to constantly talk to her about God, she raised her eyes heavenward and joined her hands in supplication. That invocation filled us with joy, for we rightly saw it as presaging the conversion of that wounded soul whom, it appeared, God wished to call at the eleventh hour.

At that point, the vicar of the parish arrived. To inspire the confidence necessary to complete the work already begun, I presented him as virtually my other self and gave him my instructions. After blessing the sick girl, I left.[35]

Rambert reports that the woman received the sacrament of the sick and died soon after.

With the Queen of the Fishwives

Bishop de Mazenod's visits with the people of Marseilles had its earthier side, as well. Indeed, it is obvious that he thoroughly enjoyed visiting with the fishwives of *la Criée* and matching their salty repartee. La Criée, the morning fish market, got its name from the fishwives shouting – *crier* in French – to hawk their fish. It still exists today, where la Cannabière, the city's main avenue, ends down at the Old Port. (De Mazenod once remarked that if Paris had its Cannabière, it would be a small Marseilles.) Early each morning except Mondays the fishing boats still arrive and the wives of the fishermen still set up their tables to sell the night's catch. Perhaps today's fishwives no longer shout quite as loudly as in the bishop's time, but the atmosphere is still boisterous and the air still filled with their salty expletives.

In the bishop's time, Elizabeth Pécout (or Sabatier – there are two versions, single and married, of her name), known by all as "Babeau," was queen of the fishwives. None too shyly she imposed her will upon all the others in the market. She used to boast, "To bring a woman to her senses is nothing for me, but to flatten a man with my fists and keep at him even when he's down in the gutter until he can't take any more, well, that's my meat." She had

---

[35] Rambert, vol. 2, pp. 12-13.

been converted by a sermon on the prodigal son during a parochial mission and subsequently converted and married her common-law husband, Joseph, the coachman. (It is not recorded if she had to "flatten" him to do so.)

Babeau not only had awe-inspiring fists, she also had a giant heart. Afterwards, encouraged by Bishop de Mazenod, she formed a religious sodality among the fishwives. They would take the bishop through the back streets to visit the poor who were sick or dying. Moreover, the fishwives were prepared to defend their bishop and his causes, should it come to that. When he was embroiled in fierce debate in 1845 defending the Jesuits against expulsion, these redoubtable women posted guard around the fathers' residence so that no one could kick out the priests that *their* bishop was protecting. And again when there was a threat on Bishop de Mazenod's life by the masonic republicans after the outcome of the 1848 elections, the fishwives mobilized to defend him – all of which gives us a good idea of how close Eugene de Mazenod was to the ordinary people of Marseilles. It also gives us an idea of how he must have changed as he went from the aristocratic homes on the Cours and the rue Papassaudi in Aix, to the fish market and the poorest streets of Marseilles. No one can accuse him of having made religion the privileged domain of the rich. Leflon recounts:

> What was most typical of Marseilles was the manner in which the fishwives of the port district showed him marks of favour without any regard for protocol. Their queen, Babeau, who was not shy, sometimes would force his carriage to come to a stop, stand in front of his door, and begin a conversation in the Provençal dialect which is more than direct, although its lilting harmonies soften what might otherwise be too blunt a remark. Her cronies would rush up to add their bit to the conversation and in his witty and hearty manner, Bishop de Mazenod would reply in rough and ready fashion, using expressions no less colourful, while at the same time slipping in a few spiritual ideas. He would then drive off again, after giving his blessing to the ladies of the fish market as they knelt devoutly on the ground.

> The women esteemed him so highly that they "had arranged to ask for him personally each time any of them became ill," and in 1848, they appointed themselves his guardians and protectors and rushed to the episcopal palace when it was rumoured that the Republicans, furious over the election results, planned to attack him. "Don't be afraid, *Monseigneur*," they told him, "We are here to guard you." Actually, he had little need of such "protection" since there were only threats, but had there been more than just threats, the determination of those *femmes terribles* would have halted the assailants . . .[36]

---

[36] Leflon, vol. 4, p. 329.

He Spoke Provençal

Bishop de Mazenod was always faithful to the Oblate motto *Evangelizare pauperibus misit me* – He sent me to evangelize the poor. And so that the poor could better understand his evangelizing message, he constantly made it a point to speak to them not only in their *langue* – their tongue, Provençal – but also in their *langage* – their way of speaking and expressing themselves. In so doing, he was something of a rarity, for others in high positions generally shunned the use of Provençal and spoke only in lofty and cultivated French. The Provençal-speaking poor, especially in the rural villages around Marseilles, considered their patois to be beyond the capabilities of the upper classes. Bishop de Mazenod was obviously amused when those uncomplicated people of the land considered it an extraordinary feat that a man of his rank could master Provençal and speak like them. Of his pastoral visit to Les Caillols on October 16, 1837, he wrote in his journal:

> Children from the parishes of St-Julien, la Pomme and Olives all came there together. It is truly a consolation for me to instruct and catechize these good souls from the country . . . . I always have reason to be satisfied upon seeing how attentive people are when I speak to them and satisfied, too, that I imposed an unshakeable rule on myself to always speak to the country people in their own language. I was told today that the villagers here, when they heard my instruction, said to one another, "What a pleasure to see our bishop speaking our tongue!" And since doing that appeared for them to be a *tour de force*, they expressed their admiration by stressing that *per d'homme ens'n, parla provençaoü, fooû ave de génie.*[37] Would that I had the touch of genius needed to reach their hearts in order that they might love their Divine Master whom I preach with all the simplicity at my command.[38]

Not only did he make it a point to speak Provençal himself, but he insisted that his missionaries do the same, because he firmly believed that the poor had the right to hear the good news of the gospel in their own language. When discussing the parochial missions preached by the first Oblate Fathers, we saw how distressed the bishop was that Father Honorat had given in to the pressure of a handful of leading bourgeois town fathers.

---

[37] Translation: For a man of his rank, one has to have a touch of genius to speak Provençal.
[38] Rambert, vol. 2, p. 23.

The 1835 Cholera Epidemic and the Constant Presence of Bishop de Mazenod

Although not as terrible a scourge as before, cholera continues to wreak its havoc in many parts of the Third World. Death is usually quick but not easy; in the worst cases, uncontrollable diarrhoea can reach a discharge of as much as four litres per hour, and death by dehydration often comes within a day. Up until the antibiotics of this century cholera was endemic throughout most of Europe. Highly contagious and almost always fatal, it came in cycles, especially where there were large conglomerations of the poor in unhygienic conditions. Marseilles was a frequent host to this unwelcome visitor.

When a severe outbreak hit the city in 1835, many wealthy Marseillais fled to the countryside and Bishop de Mazenod had every reason to do the same. He himself was just recuperating from a serious illness and was still embroiled in his troubles with the French government and the Holy See over his appointment as Bishop of Icosia. Indeed, at the time the cholera struck he did not even have the legal right to be in Marseilles, having been stripped of his office as vicar-general and deprived of his French citizenship. Yet he was there, working tirelessly, never sparing himself to bring comfort to the sick and dying. Leflon comments:

> Bishop de Mazenod's efforts were not limited to presiding over religious ceremonies, beseeching God to end the plague. . . . While fully believing in the strength of prayer and the word of God, he felt that he had to set an example of courage that would be as effective as it was affective, in maintaining morale, caring for the victims of the cholera epidemic and alleviating all its miseries. Whereas a sort of panic had emptied the city of half its population and had provoked discouragement among those who remained, his steadfastness and calm brought reassurance. "Our Fathers in Marseilles are not the least uneasy, any more than I am," he wrote. The feeling of security which God gave him was communicated to all those near him and it banished their fears. "Each one does his part, calmly and unobtrusively." . . . The bishop exerted himself to the utmost, administering confirmation in the hospitals and in the homes of the sick, as well as visiting the most afflicted parishes and religious communities . . .[39]

Indeed, his efforts went far beyond simply visiting the sick and bolstering the morale of the city. The epidemic called for more than spiritual and moral support; it also needed concrete initiative to bring physical relief to the stricken. The Bishop of Icosia was up to the challenge, even though some of his projects were frustrated by bureaucracy.

---

[39] Leflon, vol. 3, p. 17.

The prelate called a meeting of all the heads of the religious institutions, the directors of the Christian Brothers' schools, the mother general of the Ladies of Charity, the mother superior of the Ladies of Jesus and Mary, and the mother superior of the Ladies of St. Charles, and proposed that they take charge of the field-hospitals which were being planned. Two would be confided to the Christian Brothers at their St-Victor and Carmes schools, and would be used for men; three for women would be assigned to the sisters at the oratory on Paradis Street and at the *Allées* . . . . The Bishop then went directly to the prefect's office and the latter enthusiastically and gratefully accepted the bishop's proposal. The mayor, on the contrary, simply gave a "polite" refusal. Actually, he feared "that no one would want to go the general hospital once the field-hospitals were opened" and he told the prelate he would be resigned to establishing them only as a last resort . . . .

Meanwhile, the poor, who were being left without any help "were falling back on the episcopal palace." Bishop Fortuné and his nephew were reduced to selling their silverware, for lack of receiving a single "penny from all the philanthropic collections whose proceeds are disappearing into certain pockets."[40]

Victor Hugo's *Les Miserables* – Was Eugene de Mazenod the Bishop?

In 1862 Victor Hugo published the novel *Les Miserables*, in which Jean Valjean, a hardened galley prisoner, newly released, steals the bishop's silverware and is subsequently converted by the sincere goodness of the simple and holy prelate who saves him from a return to the galleys. Hugo calls his fictional bishop Msgr. Myriel, but many have seen in him strong characteristics of Eugene de Mazenod and have suggested that he was the model for the novel's kind and saintly hero. The real model, quickly recognized when the story first came out, was a Gallican bishop whom Hugo had apparently met in his youth: Bishop Miollis of Digne, brother of one of Napoleon's great generals.

A perfunctory examination of Hugo's fictional character shows that he and de Mazenod do indeed share several characteristics. (Both lived in a poor and simple manner in the south of France, both were dedicated and generous to the poor, etc.) However, the fictional hero is far too naive to have been the talented and urbane de Mazenod. In fact, Bishop Miollis' nephew Charles de Ribbes considered the fictional character too naive even to have been based on his uncle, who in real life was much better known for his simple piety and unadorned goodness than for any great learning. The nephew wrote an article, *Monseigneur de Miollis – idées et sentiments qui sont contraires à la vérité* (Bishop de Miollis – Ideas and Sentiments Contrary to

---

[40] Leflon, vol. 2, p. 18.

the Truth), in the June, 1862, issue of *Le Correspondant*.[41] In it he tried to set the record straight. As well, the bishop's biographer, Msgr. Ricard, clearly stated that Miollis was Hugo's model. Ricard also wrote a biography of Bishop de Mazenod but nowhere in it did he allude to any connection with *Les Miserables*.

Napoleon is said to have once asked Gen. Miollis what favour he could bestow upon him for his outstanding and brilliant service. Miollis told the Emperor he would greatly appreciate having his brother, a priest, become a bishop. "Why just a bishop?" came the Emperor's reply, "Why not the Archbishop of Paris?" "Thank you, Sire," the General answered, "but just a little bishopric somewhere in the mountains would do quite nicely."

The bishop-elect went for guidance to M. Émery at St-Sulpice, where he had studied. After a thorough hearing, the eminent seminary director advised him not to accept, because he did not appear qualified. Miollis thanked him humbly, agreed to refuse the honour and quietly made for the door. Émery was so impressed by the man's innate goodness and humility that he called him back and told him, "M. Miollis, I have changed my mind. I advise you to accept the honour offered to you." And so he did. He became Bishop of Digne from 1806 to 1838, a capacity in which Eugene de Mazenod knew him well.[42]

Educator of His People

In all he undertook for the Church of Marseilles, Eugene de Mazenod was animated by the guiding principles which he expressed in his journal during the retreat made just before he took the helm of the diocese:

> You alone can give strength to my soul; only you can renew in me the sacred fire of your love, which must first embrace my heart and then, through my ministry, spread to the souls you would confide to me. *I want to be a good bishop*; from the very outset of my episcopate, *I want to discharge all my duties worthily*. In a word, *I want to work effectively for the sanctification of my flock* and, *by so doing, I want to sanctify myself* to the high degree of perfection which the sublimity of my consecrated character and eminent dignity demand . . .[43]

In this reflection we see that for him, the way to holiness was through his fidelity as shepherd. He no longer struggled to compartmentalize his life into the contemplative and the active, into separate times for prayer and

---

[41] *Le Correspondant,* pp. 309-323.

[42] See *Oblate Writings,* vol. 13, p. 31, n. 24; p. 63, n. 46; p. 86, n. 65.

[43] Rambert, vol. 1, p. 749.

ministry. More and more, his life became a sanctifying oblation of service. Perhaps the vital synthesis of those principles comes through most clearly in his pastoral letters.

Engaging His People in the Most Important Contemporary Problems in the Life of the Church

Bishop de Mazenod's pastoral letters reflect the same mentality as the Lenten sermons he delivered at the Madeleine in Aix as a young priest. Regarding them, Emilien Lamirande wrote an excellent article entitled "Zeal for All Churches – Bishop de Mazenod's Teaching on the Church According to Some of his Pastoral Letters."[44] In it he shows how the bishop sought to interest the people of Marseilles in the main problems of the Universal Church. In the pastoral letters of contemporary bishops it would be hard, if not impossible, to find the degree of openness that he showed toward his people. Moreover, Bishop de Mazenod's pastoral letters convey clearly his concept of the Church.

To begin with, he was conscious of every bishop's universal co-responsibility in the Church, even if he never used the term *collegiality* (a term introduced by Pius XII and used afterwards in the Second Vatican Council). That does not mean that de Mazenod was ahead of his time, but he was certainly very open to the problems of his day and saw them within the terms of his deep faith. A man of such faith always finds the language to express his faith to the people and to be understood, even by the unlettered and the poor. A letter to Bishop Bourget in Montreal showed his conviction that each bishop is responsible for the entire Church: "Pontiff that you are in the Church of Jesus Christ and consequently having your share of the solicitude, not only for your own flock but for the whole Church . . . ."[45]

On the Unity of the Church

The mid-1830s saw Spanish politics in turmoil. The absolutist monarch, Fernando VII, died at La Granja in 1833, survived by his fourth wife, Mar'a Cristina of Naples and her two-year-old daughter, Mar'a Isabel. The queen became regent pending the coming-of-age of her infant daughter. However, the king's brother, Don Carlos de Borbona, did not recognize Isabel as Fernando's successor and claimed the crown for himself. It was the start of a civil war that lasted from 1833 to 1839 and had political repercussions for the rest of Europe.

---

[44] *Selected Oblate Studies and Texts,* 1986, pp. 307-352.

[45] Leflon, vol. 1, p. 76.

Like his brother, Don Carlos was absolutist and Catholic. He had the support of Austria and of the pope. The regent, Mar'a Cristina, allied herself with Spanish liberals, freemasons and anti-clericals, thereby gaining the support of Louis-Philippe's liberal regime in France and of Protestant England. That Rome did not recognize the regent, Mar'a Cristina, brought down reprisals against the Church in Spain. Clerics were harassed, ecclesiastical stipends discontinued, etc. A concerted attempt to set up a Spanish national church independent of Rome resulted in open persecution of dissident clergy and brought a host of Carlist refugees to Marseilles. In a circular to the pastors of Marseilles Bishop de Mazenod stated:

> Neither you nor I have, up to now, neglected to show them the solicitude that effectively satisfies the duties of hospitality which charity requires. However, in our city, day by day they are becoming too numerous for our personal resources to cope with adequately. The time has come to appeal to the charity of the faithful, in the name of the faith that is being persecuted in the person of these distinguished exiles.[46]

The problem worsened when the Church did not recognize the regent, Mar'a Cristina, while the French government did. When Cardinal Affre of Paris published the pope's encyclical reproving her actions, he had his knuckles soundly rapped by the Minister of Worship. As a result, that usually fearless champion of justice and the poor who later would be killed during peace-making attempts in the 1848 Revolution, wrote a letter counselling prudence to his fellow members of the French hierarchy. Following the reception of that letter Bishop de Mazenod observed the following in his journal about his seminary classmate:

> The Archbishop of Paris . . . has sent me his reply to the Minister's protest. It does not satisfy me at all. He believes that the objection aims only at the expressions he used to give notice of the powers he has received from the Holy See; thus, he advises us to avoid such expressions when writing our own pastoral letters. I think he is mistaken: the problem is not so much the expression as the substance itself. Thus, whatever be the vocabulary we use, the expression will always be faulted.
>
> It does not matter; I will not hesitate on that account to show myself united in mind and will to the Head of the Church. No less shall I express my horror at the schism into which they are trying to drag the poor Church in Spain.[47]

On March 29, as soon as he received a copy of the papal encyclical in question, Bishop de Mazenod had it published in his diocese. Almost

---

[46] Lamirande, *Selected Oblate Studies and Texts,* 1986, p. 312.

[47] Lamirande, *Selected Oblate Studies and Texts,* 1986, p. 313, quoted from Rambert, vol. 2, p. 109.

immediately, on April 10, he issued a pastoral letter that Father Rey considered "one of the finest that flowed from his pen from the point of view of its noble style and lofty content as well as for the strength and vigour of its reasoning."[48] He made a strong argument against national churches, showing that they will always lack the marks that characterize the true Church. The pastoral letter makes it clear that he wanted his people to know about the sad situation in Spain. What is also clear is that he wanted the hearts of the faithful to be open, like his, to the needs of the Church beyond the diocese of Marseilles:

> Yes, my dearly beloved brethren, you cannot merely watch without taking interest in the sad situation. A portion of what used to be one of the most flourishing parts of Christianity stands to be violently torn from its ancient spiritual foundations and so be separated from God's Church. How can we not be terrified at this schism which would come about in the name of a temporal power taking upon itself the right to be like a wall of separation between the bishops and the Vicar of Christ, between the faithful and him who is their common Father? . . . There is no law that can go against the law of God, no constituted power whatever, that can supersede the divine constitution of the Church.[49]

Apostolic Hopes Regarding the Church in North Africa

A trip to Tunisia in 1842 for the transfer of the remains of St. Augustine deeply impressed Bishop de Mazenod and left him with enthusiastic hope for a rebirth of the Church in North Africa. We must remember that for him, truth existed only within the framework of the Catholic Church. Therefore he saw all others, especially non-Christians such as the Muslims, as pagans who needed to be saved from hell by bringing them into the Church.

Yet when he came into personal contact with the non-Christians of North Africa, he could only admire their faith and wish all the harder that it were directed toward Jesus Christ. Indeed, he would have liked to see the faithful of Marseilles pray with equal fervour. In a long pastoral letter he stated that it would be a mistake to keep the truth captive under the pretence of not wanting to upset the nations of Islam. Again, he wanted the Church of Marseilles to be fully informed: "You, dearly beloved brethren, are imbued with the light of faith; you see more clearly and surely than do the children of this world. You understand how important is the evangelizing work of which we speak. In your estimation, the eternal salvation of a multitude of souls is at stake."[50] Eugene de Mazenod believed that Muslims could be

---

[48] Rey, vol. 2. p. 133.
[49] Lamirande, *Selected Oblate Studies and Texts,* 1986, p. 315.
[50] Ibid., p. 327 ff.

converted just as readily as any other non-Christians. To the Bishop of Algiers he wrote: "I have never considered the conversion of those poor Muslims to be any more difficult than that of the Chinese. It will be up to you to give the signal when the time comes."

Even if he was not aware of the fragility of his dream, it is clear that he wanted to share it with the people of Marseilles. Also clear is the greatness of his pastoral spirit. The Oblates would establish a mission in Algeria in 1848, but it was doomed to failure from the start because the Bishop of Algiers wanted stop-gap pastors for the French colonizers and not, as the bishop proposed, missionaries to convert the Muslims. Thus, just over a year later, he recalled his Oblates to France. Besides, Rome had asked him to send missionaries to South Africa, so it was a case of reality superseding one dream and giving birth to another.

The Unity of Christians Regarding the Anglican Church

In keeping with his views on the one true Church, Eugene de Mazenod considered Anglicans heretics. Yet, after meeting them personally and seeing them pray he was left with great admiration and a longing for their return – sentiments to be shared with his people. In the 1845 Christmas pastoral, just two months after John Henry Newman's conversion in Rome, the bishop acknowledged that the initiative sprang from the Anglicans and asked the Marseillais to pray with him for the Church of England's return to the bosom of Mother Church:

> St. Paul the Apostle, in writing to the Romans, told them that he felt in his heart a great yearning for the salvation of his brothers in Israel, a favour he prayerfully beseeched from God (Romans 10:1). Imbued with those same sentiments, a bishop of Great Britain,[51] not content to devote his own apostolic ministry and watchful care to the salvation of his compatriots, and ever striving to bring them back to the fold of their legitimate shepherd, solicits the help of our prayers to hasten that return which, in his heart, as in that of St. Paul, is the object of a most ardent desire. . . . This is not the usual question of bringing relief to bodily miseries – *these are souls*, valued as far above bodies as heaven is above the earth. These are souls redeemed by the blood of Jesus Christ . . . .[52]

At the heart of de Mazenod's love for souls and for the Church was the value of Christ's precious blood which must not be shed in vain. He appealed strongly to the Catholics of Marseilles, telling them that they were committed to the conversion of a great nation, England: "What is sought

---

[51] This was probably Cardinal Wiseman.
[52] Lamirande, *Selected Oblate Studies and Texts*, 1986, p. 332.

here is that you participate in a far greater enterprise Since the Holy Spirit teaches us that God can vivify entire nations (Wisdom 1:14), you are asked to employ a heavenly remedy for the spiritual healing of the whole of a great nation . . . ."[53] Bishop de Mazenod never used the term *ecumenism*, but he clearly lauded the efforts of Anglicans, personified in such men as Pusey, Keble and Newman of the Oxford Movement, men who in their distinct ways were in search of unity and mutual understanding.

> It is impossible not to recognize the providential hand of mercy in the religious effort noticeable today among our neighbours across the sea. It is a movement prompted from above which, helped on by ardent supplication, will grow stronger and stronger until it draws everyone into unity. To use another comparison, it is divine ferment at work in a people troubled by prolonged errors. There is every reason to hope that such ferment, under the influence of grace and increased constantly by prayer, will end up by penetrating the entire mass.[54]

The pastoral letter also recalls England's glorious heritage: "We know well that the Church of England, so renowned in history, was admirably beautiful and glorious during her spiritual prosperity. So rich in virtues was she that her island was surnamed the Island of Saints."[55]

It is well to note how open Bishop de Mazenod was in an era of narrowness and closed minds, and how open he wanted the Christians of Marseilles to be. Five years later, in 1850, he went to England to ordain a half-dozen Oblates to major and minor orders, but he would just miss getting together with, as he himself wrote, "the celebrated Newman and his Oratorians who serve a chapel where I said Mass." George Lloyd Crawley and John Atkinson, two early Tractarians and members of the Oxford Movement who were participants in Dr. Pusey's Rome-oriented Anglicanism, would later become Oblates.[56]

Christian Solidarity with the Church of Ireland

A complete failure of the potato crop triggered famine and plague in Ireland during the winter of 1846-47. When Bishop de Mazenod heard of the catastrophe, he launched an appeal to the charity of the faithful in his diocese. In a pastoral letter of February 24, 1847, he wrote: "Adjacent to England and under the same empire, lives a nation which, with its long

---

[53] Lamirande, *Selected Oblate Studies and Texts,* 1986, p. 333.

[54] Ibid., p. 333.

[55] Ibid., p. 334.

[56] Vincent Denny, O.M.I., *John Henry Cardinal Newman and the Oblates in England,* in *Vie Oblate Life,* April, 1991.

suffering and unshakeable firmness in the true religion, has become, one might say, an example to the world, to angels and to men (1 Corinthians 4:9)."[57] In making his appeal, the bishop stressed the missionary nature of the Irish nation, despite its trials and tribulations, and often because of them:

> Her poverty and suffering – the lot of her fidelity – ought to be all the more appreciated since they are the price she has had to pay for being the instrument of Providence in propagating the Faith. Her tears, at times mingled with her blood, have given birth to truth. The island's population increased extraordinarily, like the children of Israel in Egypt. Thus, an emigration, forced by necessity, has ceaselessly borne her faith to all the corners of Great Britain's immense possessions, as well as to North America, thereby laying the first foundations everywhere of Catholic Christianity and serving as a leaven by which grace is fermenting through the surrounding mass of population foreign to the true Church.[58]

He appealed to the faithful to help prevent "a nation of confessors and martyrs from being exterminated by famine," reminding them:

> Let it not be said that they belong to one empire and we to another. That would be completely unworthy of Christian charity, for as long as men will dwell on this earth, we are all children of our Father in heaven and neighbours to each other. Moreover, like us, the Irish belong to the great Catholic family. Not only is the blood of the same human brotherhood common to us all, but through the blood of our Redeemer we share the same grace and the same sacraments . . .[59]

Such openness and concern for the problems of the universal Church are simply not found in the contemporary pastoral letters of other bishops. Indeed, we can even ask whether such openness appears with great frequency in our day!

Fraternal Sympathy for the Church in Canada

An outbreak of typhus that scourged Eastern Canada during the summer of 1847 shows again how attached Eugene de Mazenod was to the clergy and people of that country and, by extension, to the universal Church. On September 6 of that year he addressed a pastoral letter for the public to the pastors, rectors and chaplains of his diocese. The epidemic, he said, was brought to the new land by Irish immigrants fleeing the ravages of famine in their own homeland. Mindful of the special bonds between Marseilles and Canada, since the Oblates, his spiritual sons, were formed in the "see of St. Lazarus," he noted that even Bishop Bourget had been stricken and one of

---

[57] Lamirande, *Selected Oblate Studies and Texts,* 1986, p. 342.

[58] Ibid., p. 343.

[59] Ibid., p. 344.

his vicars-general had died of the disease. After lauding the venerable and saintly bishop of Montreal, Bishop de Mazenod continued:

> It is true that I have a special reason for taking wholehearted interest in everything that is happening in that region of America. At this moment I feel all the anguish of fatherhood because I know the dangerous situation facing those whom grace has given me. With so much happening I learned of the blessings which the Lord showered on their apostolic labours. I was so consoled upon learning that one of them was presented by the unanimous vote of the Canadian episcopacy and has just been appointed by the Supreme Pontiff as the first bishop of a newly established Church. Hence, I cannot but associate myself to the sorrows as well to the joys of that country. Such particular reasons aside, one has to be touched by the ordeal visited upon an important segment of Christianity, French in origin, constant and steadfast in fervent faith since its foundation, despite the presence and domination of heresy – Christianity which through its daily advance and conquests appears destined to preserve or convert England's vast possessions in North America to Catholicism, making the Word of God heard, whether among settlers of the ever-growing cities or among savages in the depths of the primeval forests covering that part of the New Word.[60]

(It must be remembered that Bishop de Mazenod used the term "savage" for native Americans in accord with the usage of the times.)

Bishop de Mazenod was deeply hurt that his letter was coolly received by some of the clergy in Canada, especially by his own Oblates (not least among them Father Allard who would later head the African mission). Some resented what they saw as ploys by the bishop to jockey Father Eugene Guigues into position for the newly created see of Bytown (later to become the nation's capital, Ottawa). They felt that such an episcopal appointment would spell the eventual end of the Oblate mission in Canada. And indeed, de Mazenod himself was at first opposed to Guigue's appointment. However, after prayerful discernment and after consulting with Bishop Guibert, he could write to the bishop-elect on June 7, 1847:

> I could have been troubled by representations stemming from the love our Fathers have for the Congregation and for you, but never have I repented cooperating in something that I believe, before God, to be good, opportune and advantageous for the Church, and very honourable for our Congregation which could suffer no detriment but which, on the contrary, should derive great advantages from such a measure. . . . I see in your promotion a benevolent disposition of Providence towards the Congregation.[61]

---

[60] Lamirande, *Selected Oblate Studies and Texts,* 1986, p. 347.
[61] *Oblate Writings,* vol. 1, p. 169, n. 84.

About the lukewarm Canadian reception that greeted his pastoral call to help the Church in Canada, the Founder complained in a letter to Father Guigues, dated December 10, 1847:

> (I am surprised by the silence) you have all maintained – the Bishop of Montreal included – about the great outpouring of charity I invoked in favour of our brethren in Canada. I am the only bishop in the world who put himself to such trouble at the time of your affliction. In our land the circular I published caused quite an stir. For that country so far away, yet so close to my heart, I called for public prayers asking God to bless and preserve the devoted priests who for the people were exposing their lives to the contagion that had already stricken so many of the clergy. My people responded to the invitation with so much fervour; my clergy were so united to my sentiments that we can rest assured of having touched the heart of God. Indeed, I have not heard of the death of a single priest since we began to invoke the Lord and it is notable that all our Fathers who were infected with the sickness have recovered their health.
>
> Well, no one has breathed a word – not the least little word – of thanks. I have not had a jot of consolation to relate to those who so charitably shared my grief and care. Under the circumstances, you must admit that you have not been very considerate. Surely you received my circular by the end of September or the beginning of October. I would think that the Bishop of Montreal could well have replied with a few words to edify and encourage my people who truly deserve such a reward.[62]

In-fighting and hurt feelings aside, the important point to note is Bishop de Mazenod's constant effort to open the hearts of his people to the life and concerns of the Universal Church. In that he was admirable and, to a point, unique.

Deepening the Christian Life of the Faithful

Saint Eugene de Mazenod was concerned with the sanctification of his faithful. Voicing that concern to Father Courtès, he said that Oblates should be men who "dedicated their lives in the service of the Church and *the sanctification of souls*."[63] And in the preface of his rule he laid down the principle that guided him and should guide all Oblates: "We must lead men to act like human beings, first of all, and then like Christians and, finally, we must help them to become saints . . . ."[64] In a pastoral letter of February 20, 1859 – two years before his death – he wrote, "We are deeply concerned to work for your sanctification which, before God, is what we have most at heart." The reasons he gave for that deep concern to sanctify his people

---

[62] *Oblate Writings,* vol. 1, p. 183, n. 91.

[63] Ibid., vol. 7, p. 196, n. 344.

[64] *Preface to the Oblate Constitutions and Rules,* p. 12.

were: "our paternal affection," "The love of Christ impels us (2 Corinthians 5:14)," and, "It is God's will that you grow in holiness (1 Thessalonians 4:3)."

Bishop de Mazenod's pastoral letters generally prefaced the season of Lent, so most of them are dated in February. They include: "The Servant of God" (February 2, 1842), "Living in Union with Christ" (February 8, 1846) and "The Christian" (February 2, 1850).

In his pastoral letter of January 30, 1853, he said that growing in holiness demands permanent conversion. Then he went on to explain the role of Lent in that conversion. He further showed the means which the Church offers her sons and daughters for that conversion:

Religious Teaching and Meditation on the Word of God.

It is well to point out here that meditation on the Word of God was very strong among the Oblates during the last century. When studying the Latin text of the preface to the Oblate Constitutions and Rules, one can see how Fathers Courtès and Albini quite spontaneously used the vocabulary of the Vulgate, which means that although they did not have access to the studies we have today, they were certainly very familiar with the Scriptures through their meditation on them. It is interesting to note the wide difference between their *meditation* on the Scriptures, which had depth and was full of life, and the more widespread *formal study* of Scripture, which was very disappointing during the 19th century.

Parochial Missions

They were de Mazenod's first apostolate and he underlined the continued importance of their role in sanctification.

The Sanctification of Sunday

This theme was also taken up in a pastoral letter dated February 2, 1839.

The Sacraments (Especially Penance and the Eucharist)

He told the faithful how the sacraments give strength and quoted Isaiah 12:3: "With joy you will draw water at the fountain of salvation."

Liturgical Celebrations

Bishop de Mazenod stressed that the central point of all the liturgy is the paschal mystery. All other feasts – Christmas, for example – prepare the Christian to celebrate the passover with Christ. His letters insist repeatedly on that point. Thus, we see that making the paschal mystery central is not a recent discovery, as some might think. Indeed, it was part of Olier's teaching and Bishop de Mazenod was imbued with it. The main purpose of the liturgical celebration, he added, is to unite the faithful with Christ.

Devotion to Mary

Mary has a particular place in the sanctification of her sons and daughters. In his pastoral letter of July 8, 1849, he wrote:

> After that which directly concerns God, nothing is more precious for true and enlightened piety than whatever concerns the honour given to the Blessed Virgin Mary. Here we encounter all that exists in a son toward his mother. And what a Mother! She gave us him who is the world's life and salvation; she engendered all of us spiritually at the foot of the Cross through the pangs of the passion and death of the God-Man, the blessed fruit of her womb. She is rightly called the new Eve and the co-redemptrix of the human race.

> God's own glory is enhanced in Mary . . . . We glorify him in the masterpiece of his power and glory; we praise him, because among all the marvels of power that prove his infinite greatness, he has produced someone who sums up in herself alone, better than all other persons put together, his perfection so worthy of adoration.

> Furthermore, the greatness of the Blessed Virgin consists especially in her dignity as Mother of God. That is the reason for all the prerogatives with which she is endowed and for the greater devotion we offer her. Thus, it is the Son whom we honour in the person of the Mother.[65]

In his acts of visitation to the Oblate Marian shrines Bishop de Mazenod constantly cautioned that Marian devotion always conform to Church teaching to avoid the exaggerations of popular piety so prevalent in his day. He concluded this pastoral letter, saying, "In our homage to Mary it is impossible to overstep the limit, provided we consider her a creature, because God then always remains the supreme end of all our homage."[66]

Almsgiving

Sharing one's personal goods is another help he cited toward sanctification.

---

[65] *Selected Texts*, p. 128, n. 107.
[66] Ibid., p. 129.

The Apostolic Commitment of the Faithful

In his pastoral of February 18, 1848, he invited the faithful to have "une âme d'Église." In English we would say, to have "a living sense of Church." He then went on to explain that he meant having an openness to all who have been redeemed by the blood of Christ.

First, he spoke of the individual duties of a Christian (the commandments of the Church, for example); then he added that there were other duties that prevailed over the first set and were more important. Here he meant *the apostolate*:

> The apostle is more perfect than the coenobite. Do not be amazed, then, if we come to associate you to our ministry and invite you to share the crown of the apostolic men, glorious instruments of eternal salvation of the souls created in the image of God and redeemed by his Blood.

Furthermore, he added, "Faith is essentially communicative in the same way as charity is the willingness to help." Today we are accustomed to such ideas, but they were hardly common in the 19th-century teaching of bishops. In the same pastoral he presented some means of the apostolate for ordinary Christians: *good example* (today we would call it witness), *prayer, and the Word*.

Regarding the Word, the bishop urged the ordinary Christians of his diocese to speak: "The Christian strongly imbued with the truth of faith is, like Job, full of discourses" (cf. Job 32:18).

Bishop de Mazenod then went on to give some advice on how to express Christian truth: *in a delicate manner*, so as not to hurt people; *not in long discourses* that might antagonize or bore the listener; *in a simple and concrete presentation*.

Bishop de Mazenod thought so highly of the faithful of his diocese that he did not hesitate to call them to a deep Christian faith, stressing that holiness and apostolate go together. The expressions he used may be dated, but the content of his message is as meaningful as ever. He was a missionary and teacher, through and through, never counting personal cost nor afraid to make decisions. As an ultramontanist he had always supported papal authority, yet he did not deem it necessary slavishly to do everything the way it was done in Rome. Nor did he see any reason to call constantly on Rome for decisions that he were within his jurisdiction to take. As much a man of authority as of tradition, he was well versed by his uncle and grand-uncle[67] in the customs and traditions of the Church of Marseilles, making

---

[67] The grand-uncle had been vicar-general to Marseilles' famous and saintly Bishop Belsunce.

him all the more sure-handed in the decisions he took and the traditions he upheld. As a bishop he was obedient to the pope, yet no one could ever accuse Eugene de Mazenod of being a sycophant or of treading lightly and diplomatically to further his career. That explains why he had no patience with some of the younger "career bishops" whose posture he derided when they tried to make a show of how attached they were to the Holy See. When faced with a long list of minute questions on minor details which the Bishop of La Rochelle submitted to Rome, Bishop de Mazenod wrote in his journal on March 2, 1850:

> At this moment I have a list of questions put by the Bishop of La Rochelle to the Sacred Congregation of Rites. It is really quite unbelievable! . . . I do not understand such things. By dint of wanting to show how Roman they are – as though we were not – our young bishops fall into childishness. They do not know, as we do, how they are made fun of in Rome. Just lately, when a question was submitted about what percentage of real wax a Mass-candle should contain, the Dean of the Sacred Congregation was heard to question whether it was really necessary to query Rome on such matters.[68]

Restoration and Progress of the Diocese

Bishop de Mazenod never feared being an innovator when he felt that change was necessary for the spiritual interests of his diocese. We will now look at some of his efforts to restore the Diocese of Marseilles and bring it to flourishing Christian life.

New Parishes

Space does not permit a litany of all of Eugene de Mazenod's accomplishments for the diocese, but we can get something of an idea from the fact that while he was vicar-general and bishop of Marseilles, 38 new parishes were established – roughly one per year throughout that time. However, most of them came after he took over the diocese, after King Louis-Philippe in 1837 eased the restriction of the Concordat of 1801. Even then, the red tape involved in setting up a new parish was formidable. All churches were State property; and the project of a new parish had to be presented to the civil authorities for approval. Since those giving the permissions were bourgeois businessmen more interested in the profit of Sunday markets than in religion, changes did not come without some people digging in their heels and without some feathers getting ruffled:

---

[68] Rey, vol. 2, p. 337.

The first to be called upon to state its opinion was the parochial council of the parish that was to be dismembered and, naturally, it defended its interests. The municipal council, the next to be consulted, objected to the financial burdens that would be placed upon the municipal budget and, in addition, acted as a sounding-board for the grievances which the people under its jurisdiction sent to it. The creation of a new succursal parish would have adverse effects upon the interests of the merchants of shopping centres by drawing Sunday customers elsewhere, thereby lessening the value of land and buildings.

At times the pastor, the parochial council and the municipal council formed a block to register their refusal. That was the case in Aubagne where, in spite of opposition, Bishop de Mazenod succeeded, in 1838, in erecting the succursal parish of St. Peter. However, people's minds were so inflamed that through fear of an "explosion" the prelate had to wait until things cooled down before attempting the same operation in favour of Baudinard which, up to then, had been attached to the angered city.[69]

At other times the bishop had to go into a community to pacify the population that wanted to separate from an established parish. That was the case in the hamlet of Lascours which stopped supporting the parish priest of Roquevaire, who came to Lascours periodically for Mass. Bishop de Mazenod related in his journal:

> The men came to meet me while the women waited in the church. I spoke to those good people who really deserve some consideration . . . A bishop had not appeared since the time Bishop Belsunce was carried there in a sedan chair almost a century before. My paternal approach disposed their hearts to trust me. They are peacefully awaiting the result of my good will toward them and I shall sincerely make every effort to get them a chapel with a resident priest.[70]

Charitable Societies and Social Works

In the late 1840s Marseilles was in the midst of a population explosion but its economic and social evolution did not match its demographic change: the rise of a proletariat class, for example, did not define itself as clearly as in other places through social crises and labour unrest. Given the mentality of the times and the city's social condition, Bishop de Mazenod acted more on a charitable level, helping the destitute in their misery, than on a social justice level, attacking the root of their poverty. Accordingly, we should not be surprised if we do not find treatises on social justice among his writings. Instead, the Founder had a deep and compassionate understanding of charity and firmly believed it must be religious in character. Leflon observes: "The

---

[69] Leflon, vol. 3, p. 57.
[70] Ibid., p. 57.

destitution which was rampant in a whole segment of the Marseilles population and which so often distressed him when he went to the poor quarters to
confirm sick people in their homes, was not his only motive for relieving
extreme poverty. For him, this was an essential mission of the Church ... ."[71]

We can say that given the particular circumstances of a prosperous port such
as Marseilles and Bishop de Mazenod's own aristocratic background, he
was more focused on charity than on the problem of social justice, the
problem of *unjustifiable* destitution. He was not truly aware that the situation itself was unjust, as we would analyze it today. We know that at one
point Eugene de Mazenod had been sympathetic to the views of Félicité de
Lamennais, the foremost Catholic liberal and social writer of the age. Had
that relationship continued, perhaps his outlook would have broadened on
social issues, but when de Lamennais refused to bow to Rome and was
excommunicated they were no longer in contact.

Thus while Bishop de Mazenod showed tremendous openness and
missionary zeal as the shepherd of Marseilles, he also had his limitations.
Like the rest of the French hierarchy – and most of society in the 19th
century – he had not become aware of the fundamental demands that justice
makes on all persons, believers and non-believers. That would be a growing
phenomenon of the 20th century, but it was rare among Catholics 150 years
ago. Nonetheless, the social action inherent in so many of the charitable
works he initiated in Marseilles is striking.

We cannot help but note *how keenly he was challenged by the deficiencies*
he saw in pastoral works related to the poor. He saw clearly through the
pomp and sham of some elite "Catholic" charitable societies wherein well-
to-do participants were more interested in the social advantages of having
their names boldly inscribed on the roster of a prestigious association than
in getting personally involved. In 1838, for example, after presiding over
the "edifying" annual meeting of the *Messieurs de l'Étoile* (the Gentlemen
of the Star), he commented sadly in his journal:

> (It) discloses how destitute we are, for it is in this group that is found all
> that remains of the practising Catholics among men of high society in
> Marseilles, and certainly their total is not large if one may judge from the
> number we counted this morning. Most were persons of mature years;
> there are few, if any, young men. After all, what is about a hundred men
> from all sections of the city? Those were the thoughts going through my
> mind while the others were going into raves about the fine gathering. I
> almost forgot to add that the association lists about four hundred names on

---

[71] Leflon, vol. 3, p. 96.

its roster. If they were all genuine Catholics, we would have had more than a mere hundred at the gathering this morning.[72]

Institutions Founded by Bishop de Mazenod

Bishop de Mazenod established and encouraged charitable organizations and social works of all kinds. He was obsessed by the plight of the poor, crammed together in the port-side slums of Les Carmes and Les Accoules. Even more than the social and moral woes – the tragic evils of any large city – their neglect of religion haunted him to the point of anguish. Thus he tried to establish religious works to care for the whole person at all ages and in all levels of society, welcoming every initiative to fill diocesan needs. In his journal, he set out the principle that guided him in welcoming or establishing religiously-oriented social works:

> My system is to support the zeal of those who want to dedicate themselves to a life of perfection (through the works of charity). It will be positive, even if such associations last only the lifetime of those who took the initiative.[73]

> My policy is to lend myself to all inspirations. If God wills them, nothing will be able to prevent them. And if God does not will them, they shall fail of their own accord without any interference from me.[74]

Father Timon-David has noted that, guided by this principle, Bishop de Mazenod welcomed a wide variety of initiatives to the diocese. Among the works he established or encouraged to cope with the multitude of diocesan problems are those that follow here. It is worth noting that several of them were initiated while he was still under government interdict and in the midst of his Icosia crisis of 1832-36.

The Society for Orphan Boys, 1835

This was a home for orphans and street children. The cholera epidemic had left large numbers of children to shift for themselves and survive by their wits, much like today's youthful gangs in Naples, Sao Paolo, Mexico City, Manila and wherever else there are large concentrations of the poor.

The Providence Society, 1835

Poverty reduced many girls, orphans especially, to prostitution, a busy profession in a port city. To keep young girls from heading toward that life, the bishop had the Visitine Sisters take over the training of girls for a

---

[72] Leflon, vol. 3, p. 95.
[73] December 27, 1842, *Vie Oblate Life,* 1982, p. 76.
[74] November 4, 1848, *Vie Oblate Life,* 1982 p. 76.

respectable life, especially those orphaned by the cholera epidemics of 1835 and 1837. This work was financed by people of the city's high society.

> Bishop de Mazenod declared that he was especially gratified (by this society). "It is somewhat of a miracle," he wrote on January 4, 1839, after presiding over a meeting of 475 patronesses and hearing Father Fissiaux' report. The prelate had, in truth, been singularly well inspired in confiding the orphan girls to a man whose devotion equalled his initiative, balance and organizing ability. Like Timon-David, Fissiaux, whom Bishop de Mazenod called, "the excellent Fissiaux", was one of the best and most esteemed of the directors of the prelate's societies.[75]

The bishop was anguished, however, that he could not do even more. Returning home from the orphanage, content to see "the happiness those saintly girls enjoy there," he wrote in his journal:

> On the way, I met some poor wretches who certainly are not walking in the path of righteousness. This contrast produced a feeling of indignation and revulsion in my soul which I could not possibly express. The lack of being able to reach such a large number of souls like them, the sorrow of seeing them lost without it being possible for me to do anything to turn them from vice and help them to save their souls, makes it a real suffering and an affliction for me to be shepherd of a flock in which so many sheep are strangers to their bishop. Of them it could be said: *non sunt ex hoc ovili*; the truth is that they no longer belong to Christ. . . . Saying that all bishops, from the pope down, are faced with the same tragedy is no consolation.[76]

The Working Boys' Society, 1835

Promoted by Father Jean-Joseph Allemand, its usefulness was limited by its scope – the working youth of the middle class.

St. Raphael's Society for Working Boys, 1835

The 1835 cholera epidemic made it clear that something similar to Father Allemand's society was necessary for poor boys. Father Caire, with Bishop de Mazenod's enthusiastic approval, launched what we would recognize today as a true social apostolate, even providing accommodations and workshops for the training of young apprentices. The good priest had no dearth of ideas, but his eccentricity and lack of organizational skills greatly undermined the success such a project could have had. Father Timon-David said of him, "as odd a man as one had ever seen . . . who based everything on principles of his own invention, principles which most of the time ignored life's realities."[77] Nonetheless, Bishop de Mazenod practised his principle

---

[75] Leflon, vol. 3, p. 99.

[76] Ibid., p. 95.

[77] Leflon, vol. 2, p. 582.

of not discouraging people of good will, deeming this shelter so necessary that he did nothing to thwart the initiative of its founder. "Regrettable as it may have been, the failure of his society presaged the new orientation which youth organizations were to take in the diocese. Others would more or less successfully enter upon the course. Groping, even errors, generally precede the most fruitful realizations of the future."[78]

The Refuge for Wayward Girls, 1839

This "Home for the Madeleines" had been limping along since 1820, before the Founder arrived in Marseilles. The preoccupation he reveals in the entry from his journal quoted above, together with the initiative of a group of women who strongly supported this work, impelled him to put it in the hands of the Sisters of the Good Shepherd in 1839.

The Guardian Angel Society, 1839

Bishop de Mazenod had frequent clashes with the powerful and anti-clerical bourgeoisie. Still, when he noticed that it had never occurred to any of them to provide assistance to the destitute descendants of ruined bourgeois families, he founded the Guardian Angel Society.

House for Deaf-Mutes, 1839

This was another work established by the tireless Abbé Fissiaux, with the help of two nuns, and based on the proven methods of Father Sicard in Paris.

The Industrial and Agricultural Reform School, 1839

This apostolate had all the earmarks of a modern social service. It was started in order to rescue and rehabilitate juvenile offenders from the hardened criminality to which prison had exposed them. Again, it was the Abbé Fissiaux who established it, but reluctantly so this time. Only the bishop's express command ("In the name of God, go to reclaim the land covered with thistles and thorns") got him to launch a work that required extreme courage and a good dose of unrequited love. The 19th-century magazine *Le Correspondant*[79] told how the Abbé Fissiaux embarked on such a daunting undertaking. And about the first group of teenagers to arrive – boys who had already spent at least a couple of years in prison – Bishop de Mazenod himself wrote in his journal on March 7, 1839:

---

[78] Leflon, vol. 3, p. 108.
[79] *Le Correspondant,* 1843, pp. 80-100, n. 2.

Foul rags scarcely covered the emaciated limbs of those unfortunate prisoners. Their arms, still so young and frail, bore the marks of the chains that had bound them. Their feet were bloodstained and their hair matted. They were crawling with lice. All of them were victims of a frightful disease, the sad result of deplorable habits and vile communication with human monsters. There was not a trace of religion or trustworthiness in the souls of those degraded creatures.[80]

Beginnings certainly did not augur very well. Later, the bishop wrote:

For more than a year, each week was marked by a revolt. . . . On two occasions some of the personnel barely missed becoming martyrs of their devotedness, and it was only by a providential accident that they were not murdered. Our youngsters themselves admitted later that their idea at the time was to make us renounce our undertaking, preferring the idle life and sinful diversion of prison to a laborious life.[81]

Borrowing from the most successful methods in juvenile rehabilitation from Paris, Bordeaux and Mettrai (where there were no walls and minimum security), Fissiaux gradually defined his own system and perfected his organization. The institution moved into its proper buildings in October of 1840 and progress became noteworthy. The boys began to take interest in the useful trades they were learning and improved agricultural methods were taught to the sons of farmers in the fields and gardens. The school even boasted a band! Bishop de Mazenod took great pleasure in his visits to the institution. Of the first 18 graduates of the school, only 3 fell back into crime. Figures show that from 1839 to 1842 the institution housed a total of 255 boys: 13 were less than 10 years old; 209 were between 10 and 16, while 33 were over 16.

It is worth noting as well that the bishop urged Father Fissiaux to found his own congregation to help him carry out this very special apostolate. That he did, calling it the Congregation of St. Peter in Chains. Eugene de Mazenod happily conferred the habit on the first novices.

Society of Les Petits Savoyards,[82] 1841

In our day, sweeping chimneys is a rather clean mechanized job using efficient vacuum hoses, but in 19th-century France it was the dangerous domain of soot-covered little boys from the mountainous Savoie region who could slide in and out of tight spots and had trained ground-hogs on a string to go even further. In deplorable social and moral conditions, they ranged

---

[80] Leflon, vol. 3, pp. 99 ff.

[81] Ibid., p. 100.

[82] Chimney-sweeps.

throughout France looking for chimneys to clean. Bishop de Mazenod began by inviting them into his house, but soon realized that they needed more than a good meal. So he entrusted their care and instruction to Father Caire and sought financial assistance from the faithful of the city to float the society.

The Society of the Servantes,[83] 1841

Directed by the Sisters of Hope from Bordeaux, the society came closer to what we would see today as a social service. It purpose was to rescue from the streets of Marseilles the servant girls from mountain villages, who had come to the city unaware of what awaited them or who found themselves homeless after being dismissed by their employers. The society's purpose was not only to provide shelter but also to be a placement service, finding work for the girls under materially and morally favourable conditions. In 1845 the Sisters of Compassion took over the work of this society.

Establishment of the Sisters of Charity, January 24, 1843

When charitable funds from the municipality of Marseilles all but dried up, Bishop de Mazenod brought in the Sisters of Charity of St. Vincent de Paul to visit the destitute sick, dispense help to them in their homes and provide free medical aid to those unable to get it elsewhere. While at first ruffled by the move, the city fathers soon put their resentment aside when they saw the efficiency of the Sisters and even placed them in charge of the municipal Board of Welfare.

Creation of a New Congregation, The Trinitarian Sisters of St. Martha, 1845

Founded by Margalhan Ferrat, the new society assured home care for the sick in rural areas.

Establishment of the Sisters of the Holy Family, 1845

They did essentially the same as the Trinitarians, but in the city of Marseilles itself rather than in the country.

The Sodality of Ste-Anne, 1845

This was the sodality of fishwives headed by the renowned Babeau. It all began when the Queen of the Fish Market marched her *commères* in, one by

---

83 Servant girls.

one, to confess their sins and "get religion." As the number of penitents increased, their confessor, Father Barelle, realized a sodality was needed to follow up such conversions and to provide them with continuing religious education. Mixing ardour with shrewd psychology of the Marseilles mentality, Babeau eventually had 900 members in the sodality! Years later, on August 1, 1858, after a long day of celebrating the Feast of Sainte Anne with the fishwives, the bishop's comments in his journal about the events show that their "popular religiosity" was very Marseillaise in character:

> When I told them I had also come to celebrate my 77th birthday with them, some shouted out loud, *"Longue mai!"*, which means, may you still live a long time. Others cheered, *"Que le boeun Dieou vous conservô pourqu'es vivro cent ans."* (May the Good God preserve you so you live a hundred years.) I gave out Communion for more than an hour to those good women who today are a source of edification for the city. There were more than a hundred *pétards* (block-buster firecrackers) shot off during the day. At five o'clock, I returned to bless the beautiful statue of Sainte Anne which they had donated. In the morning and in the evening I spoke to them in Provençal, much to their satisfaction. In the evening I was obliged to restrain the outbursts of this large group of women who, when I had finished speaking, began to shout, *"Vive le Monseigneur!"* I officiated at Benediction of the Blessed Sacrament.[84]

We have already seen how the fishwives of the Sodality of Ste-Anne also took care of the sick and dying in the slum neighbourhoods where they lived.

The Conference of St. Joseph, 1846

With the bishop's blessing, the formidable Babeau convinced her husband, Joseph the coachman, of the need to form a religious society of working men. Each Sunday the men gathered to pray, sing hymns and listen to a catechetical conference, while the first Sunday of every month was a day of general Communion. A year after its inception, the "Conference" numbered 1,000 burly adherents; by 1865 – four years after the Founder's death – this society had 2,000 members.

Young Christian Workers Apostolate of Father Timon-David, 1847

On the eve of his ordination, Joseph-Marie Timon-David had made a private vow before God to serve the working class all his life. As a young diocesan priest of Marseilles, he was strongly aware a proletariat was emerging and seeking its voice. The zealous priest recognized the impor-

---

[84] Nogaret, *Vie Oblate Life*, 1982, p. 78, and partially quoted in Leflon, vol. 3, p. 104.

tance of coming up with new forms of apostolate, especially for young workers.

Bishop de Mazenod not only comprehended the new situation but understood Timon-David's very special vocation and willingly granted him the freedom he asked for – that freedom to respond to the Lord's call that, as a recently-ordained priest, he himself had asked for and received from his bishop in Aix. Therefore, with remarkable understanding he freed Timon-David of parochial and other responsibilities, so the youthful priest could devote his time and efforts fully to this new apostolate. The work grew: frequently there could be as many as 300 young working men at the Sunday conferences. The tireless Timon-David preached over a hundred retreats and gave numberless conferences. In his lifetime he would go on to write over 200 books and pamphlets, along with 55 printed volumes of letters. He died of a heart attack while working at the age of 69 in 1891.

This new proletariat apostolate grew to the point of overwhelming its founder. Timon-David went to tell Bishop de Mazenod he had decided to entrust it to some religious institute. The prelate was adamant in his disagreement, telling the young priest it would be a wrong move. "If you were to do that," he insisted, "you would lose your place in the apostolate and the apostolate itself would lose your impetus and ideals. The solution is that you will have to found your own religious society to help you with the work." Such an idea had never crossed Timon-David's mind, so he was understandably dumbfounded. At the end of the conversation, when he asked for a blessing, Eugene de Mazenod replied, "I bless you, but I do not bless your project of handing your work over to another institute. Go out and found your own."

Here we see how Bishop de Mazenod recognized an emerging situation that demanded action. As he saw the needs, it was not a case of putting new wine into old wine skins or new patches onto an old suit. It called for a completely new approach. The bishop found the man to do the job and encouraged him to think in new terms. Father Timon-David founded his religious society, a very local group, *Les Réligieux du Sacré-Coeur*, approved by Pius IX in 1876. Known in French as *les Pères de Timon-David*, the tiny society never numbered more than a hundred members. In 1990 there were 60 members, mostly priests, and almost exclusively in Provence. Their numbers, however, are not important here. What is important is that they fulfilled the mission in the Church that de Mazenod confided to them. Timon-David always kept a great love and respect for his mentor. Of him, he wrote: "Under his impulse and the many facilities he provided for initiatives, and thanks, too, to his wise counsels and orientations, works multiplied to infinity during his long episcopate."[85]

Conclusion

A missionary by vocation, Eugene de Mazenod remained one all his life, devoting himself by preference to the poorest and most abandoned souls. He loved them and was loved by them. They understood him. For his part, he constantly sought to make his mission more effective and Christ-centred. What he wrote in a pastoral letter of February 7, 1847, epitomized his long episcopacy:

> Charity embraces everything and, whenever necessary for new needs it invents new means: whether they be spiritual aids or temporal helps, they are all given generously in the name of Jesus Christ.

---

[85] *Vie Oblate Life*, 1982, p. 76.

Eugene's father, Charles Antoine de Mazenod Brilliant and conservative, he became a president of the Court of Accounts in Aix at the age of 26. He married at 33.

Eugene's mother, Marie-Rose Joannis Bourgoise, rich and 15 years younger than her husband. They eventually divorced.

Revolutionary Violence The lynching of de la Roquette and Pascalis in front of the de Mazenod home on December 14, 1790. Eugene's father escaped the same fate by slipping away to Nice earlier.

Eugene de Mazenod at 23 This pencil drawing was based on an engraving made in Paris in 1805 by Gilles-Louis Chrétien.

St-Sauveur Cathedral in Aix-en-Provence Thoughts of a priestly vocation had all but disappeared. Yet after four years of frivolity, Eugene felt an unease that set him searching for something more to life. Finally, during the liturgy of Good Friday, 1807, he was profoundly struck by Jesus' sacrifice. It was a turning point in his life that he described fully in his retreat notes of 1814.

The *Enclos de Mazenod* on the outskirts of Aix Because of Napoleon's campaign to de-Christianize the youth of France, Eugene saw all the young people as among the most abandoned. Consequently, he founded a Sodality of Christian Youth. The boys frequently met on the grounds of the *Enclos,* a family property. Eugene's youth work caused recurring friction with city pastors and once, at a Confirmation service in the Cathedral, precipitated a riot.

St-Sauveur Cathedral in Aix Eugene wanted to remain free of parochial strictures. He saw the parishes as barely responding to the needs of old Catholics and doing nothing at all for the youth. He was convinced he was called to evangelize the most abandoned.

Eugene de Mazenod at 34

Interior of the Church of the Madeleine It was here on the first Sunday of Lent, 1813, that the Abbé de Mazenod gave his famous instruction to the poor of the city.

The municipal prison in Aix Provence was a hotbed of Jansenism. Priests even denied the eucharist to the condemned. Unlike the others, the Abbé de Mazenod would even celebrate Mass in the prisoner's cell and accompany the person to the gallows, set up next to the Court of Accounts. He also attended the abandoned Austrian prisoners of war and nearly died after contracting typhus from them.

A room at last When Mme Gontier's girls academy finally vacated the monastery, this became Eugene de Mazenod's room on the ground floor.

Father Henri Tempier After he almost died of typhus, Eugene de Mazenod realized he could not work alone effectively. Needed was a group of like-minded priests working out of a community. One of the first he invited was Father Tempier.

The Church of the Mission Eugene's new society of priests needed a home. Thus he bought the former Carmelite convent, confiscated during the Revolution.

The interior of the Church of the Mission

The passage-way that was Father de Mazenod's room This space served as de Mazenod's room at the Church of the Mission for five months. Beyond it was the common room, which also served as a dormitory for Fathers Icard and Tempier. At nightfall a candle was set in the doorway to give light to both rooms.

The streets of Grans The missionaries walked the 30 kilometres from Aix to Grans to preach their first mission there, from February 11 to March 17, 1816.

Barjols Fathers de Mazenod, Deblieu, Maunier, Mie, Aubert and Moreau preached here between November 8 and December 20, 1818. The Founder set up an arbitration board to settle disputes between those who had their property confiscated during the Revolution and the new owners.

The former de Mazenod country estate at St-Laurent du Verdon Here during 13 days in mid-September of 1818 Father de Mazenod wrote the Oblate rule, made necessary when the society began to branch into several communities. He based the rule largely on that of St. Alphonsus, yet gave it his own charism so that an Oblate could never be mistaken for a Redemptorist.

Interior of the church at Barjols For many years after the mission, the people of Barjols kept enshrined in the church the hangman's noose which Father de Mazenod had worn in the penitential procession. It was their reminder of God's infinite mercy.

The mission cross This still stands at the lower end of the town square in Barjols to comemorate the Founder's mission of 1818.

The names of the missionaries inscribed on the base of the cross During the mission, to thwart de Mazenod's outstandng success, jealous canons of the Cathedral barred the doors, locking out the people on the last night. The bishop then postponed closure of the mission until the following Sunday.

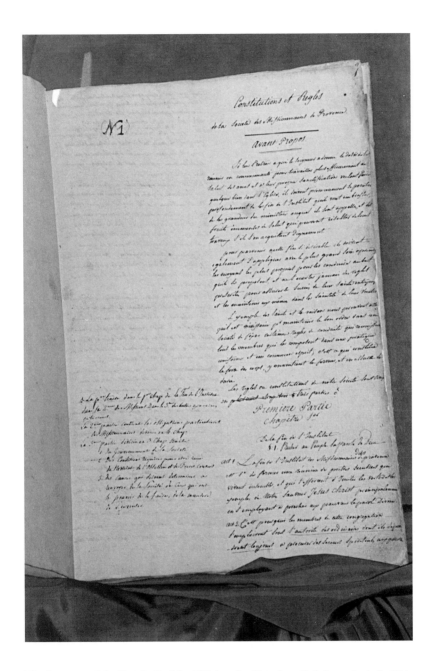

The first page of the first draft of the Oblate rule. Note the wide left margin, to facilitate later editing.

Father Marius Suzanne at 27 The superior of Les Accoules was doing marvels, when for no apparent reason the Founder harshly deposed him.

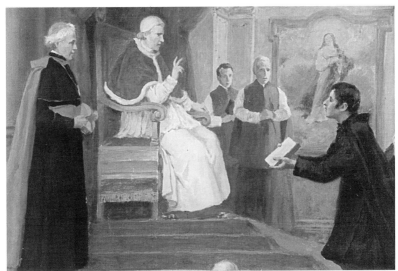

The audience with Pope Leo XII Father de Mazenod's tiny congregation lived precariously beneath the sword of Damocles. What it needed was protection that went beyond diocesan limits. Yet with only 25 members, he hesitated to seek papal approval. Finally, with a push from Father Albini, Eugene set off for Rome, arriving on November 25, 1825. After almost a month with no progress he took matters into his own hands and, without an appointment, succeeded in meeting with the pope.

Marseilles as it appeared toward the end of the 19th century. When Bishop de Mazenod took over the see in 1837, Marseilles was the second most populous city in France and the busiest port in the country. Despite a population explosion, unemployment in the city did not reach Paris' 40 per cent figure, but living conditions for the poor where hardly less abominable. The poor congregated about the port in unsanitary conditions of squalor. Cholera was a frequent and grim visitor.

Pope Leo XII At first the pontiff was inclined to grant only a *laudanda,* but when de Mazenod told him of the Oblates' missionary work Leo took a personal hand in expediting the process of full approval. It came, along with the name "Missionary Oblates of Mary Immaculate."

Canon Fortuné de Mazenod, Eugene's uncle   Fortuné taking possession of the see of Marseilles, August 10, 1823. Eugene (seen here behind his uncle) and Tempier became Fortuné's vicars-general.

Eugene de Mazenod as Bishop of Icosia (Painting by Joseph Dassy, ca. 1833) In an effort to bolster the Congregation and save the Marseilles diocese from being suppressed, Fortuné convinced Pope Gregory XVI to ordain Eugene a bishop. The ceremony took place secretly in Rome in late 1832, but when the weak pope withdrew his support, it had serious political consequences that lasted almost four years.

The bishop's residence in Marseilles, as it appeared in Eugene de Mazenod's time Until age and illness caused a change, Bishop de Mazenod lived in simple quarters on the ground floor where he could be closer to the people. Each morning the doors were open to all comers — there were no appointments — with everyone taking his or her turn in line. The poor even brought their own lunch so as not to lose their place. The edifice now holds government offices.

The Cathedral of Marseilles, begun by Bishop de Mazenod Beside it to the right is the truncated former cathedral, called *l'ancienne Major.*

The main altar of the Cathedral in Marseilles

The backstreets of Marseilles Until shortly before he died in 1861, Bishop de Mazenod was a familiar figure to the poor who lived in the tangled web of backstreets that make up the slum area of *les Accoules,* just above the port. Often the fishwives of the Sodality of Sainte-Anne led him into this labyrinth to the bedside of some dying person.

Bishop Ignace Bourget Bishop Bourget arrived in Marseilles on June 21, 1841, enroute to Rome. Throughout France he had tried unsuccessfully to find missionaries for Canada. When he discovered that Bishop de Mazenod was the founder of a society of missionaries, he begged him to heed the call of Canada. The rest is history. Soon Oblates were on their way to Canada, Sri Lanka and South Africa.

The Shrine of Notre-Dame de la Garde Even as late as the 1960's many Oblates still left for their overseas missions by ship via Marseilles. To see them off, just before they embarked, their fellow Oblates gathered at the shrine of Notre-Dame de la Garde for the farewell ceremony. On the ship, just as they were losing sight of land but could still see the glimmering gold statue of the Virgin atop the shrine, the missionaries gathered on the bridge to sing a final *Salve Regina* to the *Bonne Mère*.

Saint Eugene de Mazenod's tomb in an apse chapel of Marseilles Cathedral.

Bishop de Mazenod, ca. 1854 From a daguerreotype of a Eugene Lagier painting. In an Aix flea market on April 12, 1956 Oblate Father Charles Séty bought the plate, with the Founder's hand-written dedication to his sister, Charlotte Antionette ("Ninette"). He paid about $2.00.

Notre Dame de la Garde For centuries there has been a shrine to the Virgin atop the hill overlooking Marseilles. Bishop de Mazenod replaced the crumbling chapel of his day with an imposing basilica, which was completed after his death, in 1861. This statue of the bishop is in the entrance.

Eugene de Mazenod at 76 This is a copy of an 1858 portrait by Lagier.

Gone are all the insignia and decorations, just a simple cape and a simple cross. The face is marked by many trials; there is great serenity and meekness in the look, and no illusions. In earlier portraits of the young de Mazenod the eyes blazed; they now have a warm ember glow.

VII

Superior General

The Founder of the Oblates as Animator

At the very outset of his tiny society, Eugene de Mazenod was elected superior general of the Oblates for life. Throughout that life, his letters show us his constant efforts to animate the congregation and keep it true to its charism. Already in the group's crisis of 1823, precipitated by the Founder's move to Marseilles to serve with Father Tempier as Bishop Fortuné's vicars-general, he had made it clear that all he had done was for the good of the congregation. In its chapter of 1824 the congregation acknowledged that fact. His letters also avow it. As early as 1817, writing from Paris on August 22, for example, he stated that to remain faithful to his missionary vocation he had refused important posts: "Nothing has been able to seduce me. For you I have sacrificed what the world calls one's fortune, and I am well pleased. I do not refer to the two positions of Grand Vicar in the provinces, for they were not worth counting or comparing with *our holy mission* and *our dear Congregation*, but to something more."[1]

Still in Paris a couple of weeks later, on September 7, 1817, he wrote something to Father Tempier that would be repeated in several other letters – that his efforts to have Fortuné de Mazenod named bishop of Marseilles were purely for the good of the congregation:

> With regard to all this, I assure you that I *consider only the greater good of our works* and that I am not merely thinking of the honour that can accrue therefrom for my uncle. That is so true that I would not stir an inch to have him named elsewhere. . . If my uncle becomes bishop of Marseilles, I hope you will believe I used my time rather well in favour of our work, because it will be the best thing that could have happened . . . .[2]

Father de Mazenod was in Paris all that time, seeking governmental approval of his society. The process dragged out, and certain pastors in Aix

---

[1] *Oblate Writings*, vol. 6, p. 36, n. 22. De Mazenod probably refers to his refusal to become Bishop Latil's vicar-general. This would have quickly catapulted him to an episcopal see, since Latil was a member of the governmental commission set up to appoint bishops, and was, as well, chaplain to the king's brother.

[2] Ibid., p. 37, n. 23; cf. also p. 116.

began to circulate the rumour that he was unsuccessfully seeking personal advantages. In reply, he wrote to Father Tempier on November 24, 1817, giving three reasons for not accepting the honours offered him: affection for his confrères, concern for the souls of the young, and fidelity to his vocation:

> As for the honours it amuses them to say that I am unsuccessfully seeking, they must know that I had only to stoop in order to make them mine. If they only knew all the strength and depth *of the affection I have* especially for you, who are my brothers, my friends, my other selves and, moreover, *my concern for all the souls of the young* so cruelly forsaken until I undertook to lead them in the right path by the same means that are at the disposal of those parish priests – means that they could and should use, as I have done, by the grace of God – in the same way that you have done by combining your efforts with mine. If they knew my feelings in that regard they would no longer be surprised that I renounce the honours offered me and *return as a simple priest to this cherished family* in order to undergo once more all the perfidious attacks I have already experienced. When one prefers eternity to temporality, poverty to riches, work to repose, when one is more concerned with the sanctification of souls than with all the kingdoms of the earth, one returns with joy to a community where peace, union and all sorts of virtues reign, and one does not pine for the princely houses, canonries, grand vicariates, etc. – and one cares so little for all those things that one refuses them, as I insist I have done, without effort, without regret; on the contrary, with joy and satisfaction.[3]

In 1825, when he was about to leave Marseilles to seek papal approval of the congregation in Rome, he wrote to Father Pierre Mie at Nîmes on October 25: "I shall not forget you at the tomb of the holy apostles. I implore you not to forget me in your prayers during my journey which I undertake reluctantly, *but out of love for the Society.*"[4]

Writing from Rome on October 14, 1832, just ten days after Gregory XVI had him secretly ordained Bishop of Icosia *in partibus*, Eugene de Mazenod explained to the fathers and brothers of the scholasticate in Billens, Switzerland, that he had accepted to become a bishop so as to be better able to protect the congregation:

> You will readily understand that this high dignity, this great character that has been bestowed on me, does not relax a single bond binding me to our Congregation; instead, the overriding consideration for submitting my will has been *the awareness of the good that would flow from it for the Congregation* when the moment comes (and God leave us undisturbed for many a year yet!) when we shall have the misfortune to lose the protector whom the Lord has preserved for us among the ranks of the chief pastors

---

[3] *Oblate Writings,* vol. 6, pp. 46-47, n. 30.
[4] Ibid., p. 187, n. 202.

in the person of my venerable uncle, the bishop of Marseilles. Confined as we are and still little known, it is my opinion, shared by those Oblates whom I was bound to consult, that it would be very advantageous if we could, when the need arose, indicate that this small, unknown and newly-born Society, which has had to begin its growth in the midst of thorns, has as its representative a bishop elected by the Supreme Head of the Church.[5]

He Kept a Hand on the Day-to-Day Operation of the Congregation

Despite the rule stating that any member of the society could be the head of a parochial mission, it was invariably the Founder who, de facto, set up the programs and schedules and chose the men for each mission. Even after he went to Marseilles as his uncle's vicar-general, and after he became bishop, that practice, born of the zeal to animate and inspire his missionaries, continued.

After the July Revolution of 1830, as we have seen, parochial missions were prohibited by the new anti-clerical government. When the ban was relaxed, the Oblates returned to preaching missions with great enthusiasm and vigour. By then Eugene de Mazenod was already a bishop *in partibus*, but it did not prevent him from maintaining a very concrete interest in the method and content of the Oblates' preaching. Even after he officially took over the see of Marseilles on October 2, 1837, his interest in animating the congregation did not let up. In his letters there are many clear examples.

In January, 1837, for example, while the Oblates were preaching five missions at the same time, the Founder answered in great detail Father Courtès' queries about the faculties generally granted by bishops. He insisted on being fully informed always of the state of missions in progress and did not hesitate to call to task any superior of a mission who was remiss in writing. Thus, on January 27, 1837, he wrote to Father Mille who was in charge of a mission at Fontevieille, near Arles:

> My dear Father Mille, so far I have received only one letter from you though half of your mission is over. During this same period I have had four from Father Honorat who is as busy at Entraigues as you are, but keeps up our old custom. Since you could not be unaware of it, I do not know to what I must attribute such a prolonged silence. I am very upset and can explain it only on the supposition that you are sick; but if you are not well, why not entrust one of your confrères to fulfil your duty?
>
> I write only so that you know how upset I am, as are the other Fathers When you reply, tell me whether you received the circular informing you of Father Richaud's death. It is strange that no one has received it – would it be the same with your letters? – in which case you would be exempt

---

[5] *Oblate Writings*, vol. 8, p. 78, n. 439.

from my reproach. But even in that case, write to me, especially as I will not have the opportunity of seeing you on your return. You will set out straight for Aix where you will pay your respects to His Grace the Archbishop and orally give him an account of the blessings showered on your mission by the Lord. From there you will promptly leave for Notre-Dame de Laus where you will go with Father Pélissier (keep these details to yourself; I do not want Father Marcellin to write to him about it). You will make your arrangements at Laus while waiting to start the mission of Mane which you will preach together with Fathers Gignoux and Chauvet. Father Marcellin will wait at Aix for Father Honorat to take him and Father l'Hermite along to the mission at Maussanne . . .[6]

The second paragraph shows that even though he was a bishop in Marseilles he was also very much in charge of the Oblates. The way he assigned the priests to their various tasks makes that obvious. Not only did he assign tasks, he also had the last word in accepting candidates, as another letter, also written to Father Mille, on November 13, 1837, demonstrates:

I am about to leave for Paris, dear Father Mille, and I am writing only to approve your plan, for I have absolutely no time to write you anything else. If you think that the bishop of Gap does not object to your mission in Banon, go ahead . . . .

If Father Baron can obtain what he desires, I would willingly accept him, despite his infirmity which can be cured with some applied remedies. But you must be careful that His Lordship the bishop does not give him to us in exchange for Father Allard. The latter must come before anyone else. I esteem him infinitely. Good-bye. My address in Paris for urgent matters is: Missions Étrangères, rue du Bac.[7]

After the ban on the parochial missions was lifted, Bishop de Mazenod kept strongly insisting on the importance of respecting the traditions and ceremonies that had made Oblate missions such a resounding success in the past. Writing a long letter to Father Eugene Guigues at Notre-Dame de l'Osier on November 5, 1837, he dealt in detail with the practices he considered essential and which were to be omitted on no account. Here is an excerpt:

I urge you not to deceive yourself to the point of believing that the Fathers of l'Osier are wiser that their predecessors in the work of the holy mission. Do not change anything in your customs without having obtained my consent. All the local and temporary superiors of missions must know quite well that I never intended, nor was I ever able to give full powers to anyone and that they cannot suppress at will what has been hallowed by our tradition.

Among such practices are some that are considered essential and others that can be taken as contingent. What is prescribed in the Rule, for

---

[6] *Oblate Writings*, vol. 9, pp. 12-13, n. 604.

[7] Ibid., p. 75, n. 653.

example, the entry of missionaries into a place they are going to evangelize, cannot be suppressed, even temporarily, except by an explicit authorization from me. Obligatory in the missions are: the consecration to the Blessed Virgin, the renewal of baptismal promises, the promulgation of the law, the procession of the Blessed Sacrament, the funeral service and the instruction after the Gospel of the *Requiem* High Mass, as well as the procession and absolution at the cemetery, the first procession known as the penitential procession, the exercise preparatory to the act of contrition and the separate act of contrition of both sexes, the general Communion. . . .[8]

Another letter, written to the same Father Guigues a couple of months later, on January 26, 1839, continued with the same theme, and shows how firmly the Founder, even as bishop, kept his hand on the tiller:

Where my authorization must be obtained, I will never agree in any case whatever, that my silence may be taken for consent. Such a method is inadmissible. Only whatever I approve formally is authorized. I act in such a manner that I give a prompt reply, but should I happen to delay, one has to wait patiently and, if in a hurry, send me a reminding letter to which it could happen that I deem myself not yet bound to reply for reasons which I am not obliged to reveal, in which case, the issue remains pending. This is a lesser evil than to risk acting against the superior's will, or at least without his authorization. Remember this rule well so as never to deviate from it.

With regard to the ceremonies you would like to have suppressed, I would have much to say if it were possible to do so verbally, but the pen is not as supple as the word – it can hurt and that is not what I want to do when I have a remark to make. I will limit myself to telling you that if you held a little less to your views – if you had more respect for those of your superiors, which at least have the Church's approval – you would act precisely in that spirit of faith which you admit you do not possess; the good Lord will take the trouble of proving to you that at Grenoble, as elsewhere, he blesses both fidelity to the Rule and simplicity.

It would be understandable, were it simply a question of modifying a custom, but to change one thing now, then something else, that will never happen as long as order remains in religion and some religious are still willing to preserve our Congregation's traditions. Bishops and cardinals carry the processional cross for jubilees and in times of disaster; why should a missionary blush to bear that precious burden when it is a question of drawing God's mercy on his errant people? Does he not realize that it is in complete conformity with the spirit of Jesus Christ to do public reparation in the name of the sinners he has come to save? I am not speaking of going bare-footed – that was never prescribed – but of the ceremony itself and the sermon on the subject. Can it be that we do those things without a spirit of faith? What an accomplishment!

---

[8] *Oblate Writings*, vol. 9, p. 71 ff., n. 652.

Good-bye, my dear son. A quarter-hour's meditation will put you back on the right track.[9]

Even while taken up with the problems of Marseilles, the Oblates' Founder was preoccupied about such details as the steeple on the mission church in Aix. On March 13, 1843, he wrote to Father Courtès: "Your news about the danger of the steeple is very bad. It is useless to hope that anyone will contribute to its repair; the entire expense will be ours. Therefore, you will have to ascertain if the spire is absolutely necessary. We have no obligation to beautify the town . . ."[10]

Although he had been the bishop of Marseilles for seven years when the following letter was written to Father Courtès on February 22, 1844, it was still he, Eugene de Mazenod, who as superior general decided all the assignments.

> The Pastor of Brignoles, my dear Courtès, was just in Marseilles and I was extremely happy with his good manners. He truly deserves that we do everything possible to satisfy him. He has announced the mission for the second Sunday, and the news was welcomed with great pleasure. I hope that, in the Lord's goodness, this mission will be successful. Take good care of yourself until then. You will have good men to work with, so arrange what is to be done. Father Magnan will be there on the 27th and 28th. Father Martin's health is better. I have written so that Father Dassy will not be late in getting there. Good-bye.[11]

Animating the Oblates to Preserve Their Charism

In 1852 we find the 70-year-old de Mazenod insisting as much as ever that Oblates, by vocation, are missionaries to the poor and the most abandoned; they are not to be orators adulated by the upper classes. He felt strongly that preaching fine Lenten series in grand cathedrals and elitist churches was out of place for them. In a letter to Father Hector-Louis Merlin, dated September 10, he showed his pique when he wrote:

> How is it that no one has seen fit to tell me . . . that there was no need to preach in (Étain), seeing that the pastor has received so much help from the Jesuits, Dominicans and Redemptorists? . . . Why go and compete with all those Orders that have provided men for a given place? *Let us go by preference to the most abandoned places.* . . . I greatly insist that you tell (the pastor) that we cannot preach a Lenten series in his parish. That is so typical of parish priests. All they want is to have Lent taken care of, while my way of seeing things is quite the opposite. By that I do not mean that I will not be sending you anyone. On the contrary, I have selected for you

---

[9] *Oblate Writings,* vol. 9, p. 82, n. 657.
[10] Ibid., vol. 10, p. 8, n. 791.
[11] Ibid., p. 58, n. 835.

one of the most pleasing and soundest men in the Congregation.[12] I shall write to tell him to go to Nancy. *But in God's name, let there be an end to such all-too-human considerations that insinuate themselves speciously and in every other way.* Do not worry so much about our reputation in terms of talents and brilliant preaching. Worry, instead, about virtue, regularity, good discipline and edification . . . .

Reflect on where pretentiousness could lead. God wants none of it and does not bless it. In our time we did not make that our objective, and the Lord worked marvels through our ministry. Do what you can in the measure that God has endowed us, and do not dream of the rest. If others display more talent, let them delight therein, if the want. For ourselves, we will continue to keep on foot-slogging. Our Rules are there to reassure us. I repeat: if we go beyond that we are in the illusion of vanity – and vanity leads to pride and pride chases people from the Congregation and drives souls to the devil. Pride drives men from every religious Order. I even know of several Jesuits who left their Order through that gate of hell.[13]

A few months later, on January 21, 1853, in a letter to Father Charles Baret at Nancy, Eugene again underscored that Oblates are sent to preach to the poor, not to give brilliant sermons to the upper classes. He made an exception for this young priest, but only so he could learn from the example of an older experienced diocesan preacher in Paris. The introduction, moreover, also makes it clear that the Founder expected every Oblate to write to him from time to time:

(Your letters) give me such pleasure that sometimes I am tempted to complain that you bring me that pleasure all too rarely. I have thought about your request to preach an Advent series in Paris. I would have had some hesitation in replying, were it not that you will be spending your time with a venerable priest who offers you the privilege of his company and the help of his kind and friendly observations. We will thus be able to consider this series of sermons as an occasion to test your strength and a means of improving yourself in the art of preaching well. Given this consideration, and under such conditions, I see this as being a good opportunity for you, *even though it is a little outside your calling.* In Paris, those to whom we preach are not abandoned souls, and in such an audience it can very well happen that we do not see the marvels of God's grace that take place during our parochial missions. No matter, the motivation is quite legitimate and, provided that it does not take on undue importance, I authorize your project . . . .[14]

As the letter to Father Baret shows, the Oblate Founder was not at all sold on the effectiveness of Advent and Lenten series delivered in the great cathedrals and basilicas of France. Indeed, he considered them to be

---

[12] Father Revol.

[13] *Oblate Writings,* vol. 11, p. 102, n. 1120.

[14] Ibid., p. 114, n. 1132.

generally outside the calling of his missionaries since they were primarily aimed at the rich and of little worth for the poor. On August 16, he rescinded the permission to Father Baret given in the previous letter because his proposed mentor would be absent from Paris. De Mazenod concluded his letter, saying: "Let us evangelize the poor. That is worth more. And besides, that is more in conformity with our vocation and with the Congregation founded for such ministry."[15]

Overseas Missions

In Chapter 2 we saw how even as a newly ordained priest, Eugene de Mazenod's ardent love for the Church and for the salvation of souls led him to listen to God's call through the events around him. It was a principle he would carry through life. We saw him, early on, answering the call of the pope, who was "convinced that, given the wretched state in which France finds herself, only missions can bring people back to the Faith which they have abandoned."[16] To that end he founded the Missionaries of Provence. Later, after his tiny 25-member society gained approbation as a missionary congregation of the universal Church, events pointed to a far vaster field. Eugene de Mazenod was convinced that his Oblates were destined to be oversees missionaries, but where?

The great opportunity came in 1841 when Bishop Ignace Bourget of Montreal visited Marseilles on his way to Rome. The Canadian prelate had fruitlessly canvassed the mission societies of Paris for recruits. Not until he spoke with Father Tempier at the episcopal residence in Marseilles did he even have an inkling that Bishop de Mazenod had founded a missionary congregation. One thing led to another and the rest is history. The first Oblates arrived in Canada in 1841. It was the start of a new chapter in the annals of the Oblate congregation.

Incredibly, in the next decade de Mazenod's tiny band would spread over the length and breadth of the North American continent:

Then there was Plattsburgh, New York; and Pittsburgh, Pennsylvania – the list goes on. Moreover, before long, there were Oblates in far off Ceylon (Sri Lanka) and Southern Africa. The congregation had stretched itself to the limit.

The Founder had some very clear convictions about Oblates in overseas missions. He readily perceived that it was a special vocation and not for

---

[15] *Oblate Writings,* vol. 11, p. 160, n. 1163.
[16] Letter of invitation to Father Tempier.

every Oblate. We can recognize several characteristics of the overseas missionary in his way of thinking.

Being an Overseas Missionary Is a Special Vocation That One Accepts Generously

In contrast to some later Oblate superiors general, Eugene de Mazenod never ordered anyone to an overseas mission under obedience. He certainly twisted the occasional arm, yet he recognized the uniqueness of such a vocation and knew that to be effective it must be embraced generously. Thus, for example, his first choice to head the missionary group for southern Africa was Father Bellon. When he begged off for health reasons, the Founder chose Father Allard.

> In his *Instruction on Foreign Missions*, written in 1850 and published three years later, after the General Chapter updated the Constitutions to take into account its division into provinces, he wrote:
>
> Not all the members of the Congregation are fit for foreign missions, but only those *in whom the characteristic signs of that sublime vocation are to be found,* and who, under the inspiration of grace, feel an inclination to such ministry. Hence, they may be chosen for this excellent work if they are inflamed with an ardent desire of spreading the Faith, if they appear to be men of charity and of good will, resolute and cheerful at work, firm and unwavering in suffering, sociable, healthy and of a physical constitution fit to bear the strain of toil and capable of facing straightened conditions of life.[17]

Personal inclinations were taken into account. What was important was that the member chosen for an overseas mission be inflamed with an ardent desire to spread the Faith, that he be sociable – a man of charity and good will, resolute and cheerful, that he be firm and unwavering in suffering, that he be healthy and physically fit to bear the strain of toil, and that he be capable of straightforwardly facing the conditions in which he found himself.

Sent to the "Pagans"

For the Oblate Founder, overseas missionaries had to be new church-builders, not just consolidators of existing communities. Like St. Paul, he believed that "there is no chaining the Word of God" (2 Timothy 2:19) – that it was too powerful for anyone to dare impose limits. Oblates therefore must evangelize every type of non-believer, without exception. He saw no inherent obstacle, for example, in converting the believers of Islam to the

---

[17] *Instruction on Foreign Missions,* p. 5.

Cross. In a letter written to Bishop Pavy of Algiers on January 5, 1849, he asked the prelate to let the Oblates be free to evangelize according to their charism. "I have never thought that the conversion of those poor Muslims was any more difficult than that of the Chinese. . . ."[18]

Ceylon (Sri Lanka)

The Founder was driven by the call to go to the "pagans," as non-believers were called then. In 1845, when Bishop Horace Bettachini of Colombo vainly sought missionaries for Ceylon, Bishop Berteaud of Tulle, in France, told him, "Go to Marseilles. There you will find bishop whose Congregation is still small, but he has a heart as big as St. Paul's, as big as the world. Make it clear to him that it is a matter of saving those poor, poor souls – insist on that point! When he hears that he will be unable to resist."[19] Bishop Bettachini was not disappointed. Soon missionaries were being sent to that far-off isle in the Indian Ocean. And always, the Founder's preoccupation "to go to the pagans" comes through strongly in his letters. In 1850, he wrote to Father Étienne Semeria:

> I search in vain in your letters to see what work you are doing, and until now you have not told me of a single conversion. Frankly, I only agreed to send missionaries to Ceylon in the hope of seeing them used for *the conversion of souls*. For the Italian and Spanish missionaries who are looking for their daily bread, it is all right to win it by serving parishes, but our Oblates are called to a different ministry . . . .[20]

In another long letter to Father Semeria, dated April 2, 1850, in which he spoke of financial allocations for the missions and told the superior of the Ceylon mission that two more missionaries would be sent, the Founder asked with obvious impatience:

> Are we never going to start working for *the conversion of unbelievers*, of whom there is such a huge number on your island? I long to see you storm the fort in that country where, it seems, it has been left in peace for a long time. Say something! Tell me everything about all this and give me your views and hopes on the matter. I know you have work to do among your bad Christians, as your last letter proves, in which you tell me of the many homes you have put in order and the illicit liaisons you have brought to an end in your country, but you must also work for the conversion of the unbelievers.[21]

---

[18] *Oblate Writings,* vol. 4, p. 165, n. 4.
[19] Ibid., Introduction by Yvon Beaudoin, O.M.I., p. XXIII
[20] Ibid., p. 48, n. 14.
[21] Ibid., p. 54, n. 15.

In yet another extremely long letter to Semeria in Jaffna, dated March 12, 1851, the Founder told him that he and Alexandre Taché were to be appointed coadjutor bishops in their respective missions and Jean Allard named Vicar Apostolic of Natal. He then went on to remind the superior of the Ceylon mission:

> All the missions that we have given this year have done great good everywhere. It is this that makes me desire even more that the numerous subjects whom I send to Ceylon should at last launch an attack on idolatry and disbelief. I cannot be satisfied while so much enthusiasm and devotion does nothing but support the sad, old and decrepit Christian population. *What I want are new Christians made in a new mould.* I have said that here and I will repeat it, just as I have said it to you on previous occasions.[22]

To the Ceylon missionaries he wrote when he was 69 years old: "I have heard that you have done much good work, but there will be a great deal more for you to do when the moment arrives for you *to attack infidelity and idolatry.* I do not know whether I will have the joy of seeing it before I die, but I will always hope so."[23]

Almost all the Oblate Founder's letters to Semeria were filled with detailed news of the congregation. The one of September 19, 1851, was no exception. After dealing with many topics about the Oblates in general and the Ceylon mission in particular, he went on to imply that evangelization will take place through persistent work and not by wishful dreaming about having a band of super-missionaries. He also reiterated his call to work for a new Church rather than trying to change the ways of the old conservative and entrenched Catholics who traced their Catholicism to evangelizing efforts from Goa in the 16th century:

> (The missionaries) will have a little more difficulty, but they will manage in the end. That will be easier than sending you men like St. Francis Xavier, as you ask. That would be asking too much and I would be afraid of dampening the enthusiasm of our good Oblates if I offered them no alternative but to become St. Francis Xaviers, or else expect to do nothing. Be patient, and *when you are ready to launch an attack on idolatry you will see that you have less difficulty and more consolations in that work than in battling with those degenerate Christians who discourage you so much.*[24]

The superior general of the Oblates obviously had little patience with the old "Goan Catholics" and when the Goan clergy opposed giving Communion to children, he replied to Bishop Semeria on January 7, 1853, very

---

[22] *Oblate Writings,* vol. 4, p. 61, n. 16.

[23] Ibid., p. 66, n. 18.

[24] Ibid., p. 82, n. 23.

much along the lines of the letter just quoted: "With things as they are, it seems to me difficult to bring people to healthy ways of thinking about religion. And so, *a new generation must be formed*; you must dedicate all your care to them and fortify them against the ingrained habits of their parents by instilling good habits in them . . . ."[25]

Yet another letter to Bishop Semeria on October 10, 1857, shows both his joy at the conversion of persons in the middle of the island and the little enthusiasm he held out for success among the Goan Catholics: "Father Chounavel's letter interests me greatly. With pleasure I saw in it what I desire most of all, namely, that he has managed to obtain conversions of pagans in the centre of the island. It seems to me that I have more zeal for them than for all those bad Catholics who are always on the point of revolt and threaten to go over to the schismatics."[26]

Less than two years before his death, de Mazenod wrote to Father Christophe Bonjean in Ceylon, on November 19, 1859: "My great regret is that despite my wishes, people have thought too late about getting involved in the conversion of the pagan natives. Those people would give you more consolation than the long-standing Christians who are so ill-disposed and so weak in their faith."[27]

Despite his insistence on evangelizing the non-Christians, the Founder of the Oblates did not propose as a general principle that "old" Christians in Ceylon be abandoned because of their lack of fidelity and that "pagans" be evangelized in their stead. His judgment that it would be better for the Oblates in Ceylon to build new communities among the pagans was based on the reports he received. Certainly, he did not reject the "old" Christians out of hand, as is evident in a letter he wrote to Colombo on April 27, 1852, to Bishop Bravi, a difficult man who constantly found fault with the Oblate missionaries:

> I must thank you once again for your fatherly kindness towards our Oblates of Mary. Give them time to gain a little experience of the country. They have no lack of talent, which goes well with virtue. If the English want things otherwise, I care little, firstly, because I do not greatly value the judgment of those gentlemen on the qualities suitable for missionaries and also because the Oblates, who were sent to Ceylon by the Sacred Congregation of Propaganda, have as their principal mission the conversion of unbelievers *and the instruction of those ignorant people*

---

[25] *Oblate Writings*, vol. 4, p. 104, n. 31.

[26] Ibid., p. 139, n. 44.

[27] Ibid., p. 146, n. 49.

who call themselves Christian but are not so, either in principle or in practice.[28]

The Founder clearly did not pull principles out of thin air. Instead, he proposed decisions based on facts gleaned from the reports sent to him by the Oblates in the field.

Southern Africa

De Mazenod's frustration with the slowness of conversions in Africa boiled over at times, especially in the case of Bishop Jean Allard, the first vicar apostolic of Natal. Allard had previously been a strict and meticulous novice-master in Canada and always tormented by extreme scruples. Indeed, as a scholastic he had been haunted by remorse at the thought that the seeds from a bunch of grapes he had thoughtlessly picked and eaten in a vineyard could possibly have produced a great number of new vines for the proprietor, a poor old woman.

It was only natural that such scrupulosity filled the man with self-doubt, which made him withdrawn and hampered his learning English or Zulu. Not only did he keep to himself, but frequently he kept his missionaries from getting close to the people as well. Furthermore, Allard expected Oblates to endure every kind of hardship simply because they were missionaries. Thus when he did send them forth it was always on foot – on regular round trips as long as 1,000 kilometres – even though horses were available! Before long, most of his original group had lost heart and either left Africa or the priesthood. One of the originals, Father Logegaray, even joined the Calvinist Evangelical Mission Society and ended his days killed tragically as a white hunter.

Since the Founder was so convinced that the Word of God could conquer all, it is not surprising that he often lashed out bitterly at Allard's lack of results in converting the "pagan" Zulus. One can feel his fury in the letter he wrote to the hapless bishop on May 30, 1857 – five years after the Oblates' arrival in Natal. Today, some of the terms the Founder of the Oblates used do violence to our sensitivity, but we must remember that times and expressions have changed. Today *Kafir* has the overtones of a racist slur, but in the 19th century it was an acceptable term for the natives of South Africa.

> There is a matter of extreme concern in the lack of success of your mission to the Kafirs. There are few examples of such sterility. What! Not a single one of those poor unbelievers to whom you have been sent has opened his eyes to the truth you are bringing them! I have difficulty in consoling

---

[28] *Oblate Writings*, vol. 4, p. 98, n. 30.

myself, since you were not sent to the few heretics who inhabit your towns. It is to the Kafirs that you have been sent, it is their conversion that the Church expects of you. It is, therefore, to the Kafirs that you must direct all your thoughts and efforts. All our missionaries must know this and take it to heart.[29]

As a result, Bishop Allard began to search frantically for results, first here, then there, never giving himself or his missionaries enough time in any given place to achieve something of true consequence. It is hardly surprising that the first Zulu mission proved an utter failure. Finally, abandoning the Zulus, he went to the Basotho, where King Moshoeshoe received him generously and the conversion of the Africans to the Faith by Oblate missionaries truly began.

Bishop Allard's difficult character continued to provoke problems among the Oblates and among the Holy Family Sisters who worked with him. This finally precipitated his retirement to Rome in 1874, where he lived an exemplary and novice-like religious life. On September 26, 1889, he was found dead at his prie-dieu in the chapel.

The Marvellous Deeds of the Missions

From his letters to the missionaries abroad, we can see clearly that the Founder was evangelized by their deeds. The Oblates let him discover in them the marvels of the Lord. He greatly admired their apostolate, in which he could recognize the great deeds of the Apostles, such as are to be seen in Peter's discourse on Pentecost:

> But Peter, standing up with the eleven, lifted up his voice and spoke out to them: "Men of Judea and all you who dwell in Jerusalem, let this be known to you, and give ear to my words. These men are not drunk, as you suppose, for it is only the third hour of the day. But this is what was spoken through the prophet Joel: 'And it shall come to pass in the last days, says the Lord, that I will pour forth of my Spirit upon all flesh; and your sons and your daughters will prophesy, and your young men shall see visions, and your old men shall dream dreams. And moreover, upon my servants and upon my handmaids in those days will I pour forth of my Spirit, and they shall prophesy. And I will show wonders in the heavens above and signs on the earth beneath, blood and fire and vapour and smoke. The sun shall be turned into darkness and the moon into blood, before the day of the Lord comes, the great and manifest day. And it shall come to pass that whoever calls upon the name of the Lord shall be saved.'"

Acts 2:14-21

---

[29] *Oblate Writings,* vol. 4, pp. 205-206, n. 26.

To Father Henri Faraud in Arctic Canada, the Founder wrote a long letter on May 28, 1857. In it he tells the missionary:

> With lively interest and unflagging attention, I have just read, in one sitting, your admirable account of La Nativité Mission, sent on December 6 of last year. How can I express to you all the feelings it awakened in my soul? I felt called, first of all, to give thanks to God for his continual help and for the miracles that he deigns to work by means of your ministry. Then, in spirit, I pressed you to my heart, touched to the point of tears by all that you have had to suffer to conquer those souls for Jesus Christ who, in all your many difficulties, has clothed you with his power and sustained you by his grace. Moreover, what a reward you will have beyond this world, when one thinks of the wonders that have been wrought by the power of your ministry! *One has to go back to the first preaching of St. Peter to find anything similar.* An apostle, just as he was, you were sent to proclaim the Good News to those savage nations, the first man to speak to them of God, to bring them to the knowledge of Jesus Christ, to show them the way that leads to salvation, to give them rebirth in the holy waters of Baptism – one can only prostrate oneself before you, so privileged are you among your brothers in the Church of God by reason of the choice he has made of you to work those miracles . . . .[30]

In 1847, when his reserve of candidates for overseas missions had been expended, de Mazenod asked Father Pascal Ricard, the frail and bed-ridden superior at the shrine of Notre-Dame des Lumières, literally to rise from his sick-bed to accompany a young priest and two young scholastic brothers who were close to ordination – Georges Blanchette, Casimir Chirouse and Charles Pandosy – on a perilous journey to found a mission in the Oregon Territory. So hurried was their departure that Father Ricard did not even have time to go home to bid farewell to his parents. It was a case of not turning back after putting one's hand to the plough. On January 8 of that year the Oblate Founder wrote Ricard:

> So there, my dear Father, is where you are called by Divine Providence. . . . I say nothing of how magnificent in the eyes of Faith is the ministry you are going to fulfil. One must go back to the birth of Christianity to find anything comparable. It is an apostle with whom you are associated and the same marvels that were wrought by the first disciples of Jesus Christ will be renewed in our days by you, my dear children, whom Providence has chosen amongst so many others to announce the Good News to so many slaves of the demon, who huddle in the darkness of idolatry and who do not know God. *Truly, this is the real apostolate which is renewed in our times.* Let us thank the Lord for having been deemed worthy to be such active participants therein.[31]

---

[30] *Oblate Writings,* vol. 2, p. 146, n. 234.
[31] Ibid., vol. 1, p. 148, n. 74.

For the Founder, overseas missions were the true mission of the Apostles. Writing again to Father Ricard on December 6, 1851, he stated:

> Foreign mission, compared to our missions in Europe, have a special character of a higher kind, because that is the true apostolate of announcing the Good News to nations which have not yet been called to the knowledge of the true God and of his son, Jesus Christ. . . . *This is the mission of the Apostles: Euntes, docete omnes gentes!* That teaching of the truth must penetrate even to the most backward of nations so that they may be regenerated in the waters of Baptism. You are among those to whom Jesus Christ addressed those words, giving you your mission as he gave them their mission.[32]

He Took the Opinion of His Missionaries into Account

It seems almost paradoxical that a man as headstrong and determined as Eugene de Mazenod would heed the opinion of his overseas missionaries. Yet such was the case. His *Instruction on Foreign Missions* was only written after nine years of accumulated reports on the Oblates' experiences in the field and was added to the revised rule in 1853. In no way is it a theoretical or ethereal set of directives dreamt up by someone comfortably ensconced behind a desk in the rear echelons, with only a vague inkling of what might really be going on at the front. Instead, he proposed a concrete code in the light of the information he had received. And in the very first edition of the rule he had even left a blank page where directives for the brothers in the congregation should have appeared, because as yet he had no experience upon which to base himself.

Here it is well to recall once more Eugene de Mazenod's directive to the Ceylon missionaries to build new Christian communities rather than fritter away their energies in fruitless ministry to the stodgy and conservative old Goan Catholics of the Island. It was a directive based on the reports he got from Bishop Semeria. Moreover, to Father JB Honorat in Canada, the Founder wrote on January 17, 1843: "You must not be afraid to question me when you believe I have given a decision which presents some problems. It will probably be because I was insufficiently informed."[33] Writing again to Father Honorat, but this time to chide him, the Founder presented Father Semeria as an exemplary missionary who wrote monthly letters and thus kept him fully informed in order to make knowledgeable decisions: "It is as if I were on the scene. One can thus make a judgment and reach decisions."[34]

---

[32] *Oblate Writings,* vol. 2, p. 29, n. 157.

[33] Ibid., vol. 1, p. 34, n. 15a.

[34] *Letter of July 12, 1849,* in *Oblate Writings,* vol. 1, p. 223, n. 121.

To Father Semeria in Ceylon, he wrote on January 21, 1852: "How admirable you are in your correspondence! I am delighted by your exactitude and your letters are full – I always re-read them several times."[35]

Oblate Hospitality

Among the early missionaries it was customary never again to return to one's native France. They went overseas for life. Virtually the only exceptions were Oblate bishops on their way to Rome or in France on Church business. But no matter whether the missionary was bishop or priest the Oblate Founder showered hospitality on him. In several entries of his journal he mentions how he stayed up into the small hours to speak eagerly with the person.

A letter to Fathers Végreville and Moulin and to Brother Dubé at Ile à la Crosse, in Canada's vast North West Territories, recounts an incident involving 28-year-old Father Vital Grandin who had come to Marseilles from western Canada to be made a bishop at the hands of Bishop de Mazenod: "The day before yesterday, an hour-and-a-half after midnight, we were still talking about your mission and about all of you with this excellent and, I will say more, this angelic new bishop. Here he has won all the hearts, and I am not surprised. It is impossible to display, without being aware of it, more virtues than he does."[36]

Vital Grandin's episcopal ordination took place on November 30, 1859. For that occasion the Oblate Founder, who was then 77 and only a year-and-a-half from death, outdid himself in warm hospitality, even writing a pastoral letter of invitation to the entire Marseilles diocese, stating, among other things:

> This great ceremony ... gains special significance from the mission of him who will be consecrated. He is an apostle called to the furthest limits of the earth. . . . In a ministry that has already lasted many years, he has undergone privations and sufferings of every kind, sufferings that are met at every instant in those lands so close to the North Pole; they do not frighten him. We invite the priests and faithful of Marseilles to come and join their prayers with ours and those of this young prelate.

During Grandin's stay in Marseilles, his exuberant superior general wanted to regale this quiet and unassuming missionary son who had suffered such hardships in Canada's uncharted northwest. Thus, it is told, he had a magnificent pike stuffed and prepared for dinner along with a very decent

---

[35] *Oblate Writings,* vol. 4, p. 87, n. 26.
[36] Ibid., vol. 2, p. 221, n. 270.

wine. During the course of the meal, de Mazenod commented, "I am sure, my son, that you never eat such a fish in your poor mission in the North, eh?"

There was silence for a moment; then came Grandin's hesitating but humbly forthright reply, "Well, no, not really, Monseigneur. You see, we must fish a great deal through the ice to provision the missions for the winter, so the pike are frozen and stored to feed the sled-dogs. We only eat the trout and the char."

Eugene de Mazenod's Method

Through Saint Eugene de Mazenod's letters and the testimony of his life a method emerges, not only in his own way of living but also in the directives he set forth for all who would be Oblates in the future.

Examine the Situation with the Eyes of Faith

Throughout the Founder's life, he looked at his own situation with the eyes of faith and discovered in it how the Lord was calling him. That fact comes through from the very beginning in his options and in his first choice of men to help him accomplish his mission. In the preface to the Constitutions and Rules, he wrote

> The Church, that glorious inheritance purchased by Christ the Saviour at the cost of his own blood has, in these days, been cruelly ravaged. . . . Did we not know that the sacred deposit of faith is to be preserved intact to the end of time, we would hardly be able to recognize the religion of Christ from the few remaining traces of its past glory that lie scattered about . . .

> The sight of these evils has so touched the hearts of certain priests, zealous for the glory of God, men with an ardent love of the Church, that they are willing to give their lives, if need be, for the salvation of souls.

It is important to note that the Oblate Founder not only examined what was strictly religious but also considered the circumstances. Remember the mediation boards he set up in the early parochial missions to arbitrate differences between returning nobles and the bourgeoisie – something necessary, given the situation after the Revolution.

Another example is to be found in what Eugene de Mazenod said in the *Instruction on Foreign Missions* about training people for the duties of civil life (the original reads: *les nécessités de la vie sociale*) and the responsibility of the Oblate brothers in that regard. What the Founder proposed was only a beginning. Moreover, in retrospect and in the light of today's missiology (which has its own tensions in the area of evangelization between respect for cultural values and fidelity to the gospel) one might well question thrust of his directive. In Canada a controversy has been going on for several years concerning the wounds inflicted upon the First Nations by well-meaning missionaries who tried to assimilate the Natives into a European-type of Christianity and by so doing left them virtually bereft of their own culture. In 1992 the Canadian Conference of Catholic Bishops made a statement that might well reflect upon the Founder's way of seeing the missionary's role. The statement said, "The missionaries' commitment to the European expression of Christianity made it difficult for them to recognize the spirituality of the aboriginal peoples."

One thing is certain: de Mazenod had an abiding concern to prepare the Native as a whole person for a life of Christian quality. We have already seen that the Founder of the Oblates was a product of his times. Although he was far more concerned than the average bishop about the quality of Christian life for the Native peoples, his concept was definitely European in its framework. Nevertheless, it does show his deep social concern, as the following directives evidence:

> Far from thinking it incongruent with their ministry to train the inhabitants of the woods to the duties of civil life, the members of our Society will consider it as intimately connected with the mission's welfare and as most fit to obtaining better results. Every means should therefore be taken to bring the nomad tribes to abandon their wandering life, and to select places in which they may learn to build houses, cultivate fields and practise the elementary crafts of civilized life. In preparing men destined for the foreign missions, superiors will try to find one, or even more, who may be suitable for this kind of work. They will also strive to give them lay brothers well versed in the different mechanical arts, who will thus be able not only to help *but to take the place of the missionaries themselves.*[37]

This shows that the Founder saw that the brothers had responsibilities in their own right and were not simply priest's helpers.

Respond with Generosity

The preface of the Oblate Constitutions and Rules embodies the generosity of de Mazenod's own response and the response he expected of his Oblates.

> They are convinced that if priests could be formed, afire with zeal for men's salvation, priests not given to their own interests, solidly grounded in virtue – in a word, apostolic men deeply conscious of the need to reform themselves, who would labour with all the resources at their command to convert others – then there would be ample reason to believe that in a short

---

[37] *Instruction on Foreign Missions*, p. 13.

while people who had gone astray might be brought back to their long-unrecognized responsibilities.[38]

To Father Tempier he wrote as early as August 22, 1817, even before he had written the rule: "Each Society in the Church has its own spirit; a spirit inspired by God according to the circumstances and needs of the times in which God is pleased to raise such supporting corps, or perhaps it would be better to say, such elite corps, which precede the main army on the march and excel in bravery, thus gaining the more brilliant victories."[39] Frustrated by the lack of zeal in some candidates, he gave the following counsel for the formation of the scholastics to Father Charles Bellon:

> Let our training be manly, serious and totally saintly. It is a question of forming men who are to be imbued with the spirit of Jesus Christ, who can fight the terrible power of the devil and of his destructive reign over the people – men who can build up the world so as to bring it to the truth, who can serve the Church in the loftiest and most difficult apostolate. Can we achieve such results with men who are not generous, men devoid of courage, men who have fallen into a rut? If (a young man in formation) does not have fervent and noble aspirations now, how can we expect that he will discover them later? . . . The person who cannot imitate the detachment proposed by Jesus Christ and practised by the saints is not good for very much. How lax we are! We finally get there only by dint of much reasoning when we should be soaring as though by supernatural instinct.[40]

No "Smouldering Wicks" in the Congregation

In the Founder's journal there is an entry that exemplifies the spirit he sought in his Oblates. Father Ambroise Vincens, the spiritual director, interceded by letter on behalf of a novice, saying that the young man in question was perhaps still only a smouldering wick but that he had hopes of some day seeing him catch fire. To push him hard now, he thought, might forever extinguish that wick. The Founder did not reply to Father Vincens immediately but penned something in his journal that he probably would not have put quite as bluntly in a letter. The bluntness, however, shows us how forceful were his convictions: "I have no use for smouldering wicks in this Society. I want you to burn, to give heat, to give light, or to get out."[41]

---

[38] *Preface to the Constitutions and Rules,* (English), p. 10.

[39] Rambert, vol. I, p. 237; and *Selected Texts*, p. 503, n. 448.

[40] Yenveux, vol. 4, p. 43, vol. 8, pp. 91, 196-198, and *Oblate Writings,* vol. 10, p. 84.

[41] Rey, vol. 2, p. 238.

Evangelize with Vision and Daring

When the Oblate Founder composed the original rule in French in 1818, he wrote, "We must spare no effort . . . ." In 1826, when Fathers Albini and Courtès, both accomplished Latinists, translated it for official presentation in Rome, they used the Latin phrase *"Nihil linquendum inausum"* – "to leave nothing undared" – which more vividly conveys Saint Eugene's thought than do his own words.

For Eugene de Mazenod, daring, inventiveness and creativity – all wrapped in charity – were essential. In another letter, written on March 1, 1844 – three years after the tiny band of Oblate missionaries arrived in Eastern Canada – he chided Father Honorat for not jumping eagerly at an opportunity to push forward, to open the vastness of Canada's far-flung Northwest to evangelization:

> You have to be truly enterprising when you are called upon to conquer souls. I was fuming to find myself separated from you by 2000 leagues and unable to make my voice reach you in less than two months. And yet, your letter of February 2 arrived today, March 1. God grant that you may at least have received mine which not only approved such a great project but applauded it with delight. This was not something tentative to be tried. You should have gone there with the firm resolve to overcome all obstacles, gone there to stay, to take root! How could you hesitate? What more beautiful mission can there be than that! Ministering in the lumber camps, in missions to the Savages, getting set up in a city which is wholly of the future. A beautiful dream coming true, and you would have let it escape! The thought makes me shiver! Gather up all your courage in your hands once again and get yourself properly set up. Urge each one to do his duty. It is only thus that you will bring upon yourselves the blessing of God . . . .[42]

(Again, we should remember that de Mazenod intended nothing disrespectful in using the term "savages." It was in line with the usage of the times.)

Eugene de Mazenod was truly a "holy adventurer." When the youthful trio of Oblates set out for Oregon with their moribund superior in 1847, they did so without even taking sufficient money to get them there! As he had told Bishop Bourget several years earlier, "One must leave something to Providence."[43] Writing to Father Guigues the same year, he urged him, "never let yourself be beaten down by difficulties."[44] Even on his deathbed, the holy daring, the dynamism and the vibrant force of his character showed through.

---

[42] *Oblate Writings*, vol. 1, p. 79, n. 32.

[43] Ibid., p. 122, n. 58.

[44] Ibid., p. 174, n. 86.

As the end approached, surrounded by his grieving Oblates, he twice asked them: "If I should doze off and you see that things are getting worse, please wake me up. I want to die knowing that I am dying."[45]

"A Man of Desires"

The Oblate Founder had a grand vision. To Father Jean-Baptiste Honorat, superior of the missionaries destined for Canada, he wrote on October 9, 1841 – even before the little group had set sail from France – that he considered himself "a man of desires."[46] "I anticipate the future of that conviction.[47] I am not a prophet, yet I have always been a man of desires, some of which have been heard and fulfilled . . . ."[48] He may not have considered himself a prophet, yet he foresaw that "Montreal perhaps is only the gateway leading the family to the conquest of souls in several countries."[49] Elsewhere he would forecast that "Bytown (Ottawa) is a city of the future"[50] and that "Red River (St. Boniface and Winnipeg) will be the springboard for evangelizing the entire north of the American continent."[51]

Eugene, whose full name was Charles-Joseph-Eugene de Mazenod, considered himself as daring as his patron saint. On his 48th birthday, August 1, 1830, he wrote to Father Tempier from Fribourg in Switzerland:

> The great works of a saint like Charles Borromeo have always excited in my heart more satisfaction and joy than admiration. Heretofore I did not utter it for fear of pride. I did not dwell on such a thought but, fundamentally, I have never managed to ward it off. I have never been able to dispel from the depths of my being that in his place I would have done as much. Again yesterday, when the solemnity and length of the ceremonies on the Feast of Saint Ignatius, at which they asked me to preside, and the circumstances of it being the last day of my forty-eighth year, aroused in me more devout thoughts and holy desires and allowed me also the time to reflect under the aegis of Jesus Christ present and exposed, how deep in my soul I plunged! How diverse and mixed were my feelings! . . . I finished off by asking God to take me out of this world if I am not to do anything more that what I have already done.[52]

---

[45] *Circular no. 9*, Father Fabre, on the death of the Founder, p. 11.

[46] The late Father Angelo Mitri, O.M.I., while Postulator General for Oblate Causes, wrote an excellent article in French precisely on this point. Entitled *Le Bienheureux Eugène de Mazenod, homme des désirs, et l'oblat*, it appeared in *Vie Oblate Life* 1982, pp. 213-231.

[47] He had just mentioned at some length the great impact and growth he expected the Oblates to have in Canada.

[48] *Oblate Writings*, vol. 1, p. 16, n. 9.

[49] Ibid., p. 15, n. 9.

[50] Ibid., p. 79 n. 32.

[51] Ibid., p. 111, n. 50.

[52] Ibid., vol. 7, pp. 204-205, n. 351.

Seven years later, though still confident he must be daring, his enthusiasm had been tempered by the Icosia crisis. His retreat notes from 1837, made before taking over the see of Marseilles, tell us that "there was a time when I felt such vigour of soul on reading the life of St. Charles that it did not seem beyond my power to do as much as he did, were I in his place. I am less rash today . . . ."[53]

How Eugene de Mazenod Saw Himself in His Relationship to the Congregation

The fifth volume of *Oblate Writings*, containing the letters Eugene de Mazenod wrote to the Sacred Congregation of *Propaganda Fide* and to the Society for the Propagation of the Faith in Lyon, provides a clear understanding of how he saw himself in relation to the Oblate congregation. Only once in that correspondence, in his last letter to Cardinal Prefect of the Sacred Congregation, written on March 27, 1861 – just two months before his death – did he refer to himself as the "Founder": "Firstly, I can only be very grateful to the bishops of Canada who made the choice and to Your Eminence who agreed upon this priest for the See of Vancouver from the Congregation of the Oblates of Mary, *of which I am the Founder and Father.*"[54]

The Congregation – A Grace From and Gift to the Church

The Founder saw the Oblate congregation as a channel of grace for himself and for all its members. On July 14, 1860, he wrote to Father Louis Soullier, who would later become superior general, that the congregation was confided to him by God. Written less than a year before his death, the letter highlights the stewardship of the mysteries of God: "I would like to make use of you according to the enlightenment that the Lord gives me for governing *the Congregation he has entrusted to me.*"[55] The congregation is a gift from God and is destined to exist for the Church. His faith-filled attitude convinced him that the Church was its founder. A letter sent to *Propaganda Fide* in Rome on September 14, 1833 shows his complete confidence in the Oblate congregation, for the very reason of its ecclesial foundation: "Since, thanks be to God, regular discipline is a feature *of this Congregation founded by Pope Leo XII*, the Holy Father could rest assured

---

[53] Leflon, vol. 4, p. 318.
[54] *Oblate Writings*, vol. 5, p. 158, n. 78.
[55] Ibid., vol. 12, p. 190, n. 1455.

regarding the virtue and exemplary life of the men chosen for the Mission."[56]

Recall, too, his letter on March 20, 1826 to Father Tempier while still overwhelmed by the hand of divine providence in the approbation: "The pope *not only approves the Congregation, he founds it: Constituimus . . .* it was the pope himself who said more in favour of our case than I could ever have done."[57] For Eugene de Mazenod the congregation was a source of grace. In a letter after his retreat, dated November 4, 1831, and written to Father Courtès, he stated: "Perhaps as never before have I grasped the value of the favour that God has shown us, and as never before have I come to *appreciate the means that God puts at our disposal in the Congregation* to serve him as we should and sanctify ourselves."[58]

Stewards of the Mysteries of God

Like St. Paul, Saint Eugene de Mazenod considered himself a "steward of the mysteries of God" (1 Corinthians 4:1). Even though he was the founder and superior general of the congregation, in his mind he was not its owner. It had been confided to him for the good of the Oblates and for the glory of God. Moreover, he expected each Oblate to live in such a way that each could say with pride and thanksgiving, "the congregation is mine," making each one, like the Founder, a steward of the mysteries of God.

The congregation existed not for itself but for the service of the Church. Once, in a letter of reprimand to Father Honorat about the lack of discipline and fraternal charity in the contentious Canadian mission group, of which Honorat was the superior, the Founder wrote, obviously vexed:

> Do not imagine there is a single mission in the world without its problems . . . but nowhere do they behave as in Canada. There everyone rises up as a teacher or doctor, vying with one another to give lessons to the superior who, by the way, is not a child. Nor are they content to make an observation respectfully and then leave the matter to his wisdom; instead, they return to the attack again and again.
>
> It was never my idea to make *a gift to the Church* of a society of insubordinate priests, without deference or respect for their superiors, detractors of one another, grumblers void of the spirit of obedience, each reserving the right to judge according to his prejudices, his likes or dislikes, sparing no one, commenting thus not only amongst themselves but even with strangers whom they carelessly take into their confidence.[59]

---

[56] *Oblate Writings,* vol. 5, p. 6, n. 2.

[57] Ibid., vol. 7, pp. , n. 231

[58] Ibid., vol. 8, p. 43, n. 407.

[59] Ibid., vol. 1, July 12, 1849, p. 223, n. 121.

Here, his comment reads like a photographic negative showing the reverse of what should be. Even so, his great consolation lay precisely in the fact that the congregation was formed for the Church. To Father Pascal Ricard he wrote on October 29, 1850: "I have entered into my sixty-ninth year. If I had to die today, the reason for my greatest consolation would be that in the Church of God I leave behind a family so numerous and so devoted to the Church and to the salvation of souls."[60] And on his deathbed his words became the cherished legacy of every Oblate of Mary Immaculate: "I die happy . . . I die happy because God deigned to choose me to found in the Church the Congregation of the Oblates. Among yourselves practice charity, charity, charity. And outside, zeal for the salvation of souls."[61]

The Congregation Is Entrusted to Every Oblate

In letters to *Propaganda Fide* in Rome or to the Society for the Propagation of the Faith in Lyon, Bishop de Mazenod usually referred to himself as "the superior." So he writes, "I therefore feel it my duty to address this request to you myself since they are missionaries who belong to the *Congregation of which I am the superior.*"[62]

More often, however, he referred to the society as the one "to which I belong,"[63] or with his favourite designation: "Our Congregation." (for example: "I cannot close my letter without renewing the expression of gratitude *of our Congregation* for the kindness you show it whenever the occasion arises"[64]).

Eugene de Mazenod deemed it especially important that members share his interest in and his responsibility for the congregation. If, in truth, they were "stewards of the mysteries of God" each should be able to say "the Congregation is mine." Thus, in addition to saying "our Congregation," he stressed that every Oblate was on an equal footing of ownership. Accordingly, to Father Lavigne at Notre-Dame de l'Osier he wrote on February 9, 1847: "I will tell you that I have no servants in the Congregation; I have only well-loved sons who are foremost in my heart, whom I mention before God, even though I cannot write to them all as often as I would like."[65]

---

[60] *Oblate Writings*, vol. 1, p. 244, n. 135.
[61] *Circular no. 9*, Father Fabre, on the death of the Founder, p. 9.
[62] *Oblate Writings*, vol. 5, July 31, 1842, p. 166, n. 80.
[63] Ibid., p. 10, n. 3.
[64] Ibid., April 17, 1855, p. 279, n. 162, and April 14, 1856, p. 284, n. 168.
[65] Ibid., vol. 10, p. 153, n. 922.

Father Ancel was a difficult and recalcitrant priest who later left the Oblates. He had joined the congregation after having trouble getting along with his colleagues in the diocesan clergy. Soon, however, he was also at odds with his Oblate confrères in Ajaccio, Corsica, and thereupon accepted a position outside the congregation without seeking anyone's permission. There followed an angry letter to the superior general in which he made reference to "your Congregation," whereupon de Mazenod wrote him the following on October 17, 1840:

> You look after your own interests not only outside of but in formal opposition to the obedience you have vowed and which binds you to your lawful superiors, and it is after having settled on an illegitimate, illegal and anticanonical measure that you inform me without embarrassment that you have accepted a post on your own authority outside of *this Congregation which you call mine, as if it were not as much yours as it is mine, as if you had not solemnly sworn in the presence of Our Lord Jesus Christ to live and die in her bosom* . . . .[66]

A Spirit of Thanksgiving

A text which the superior general of the Oblates often quoted in his letters was from St. Paul's epistle to the Philippians, Chapter 1, verses 3-11. Frequently we see it quoted verbatim, at other times we find only verse eight: "God indeed is my witness how I pursue you all with my affection in the tenderness of Christ." In the letter of obedience appointing Father Honorat superior of the group of missionaries heading to Canada, we read:

> As for me, I give thanks to God each time I think of you, in all my prayers, supplicating him with joy for you all because of your communion in the Gospel; confident also in that He who has begun good work in you will bring it to completion, until the day of Christ Jesus, as is rightful for me to believe as well as for you whom I bear in my heart. God indeed is my witness how I pursue you all with my affection in the tenderness of Christ; and I ask that your charity may abound more and more in knowledge and in every sentiment through Jesus Christ, to the glory and praise of God.[67]

Saint Eugene de Mazenod gave thanks for the works accomplished by the Oblates. His letters to the missions are replete with thanksgivings. For example, in a paraphrase of Paul, he wrote to Father Christophe Bonjean in Ceylon on November 19, 1859, saying, "I never cease blessing the Lord for all the good you are doing together with our dear and venerable Vicar . . . ."[68] A similar passage can be found in his journal: "Blessed be the Lord for all

---

[66] *Oblate Writings,* vol. 9, p. 150, n. 714.
[67] Ibid., vol. 1, September, 1841, p. 14, n. 8.
[68] Ibid., vol. 4, p. 147, n. 49.

the good performed by our dear Oblates. May our Immaculate Mother increase the number of vocations so that their good work spread and grow more and more."[69] And to Fathers Gondrand and Baret, calling them "my dear sons," he wrote on April 16, 1850: "I bless the Lord for the success he bestows on your preaching."[70]

United by Christ

Paul speaks of union with Christ as "your communion in the gospel." In the same way, Saint Eugene saw himself and his Oblates as "companions in grace" (Karl Barth's expression), participating in the grace of proclaiming the gospel. He spoke of "supplicating with joy for you all because of your communion in the gospel," which means that his Oblates, all of them together, are missionaries – and missionaries, moreover, with him. To scholastic Brother Charles Baret, upon his oblation at Notre-Dame de l'Osier, the superior general wrote on August 18, 1843: "I do not know you personally, but since the affection that unites me with my children is essentially supernatural, it is enough for me to know that the Saviour Jesus Christ, our common Master, has received your vows, has adopted you and has marked you with the seal that makes us what we are, *so that we are united in the most intimate bonds* of charity and that I am bound to you forever, as you are to me."[71]

The Primacy of Personal Relationships

We already know that Eugene de Mazenod had several closer friends among the Oblates, such as Tempier, Suzanne, Guibert and Courtès. But his concern and interest extended to all members of the congregation. Trying to get each Oblate to be the best he could be, however, sometimes resulted in heavy-handed measures when he pushed too hard. Still, he acted out of love, very much like a father who sometimes pushes a son too hard. One recurring manifestation of his love and concern for each Oblate can be found in the way he always defended them fiercely when they were in any conflict with local bishops.

That was the case, for example, in Oregon, where the Oblates had been hampered and constrained in their apostolate by the bishops of Vancouver and Oregon. There, the Founder argued before the Sacred Congregation of *Propaganda Fide* that his missionaries would be better off working as

---

[69] *Missions,* 1873, p. 43. The journal entry is dated December 5, 1854.

[70] *Oblate Writings,* vol. 11, p. 9, n. 1041.

[71] Ibid., vol. 10, p. 27, n. 811.

together in their own allotted vicariate. Bishop de Mazenod was a personal friend of Cardinal Barnabò; hence his complete honesty. He could not have been as frank with other persons in the Roman Curia:

It may very well be that His Excellency the bishop of Vancouver, an assuredly upright man but hardly gifted, as you will have already realized, has come to Rome with a completely different plan drawn up together with his two confrères in Oregon, who have proved themselves to be very unwise administrators (I express myself so frankly only when writing to you). He will have presented principles for your consideration that are quite different. It is up to the Sacred Congregation to decide in its wisdom if the special interests of those prelates, brothers and friends, are to be preferred to the good of that mission.[72]

The Founder was clearly preoccupied with the health of his Oblates, wherever they might be. In another letter written to Cardinal Barnabò, on August 12, 1860 (less than a year before his death), we read:

What I felt I had expressed was only that Your Eminence suggest or order two missions in the Colombo Vicariate, no matter which, to be set aside and served by two Oblate missionaries, obviously under the jurisdiction of the Apostolic Vicar of Colombo. I presented Your Eminence with the reason for this, and I will not repeat it. However, I do insist that most of the missions in the Vicariate of Jaffna are unhealthy and excessively tiring and that our Fathers, without excepting the Apostolic Vicar, have all contracted fever which weakens their constitution and ends up killing them. Bishop Bettachini has been a victim, as have our Fathers who passed away, along with the one who is on the verge of death.

It is, therefore, quite natural for me, as Father of the family entrusted to my care, to be vigilant over its existence, and alarmed when I see its members decimated by an unhealthy climate and the excess of their work. For that reason I ask that missions in the healthy vicariate of Colombo be assigned to them in order that the superior of the Oblates have the opportunity to send those men there who need a change of air. Any bishop other than Bishop Bravi would have found this a very simple measure to carry out....[73]

Another example of the importance he placed on personal relationships can be seen in the episcopal ordination of 28-year-old Vital Grandin. When the youthful missionary was named coadjutor to Bishop Alexandre Taché in Red River, Eugene de Mazenod insisted that Grandin leave Canada for Marseilles so that de Mazenod, as bishop, superior general and spiritual father, could himself do the consecrating. On the night of the episcopal ordination, November 30, 1859, the aged superior penned this entry in his journal. The pride and love he had for this son is plain to see:

---

[72] *Oblate Writings,* vol. 5, p. 41, n. 13.
[73] Ibid., p. 41, n. 13.

Once again, this has been one of the most beautiful days of my life. I have consecrated to the episcopate, with the assistance of the Bishop of Fréjus *(Jordany)* and the Bishop of Cérame *(Jeancard),* our good, virtuous, excellent Father Grandin. He made his novitiate for the episcopate in the terribly arduous missions of those vast and icy regions that fall within the diocese of St. Boniface, during five years of superhuman labour. . . . I previously expressed all the joy I felt at the arrival of this young man who had already received from me the tonsure, minor orders, the sub-diaconate, the diaconate and priesthood. . . . What a fine spirit, what good judgment, what simplicity, what attachment to the Congregation, his mother! What detachment from all the things of this world! What sacrifice of the dearest bonds of affection which, nonetheless, he keenly feels! What a good heart! In a word, what devotion with all that he vowed implies. It is impossible not to love such a man and I am happy to see that he has drawn to himself the esteem and the affection of all who have come near him. As for me, I will not attempt to express the joy and happiness I felt in consecrating such an angel to the episcopate. The memory of his visits to our various communities will not fade. He has given a constant example of the most perfect regularity, bishop-elect, though he was, asking permission for the most minute things. And on the day before his consecration, he wanted to kiss the feet of the entire community of Mont Olivet but, to my great regret, the local superior would not permit it . . . .[74]

To further illustrate the Oblate Founder's personal interest in each member, let us take the example of two Oblates in the first contingent of missionaries to Canada, Fathers Honorat and Telmon. Both cases show him at times pushing too hard, but his interest in each cannot be denied.

Father Jean-Baptiste Honorat

Of Father Jean-Baptiste Honorat, the Founder once wrote, "Certainly, I love him dearly, but all his life has been my martyrdom."[75] Honorat was the superior of the first mission group that went to Canada in 1841 and faced constant dissension within his group. The members were of strong and individualistic character and Honorat was no match for their forcefulness. A constant irritant was the brilliant Father Antoine Telmon, and many of the other missionaries sided with him in his frequent clashes with Honorat. De Mazenod's concern about the constant bickering within the group and, worse, the way they were openly airing their grievances with outsiders, caused Honorat to be on the receiving end of a good many reprimands from Marseilles – reprimands meant to be constructive but which nevertheless stung sharply and wounded deeply. After one that was particularly harsh, Honorat replied on January 30, 1844:

---

[74] *Oblate Writings,* vol. 2, p. 221, n. 270.

[75] Ibid., vol. 1, p. 65, n. 28.

Why are you always writing to me in this way? Reproaches, always reproaches, and nothing but reproaches. So much so that for several reasons I shall have to burn your letters which, however, should be so dear and precious to me. Oh, you do not know me! . . . But you do know that I left France out of pure obedience. Taking into account the persons you sent, only I would have agreed to go No, I am not a fool. Only to please you did I reluctantly agree to go along with such a group. I foresaw all that would happen, and yet I accepted to go. From the moment of that decision, there has not been a moment when I have not endured suffering worse than death. And you take nothing of that into account.

I have a heart – a heart you know nothing about – that is wounded and continually crushed. But you cannot destroy it. Put me down, reduce me to any of our communities – no matter which – to whatever state and for whatever reason, and I will be grateful to you . . . but do not write to me this way . . . . Never, my Father, have I worked so much in my life at so many things and with more honest and purer intentions. I say that before God. I have the witness of a good conscience. My will is only for God and the Society. I refuse no work. I believe I have acquired experience. You ought to know me. Trust none of those biased persons. Consult your heart and mine, and then take your stand.[76]

The facts are somewhat coloured by Father Honorat's depressed state of mind when writing the letter. Actually, we know from other writings and from his biographer that he willingly accepted to head the Oblate mission in Canada. Honorat's own letters at the time of his appointment show his enthusiasm at the prospect before him, but later, the constant sniping from his subjects and the superior general's reprimands combined to get to him. The truth was, however, that the Founder did think highly of Father Honorat's work, even while the latter was still in France. Before sending him to Canada he had commented to Father Mie that "I know this dear Father's solidity of principles. One can say anything to him without fear. Acting only for the sake of God, he gives himself with simplicity to all that obedience prescribes."[77]

Unfortunately, in the Founder's concern to help Father Honorat develop his leadership qualities he went too far with the blunt and acerbic manner of his corrections. Finally, exasperated by the in-fighting among members of the mission group in Montreal, Bishop de Mazenod sent Father Guigues across the Atlantic as official visitor. When Guigues opened up a new mission largely directed toward the Native peoples on the Saguenay, Father Honorat was relieved as superior of the entire group and named superior of the Saguenay. On September 25, 1844, Bishop de Mazenod wrote to Father

---

[76] *Oblate Writings,* vol. 1, p. 65, n. 28.
[77] Ibid., vol. 6, p. 174, n. 183.

Guigues lauding Father Honorat's virtue and competence yet concerned about his tendency to let money slip through his hands:

> Excellent idea to have named our dear Father Honorat as superior. He altogether deserves such a mark of confidence. You would not believe the admirable letter he wrote me about your arrival. I recognize therein his virtue. But do not forget to put limits on him, very narrow limits in the administration of his new community's finances. You know his failing; he is incorrigible. This good Father would ruin the finances of the most opulent state, so no weakening on that point.[78]

In another letter, written to Father Guigues on December 5 of the same year, the Oblate superior general grudgingly admitted that he had been too hard on poor Father Honorat: "Of Father Honorat I expected nothing less than the good example he gives. No one has ever rendered more justice than I to his religious virtues. The burden that I was obliged to impose upon him was too heavy for his shoulders. Now he is relieved. In his new post he will do well."[79]

Throughout these and other letters we see his concern for and knowledge of each Oblate as a person. Yet something else also comes through, especially in his treatment of Honorat – something he himself admitted was a stumbling block – his grudging difficulty to admit he had erred or overstepped himself. As early as 1812-1813, just recently ordained and before he began organizing the tiny society that would eventually become the Missionary Oblate Congregation, according to his spiritual notes, he had taken the resolution "to pronounce those words that are so difficult for me to say: 'I am wrong, I made a mistake.'"[80]

Father Antoine Telmon

The entry in the Founder's journal for May 17, 1837 is a personal and confidential reflection on an Oblate in the field. It reads as follows:

> Ah! how much our dear Father Telmon needs to work on his temperament. ... Still, I must admit I was pleased with the way he took my remarks and reprimands. Granted, I spoke to him with a great deal of kindness and discretion, without, however, concealing the truth from him. It is dangerous for a young man not yet sufficiently grounded in virtue to be so successful in everything he does, who thus becomes the object of everyone's admiration. Selfishness and pride creep in and he grows blind to his own defects. The reprimands of superiors who notice such defects then become unbearable because they are considered unjust and the result

---

[78] *Oblate Writings,* vol. 1, pp. 106-107, n. 46.

[79] Ibid., p. 111, n. 50.

[80] *Écrits spirituels,* p. 38, n. 15.

of jealous prejudice. Respect and obedience are soon jeopardized, murmurs, complaints and more, enter the picture and a person can go far out of line like that. Such, exactly, is Father Telmon's case. He was very successful in everything in Corsica and everyone vied to praise him. It has come to the point where the bishop happened to tell me the other day that Father Telmon was necessary for the diocese and that there would be a general upheaval were I to recall him. Father Telmon needs much more virtue than he now possesses to resist such enticements. He has suffered the consequences thereof and I pray God he will realize them and remedy them in time.[81]

Here, again, we see the Founder's concern for the spiritual growth of an individual Oblate. These are his private thoughts and preoccupations – they do not appear in any administrative letter. Moreover, this entry in his journal ends with a prayer for Father Telmon. The same concern is evidenced in a letter that the Founder wrote to Father Honorat concerning Telmon. Now, however, the tone changes: it is an administrative counsel:

Obviously you do not know your people and you write under the impression of the moment which is soon replaced by another which is quite the contrary. And on this subject, I would like to ask you where you find that the superior general desires to correspond with members of the Society solely through the intermediary of the local superior? That is what one must conclude from your recommendation, repeated several times, that any advice I might have to give to the Fathers of your community, and especially to Father Telmon, should be sent through you. But that cannot be, my dear friend, and I will do that less than ever since I now know that in my letters to you, you suppress the communications that I insert precisely for such-and-such a person, or for all in general. You reserve the right to judge the opportuneness of my observations, my remonstrances, my reproaches. You understand that this cannot be.

The manner in which you speak to me of Father Telmon in your last letter worries me. With such an attitude, it would be very difficult to draw out the best in this Father who could, nevertheless, be so useful to you. You cannot keep something from being noticed when it preoccupies you so. I am afraid that you will end up giving the impression that you are more afraid of his superior talent than of the abuse he might make of it. You have to realize that he is no longer a child and you will not obtain much through the use of your authority, especially if he has grounds to believe that you are deluding yourself. Believe me, I have told you often that it would be better to come to an amicable agreement.[82]

The superior general's concern is obvious. It comes through very differently in each individual case, but it is there.

---

[81] *Selected Texts*, pp. 103-104, n. 84.
[82] *Oblate Writings,* vol. 1, p. 50, n. 20.

The Founder's Love and Affection for the Oblates

In Chapter 5 we saw that a cursory reading of many of Eugene's letters to Oblates might by today's standards leave the impression that his affection had overflowed into gushy sentimentality. From the outset, however, we must remember two things: Eugene de Mazenod came from Provence – a man born to the warm Latin temperament and expression of the *Midi* – and he came Europe's Romantic Age, with its flowery – even theatrical – way of expressing itself. We can already see this theatricality in his letters from Palermo, especially at the death of his "second mother," the Duchess of Cannizzaro. But it goes a lot deeper than that.

"Combien de Corps Pour un Optimum d'Esprit?"

Often, in speaking of his affection for the Oblates, Eugene de Maze-nod said that *his love was a special gift from God.* That expression has its echo in Teilhard de Chardin's reaction to a prevalent *machista* attitude that disdains whatever is material, "sentimental" or too-human in the Church of Jesus. We cannot deny the attraction of creature comforts, material things and human affection. We can chose how we face the situation: either succumb hedonistically to the temptation and charm of creature comforts and give in totally to our affections, or harden ourselves, distrusting creatures and squelching any hint of affectionate relationships.

In the strict and severe religious formation of a generation ago, the second was the obvious choice. In a world of solemn liturgies and coldly intellectual sermons, how very often was it drummed into the seminarian: "Watch your emotions!" "Don't express your affections too warmly!" "Be careful of particular friendships!" and so forth.. For one formed on the basis of such counsels, it becomes difficult indeed to be comfortable with the warm affection that Eugene de Mazenod so often expressed.

Teilhard de Chardin's reaction to this severe attitude was the *Tertia Via* – the Third Way – a call for passivity. However, it is a passivity that heeds God's love in our lives – letting God in and acknowledging that everything, including affection itself, is a gift of God. We cause it to bear fruit as a gift of the Lord, *not as a personal talent.* The Third Way can help us better understand Eugene de Mazenod's outlook. At the same time it is obvious that practising the Third Way requires great and deep internal freedom.

Teilhard de Chardin posed a cryptic question about internal freedom in its relation to warm affection: *combien de corps pour un optimum d'esprit?* – *how much body for an optimum of spirit?* The reply is eminently personal and can only be made responsibly by someone who is authentically free. It is not a question of limits, of how far one can go. It is, instead, the spirit taking over and transcending the corporeal. It is the *agape* that God gives us for an optimum of the spirit.

Receptivity

Texas Oblate and spiritual theologian Father Kelly Nemeck wrote and defended his thesis on Saint John of the Cross, in French at the University of Lyon. He titled the English translation *Receptivity*. It takes Teilhard's premise of passivity perhaps a step further, because it better describes what it means to be conscious and aware of God's gift of love in one's life. Such a gift belongs to God, not to me. But I am open – receptive – to it and make it fruitful precisely because it belongs to God and I am attuned to God.

Being receptive also means that one receives the Lord's gifts with open arms, all the while acknowledging that they remain the property of the Lord. For that reason I can welcome my heart's warm affection and feel at ease with it. Eugene de Mazenod never said this in so many words, yet reading his writings we find it between the lines.

Receptivity in St. Eugene's Life

There is a significant entry in his journal on September 4, 1837, upon the death from cholera of his housekeeper, Dauphin:

> I declare that I cannot grasp how those who do not love human persons – who deserve to be loved – can love God. Hence, it is understandable that I see no reason to disown or even hide the feelings within me. Let him who may be tempted to find fault with me know that I have little fear of his judgment and that I could forcefully prove to him that *I have every reason to thank God for having given me a heart that is better able to understand the heart of Jesus Christ our Master*, who made, animates and inspires mine better than those cold egoistic logicians who apparently put their heart into their brain and do not know how to love anyone because, in the final analysis, they love only themselves . . . .They try to impose on us a type of perfection more worthy of the Stoics than of true Christians! Let us love God because of his infinite perfection; let us also love him because he has loved us first.[83]

Eugene de Mazenod clearly considered his capacity for warm love and affection to be a special grace from God. On April 24, 1855, writing to Father Antoine Mouchette, the spiritual director of the scholastic students at Montolivet, he confided, "I love my sons more – immeasurably more – than any other human person could love them. *That is a gift that I have received*

---

[83] *Selected Texts*, pp. 381-382, n. 327.

from God, for which I do not cease to thank him, for it flows from one of his most beautiful attributes and because I have reason to believe that he may perhaps not have granted it to anyone else in the same proportion as he has to me."[84]

And again to Father Mouchette, two years later, on March 22, 1857:

> Often I have told the Lord that, since he gave me a mother's heart and sons who merit my love in so many ways, he must allow me to love them immeasurably. I do this in good conscience. It seems, dearly beloved son, that the more I love someone like yourself, the more I love God, the source and bond of our mutual affection. This sentiment is a permanent feature in my soul. I bear it with me wherever I may be. . . .[85]

In a letter already mentioned, written to Father Christophe Bonjean of the Ceylon mission on November 9, 1852, Bishop de Mazenod expressed much the same conviction:

> We have never seen each other but you must admit, my dear Father, that we already love each other a great deal. For me *it is an instinct that God gives me,* or rather, a quality for which I thank him daily, that my heart is entirely bound to all those whom his goodness gives me. Nothing makes me understand the love which God has for all his children more than the feeling I have for all those who belong to me and to whom, for my part, I am entirely devoted . . . . Thus it is, my dear Father, that without having had the consolation of seeing you I love you with all my heart.[86]

Expressions of his Affection

To Father Henri Faraud, Bishop de Mazenod wrote on May 10, 1848:

> There is a father beyond the great lake whom you must not forget. Rest assured you are always present to me, whatever the distance separating you from him, not only at the holy altar where each day he offers the Holy Sacrifice for the family and all its members, but during the day's routine and in the frequent conversations wherein the names of his children, their ministry, their strenuous labours and all the good they do are constantly present in his memory or on his lips. Why then, dear son, when Father Aubert writes me, do you not add some lines to his letter or, better still, why not write directly and tell me about yourself and narrate what you have done for the glory of God? Twice a year, there being no means to correspond more frequently, is not difficult to manage and you would give me so much pleasure, so much benefit.
>
> You do not know me very well if you do not know how much I love you. So, make up, my dear child, for your past negligence by writing down your story for me, since your departure for the missions up to the day your letter

---

[84] *Oblate Writings,* vol. 11, p. 266, n. 1269.

[85] Ibid., vol. 12, p. 49, n. 1345.

[86] Ibid., vol. 4, n. 49, p. 147.

is dated. For that you take a large sheet of paper and you write on all four pages – and more, if necessary – or continue in a second letter from where your story leaves off. There is no detail to which I am indifferent All that comes to me from my children interests me in the highest degree. Give me that pleasure, my dear Father Faraud. I ask it in return for the good I wish you, for the friendship and the paternal love I have for you.[87]

Four years later, on May 1, 1852, he wrote again to Father Faraud:

It does not matter, my dear son, that you are at the end of the world, for you are always present to my heart, which feeds on the love I feel for you. Believe that this is the feeling uppermost in my soul. I ask you a favour: never imagine that if by chance I have made any little observation that might possibly be taken as a reproach, that my esteem and my affection for you could ever be lessened by the tiniest degree. You could never love me with one-hundredth of the love with which I love you. *God, who destined me to be the father of a large family, has made me a sharer in the immensity of his love for humankind.* So do not delay in answering me.[88]

Similar expressions can be found in a letter to Father Telmon, written on December 18, 1848. Telmon, who frequently had problems getting along with his confrères, had just grieved the Founder by his bitter complaints:

Just the sight of your handwriting made me tremble with joy. When I see the writing of those I love it has more effect on me than their portrait would have. You act, nevertheless, as though you had no idea how much I love you. Otherwise, would you remain so long without writing me and, when you do write, would you write as you do? Not only are you unconcerned about afflicting me with complaints and incessant grumbling but not one of your letters fails to include some painful barbs directed at me which wound the most sensitive part of my heart, that part wherein lies the tender affection that I have for you . . . . I implore you, dear son, never say such things to me and, moreover, never think them. It is now twenty-seven years since I adopted you and since you have been living in my heart – and you are on the verge of believing that my idea is to abandon you! If you were fair you would say: my superior, my Father, loves me so much despite the bitterness I have caused him, and despite my behaving in a manner for which he could reproach me, his heart has never changed . . . .[89]

In a long letter covering several administrative points about the Ceylon mission, Saint Eugene also expressed his affection for Father Semeria and the Oblates who were announcing the Good News in that distant island: "Remember me to each of the Fathers individually. I wish I could write to each of them directly but that is impossible. Therefore, let them know, at least, that they are all in my thoughts and have a special place in my heart. I

---

[87] *Oblate Writings,* vol. 1, n. 95, p. 192.
[88] Ibid., vol. 2, p. 40, n. 165.
[89] Ibid., vol. 1, pp. 206-207, n. 106.

bless them and you, too, my son."[90] When the Founder sent young Father Vital Grandin to the Red River mission he wrote the following to Father François Bermond, the superior in St. Boniface: "I often speak about you with Father Rey; he can tell you I love you and I can repeat it. But will you one day be so good as to say the same to me? It would bring me extreme happiness, for I live only by the heart."[91]

Similarly, the Founder wrote to Father Ambroise Vincens on March 9, 1853: "What, in your goodness, you told me at the end of your letter was a balm for my heart, a balm that it savoured with inexpressible consolation. May you be blessed, my son. You know well, whether or not I concur with the sentiments you express, that my life is to follow my heart."[92] And to Father Dassy at Bordeaux he wrote on January 10, 1852:

> As for the delightful Father de l'Hermite, what a treasure I have given you in him! I do not know how my heart is equal to the affection which it nourishes for you all. *It is a prodigy which is something of an attribute of God.* I love my new children, such as Father de l'Hermite, beyond all telling, without slackening in any way the love I have for our veterans such as you, for example. No, on this earth there is not a creature to whom God has accorded the favour of loving such a great number of persons so tenderly, so strongly, so constantly. It is not simply a question of charity; no, it is a maternal sentiment toward each of you individually, without prejudicing any of the others. Not one of you could be loved more than I love him. I love each one fully as if he were the only beloved and I experience that really exquisite feeling for each one. It is wonderful! So fortunate do I count myself in being able to enjoy such a privilege that I sometimes wonder if God is not already giving me a payment in this world for what little I have done for his glory.[93]

Such expressions of affection help us understand why Saint Eugene suffered so much at any Oblate's death. When he received word from Texas that Father Hippolyte de Lustrac and Brother José Garc'a had succumbed to yellow fever and that the superior, Father Auguste Gaudet, was near death from the same fever, a cry of agony rose from the depths of his soul. We hear it in a letter of November 26, 1858:

> What a terrible blow, my dear children! I am not made for such unhappiness and I have the feeling that I will never get used to it. The loss of dear Father de Lustrac and the poor Brother was enough already. And now I will have to wait for your next letter under the crushing burden of the threat to the life of our good Father Gaudet . . . . What has happened to

---

[90] *Oblate Writings*, vol. 4, p. 102, n. 30.

[91] Ibid., vol. 2, , p. 74 n. 192.

[92] Ibid., vol. 11, p. 175, n. 1187.

[93] Ibid., pp. 69-70, n. 1095.

him? . . . Would you be so kind as to tell me by the first possible post? How long these days of waiting are going to seem to me! In the name of the good God, reassure me as soon as possible. For my heart, hours are like days and days, like weeks.

Cruel Texas missions! What terrible wounds you inflict on my soul! This is the fifth victim you have devoured and what has become, I repeat, of the sixth whom you have struck with such fierce blows? My God, forgive me this cry of anguish! I do not presume to murmur against the dispositions of your Providence, and I know with an assurance that is more than confidence that you only call to yourself those whom you take away from us in order to reward them with eternal happiness, but this heart you have given me, so sensitive and so loving, could it not be torn apart by so early a separation?[94]

Physical Expression of the Founder's Love

Eugene de Mazenod's regal mien and his brusque manner often made him seem icy and overbearing. Sometimes it was even more than brusqueness. Indeed, it could be like the blast of a *mistral* wind, as many attested. Yet the poor and others who knew him well knew he held no malice. Timon-David gives us an account of a late-night encounter with the bishop, one that did not begin very auspiciously. After climbing the stairs to the second floor, the timid and dejected young priest thought better of disturbing the aged prelate, whose hunched figure was outlined by a lamp as he sat in absorbed attention behind a huge desk. The priest tip-toed away from the open study door and had almost reached the end of the corridor when a stentorian voice boomed out of the study. Timon-David recounts:

"Who's there?"

At that question, made snappishly, I started meekly towards his door.

"It is I, Monseigneur."

"Who told you I was here? Can't a bishop have a moment's peace?"

I didn't know which way to move and my knees were knocking. I then replied, "I'm sorry, Monseigneur. I'll leave."

"No, as long as you're already here, wait for me in the hallway." A moment later I heard a formidable *"Entrez!"* Stammering, I tried to explain what had brought me there, and as I went along there were clear signs that his heart was softening. The storm was passing. He became kind again, then affectionate and, finally, fatherly.

"But my child, when you have troubles like this, why don't you come and tell me about them? Am I not your father?" And with those words he

---

[94] *Oblate Writings,* vol. 2, p. 202, n. 260.

embraced me and my cheeks were moistened by his tears. No one I ever knew could mesmerize me as he could.[95]

The Grace of Jesus' Example

When Eugene de Mazenod thought affectionately of his Oblates, it was progressively with the perspective of the apostolate, in an attitude of faith. The letters he wrote toward the end of his life attest to that far more clearly than those written at the beginning. We can see the purification that came from the trials of his dark night. Frequently, the warm expressions of affection are the same, but after the long years of catharsis they are always placed in an apostolic context and in an attitude of faith. In the affection he had for his Oblates, he discovered more and more a loving Jesus Christ, and that he was called to love as his Master loved. Following the entry in his journal on the housekeeper Dauphin's death, Saint Eugene went on to write, "Let us study Saint John, fathom the heart of Saint Peter and his love for his divine Master, and especially, let us deeply probe all that flows from the loving heart of Jesus Christ not only for all humankind, but especially, for the Apostles and Disciples, and then let them dare to come and preach to us a love that is speculative, without feeling or affection."[96]

Like Jesus before the tomb of Lazarus, Eugene de Mazenod was not afraid to let his sorrow show. When news arrived from Nancy of 48-year-old Father Eugene Dorey's death, on the heels of the demise in quick succession of Fathers Victor Lacombe, 29 (Jaffna), Jean-Paul Pasqualini, 30 (Ajaccio), Casimir Chauvet, 43 (Romans) and Bartholomé Duperray, 27 (Brownsville), he was torn apart. In a letter to Father Jean-Baptiste Conrard, dated March 19, 1855, he wrote:

> I am overwhelmed! Before opening your letter, as I was holding it in my hand, I said to Father de l'Hermite who was alone with me, "I always open letters from our men with some apprehension." And I was not wrong! What a blow after so many others! I must drink the chalice down to the very dregs. May God give me the strength to bear up under it. If I were more virtuous I would rejoice to see our little family provide heaven with such a large number of elect, for all of our men die in the Lord's peace in the midst of the most holy ministry – mostly victims of their own charity, true martyrs of the first of all virtues. But since the Lord has given me the heart of a father to an eminent degree, if I feel all the consolation, I also experience all the weakness. I most certainly love you with a supernatural love, but I also love you in the manner of, and I dare to say even more tenderly than an earthly father. Thus, even though I do rejoice in the Lord over the blessed predestination of all of my children whom the Lord calls

---

[95] Leflon, vol. 4, p. 309.
[96] *Selected Texts*, p. 383, n. 327.

to himself, my heart is nevertheless torn in a cruel way. And that, to the point where yesterday I marvelled that I could even resist.[97]

When the news of Father Dorey's death came after so many other deaths and Father Casimir Aubert's stroke, he wrote, ". . . like a hammer blow which plunged me into a new sea of sorrow. . . . May I now say to our Master that it is too much!"[98]

Two months later, in a letter written to Father Jean Jeanmaire at Nancy on May 25, 1855, we find the Founder still grieving the loss of so many young Oblates, two of whom – Chauvet and Duperray – had died continents apart but on the same day. He said:

> Such preoccupations are great enough to overwhelm those younger and less strong than I . . . . Everyone is astonished at the vigour the good Lord grants me. But what would it take for this fine appearance to vanish? A grain of sand or a drop of water! I therefore do not count on the longevity that everyone is entertaining enough to accord me, but I use the good health that the Lord grants me to fulfil as best I can the responsibilities laid upon me, acknowledging all the while that I am powerless to be adequate therein according to my wish and the need.

> The loss of our men is the only cross that my poor heart cannot bear to support. These are always open bleeding wounds that will heal only with my own death. Never will others understand the furnace of love that God has put into my heart, a heart which may perhaps give forth too much of what rightly should belong more to God. But I am not going to be scrupulous about that.[99]

The Grace of the Oblate Bond

Eugene de Mazenod frequently expressed his love of the Oblates in prayer. In another letter on December 2, 1854, again to Father Mouchette, the spiritual director of the scholastic community at Montolivet, he asserted that brotherly love is a characteristic of the Oblate charism:

> How very often I attend to your interests before the good God . . . Such love – which is more than simply a paternal love of the head for the members of the family – such cordial affinity of the members for their head which establishes between them a relationship springing from the heart and forms true family ties between us – father to son, son to father – *this I have not come across anywhere else. I have always thanked God, for it is a particular gift which he has deigned to grant me*; for it is the temper of the heart that he has given me, this expansive gift which is my own gift and which pours itself out on each one of them without taking anything

---

[97] *Oblate Writings*, vol. 11, p. 259, n. 1260.

[98] Ibid., p. 259.

[99] Ibid., vol. 11, p. 271, n. 1273.

from the others, just like, I make bold to say, God's love for humankind. *I say that it is this sentiment, which I know comes from Him who is the source of all charity, that has evoked in the hearts of my children the reciprocity of love which forms the distinctive character of our beloved family.* May this help us mutually to appreciate the beauty of our vocation and may it be attributed to God for his greater glory. That is the most ardent wish of my heart.[100]

Charity Is the Pivot

In a letter of July 29, 1830, from Fribourg to Father Guibert at Notre-Dame de Laus, the Founder takes up much the same theme, one that would carry right through to his deathbed 30 years later:

Charity is the pivot on which our whole existence turns . . . . Charity for our neighbour is an essential part of our spirit. We practice it first amongst ourselves by loving each other as brothers, by never considering our Society other than the most united family on the earth, by rejoicing just as much over the virtues, the talents and other qualities that our brothers possess, as if we ourselves possessed them, in bearing with mildness the little faults that some have not yet overcome, covering them over with the mantle of the most sincere charity, etc. In regard to the rest of humankind, we consider ourselves only as the servants of the Father of the family, commanded to console, assist and bring back his children by working to the utmost, in the midst of tribulations and persecutions of every kind, without claiming any reward beyond that which the Lord had promised to faithful servants who have worthily fulfilled their mission.[101]

Conclusion

In the letters quoted we see how keenly aware Saint Eugene was of God's gifts – heart, health, unity, the list goes on. How clearly he saw that God had showered him with special gifts. He thanked the Lord and did his utmost to develop those gifts. His warm affection for the Oblates was eminently theocentric. With such a mentality the Founder was faithful to his duty as superior general. It is an example that gives Missionary Oblates direction in their own lives, without having to imitate their Founder's style or expressions of affection. But like him, they too must seek to develop all the qualities they receive as gifts from the Lord, including the richness of their sensitivity. Just as Eugene de Mazenod could accomplish this following his long dark night of purification, so all Oblates should be challenged by his grace to fulfil their own gifts for the mission.

---

[100] *Oblate Writings*, vol. 11, p. 262, n. 1264.
[101] Ibid., vol. 7, pp. 202-203, n. 350.

Eugene de Mazenod did not try to root out his feelings. Instead, he brought together his qualities, his talents and his duties. It brings us back to Teilhard's question, *combien du corps pour un optimum d'esprit?* The answer, as Eugene gradually discovered, is personal. It is a grace-filled gift from God that comes with maturity and true freedom.

Eugene de Mazenod's personality went through progressive changes in the day-to-day experience of living in a society that was itself changing. Nothing better illustrates this than the three portraits shown here, as different as the dates on which they were made. The first shows a young priest, characterized by provocative austerity: neglected hair-styling, drawn face and piercing eyes, the composite revealing the resolute look of a Restoration missionary, ready to hurl himself into the struggle for souls in order to reshape a society spiritually deformed by the Revolution. The second portrait, made when he became Bishop of Icosia, accentuates his self-assurance. He is every inch a bishop of the time of Charles X: long sideburns, innate authority, firm determination; less austerely dressed, he reflects his aristocracy, although he still retains the same intensity and the same lack of gentleness found in the first portrait. Completely different, however, is the photograph of an old man marked by his trials; it leaves an impression of a man of fatigue and sad weariness. The strength and forcefulness are still there, but one guesses that he lacks any illusions about human capabilities and that in him mingle meekness and serenity; in the deep-set and half-closed eyes, what was once a flame has become a glow.[102]

---

[102]From Leflon, vol. 4, p. 306.

VIII

Missionary Oblate

The French School Of Spirituality

France, embroiled in the bloody Thirty Years War during the first half of the 17th century, found herself besieged from all quarters. Though she was a centre of power in Europe, and in the forefront of Europe's new war technology, with superb cannons and military skills, France was also surrounded by powerful enemies: the English, the Dutch and the Hapsburgs. Add to that a bloody civil war and it appeared the nation was about to break apart. At the same time, France was experiencing a tremendous cultural and artistic explosion. The humanism of the Renaissance, sparked by the rediscovery of Greek and Roman civilizations, appeared about to lay the Middle Ages and Christianity permanently to rest. This was the time of giants like da Vinci, Michelangelo, Rabelais, Cervantes, and Shakespeare, of Velázquez, El Greco, and Rubens, a time when Nicholas Copernicus argued for a revolutionary heliocentric system of astronomy and Galileo defended him. Little wonder that in France respect for human reason rose to dizzying heights and everything acceptable had to withstand the test of experimentation. Eminent thinkers called for a tabula rasa – a return of humanity and civilization to a blank tablet on which would be engraved a glorious renewal.

Philosopher René Descartes was far from alone in calling for a new approach. A group led by Cardinal Pierre de Bérulle (1575-1629) sought to renew the way people saw themselves as Christians. Collectively, the movement came to be known as the French School of Spirituality. Susan Muto, in her preface to *Bérulle and the French School,* describes a *school* thus:

> In the Roman Catholic tradition a special school represents and articulates the common ways of the faith – repentance, prayer, meditation on scripture, devotion to the sacraments – but its expression of these foundations includes a distinctive typology of styles and emphases. Special schools thus contain the essentials of a gospel, a Christian and church-oriented spirituality, but they enable people so attracted to them to personalize these basics in a special, even intense manner that at once

awakens them to God in a new way and facilitates their ongoing formation.[1]

Those Who Shaped the French School

Many elements came together to give the French School its extraordinary vitality. Among them were Cardinal Bérulle's own founding of the Oratory (1611) and his introduction of the reformed Carmelites to France (1604), thus exposing French thought to St. Teresa of Jesus through Mother Madeleine de St-Joseph, the first French prioress. At the same time, the Abbés Charles de Condren (1588-1641) and Jean-Jacques Olier (1608-1657) founded and inspired the Sulpicians, who to this day have been the predominant formators of the French clergy. It was Olier who began the Seminary of St-Sulpice in Paris in 1641-1642. The Founder of the Oblates would do his priestly studies there, not in the impressive original building on the Place St-Sulpice beside the magnificent church of the same name – that building was confiscated in the Revolution and later demolished by Napoleon – but in another edifice on the adjacent rue du Pot-de-Fer, now known as rue Bonaparte.

Other notable contributors to the vitality of the French School of Spirituality were St. John Eudes, founder of the Eudists and of the Sisters of Charity (who inspired the foundation of the Good Shepherd and the Little Sisters of the Poor), St. Vincent de Paul and the Lazarists, along with their feminine arm, the Sisters of Charity of St. Vincent de Paul.

At the heart of this Christian renewal – which some have likened to a Copernican revolution – was one very essential intuition: one's personal experience of Jesus Christ. Since the scientific and humanist spirit would not concede that the idea of God could be the subject of experimentation, one had to deal, first and foremost, with Jesus as a person. After all, Jesus had an historic existence of which we have empirical evidence. And through Jesus, one could retrace "the way" to God (John 14:6). Louis Cognet, an incisive researcher into French theology, wrote: "The Incarnate Word was to be God's essential manifestation: in him the incomprehensible God becomes understandable, the ineffable God makes himself heard, and the invisible God becomes visible. Thus, it is pure illusion to try to reach God other than through this essential manifestation."[2]

---

[1] *Bérulle and the French School*, Paulist Press, New York, 1989, p. xv.
[2] *Histoire de la spiritualité chrétienne*, Abier, 1966.

About the inherent tensions in the French School's mysticism and on the experiential tightrope it had to tread, William Thompson commented:

> One of the greatest sources of renewal . . . must be the breakthroughs in mystical thought and practice. On one level, surely, this mystical renaissance can be seen as a creative alternative to the dogmatic aridity of the prevailing school theology. It represents a deep effort to remain in tune with the experiential sources of faith and theology. On another level, too, it can be seen as a reaction against what is perceived to be an excessively humanistic trend in the Renaissance period. In other words, this mysticism is a tension-filled reality moving between two extremes. At times it fell into those extremes.[3]

The founders of the French School of Spirituality, especially St. John Eudes, pondered deeply St. Paul's words about all Christians forming but one body with Christ. Accordingly, every aspect of reality must be incorporated in Jesus Christ, thus making world history the building of Christ's mystical body.

The French School – Not a Philosophical Exercise

Although the Oratory produced several great philosophers – among them, Malebranche (1638-1715) – it was a movement primarily characterized by a rejection of abstract philosophical research. In its place, members actively sought to have the world know Jesus as he is. The richness of the French School was exemplified by the devotion to the Sacred Hearts of Jesus and Mary, begun by St. John Eudes. It found its essential expression in giving thanks to God for the love of Jesus toward all persons, known in religious experience, and for the union of all believers in the prayer of Jesus who seeks to present us all to the Father. Thus two concurrent lines run through the spirituality of the French School: adoration of the immense mystery of God – Jesus is the perfect representative worshiper of the Father – and devotion to the loving attitude of Jesus and Mary. In this spiritual understanding, Mary's innermost being is grounded in the life of Jesus within her. The same applies to the disciple. Thus it is easy to see why Eugene de Mazenod was partial to the prayer *O Jesus vivens in Maria*:

> O Jesus living in Mary, come and live in your servant:
>
> in the spirit of your holiness, in the fullness of your power,
>
> in the reality of your virtues, in the perfection of your ways,
>
> in the communion of your mysteries;
>
> have dominion over every adverse power,

---

[3] *Bérulle and the French School,* Paulist Press, New York, 1989, p. 9.

in your own Spirit, to the glory of God the Father.[4]

From that prayer we can see that the spirituality of the French School sought to continue in its time the respect that Jesus had shown for the men and women of his time. It did so mainly through a three-part focus on the Incarnate Word. *Adoration*: I bring Jesus before the eyes of my mind. *Communion*: I bring Jesus into my heart. *Cooperation*: Jesus in my hands and on my lips – in other words, applying one's new-found love to everybody that one meets and everything that one does.

Reaching Out to the World

The spirituality of the French School was essentially mystic, not metaphysical. Nonetheless, in its union with Jesus it sought to reach out into the world, to confront society's problems. Bérulle, for example, opposed the worldly and unprincipled Cardinal Richelieu and reconciled King Louis XII with his mother. St. John Eudes attacked the enslavement wreaked by prostitution and in later life entered into the reform of seminaries. St. Vincent de Paul and his nuns became the champions of the destitute and of foundlings. He was also deeply involved in priestly reform. The Council of Trent had legislated the foundation of seminaries, but it had never become law in France. Thus, Vincent de Paul railed:

> The church has no worse enemies than her own priests. Heresies have come from them . . . and it is through them that heresies have prevailed, that vice has reigned, and that ignorance has established its throne among the poor people; and this has happened because of the undisciplined way of life and the refusal to oppose these three torrents now inundating the earth with all their might.[5]

It is easy to see how, 150 years later, this must have strongly influenced an ardent and impressionable young Eugene de Mazenod and how it would form a part of his spiritual makeup for life.

While Ignatian spirituality stems from the same period in history and has several elements that coincide with the spirituality of Bérulle, it differs markedly from the French School in its approach to meditation and contemplation. St. Ignatius tended to set up a scene for the imagination: to imagine, for example, Christ's Nativity, putting oneself in that scene, imagining what it must have been like to be a shepherd or one of the magi, searching the whys and wherefores of their actions and thought, etc. The French School

---

[4] *Oblate Prayer Book* (English), p. 23.
[5] André Dodin, *Entretiens spirituels aux missionnaires*, Paris, Seuil, 1960, p. 502.

concentrated on trying to unite oneself to Jesus Christ, the Incarnate Word, to worship God as he does, and to reproduce within one's own mind and heart the attitude, the sentiments and the spirit of Jesus himself.

The French School on the Priesthood

We get a clear idea of the French School's teaching on the priesthood from Father Olier's book *Traité des saints ordres (Treatise on Holy Orders)* and from de Condren's *L'idée du sacerdoce et du sacrifice (The Idea of Priesthood and Sacrifice)*. Here are some excerpts and commentary:

The priest must reproduce the features of Jesus Christ the Priest in his own life.

> It is the priest who gives continuity to the life of Jesus Christ, our head.[6]

> Accordingly, in the Church, the priest is a living Jesus Christ . . .who is endowed with a plenitude of grace and divine riches, not only for his own perfection but for that of all the people.[7]

In the exercise of his priesthood, Jesus Christ is the perfect worshiper of his Father. He is totally dedicated.

> "What a life is yours, O Divine Priest! I see in you only priesthood. Everywhere I see nothing but sacrifice . . . all your life breathes consecration."[8]

Olier presents the resurrection of Christ as the culmination of the salvific sacrifice. That was to be a key concept in the life of Saint Eugene de Mazenod. Indeed, as bishop of Marseilles, his pastoral letters repeatedly insisted on the Resurrection as the most important feast of the liturgical year.

To reproduce Christ's features, the priest must be totally consecrated.

> That is why priests must have a great devotion to Our Lord in his Resurrection, for on that day he was proclaimed priest. Moreover, it is in that mystery that he established the priesthood and the graces of priesthood. And since, on that day, he triumphed over the world, the flesh and sin, and was thus completely consumed in God his Father, it is fitting that on that day, too, he also wished to share that grace with everyone – especially with priests who, like him strive to be hosts consecrated to God.[9]

---

[6] Olier, *Traité des saints ordres,* Paris, 1929, p. 420.
[7] Ibid., p. 421.
[8] Condren, *L'idée du sacerdoce et du sacrifice,* Paris, 1925, p. 443.
[9] Olier, *Traité des saints ordres,* Paris, 1929, p. 436.

The priest can only be dedicated in so far as he is the giver of God.

Everything can only be explained and take place through the mutual gift of the Father and the Son and by our response to that gift:

> When the Father gives himself to the Son, he also gives himself to all who are submitted to the Son; when Jesus gives himself to the Father he also gives to him all who are united to him [Cf. John 17:6 and 14:20]. Thus, by this adorable sacrament there takes place a perfect communion and a complete society formed by God with humankind, and humankind with God. And it all comes about only through the ministry of priests and through priestly virtue.[10]

Conclusion

The essential goal of the French school was embodied in the dictum of St-Sulpice: *Vivere summe Deo in Christo Jesu!* – to live entirely for God in Christ Jesus! That, according to Olier, is the first and final end of seminary training. The fundamental point of this doctrine on the priesthood is that the priest is dedicated – *given* – with and like Christ. "Since a priest should be entirely consumed in Christ, it follows that his heart must be continually filled with the marks of his faith and be in a perpetual state of adoration, love and reverence – a heart that, like the Eucharistic host is completely given to God's praise. In a word, a priest's sacrifice must be a perfect holocaust."[11] In speaking of the priesthood, the key words used by the French School of Spirituality are: *gift, victim, host, sacrifice* and *oblation.* Eugene de Mazenod would especially bring the last of these – oblation – into his own life and into the life of the congregation he founded.

Missionary Oblate

Eugene de Mazenod's Spiritual Perspective

Although the French School of Spirituality of St-Sulpice left a definitive mark on Eugene de Mazenod's spiritual outlook, it is obvious that he had not exactly arrived at the seminary without the stamp of earlier influences. Indeed, his spiritual life had already been broadened and enriched by his considerable experience. We have already seen, for example, how the call to be sent to the poor had been deeply anchored in his heart by Don Bartolo in Venice and later, as a young layman in Aix, by his work among prisoners.

---

[10] Olier, *Traité des saints ordres,* Paris, 1929, p. 461.
[11] Ibid., p. 507.

We can truly say that Eugene first heard the call of the Church through the needs of the poor – it was not just something he encountered in the halls of St-Sulpice. Instead, it was the aspect of Jesus Christ that he discovered in a very special way in his Good Friday conversion experience of 1807. Realizing the Christ had shed his precious blood out of love for all humankind and, at the same time, seeing so many people who did not know Christ as their Saviour, impelled Eugene to go to the most abandoned. While he did at times speak in the Sulpician manner of Christ as the *Priest* who is totally dedicated to the glory of the Father, the heart of his vocation and his spiritual perspective led him to follow Jesus as the *Saviour* unconditionally throughout his life. In July, 1816, just months after establishing his little band of missionaries, we see him already insisting that stress must be put on the fact that Jesus Christ is *Saviour*.

> I want you to change the end of our litanies; instead of saying *Jesu sacerdos* (Christ the priest), we must say *Christus salvator* (Christ the Saviour). Such is the aspect under which we should contemplate our divine Master. Our particular vocation is such that we are associated in a special way with the redemption of humankind. . . . Would that we endeavoured, by the sacrifice of our entire being, not to render his redemption useless, neither to ourselves nor to those we are called to evangelize.[12]

Eugene de Mazenod's Spiritual Credentials

There were three major influences from his childhood and youth which would constantly act as a modifying force throughout his life:

The Tutoring of Don Bartolo in Venice – The Ignatian Approach

Remember Eugene, the boy, barely into his teens, leading a quasi-monastic life in Venice. The suppression of the Jesuits had frustrated Don Bartolo's wish to enter the Company of Jesus, but he was a Jesuit at heart and well-versed in Ignatian spirituality. He schooled Eugene in Ignatian meditation with active reflections on Scripture and on the virtues applied to his life situation. Moreover, the call to be sent to the poor and the attraction of overseas missions had already been anchored in his heart in Venice.

Exile in Palermo – St. Alphonsus

While in exile in Palermo during his late teens, Eugene had a passing acquaintance with the life of St. Alphonsus. Eventually, after coming to

---

[12] Rambert, vol. 1, pp. 190-191, and *Selected Texts*, pp. 28-29, n. 6.

know the saint's spirituality and moral theology in Italy, that interest would lead him, as a zealous parochial mission preacher, to introduce Liguorian moral theology to France. It would also mature and enter into both the rule and into his lifelong spiritual outlook. Later, as a young priest, after he had delved more deeply into St. Alphonsus' moral theology in Italy, he would write:

> Our particular vocation is such that we are associated in a special manner with the redemption of humankind; the Blessed Liguori also put his Congregation under the protection of the Saviour. Would that we would endeavour, by the sacrifice of our entire being, to render his redemption useful, both to ourselves and to those whom we are called to evangelize.[13]

Reacculturation in France – A Return to Ignatius

We saw that Eugene returned at 20 to Aix, to disillusionment, to family problems and to a whirl of shallow pleasures. Nevertheless, a healthy new longing took hold of the young man; it was at this point that he met Father Magy. The ex-Jesuit further schooled the young de Mazenod in Ignatian spirituality, leading him to listen more closely to what the Lord had to say to him.

How Saint Eugene de Mazenod Linked Prayer and the Apostolate

Groping to Find His Way

Even after ordination Eugene was still not sure what direction the Lord wanted his priesthood to take. He even contemplated monastic life, setting up a Trappist-like regimen with Brother Maur while living with his grandmother on the rue Papassaudi in Aix.[14]

> In his first years as a priest Father de Mazenod struggled to find a balance between contemplation and action in his life. At first he tried to remain faithful to the schedule of a good seminarian. Then he gave himself over to frenzied apostolic activity .... As he grew in the Lord, his attitude became simpler; the question was less a problem of balance and more a challenge to "cooperate with all his heart" with God's Will.[15]

With age and maturity Eugene became much more flexible, but that was not the case in his early days of ministry. Then he saw his life as

---

[13] Rambert, vol. 1, pp. 190-191, and *Selected Texts*, pp. 282-29, n. 6.
[14] See Chapter 2.
[15] Oblate prayerbook *(Vade Mecum)*, (English), p. 20.

compartmentalized: so much time for activity, so much for prayer, so much for rest, etc. The early years were a time of countless rules and detailed regulations for himself and for others. In 1815, for example, he drew up the following long list. Today it might evoke a smile, but it was deadly serious for Eugene. The list also shows how full he kept his days.

My Relationship with Persons Outside the Community

• Such relationships must always be subordinated to the duties I must fulfil as head of the Mission house and in charge of youth work.

• I am, first of all, the servant of my brothers, then of the young people, and only then, of everyone else.

• Accordingly, I will not give in to the extreme repugnance I have for sitting in the confessional; and I will take greater care not to let that repugnance be noticed by others. Do not women, too, need confession? Should I not look after their welfare, as well? Thus I will keep to the days established, and on those days I will go to the confessional with the same joy as to the other exercises, because such is the will of God. Indeed, it would perhaps be more perfect to graciously welcome the women who present themselves.

• The Congregation of Young People could suffer because I do not pay sufficient attention to administering it. Thus, on Thursdays I will give it all the time that confessions of the youth permit.

• On Mondays I will take care of missions.

• On Tuesdays, the temporal interests of the house, be it time spent with the bursar or with persons outside the community.

• Wednesday morning: confessions of women.

• Thursday: confession and instruction of youth.

• Friday: correspondence.

• Saturday morning: confessions of women.

• In the afternoon: confessions of young people.

• Sunday morning: confessions . . ., the congregation, services in the church.

• Less rigor toward my mother and more compliance with everything I can do to afflict her less, without however allowing order, regularity and the spirit of mortification to suffer. I shall have to try convincing her that I am not out to kill myself.[16]

The Unifying Principle

Gradually, Eugene de Mazenod came to realize that the spiritual life was more than just relentless and rigid timetables whereby he regimented

---

[16] Rambert, vol. 1, p. 202.

himself and others. His nature was such that he would still keep falling into the trap of overly strict and detailed regulations, but more and more, he began to learn from such experiences. Having exhausted himself physically by all his ministry in the Mission church and by preparations for the great parochial missions that his little society was about to launch, he found himself under doctor's orders to go to Bonnevaiane, near Marseilles, in July 1816, to recuperate. It was a time of quiet discernment, a kind of holiday retreat with the Lord. His notes of that stay indicate that he made an act of total dependence on God's will. The following text is rather lengthy, but worth quoting in its entirety, for it shows that Eugene's act of dependence was something done in perfect freedom and in union with God:

> I am going to try to profit from it by seriously examining my interior life. The work I am forced to do prevents me to think about myself – truly leaves me no time – when I am in the city or giving a mission. What happens then? I become daily more miserable and, having never been endowed with many virtues, I am left in rags.
>
> This is distressing. Since I am destined to work endlessly for the salvation of others, and my office puts me in continual contact with everyone, if I do not have the talent – or better, if the good Lord does not give me the grace to grow in virtue in the midst of such a tumult of tasks and to sanctify myself on the run – I am to be pitied and certainly quite badly off in my situation . . . .
>
> I must really convince myself that I am doing God's will in devoting myself to the service of my neighbour through doing things that are external to our house, etc., and then do my best without worrying if I cannot thereby do other things for which I may perhaps be more inclined or which may seem to be directly concerned with my own sanctification. If, for example, at a time when I would like to contemplate the mercies of Jesus Christ in his sacrament, I am called to hear confessions, I must leave our Lord without murmuring or without regret in order to fulfil the duty of charity laid on me by his will. Or again, even if I am tired in body and in spirit and want to get some rest through good reading or in prayer, etc., and the operation of the house obliges me to go and make odious trips or tiresome visits, then, convinced that I must give preference to what God asks over what I myself might desire, etc., I will not hesitate and will do it most willingly. So, supposing that I did have a choice, I would prefer what was required by the service God has entrusted to me to what may be more pleasing to me. Better still, I will try to love what is more in conformity with the Master's will, which alone must direct not only my actions but also my desires.
>
> If I achieve that, everything is won . . . .
>
> I must convince myself that God utilizes persons for his works, but he does not need them. Thus, by being more dependent on him and less worried about success I would much more promote the things he has deigned to entrust me with. A little more prayer, much less anxiety and calculation.

As a result of this reflection, I resolve to arrange matters in such a way that I do more *oraison* [a period of mental prayer before the Blessed Sacrament] than hitherto. It is in that context that I must get used to dealing with my affairs and those of our community, of the youth, etc.

Besides morning oraison, done in common with the others, as far as possible, I shall steal a few moments after dinner to resume this exercise before the Blessed Sacrament.

Despite the best of intentions and much to my regret, I am sometimes obliged to exempt myself from certain exercises at the prescribed times because other things get in the way, making it impossible. Nonetheless, I must find a way to supplement or avoid such a lack. I think the only way to do so is to act in perfect dependence on God's will, in perfect freedom of spirit, in union with God, by an interior attitude of adherence to what it may please him to command at each given moment, being convinced that it is what he wants me to do and not something else.[17]

It would be nice to think that the resolution of this retreat solved all of Eugene's problems. Not so. Unfortunately – or perhaps fortunately for us who can appreciate his struggles in our own lives – he was human enough to have to come back repeatedly throughout his life to renew and refocus his energies. In another retreat two years later, upon re-reading the notes of his July 1816 retreat, he commented,

God forbid that I even wish to give up serving my neighbour! Far from it! So much so that I would like, if it were possible, to do still more than what I have done thus far. The Lord is undoubtedly glorified by this since it is precisely the way that is more pleasing to him. I shall be more prudent, however, and while serving my neighbour I shall not neglect myself as I have been doing; I shall not convince myself as easily as I have done that charity towards my neighbour can substitute for everything – that it can serve as meditation, preparation, thanksgiving, the visit to the Blessed Sacrament, prayer, etc. That is an exaggeration which has cast me into the condition I recognized yesterday. It will not be difficult to correct . . . .

The essential is to arrange things in such a way that nothing suffers and that in serving my neighbour I do not neglect myself to the point of becoming lukewarm.[18]

The Concrete Application

The Oblate Founder's writings show him working out the unity and balance between work and prayer throughout his life. Trying to walk in the footsteps of Jesus who never ceased to contemplate the working of his Father (John 5:19), he wrote in his first rule: "The whole life of the members of the Society will be one of continual recollection." That was easier said than

[17] *Selected Texts*, pp. 293-297, n. 248.
[18] Ibid., pp. 298-99, n. 249.

done, however, as these entries from his retreat notes show. In 1824, in the midst of parochial missions, administration and a host of other activities, he longingly penned these words: "I need solitude, I need regularity, I need example . . . ."[19] Accordingly, in an effort to provide some of that solitude, regularity and example, he included the following in his rule of 1826: "Since the missions force us to spend nearly three-quarters of the year in the world's milieu busying ourselves mainly and almost exclusively with the conversion of sinners, we run the risk of forgetting our own needs if we do not at least in the brief intervals of this perilous ministry return to the precise observance of the Rule."[20]

Oraison, the Oblate term for a period of mental prayer before the Blessed Sacrament, usually in the evening – was something specific to Saint Eugene. It had been part of the regulations of St-Sulpice, but there it was practised only once a week. For the Founder, oraison was a special daily encounter with the Oblates in the love of Christ. Of Eugene de Mazenod and the practice of oraison before the Blessed Sacrament, Oblate spiritual theologian Father Kelly Nemeck said in a 1993 retreat he gave at Notre-Dame-des-Lumières in Provence:

> We spend hours in silent prayer before the little box on the altar that is the tabernacle. There is a mystery there that corresponds to the Last Supper discourse: "with me in you . . . and you in me." We cannot physically get into Christ but do so sacramentally – the outward sign of an inward reality. And in regard to oraison before the Blessed Sacrament, there is a relatedness in being in the same room as the sacramental presence.

> In his own life, the Founder gradually came to answer Paul's challenge hurled at the Corinthians (II Corinthians 13:5): "Test yourself," he told them. "There is only one question – no multiple choices allowed – *Do you really acknowledge that Christ is in you?* If not, you've flunked the test." Eugene's writings would indicate that he knew there is a real presence, not only of Jesus, but of the entire Trinity that indwells within a person. Communion is the sacrament of indwelling – its outward sign.

> Moreover, Eugene's intuition told him that verbally or by letter he could *communicate* with his Oblates but, more important, he could *commune* with each of them *in Jesus' love,* no matter where in far-off lands their missionary vocation had taken them. He effected such communion in and through the Blessed Sacrament. We might diagram that communion thus:

---

[19] *Ecrits spirituels,* vol. 15, p. 202.
[20] *Constitutions and Rules* (English), 1928, p. 48.

```
┌──────────────────────────────────────────────┐
│                  Jesus in the                   │
│              Blessed sacrament                  │
│                  ↗ ⇓ ↖                          │
│               ↗     ⇓     ↖                     │
│    The Founder ⇨ ⇨ ◯ ⇦ ⇦ The Oblate            │
│                                                 │
└──────────────────────────────────────────────┘
```

To Father Pierre Aubert in St. Boniface, the Oblate Founder wrote:

> Sometimes when I find myself in the presence of Jesus Christ it happens that I experience a kind of illusion. It seems to me that you are adoring Him and praying at the same time as I, and He, being as present to you as to me, we feel as if we were close to one another, although unable to see each other. I revert to it constantly and cannot describe the good and the consolation I derive therefrom. Try doing the same and you will experience it as I do.[21]

To Father Albert Lacombe in Canada he wrote on March 6, 1857: "You could not believe how much I think of our dear Red River missionaries while in the presence of God. I have only one way of drawing near to them, and that is in front of the Blessed Sacrament where I seem to see you and touch you."[22]

Such comments are repeated time and again in the Founder's correspondence, especially when writing to his far-away missionaries. To Father Vegreville in western Canada he wrote on March 25, 1857:

> It is a great consolation to have a *common centre* where we meet every day. What a delicious rendezvous is that altar on which the holy Victim is offered, and that tabernacle to which one comes every day to adore Jesus Christ and to speak with him of everything concerning us. I speak to him of all the children his goodness has given me; I pray to him to preserve you in those ideals of religious perfection of which you gave a fine example during your novitiate and scholasticate. I pray that he preserve you in holy humility among the wonders of zeal, mortification and charity that your ministry, arduous as it is, so often gives you the opportunity to perform. I pray to him also to preserve you in health so that you may long be able to still continue answering to your sublime vocation of gaining glory for God and the salvation of such abandoned souls – souls that only you, devoted servants with no other aim in this world, can save. What your reward will be, God alone can measure.[23]

---

[21] *Selected Texts,* letter of Feb. 3, 1847, p. 311, n. 263.

[22] Ibid., p. 316, n. 267.

[23] Ibid., pp. 317-318, n. 268.

Eugene de Mazenod was unique in frequently referring to the Blessed Sacrament as "the centre of the community." One hundred and fifty years later, Canon 668 of the new code, referring to consecrated persons in religious life states: "The Eucharist is celebrated and reserved so that it is truly the centre of the community."

Elements of Saint Eugene's Life in the Spirit

Looking at the Situation with the Eyes of Faith – *See*

The Founder, especially early in his spiritual life, may well have been prone to multiply resolutions and detailed timetables, yet as a founder he was never one to draw up grandiose *a priori* plans. Nor did he, once his project of evangelizing the poor got started, preordain every last detail of the work to be done. Instead, he studied the situation and listened to what his missionaries wrote in order to find the will of God in all those concrete events. The preface to the rule illustrates how he looked and listened to the Church to discover the call of God:

> Faced with such a deplorable situation, the Church earnestly appeals to the ministers whom she herself enrolled in the cause of her divine Spouse, to all in their power, by word and example, to rekindle the flame of faith that has all but died in the hearts of so many of her children. Alas, few heed their mother's urgent plea. Indeed, many even aggravate things by their own disgraceful conduct and, instead of trying to lead the people back to the ways of justice, they themselves must often be reminded of their own duties.[24]

Responding Generously – *Act*

Remember what the Founder wrote in his journal about the zeal he expected from those who wished to be Oblate missionaries: "I do not want smouldering wicks in this society. I want you to burn, to give light, to give heat or to get out."[25] Right in the preface to the rule, Saint Eugene made it clear that generosity and zeal are requisites:

> They are convinced that if priests could be formed, afire with zeal for men's salvation, priests not given to their own interests, solidly grounded in virtue – in a word, apostolic men deeply conscious of the need to reform themselves, who would labour with all the resources at their command to convert others – then there would be ample reason to believe that in a short while people who had gone astray might be brought back to their long-unrecognized responsibilities.[26]

---

[24] *Preface to the Constitutions and Rules* (English edition), pp. 9-10.

[25] Rey, vol. 2, p. 238.

[26] *Preface to the Constitutions and Rules* (English edition), p. 10.

With Daring and Creativity

The words of the preface to the Oblate rule, *nihil linquendum inausum* – nothing left undared – bespeak the daring and creativity Saint Eugene exemplified in whatever apostolate he undertook. Even charity was to be seen in that perspective. Recall that in his Lenten pastoral of 1847 he wrote what has become a watchword for Oblates: "Charity embraces all and, if necessary, where there are new needs it invents new means."

With Openness of Heart

Saint Eugene's pastoral letters expressed his constant concern for churches far beyond his own episcopal see. Recall how in speaking of Ireland's starving masses during the famine he begged the faithful to help prevent "a nation of confessors and martyrs from being exterminated by famine." Moreover, he followed with minute attention the work of Oblates in missions all over the world and in spirit shared the labours, hardships, frustrations and triumphs.

Acting with Interior Freedom

Even as a small boy of 12, under the tutelage of Don Bartolo in Venice, Eugene felt the need for inner freedom. Recall what he wrote in his journal about the rigid program of studies and prayers that the saintly Venetian priest had imposed on him: "I shall fulfil those duties at fixed times, but with the freedom of God's Spirit which will allow me to respond to the demands of the circumstances."[27] Freedom was an important value throughout Eugene's life. It would help him seek only the glory of God and keep him from getting puffed up by his own successes. He could also resolutely undertake difficult projects and respond to new calls made on the Oblates by the Church.

Being Evangelized by the Poor

We only recall how Babeau, "the Queen of the Fishwives," brought the aged bishop to the backstreet hovels of the poor and the dying or read the moving account in his journal of the death of a crippled deaf seamstress to see how greatly he was influenced and evangelized by the poor. An example is the entry in his journal for November 12, 1838: "For the third time this week I went to administer Confirmation in our worst section of the city. I always come away edified from those destitute dwellings where hard-core misery is

---

[27] Rey, vol. 1, p. 26.

attended to by such earnest charity. It is truly remarkable to see so many of the good people there, taking care of the sick of their quarter."[28] Eugene de Mazenod experienced what every zealous missionary soon discovers: the more you give of yourself to Jesus in the poor, the more you see Jesus in and through them. God will never allow himself to be outdone in generosity.

Highlights in the Spiritual Odyssey of Saint Eugene de Mazenod

Saint Eugene was most discreet about the spiritual graces he received in the course of his life. Yet, some do stand out, among them the following. They show his attachment to the person of Jesus Christ, the missionary commitment of the Oblates, and his filial confidence in Mary

Good Friday, 1807: The Beginnings of Conversion

Already in Palermo, a subtle awakening came, a feeling of spiritual exile, of being out of his element, that would explode in the Good Friday conversion of 1807, as he himself wrote seven years later in his retreat notes: "I looked for happiness outside of God and, to my sorrow, looked there for too long a time. How many times, in my past life, did my heart, torn and tormented, throw itself in desperation at its God whom it had abandoned."[29] He seems almost to be echoing the words of Augustine's spiritual odyssey, written by the great saint in his *Confessions* after he "came home":

> I learned that I was in a region unlike yours and far distant from you, and I thought I heard your voice from on high: "I am the food of grown men; grow, then, and you will feed on me. Nor will you change me into yourself like bodily food, but you will be changed into me." Late have I loved you, O Beauty ever ancient, ever new, late have I loved you! You were within me but I was outside, and it was there that I searched for you. In my unloveliness I plunged into the lovely things which you created. You were with me, but I was not with you. Created things kept me from you; yet if they had not been in you they would not have been at all. You called, you shouted, and you broke through my deafness. You flashed, you shone, and you dispelled my blindness. You breathed your fragrance on me and now I pant for you. You touched me and I burned for your peace.[30]

For Eugene, the call that "broke through his deafness," the flash that "dispelled his darkness," came, as we saw in Chapter 1, on Good Friday, 1807, when the Spirit's special grace showed itself physically in the gift of

---

[28] *Manuscript in the Oblate Postulation,* Rome, and in *Selected Texts*, p. 64, n. 40.

[29] Retreat Notes, 1814, second meditation; Archives of the General Postulation, DM IV-2, OMI Rome.

[30] *The Confessions of St. Augustine,* lib. 7, 10, 18; 10, 27; CSEL, 157-163, 255.

abundant tears. There, in the flash of that grace-filled moment before the crucifix, he discovered the depth of God's love which ransoms every soul of humankind in the precious blood of Jesus. But even more profound than the realization that Christ died for every soul was Eugene's discovery that he had died for *him* – for Eugene de Mazenod personally – that Jesus would have died for him alone, even if there had been no other souls to ransom! Like Augustine he could say "You touched me and I burned for your peace." For the young de Mazenod, Good Friday, 1807, was not a final act, yet it was perhaps the most decisive milestone in his life.

The "Strong Impulse from Without"

This was a phrase Saint Eugene used to describe the exterior force which moved him to found the Oblate congregation. Recall what he wrote to his friend, the Abbé Charles de Forbin-Janson:

> Now I ask you and I ask myself how I who hitherto could not make up my mind in this matter, suddenly find myself setting wheels in motion, renouncing my comfort and risking my fortune by launching an enterprise of which I know the worth but for which I only have a liking negated by other diametrically opposed views! . . . I see myself moved to resolve something of the utmost seriousness as if by a *strong impulse from without*. When I reflect on it, I am convinced that it so pleases God to put an end to my wavering. And in such a way that I am committed to the hilt! *I assure you that in such circumstances I am quite another man* . . . .[31]

August 15, 1822: Mary

The extant documents about Eugene de Mazenod show that he had a constantly growing filial devotion to Mary. He approached her as his mother, asking her help with all simplicity. There is little direct documentation about the circumstances of August 15, 1822. What we do know is that he received a confidence-inspiring mystic grace while praying before the newly-dedicated statue of the Immaculate Conception in the Mission Church at Aix. To Father Tempier he wrote:

> Would that I could share with you all that I experienced in the way of consolation on this beautiful day devoted to Mary our Queen! . . . I would like to believe that all the faithful who came to our church this evening shared my fervour at the sight of the statue of the Holy Virgin, and greater still, the graces which, I dare to say, she obtained from her divine Son while we were invoking her with so much affection because she is our Mother. I believe I also owe to her a special experience that I felt today; I will not go so far as to say more than ever, but certainly more than usual.

---

[31] *Oblate Writings,* vol. 6, p. 8, n. 5.

I cannot describe it too well because it comprised several things but all are related to a single object, our dear Society.[32]

The importance of this mystic experience was that by it the Blessed Virgin Mary revealed to Saint Eugene the value of his congregation for the ministry to the poor and for the sanctification of its own members. This event, along with the tradition that has built up around it, will be treated in greater detail in the next chapter.

Eucharistic Experiences

The eucharist provided special moments of grace in Saint Eugene's life. At the moment of communion he frequently experienced great consolation amidst the desolation strewn on his path. Throughout all the troubles that the early stages of the July Monarchy brought for the Oblates' mission preaching and for the Church in general, the Founder was sustained and comforted by the eucharist. To Father Tempier he wrote from Fribourg:

> Although each day I expect more bad news, it is impossible to ward off a deep feeling of sadness when it arrives, especially when domestic sorrows come along and pile themselves on top of the burden that is already too heavy to bear . . . . It seems to me that our Lord will help us by his grace to endure all our sorrows.

> This morning before communion, I dared to speak to this good Master with the same freedom that I would have entertained were I to have had the happiness of living, with this present predicament, while he walked the earth. I said Mass in a private chapel, I was not disturbed by anyone's presence. I bared to him our needs, asking for his light and help, and then surrendered myself to him entirely, seeking absolutely nothing more than his holy will. In that disposition I took Communion. Upon taking the Precious Blood, so impossible was it for me to withstand such an abundance of interior consolation that, despite my efforts not to reveal before the brother server what was going on in my soul, I could not help but sigh and shed such a quantity of tears that the corporal and altar cloth were saturated. It wasn't any painful thought that provoked such an explosion; on the contrary, I was well, I was happy, and if I were not so insignificant, I would even believe that I was loving and grateful. That state lasted for quite some time; it continued during my thanksgiving which I shortened for another reason.

> From all this I concluded that our good Saviour wanted to give me proof that he had accepted the feelings I had expressed to him in the simplicity of my heart. With that same simplicity I share with you what happened, for your own consolation and encouragement. Do not refer to it with me again, and keep praying for me.[33]

---

[32] *Oblate Writings*, vol. 6, pp. 92-93, n. 86.

[33] Ibid., vol. 7, pp. 211-212, n. 359.

No effort seemed too demanding when it came to praying before and honouring the Blessed Sacrament. On one occasion the cathedral clergy publicly announced that the customary all-night adoration at the repository between Holy Thursday and Good Friday would be cancelled – they felt that, in view of the 5:30 A.M. Passion sermon on Good Friday, it would be too exhausting. Bishop de Mazenod countered by announcing that he himself would lead the adoration, thus making it imperative that the clergy also be there in a body. It was only close to midnight – after they must surely have gotten the message of the need for rekindling zeal – that he relented and sent them off to bed. "He remained there himself until dawn, animating the prayers of the faithful by his exhortations and by readings from Louis de Grenade, and this, in spite of the fact that he was scheduled to pontificate at the Good Friday services and in spite of the fatigue which his fearful fasting of Holy Week had accentuated."[34]

Characteristics of Eugene de Mazenod's Spirituality

His Passionate Love for Jesus Christ in his Personal Life

When speaking of Saint Eugene's spiritual life we cannot help but be struck by his passionate love of Jesus Christ and his determination to follow Jesus, patterning his own life on that of the Master. The French School of Spirituality saw the Son as the perfect worshiper of the Father and Eugene wished to walk in the footsteps of Jesus. Ever since that fateful Good Friday of 1807, de Mazenod's symbol remained the crucified Christ – the sign of total self-giving. His experience of Christ's love enlightened his life while it animated his apostolate and animated his love for the Church, saved by the precious blood of Jesus. His writings show how deeply he felt the uniqueness of every soul and how the experience of divine love seared an indelible mark on him. His references to Christ are spontaneous. To Father Tempier he wrote on August 22, 1817:

> We are put on the earth . . . to sanctify ourselves while helping one another by our example, our words and our prayers. Our Lord Jesus Christ left us the task of continuing the great work of redeeming mankind. It is toward that unique end that all our efforts should be directed. As long as we will not have spent our whole life and given all our blood to achieve it, we can say nothing – especially when we have only given a few drops of sweat and a few moments of fatigue. This spirit of being wholly devoted to the glory of God, the service of the Church and the salvation of souls, is the spirit proper to our Congregation, a small one, to be sure, but one which will always be powerful so long as it is holy.[35]

---

[34] Leflon, vol. 4, p. 325.
[35] Rambert, vol. 1, pp. 236-237.

In his retreat notes of 1831, he made the following entry:

> The more I progress, the more I am overwhelmed, amazed and carried away by our sublime destiny . . . . Could anyone think that the Rule has already insisted sufficiently on the indispensable need to imitate Jesus Christ? No. It further presents the Saviour to us as the real Founder of the Congregation and the apostles who were the first to walk in the footsteps of their teacher, as our first fathers.[36]

In 1817, while Father de Mazenod's little society of missionaries was being hard-pressed by many difficulties from within and from without, and its founder was in Paris trying to obtain civil recognition for it, Father Tempier wrote him on October 19, 1817:

> Whatever we have done, how do we deserve this grace to share in the precious cross of the Son of God? Truly, I am personally quite awe-struck and feel far from deserving such a favour. It is a grace of predilection that God gives only to his saints; thus, how can we complain? Please God that his Providence might always treat us in this way and, above all, that we respond thereto! Our little family, so humiliated and despised, would soon become quite holy and then, what a harvest! . . .[37]

Father Maunier appended his support in similar terms. To their joint letter Eugene replied on October 31, 1817, encouraging them, for their mutual love in Christ, to be prepared to suffer all, as Paul had to do:

> It is for God that we suffer; we shall not let ourselves be disheartened: *ob quam causam, etiam haec patior sed non confundor.* [2 Timothy 1:12: "Therefore, I suffer as I do, but I am not ashamed."] The demon would triumph were we to fail since souls redeemed by our Lord would be abandoned. So, let us continue to strive like good soldiers of Jesus Christ: *labora sicut bonus miles Christi Iesu.* [2 Timothy 3:?: "Share in suffering as a good soldier of Jesus Christ."] What does it matter, after all, if individuals may have revolted against us? Saint Paul the apostle was treated worse than we, for not only was he abandoned by Demas, but met an Alexander who did him much evil, and all who were in Asia went away and left him [2 Timothy 4:10, 14:1, 15]. . . . And when he had to defend his case before the Emperor, no one stood by him; they all abandoned him [2 Timothy 4:16]. . . . Nonetheless, he did not lose courage and with the powerful help of God he accomplished his allotted mission and was delivered from the jaws of the lion. . . . It would indeed be foolish for anyone to desire to do good, yet not experience opposition: *omnes qui pie volunt vivere in Christo Jesu persecutionem patientur.* [Timothy 3:12: "All who desire to live a godly life in Christ Jesus will be persecuted."] St. Paul was subjected to it everywhere but, nevertheless, was helped through it by the Lord. Let us be firm in our confidence that it will be the same for us . . . .[38]

---

[36] *Selected Texts*, p. 32, n. 9.

[37] *Oblate Writings*, vol. 6, p. 43, footnote to n. 28.

[38] Ibid., pp. 43-44, n. 28.

Noteworthy throughout the Oblate Founder's extensive correspondence and writings is his generosity in trials and how he saw in them a sharing in Christ's passion. It was an asceticism in union with Christ – not simply asceticism to please Christ, for Christ takes no pleasure in seeing us suffer. It is a key, moreover, in preparing oneself, like an athlete, for the course that ends in the Kingdom with Christ.

The Spirit of the Lord

At the heart of Saint Eugene's vocation was Luke 4:18: "The Spirit of the Lord is upon me." Sharing in the very life of Jesus filled him with a great love for the poor. Like Christ, the Spirit stripped him for the glory of the Father and the salvation of people; it was his life's kenotic dimension. Sharing in the destiny of Jesus gave him greater freedom to go everywhere and to reach out to everyone. The Passion is suffering, but it is also contemplation – it fascinates because it is the manifestation of limitless love. Saint Eugene de Mazenod wanted his whole life to be a faithful, loving response – a response that would inspire his apostolate and the apostolate of countless Oblates, present and future.

His Ardent Love for the Church

Father Paul Sion was a missionary for many years in Laos. Later in Rome, until his death from cancer in 1983, he delved deeply into the Founder's life and thought and was on the commission that prepared the congregation's new Constitutions and Rules. In 1977 he wrote that Eugene de Mazenod's filial love for the Church was nowhere more patently revealed than in his preface to the rule.[39] Indeed, we know that the Founder returned to the rule time and again, so as to "engrave" it on his heart – as we read in his retreat notes of 1831 – inviting all Oblates to do the same. The first words of the preface to the Oblate Constitutions and Rules are, significantly, "the Church." And equally significant is that the Church is immediately equated with "the Saviour." Saint Eugene thereupon developed a threefold sequence: the deplorable state of the Church, the Church's cries of distress and the response of those in love with the Church.

> *The Church*, the glorious inheritance which Christ, *the Saviour* purchased at the cost of his own blood, has in our days *experienced* cruel *desolation*. The beloved spouse of the only begotten Son of God is torn with anguish as she mourns the shameful defection of her own children . . . . Faced with this most deplorable state of things, *the Church earnestly appeals* to those

---

[39] Paul Sion, O.M.I., "Our Founder's Love for the Church", in *Vie Oblate Life*, 1977, pp. 95-118.

ministers whom she herself enrolled in the cause of her divine Spouse to do all in their power, by word and example, to arouse the faith that slumbers in the hearts of the greater number of her children. But few, alas! are those who heed the urgent plea of their mother. Many even increase the evils in the church by their own disgraceful conduct . . . .

The sight of these evils *so touched the hearts of certain priests* who are zealous for God's glory and *have an ardent love for the Church* that they are willing, if need be, to give their lives for the salvation of souls.

Father Sion wrote: "The stirring pages of the preface are, first of all, the story of Eugene's own special calling and of his own 'ardent love' of the Church." The sight of those evils

"so touched the hearts of certain priests. . ." one being his own, "touched" first and foremost by our Saviour's merciful love for him. The grace of conversion so affected him that he felt turned inside out. It overwhelmed him, filling him all at once with sadness and happiness, with repentance and gratitude. Christ "made him his own", as St. Paul said, when He was furthest from his thoughts.[40] The love of his "gracious Saviour"[41] won him wholly. Being affectionate by nature and not given to doing things by halves,[42] Eugene responded to love with love, offering himself completely to his Saviour. "Only love can requite love," he wrote his sister a few months after entering the seminary.[43] How well he understood then, and would later strive to share Paul's experience:

[T]he life I now live in the flesh I live by faith in the Son of God who loved me and gave himself for me."[44]

Eugene expressed something very similar in a letter to his mother:

It seems I think of my sins solely in the endeavour to make reparation for them by giving my whole self to the service of Him whom I have so greatly offended, yet who has loved me even more."[45]

Such, then, was his response, such the ideal he set for himself henceforth, despite opposition from his family, the threat of religious persecution (under Napoleon), and his own shortcomings, not forgetting past lapses for which he was most anxious to atone.[46]

---

[40] Retreat Notes, 1814, 5th day, 13th meditation.

[41] Retreat Notes, 1812, an expression that appeared often in his notes.

[42] Cf. a letter (October 12, 1801) from Don Bartolo Zinelli to Eugene in Palermo: "My opinion of you is: your character will not let you do anything by halves; you will do much good or else much harm."

[43] Letter of March 6, 1809. In the letter he is actually referring to family affection, yet his words sum up and express just as well his spiritual disposition.

[44] Galatians 2:20.

[45] Letter to his mother, May 29, 1809.

[46] Paul Sion, O.M.I., "Our Founder's Love for the Church", in *Vie Oblate Life*, 1977, pp. 96-97.

Seeing the Priceless Worth of Every Soul

Why is it so important when we speak of Eugene de Mazenod's ardent love of the Church to place so much stress on his conversion experience? Simply because it was more than a purely personal experience meant for him alone. It was so profound that, given his generous nature, it could not help but move him to anguish at the sight of so many people – even people within the Church itself – ignorant or uncaring about the truth that the Saviour shed his precious blood for them.

Recall how as a seminarian at St-Sulpice he had put himself at the service of the Church, doing whatever he could: feeding clandestine information between the Black Cardinals and the imprisoned pontiff. During that time he also wrote: "Oh! if only we could appraise the true worth of a single human soul, one ransomed by God made man shedding his blood to the last drop . . . then perhaps we might rouse ourselves out of our lethargy, summon all our strength and be ready, if need be, to lay down our lives . . . ."[47] This love of his "most gracious Saviour" would henceforth fuel his devotional life and fire his dedication. On the eve of his priestly ordination he vowed to live in the future "for Him alone," to spend himself utterly "out of love for Him, serving him and making him known to others."[48] As a result, Father Sion stated:

> Throughout his life his concept of the Church would bear indelibly the marks of his own conversion through the grace of the Saviour. For Eugene de Mazenod the Church was not simply the divine as well as the human society instituted by Christ, it was the great family of all who, like himself, had been ransomed by the Precious Blood of the Saviour . . . .
>
> His primary desire had been to make reparation for his own transgressions; now it grew to the extent of wanting to embrace the whole Church, to love and serve the Church to the utmost of his power. "Christ loved the Church and gave himself up for her . . ." [Ephesians 5:25]. Impossible for Eugene to remain unresponsive to that love, having once realized, by a special grace, its supreme cost.[49]

In a letter written to his father on December 7, 1814, when some members of the family cast doubt on the sincerity of his motives for becoming a priest, he stated unequivocally: "I committed myself to the Church's service because she was in dire need and being persecuted . . . . That and that alone,

---

[47] *Notes: Spiritual Talks and Subjects for Meditation,* no. 29, on the conversion of sinners.

[48] Prologue to his priestly Retreat Notes, December 1811.

[49] Paul Sion, O.M.I., "Our Founder's Love for the Church", in *Vie Oblate Life,* 1977, pp. 98-99.

was my reason. There could be no other for me, given the character which God in his bounty deigned to bestow upon me."[50]

And in his memoirs Eugene would one day write: "During my seminary days, I entertained the thought of making myself as useful as possible to the Church, our Mother, for whom the Lord had given me the grace always to have a filial love. The destitution in which I saw her had been one of the deciding motives for my embracing the ecclesiastical state."[51]

Ardent Yet Discerning Love for the Church

The very love that impelled Eugene to become a priest also drove him to undertake an apostolate among the poor and most abandoned in Aix and then prompted him to found the Oblate congregation that would serve the Church well in her "most urgent needs" throughout the world. For Saint Eugene de Mazenod, the love of Jesus Christ and the love for the Church were inseparable. His Lenten pastoral letter of 1860 is an act of faith in the Church's divine aspect, the loving gift of God for the benefit of all the people:

> How is it possible to separate our love for Jesus Christ from the love we owe to his Church? These two kinds of love merge: to love the Church is to love Jesus Christ and vice-versa.
>
> We love Jesus Christ in his Church because she is his immaculate spouse who came out of his opened side on the cross, just as Eve came out of the first Adam. In his Incarnation the divine Word united himself to human nature, and that union is so perfect that there is in the Man-God only one person, that of the Word. The human race, however, assumed in only one of its members – in the new Adam who is Jesus Christ – was, through the mercy of the Most High, called to participate really and as a whole in this ineffable union of divine and human natures in the Word made flesh. Jesus Christ had to associate mankind to himself mystically so as to form one whole entity with it while allowing the personality proper to each person united to him to subsist. And just as there is only one person in Jesus Christ, so all Christians should form but one body with him, a body of which he is the head and they are the members . . . .
>
> The Church, therefore, is the prize won by the blood of Jesus Christ, and the object of his infinite love for everyone. He loved the Church more than his own life, and because of him she is dear to God the Father, who already from all eternity had loved her even to the point of giving his only Son for her sake *"sic Deus Dilexit mundum ut Filium suum unigenitum daret"* (John 3:15). Furthermore, it is to her that the Holy Spirit, who was promised by the divine Saviour, united himself inseparably as her soul, to

---

[50] Letter to his father, December 7, 1814.
[51] Rambert, vol. 1, p. 161; also *Selected Texts*, p. 72, n. 50.

inspire her, enlighten her, guide and support her, and to bring about in her the mighty works of God: *Magnalia Dei* (Acts 2:11).

All who are members of the Church live in God's spiritual house; rather, they themselves are that house which is a huge temple into which the whole world must enter and of which all stones are living stones. This temple is the vestibule and image of the eternal one. In both cases, the Spouse showers all the riches of his love upon the Bride. God himself has built this house out of divine cement.

Now, most dear brethren, we ask you: If we do not love the Bride of Jesus Christ as her children – that bride whom Jesus willed to give us as our Mother; if we do not love the family of the Man-God, his living habitation, his holy temple, his earthly city, image of the eternal city, his Kingdom, his flock the society he founded – in a word, the enterprise which has been the object of all his labours and delights here below – would that not be the same as not wanting to love Jesus himself? Does it not amount to disregarding the designs of his mercy, the rights of his love and of his power? Is it not tantamount to dishonouring him as Saviour, as Redeemer of mankind, as conqueror over hell and death, and as the sovereign master "to whom all the nations of earth have been given as heritage" (Ps. 2:8)?[52]

Sorting Out the Temporal from the Divine

Even though the Founder upheld the Church with a burning love, he generally managed very well to distinguish between its temporal and divine aspects. The pastoral letter quoted above was published at a time of rebellion in the Papal States, a rebellion that would eventually end in political unification, when Victor Emmanuel of Sardinia-Piedmont would be proclaimed king of all Italy. Despite Napoleon III's declared support of the pope, he went to war on the side of the rebellious states against the pontiff's ally, Franz Josef of Austria. Although the great French victory at Magenta hurt and infuriated Bishop de Mazenod, for it cost a great many lives and meant the virtual end of the pope's temporal rule, he could distinguish clearly between the temporal and the divine in the Church – something that many French bishops could not.

The war had been exceptionally unpopular at home, with most of the French hierarchy taking a stance in strong opposition. Indeed, some even wrote violent and vitriolic diatribes against it and against France's allies. Even Oblate Bishop Guibert – normally the consummate diplomat whose patient dealings with Louis-Philippe had extricated the Founder from the Icosia mess – joined in the heated battle. As Archbishop of Tours Guibert wrote on October 1, 1860: "So far Piedmont has more or less veiled its criminal

---

[52] *Selected Texts*, p. 73, n. 51.

projects. Actually, no one had accepted to be taken in by its hypocritical intrigues; its lies were accepted only by its unofficial accomplices."

Everyone expected de Mazenod to also join in the war of words – even though the crusty old prelate was a bare half-year from death. Hadn't he always been the tireless champion of the pope and a bishop in his own right, ever ready to defend the Church? Yet in this case there was marked reticence on his part that plainly distinguished between the power of the sceptre and the power of the keys. Perhaps the young firebrand de Mazenod would not have been capable of making such a distinction, but the mature de Mazenod could, even though it chagrined him deeply to witness this betrayal by France. His love for the Church, like any true love, had matured.

Bishop de Mazenod did not join in the battle alongside his episcopal confrères. Instead he wrote three personal letters to the emperor, reminding him frankly yet courteously that as the ruler of France he had not been faithful to his promise to the pope. The emperor replied politely to the first letter, but that was the sum of their correspondence on this matter. To Bishop Guibert, Bishop de Mazenod wrote on October 18, 1860, about to the latter's attack quoted above:

> My dear Lord, I am writing to tell you that I cannot manage to write you. Still, I would have many things to tell you, but I do not have the time to enter into details. That would take me too far afield. To tell you crudely that I regret a few expressions in your last written piece is to say too much. Quite for nothing are you losing all the advantages which your good sense and wisdom had acquired for you for the good of the Church's cause. No one could have served her better than you. It is a great misfortune that you have put yourself into a position where no one will listen to you any more. These considerations merit to be carefully pondered.[53]

The Church – A Divine Reality

Because the Roman curia was amazed that the bishop of Marseilles kept publicly silent on what was, for them, such a burning issue, Eugene de Mazenod wrote the Lenten 1860 pastoral letter already noted earlier in this chapter. It is an act of faith and love in which we see that for him the Church is not first and foremost an organization, even if the temporal position of the pope was at stake. For him *the Church is a divine reality – a mystery.* God is given up to men and women of this world through the mediation of his Son. That makes the church a family, a body.

---

[53] *Oblate Writings,* vol. 12, p. 196, n. 1462.

Saint Eugene, the man of faith, found the right language for expressing his faith in the Church through the use of New Testament images: the spouse, the family, the house, the flock, the mystery. A hundred years later the Second Vatican Council would use the same terms.

Love explains his generosity and his courage to endure trials in the Church and remain faithful. The 1860 pastoral letter is a meditation from the heart. So is the preface of the rule, written 42 years earlier. De Mazenod loved the Church because the Church is Jesus Christ communicated to the People of God in every age. Eugene's love for the Church was no sentimental flash, but a devouring and abiding flame kindled by the Spirit. It was a flame that would burn brightly – even in moments of severe trial and distress when love and fidelity meant walking with Jesus on the way to Calvary – a love that lasted to the very end of his earthly life. We can feel its heat in the letter of invitation he wrote to the Abbé Tempier in 1815:

> My dear friend: read this letter at the foot of your crucifix . . . . Stifle the voice of selfishness . . . . Meditate seriously on the condition (of people in rural districts) . . . . Consider the feeble means . . . . Ask your heart . . . and then answer my letter. Dear friend, I entreat you, do not refuse your services, given such a chance of doing so much good for the Church.[54]

All for the Glory of God

"The glory of God" appears time and again in Saint Eugene's writings and exhortations. Thus he wrote in the preface to the rule: "The glory of God, the good of the Church and the salvation of souls." That trilogy is a patrimony common to all religious, as the Code of Canon Law reminds us.[55] To seek God's glory is a basic element in the spirituality of most founders of religious institutes: *Ad maiorem Dei gloriam* (for the greater glory of God) is the motto St. Ignatius Loyola bequeathed to the Jesuits, and *Ut in omnibus honorificetur Deus* (so that God be honoured in all things) is the legacy St. Benedict left to his monks. However, the thrust of an Ignatius, the soldier who enlisted in the service of the divine King, is bound to differ from that of a serene Benedict imbued with a profound and abiding sense of divine greatness. Different, too, is the approach and attitude of Saint Eugene. It is only fitting to ask how Eugene de Mazenod, Missionary Oblate of Mary Immaculate, understood "seeking God's glory"? And what did "striving solely for the glory of God" mean to him?

---

[54] Leflon, vol. 2, p. 34.
[55] Cf. canon 573, no. 1.

The Father's Glory Is Jesus' Deepest Desire

We have already glimpsed Eugene de Mazenod's passionate love of Jesus Christ in his life and as a religious founder animated by the Holy Spirit. It was always Jesus himself who led him to seek the glory of God his Father. To grasp what God's glory meant to the Founder, we should have a notion of what it means to Jesus.

Glory is the radiation of God's being. God's aim in creation and in redemption is to manifest and communicate his glory to creatures in his Son. The Father's glory is the very meaning and purpose of the Son's life, since he is sent by the Father. To glorify God was the overriding truth of Jesus' life.

For the creature, giving glory to God means proclaiming God's greatness, thanking him, appreciating him and praising him for the marvellous things he does. Indeed, glorifying God is a joy for the believer. Because God the Father is the one and only Absolute, anything else is relative and incapable of providing a solid basis for one's life.

Eugene de Mazenod, in the footsteps of Jesus, sought God's glory as his deepest desire. Like a recurring refrain comes the phrase "for the glory of God." When he asked the Congregation of *Propaganda Fide* that Father Ricard be appointed bishop of Nesqually, he wrote: "I will feel that I have accomplished a great deal for the glory of God . . . if I obtain what I have just communicated to you."[56] To Bishop Alessandro Barnabò of *Propaganda Fide* he wrote on October 8, 1849: "I would sacrifice my life a thousand times over for the glory of God and the salvation of souls and I would rather see my hand wither than to write even a single syllable contrary to that end . . . ."[57]

The present Oblate Constitutions and Rules end with Saint Eugene's heartfelt words of encouragement, written in 1850, that show how driven he was by God's glory: "We urgently exhort . . . each and every member of the Congregation . . . to renew themselves by God's grace in the spirit of their vocation; to unceasingly undertake, under the aegis of their most loving Immaculate Mother, ever more important and effective works for the greater glory of God and for the salvation of the most abandoned souls."[58] On February 18, 1826, immediately after the pope's approbation of the congregation and its rule, the Oblate Founder wrote to Father Tempier in the

---

[56] *Oblate Writings,* vol. 5, p. 21, n. 7.

[57] Ibid., p. 33, n. 12.

[58] *Constitutions and Rules* (English), p. 141.

same tenor: "The conclusion to be drawn from this is that we must work with renewed ardour and with even more complete devotedness to bring to God all the glory that stems from our efforts; to the needy souls of our neighbours we must strive still more to bring them salvation in all possible ways."[59]

Seeking God's Glory – A Source of Freedom

Jesus is a free person: "It is not that I accept human praise," he says, "I have come in my Father's name."[60] The essential relationship in Jesus' life is with the Father, making him free to speak frankly and openly to any group or to any person, free to proclaim the Beatitudes, regardless of the world's attitude; free to question even the poor in regard to sin, free to relate to persons because he is turned to God.

The fiery young Provençal nobleman had become a priest determined to dedicate himself utterly to the service of the Church. Recall how, upon returning to Aix, he saw that the parochial institutions of the Church were failing the poor, that they had virtually abandoned the poor and that the Church of France was not sufficiently addressing the needs of a post-Revolutionary era. For that reason he felt the need to avoid entanglement in the mesh of parochial duties that converted only the converted, to be free to respond to the most urgent needs not being addressed by the establishment.

Eugene de Mazenod was sufficiently free to speak honestly to everyone and, as Founder, to send stern letters at times to certain missionaries, as he did with Bishop Allard in South Africa for not acting more like a missionary bishop. During Lent of 1813, his freedom, based on God's glory, prompted him to preach in Provençal, the local dialect of the lower classes, despite upper-crust criticism in Aix. It also allowed him, a year earlier when he was about to return to Aix from St-Sulpice, to write to his mother: "My whole life has been planned in advance and nothing will deter me from it because it is something I decided in the presence of God. . . . So, that's settled. People can call me rude if they wish – even uncivilized; it will not bother me."[61] To Bishop Barnabò he also expressed that freedom on Nov. 23, 1848: "When God's glory and the salvation of souls are at stake, there is no evil in expressing oneself with simplicity and speaking with an open heart."[62]

---

[59] *Oblate Writings,* vol. 7, p. 40, n. 224.

[60] John 5:41, 43.

[61] Oblate Postulation, Rome. Letter of April 22, 1812, file F.B. I, 8.

[62] *Oblate Writings,* vol. 5, p. 23, n. 8.

Seeking God's Glory – A Source of Peace

There is peace in Jesus' soul as he rededicates himself to obtaining the Father's glory. When a group of Greeks wanted to see Jesus, he announced to them that the hour of his suffering and death was at hand: "My soul is troubled now, yet what should I say – Father, save me from this hour? But it was for this that I came to this hour. Father, *glorify your name"* (John 12:27-28).

Being truly human, Jesus was understandably shaken by the thought of so violent a death. He prays – he beseeches God – but finally says, "Glorify your name." With those words peace reigns in his heart and in all tranquillity he can proclaim the certitude of victory: "And I, once I am lifted up from earth, will draw all people to myself" (John 12:5).

Of the many trials that Saint Eugene de Mazenod had to undergo, perhaps his four-year-long Calvary of Icosia more than any others reveals the inner peace that came to him from seeking the glory of God above all else. Being proscribed by France and silenced by Rome inflicted deep personal suffering, yet he could still note in his journal: "As long as God is glorified, what does it matter that I am humiliated, ignored, abandoned by nearly everyone? May I be still less in the eyes of men."[63] After the Icosia crisis, when Eugene was named Bishop of Marseilles, he saw it as yet another cross, and wrote to Father Tempier: "To burden me with a diocese would be the worst condemnation – the equivalent of a death sentence." Nonetheless, in his journal we read: "So be it! Just so long as it glorifies God. I could not have lost my independence and liberty more completely; humanly speaking, it is an affliction for me, but things must be considered in another light."[64] These words echo the inner peace in his letter to Father Tempier following the approbation of the rule: "I have done all I had to do. God will do the rest. We live only for him, we want only the glory of his holy name and the salvation of souls redeemed by him. When we have used all the means available to us, we ought to remain in peace and not worry about anything."

---

[63] This entry, to Msgr. Frezza, dated April 27, 1835, is quoted in *Il Fondatore degli oblati di Maria Immacolata,* by Vincenzo Anzalone, O.M.I. (Roma, Editrice Missioni O.M.I., 1961, p. 183). Father Anzalone refers to p. 617 of the first volume of Toussaint Rambert, *Vie de Monseigneur Charles-Joseph-Eugène de Mazenod, évêque de Marseille, fondateur de la Congrégation des Missionnaires Oblats de Marie Immaculée* (Tours, Imprimerie Mame et Fils, 1883). However, the passage quoted is from p. 698 of that work.

[64] Leflon, vol. 2, p. 515.

Seeking God's Glory – Denial of Self

Jesus is ever the model. In the strongest of all statements on poverty of spirit, of a heart that is poor, he proclaimed: "I solemnly assure you, the Son cannot do anything by himself – he can do only what he sees the Father doing. For whatever the Father does, the Son does likewise" (John 5:19). Long before Jesus gave us the beatitude, "Blessed are the poor in spirit," he lived it himself. And since he was poor in spirit – totally detached from himself – he could welcome and accept all the Father's wishes as he conformed his life to the Father's will.

Saint Eugene saw clearly that God's glory demanded he deny himself so as to be filled with the Saviour's infinite love. Indeed, it is in the perspective of love that he understood the call to self-denial and to take up the cross each day. Moreover, he insisted that his Oblates be attentive to that same call. To Father Tempier he wrote on April 19, 1826: "Please God that at Aix they will know how to profit from the gifts of God. For that, the missionaries must forget themselves and aim at nothing more than the greater glory of God and the salvation of these poor souls."[65] To Father Jean-Baptiste Honorat, superior of the Oblates who were establishing the first mission in Canada, he wrote that they should never "seek their own interest but only whatever pertains to the glory of God and the service of the Church."[66] Writing to Cardinal Fransoni on September 25, 1847 about the choice of missionaries for Ceylon, the Founder observed that the task was not very difficult since all of them were good. And then he added: "They are all ready to sacrifice their lives for the glory of God and to work for the conversion and sanctification of souls. That is the precise goal of their vocation."[67]

Seeking God's Glory – The Source of Missionary Zeal

To glorify God means to praise and admire him in the reality of his love for all human persons. Jesus said: "It is not to do my own will that I have come down from Heaven, but to do the will of him who sent me. It is the will of him who sent me that I should lose nothing of what he has given me; rather, that I should raise it up on the last day" (John 6:38-39). The person seeking God's will begins to contemplate, to discover God's infinite love more and more. He or she comes to share God's intense desire that "everyone be saved and come to know the truth" (I Timothy 2:4).

---

[65] *Oblate Writings,* vol. 7, p. 87, n. 237.
[66] Ibid., vol. 1, p. 19, n. 10.
[67] Ibid., vol. 5, p. 16, n. 6.

We understand how, because he loved Jesus, Saint Eugene de Mazenod always linked the search for God's glory with the salvation of souls. The Oblate Founder explicitly affirmed this link in a letter written on October 16, 1858 to the missionaries evangelizing in Ceylon. It brings out his conviction that God is glorified when human beings achieve salvation. In the letter, after congratulating his Oblates for their apostolic work, he encouraged them "to continue to bring about the glory of God by working for the conversion of those poor souls which, without you, would not be saved."[68] For St. Eugene de Mazenod and for all who are Missionary Oblates, seeking God's glory means responding to the love of Jesus Christ, contemplating infinite love and sharing God's love for all humankind.

Missionary to the Poor

Opting for the poor and most abandoned was Eugene de Mazenod's definitive choice from the very outset of his priesthood. In his memoirs he recalled how, upon returning to Aix after his ordination, he told the bishop-administrator of the diocese: "My only ambition was to consecrate myself to the service of the poor and the children. Thus, my first struggle was my work in the prisons. . . ." Much to the dismay of his noble peers he began his apostolate in Aix by working with the poor not in the noble mother-tongue, but in Proven-çal, the patois of the masses. His option for the poor which began with the prisoners and the youth of Aix and with the landmark Lenten instructions of 1813 would grow and spread over much of the world during his own lifetime It remains the Oblate congregation's option today – the very heart of its missionary thrust.

In Community

Early in his apostolate, after nearly dying from typhus while ministering to the Austrian prisoners of war, Eugene de Mazenod realized he could not achieve his goals by working alone. He needed a community of zealous, like-minded co-workers prepared to work for the glory of God, the well-being of the Church and the salvation of souls. In the preface to his rule, referring to the Church's need to re-evangelize the unlearned and the lost and to conquer the world for Christ, he concluded:

> Such are the great works of salvation that can crown the efforts of priests whom God has inspired with the desire to form themselves into a Society in order to work more effectively for the salvation of souls and for their

---

[68] *Oblate Writings*, vol. 4, p. 143, n. 47.

own sanctification. To bring all this into being, they must carry out their duty worthily, faithfully fulfilling their splendid vocation.[69]

The Founder saw his followers forming an apostolic community modelled on that of Christ with the apostles: "Jesus is our Founder, the apostles our forerunners, our first fathers! It is the Church that teaches us this, it is Peter, through the lips of Leo, who tells us this. Let us swear to be faithful, to become worthy of our great calling!"[70]

Vows and the Example of the Apostles

The Oblate Founder's vows can be seen, in part, as the outcome of his priestly formation in the French School of Spirituality at St-Sulpice (Christ totally consecrated and given to the Father and bearing humankind with him), enriched by his earlier call to be sent to the poor. However, to those two elements we must add yet another: his discovery of the apostles' role. He came to see his followers as forming an apostolic community modelled on that of Christ with the apostles: "Jesus is our Founder, the apostles our forerunners, our first fathers! It is the Church that teaches us this, it is Peter, through the lips of Leo, who tells us this. Let us swear to be faithful, to become worthy of our great calling!"[71]

Saint Eugene was convinced he had been called to be an apostle and, like the apostles, called to let himself be formed by Jesus. The apostles ("our first fathers") became the models upon whom he would form his society of priests. Increasingly, he became aware that the apostles had consecrated themselves totally to Jesus, so that they could be sent out to preach the Good News and always be at the total disposition of the Master. Thus the preface of his rule states:

> How, indeed, did the Lord Jesus Christ proceed when he undertook to convert the world? He chose a number of apostles and disciples whom he himself trained in piety, and he filled them with his Spirit. These men he sent forth, once they had been schooled in his teaching, to conquer the world which, before long, was to bow to his holy rule.

The four Gospels showed him that, at the very outset of his public life, Jesus chose companions who together with him were to be witnesses to the Kingdom he was proclaiming. Indeed, in John's Gospel, Jesus is seen choosing them even before his ministry began. Eugene obviously saw the apostles as missionaries, men filled with zeal, sharing Christ's commitment of fidelity to the Father and to the salvation of the poor.

---

[69] *Constitutions and Rules,* 1826, Mss Post.

[70] *Selected Texts*, p. 33, n. 9.

[71] *Ibid.,* p. 33, n. 9.

Essential for such an apostolic calling is *zeal* – the total giving of oneself to God. As Eugene saw it, there could be no half-measures, no middle-ground. His contemporaries, even those who were not his friends, were unanimous in recognizing his apostolic zeal. Bishop Jeancard, a true friend, wrote of him: "It is hardly necessary to describe the compassion and zeal that the situation[72] inspired in Bishop de Mazenod. In his view, *one had to devote oneself, to give and spend oneself without reserve, to die working, if success could only be gained at that price, to save so many souls who were on the way to perdition.*"[73] In 1951 the late Father Leo Deschâtelets, then Superior General, wrote circular Number 191, *Our Vocation and Our Life of Intimate Union with Mary Immaculate.* In it he stated:

> To be a missionary in the mould of Father de Mazenod is to feel the urgency with which St. Paul cried out: ". . . Woe unto me if I do not preach the Gospel"; and again, "I most gladly will spend . . . myself for . . . souls." One thing is certain: no one becomes such a missionary by half-hearted efforts; this is a standard attained only by persons who "do all in their power by word and example."[74]

Forming His Community as Jesus Formed the Apostles

Constitution 45 of the 1982 Oblate Constitutions and Rules reads thus:

> Jesus personally formed the disciples he had chosen, initiating them into "the mystery of the Kingdom of God" (Mark 4:11). As a preparation for their mission he had them share in his ministry; to confirm their zeal he sent them his Spirit.
>
> This same Spirit forms Christ in those who endeavour to follow in the apostles' footsteps. As they enter more deeply into the mystery of the Saviour and his Church, he moves them to dedicate themselves to the evangelization of the poor.

These were not the Founder's words, yet the spirit – a spirit that sees the apostles as our first fathers – is certainly his. Indeed, Constitution 45 of the new rule reflects the double question Eugene de Mazenod posed in the preface to the first rule: "How, indeed, did our Lord Jesus Christ proceed when he undertook to convert the world? And how should men who want to follow in the footsteps of the divine Master Jesus Christ conduct themselves if they, in their turn, are to win back the many souls who have thrown off his yoke?"

The community's involvement in proclaiming the Good News meant that its members had to be formed by the Master, a formation carried out in two

---

[72] France after the Revolution.

[73] Jeancard, *Mélanges historiques,* pp. 67-68.

[74] *Oblate circular* no. 19, English text, p. 25.

special ways: by being with Jesus (being totally given – dedicated – to him), and by being sent by him.

The Call to Walk With the Master

Jesus obviously formed his apostles through concrete examples and by teaching them directly. Yet the image that the synoptic evangelists used most often to represent Jesus' call to his disciples was that of walking with him. Jesus "made his way along the sea of Galilee"[75] and walked the dusty roads of Palestine. He called them to follow him, to commit themselves to walk the same road he was walking, to go the same way he went. Walking is deeply embedded in the imagery of the Israelites. Indeed, it goes all the way back to Abraham's long walk when he set out "not knowing where he was going" (Hebrews 11:8), and to the walk of Exodus, which symbolizes Israel's commitment to the covenant with God. Given their spiritual experience as sons of Israel, the apostles spontaneously retained the image of Jesus in the act of walking when he called them.

An apostle's life, therefore, consists in following Christ. This is not to be taken simply as a banal expression. Indeed, Jesus himself specified its grave implications and laid out its scope in detail. For the apostle, to follow in Jesus' footsteps and walk with him means "to take up his cross" (Matthew 10:38, Luke 9:23), "to deny one's very self" (Mark 8:34), "to sell all you have" (Luke 18:22).

St. Luke, in Jesus' encounter with three young men (Luke 9:57-62), further indicates that to be a disciple of the divine Master means: to be as poor as Jesus, to be close to the people without putting down roots that tie one to persons or places, to prefer Jesus over everyone else, to persevere, no matter how great the renunciation and despite other calls that may have some validity.

Moreover, according to John's Gospel, to walk with Jesus, also means to possess "the light of life" (John 10:27), to listen to and heed the voice of the good Shepherd (John 10:27), to serve Jesus (John 12:26).

These calls were issued in the context of Jesus' going up to Jerusalem (Luke 9:51). He was determined to live out his Exodus, for it was to that end that the Father called him. Hence he invites his disciples to commit themselves by walking the same road and, together with him, to live out the Exodus in a new way. Luke 9:51 refers to Jesus' Passover which was to be the definitive covenant between God and humankind (Luke 9:31).

---

[75] Mark 1:16; Cf. also Matthew 4:18, Luke 4:5, Matthew 9:9, Mark 2:14.

In addition, there are the statements of Paul: "to continue walking in the footsteps of Christ" (Colossians 2:6), and "racing to grasp the prize, if possible" (Philippians 2:16).

Pilgrims with Christ, free to walk, indeed, to run, assured of never being alone, men with their eyes fixed on the road taken by their Master so as to commit themselves to following him – such were the apostles formed by Jesus. And such were the Missionary Oblates whom Eugene de Mazenod wished to gather around himself to announce the Good News to the poor. In the preface to the rule he called for men "afire with zeal for men's salvation, priests not given to their own interests, solidly grounded in virtue – in a word, apostolic men . . . ." As Eugene de Mazenod saw it, the full expression of all those elements necessarily had to take place within the framework of religious vows. If the Oblate Founder spoke frequently of the evangelical counsels as a way to commit oneself to follow the apostles, it was because he realized that the Twelve had been thus formed by Christ to be filled by the Holy Spirit, as Luke tells us in his Gospel: "The Spirit of the Lord has been given to me, for he has anointed me. He has sent me to bring the Good News to the poor, to proclaim liberty to captives and to the blind new sight, to set the downtrodden free, to proclaim the Lord's year of favour!" (Luke 4:18).

Consecration to the Lord

Religious consecration was the logical conclusion of the Founder's contemplation of Jesus, the perfect worshiper completely dedicated to the Father. Accordingly, through their vows made on April 11, 1816, he and Father Tempier shared in Christ's total offering of self – his *oblation* – dedicating themselves to the Father's will and to the salvation of humankind. For Eugene, this was not just a theory – it the ideal by which he would try to live his entire life and form his followers.

In his memoirs, written around 1845, recall that he wrote:

> I stated that my intention in dedicating myself to the mission ministry, especially working to instruct and convert the most abandoned souls, was to follow the example of the apostles in their life of devotedness and self-denial. I became convinced that, in order to obtain the same results from our preaching, we would have to walk in their footsteps and, as far as we could, practise the same virtues. Hence, I considered as indispensable our opting for the evangelical counsels, to which they had been so faithful, lest our words be no more than what I have often noticed about the words of others who proclaim the same truths, namely sounding brass and tinkling cymbals. My consistent thought has even been that our little family should

consecrate itself to God and to the service of the Church through the vows of religion . . . .

Briefly put, Father Tempier and I felt that we should not delay any longer, and on Holy Thursday (April 11, 1816), when both of us had taken our place under the structure of the beautiful repository we had erected over the main altar in the Mission church in the night of that holy day, we pronounced our vows with indescribable joy . . . and we prayed that, if it were his holy will, the Divine Master would bless our undertaking and lead our present companions and those who would be associated with us in the future to appreciate the full value of this oblation of one's entire self to God, wishing only to serve him unreservedly and to consecrate one's life to the spread of his holy Gospel and the conversion of souls. Our petition was answered.[76]

In that excerpt, when speaking of the apostles, it is striking that the first terms he used were *devotedness* and *self-denial*. The term *zeal* does not appear. In a way, this is symbolic of the journey of Saint Eugene's vocation. Zeal was characteristic of him at the very outset when as a young missionary priest he was afire at the prospect facing his tiny society. The quotations from the preface to the rule, cited earlier, make that abundantly evident. It was later, when the Oblate Founder was in his 60s, that he wrote his memoirs. In them we see the wisdom which came with the distillation of a lifetime's experience. Zeal is no longer stressed, it is taken for granted. He had grown, his spirituality had deepened; now the accent was on being *offered* in order to be *sent*. Moreover, from the last part of the excerpt we also see in what sense the Founder saw the congregation as *priestly;* that is, whether priests or brothers, Oblates are are totally dedicated to the likeness of Jesus and of the apostles.

With the Virgin Mary

This subject will be treated at length in the next chapter. Suffice it here to underline the saint's strong devotion from childhood to Mary Immaculate. During his near-fatal bout of typhus, contracted while ministering to Austrian prisoners of war in Aix, the children of his youth sodality stormed heaven with their prayers. Through Mary's intercession, the young priest was restored to health after being bed-ridden for four months. Later, it was Eugene himself who petitioned the pope to place the nascent Oblate congregation under the patronage of Mary Immaculate, and to the end of his life he saw Mary at the foot of the cross as intimately associated with the Redemption.

---

[76] Rambert, vol. 1, pp. 187-188, and *Selected Texts*, pp. 39-40, n. 16.

What Oblation means to the Oblates

To express his ideal, Father de Mazenod privileged one term, *oblation*, meaning a basic attitude of offering oneself totally to God. He seems to have picked up the use of the word from two different sources. One of these was St. Alphonsus Liguori, who used the term *oblazione* to refer to the ceremony of taking vows: "*i novizi saranno ammessi all' oblazione. . .*" ("the novices will be admitted to oblation").[77] He called the members of his institute *sogetti* (subjects) or *congregati* (those of the congregation). From the 1818 rule onwards, and possibly before, Father de Mazenod always referred to members who had taken vows as *les oblats* – the Oblates. It is worth noting that this usage precedes by several years the pope's conferral of the official title, *Oblates* of Mary Immaculate. A second source for the term appears to be Cardinal Bérulle, who in his *Opuscule de piété*[78] (*A Short Study on Piety*), makes frequent use of the word *oblation*. He used it especially to express the sacrifice of Jesus wherein he gives himself totally to the Father. *This is the meaning of oblation in Oblate life.*

Oblation

Thus, we see how Saint Eugene achieved a synthesis between the priestly ideal of St-Sulpice (in the likeness of Jesus), and a missionary vocation faithful to the apostolic ideal. We know how his Sulpician formation was enriched by his call to the poor and by the discovery of the apostles' example. The outcome was taking vows on April 11, 1816 – a total consecration, with Father Tempier, of their life to Jesus in the manner of the first apostles. That consecration would be known as *oblation,* and would be characteristic of the Oblate vocation.

Emilien Lamirande, in *"Esprit d'oblation: approche historique,"*[79] gives numerous examples of how early Oblates interpreted *oblation* and states that Eugene de Mazenod, while not explicitly defining *Oblate* or *oblation,* nonetheless did insist time and again that consecration to God implied the complete giving of oneself in a spirit of generous devotion to the glory of God, the good of the Church and the salvation of souls. He added that such an attitude embodies the Oblate spirit and is its unifying bond. The article concludes:

> Even though we may be somewhat surprised to learn that our early Oblates, and especially Bishop de Mazenod, did not delve deeper into

---

[77] Cosentino, vol. 1, p. 124.

[78] *Opuscule de piété*, presented by G. Rotureau, Aubier, Montaigne, 1944.

[79] *Études oblates*, vol. 16, 1966.

certain aspects of our spirit of oblation – and in particular, that our name did not immediately prompt reflections in that direction – we believe that the fundamental elements of our spirit are expressed more frequently than a cursory glance would seem to bear out. Despite the absence of ready-made expressions, the notion itself has existed among Oblates for years in terms that are synonymous. That, for us, is proof that the idea naturally harmonizes with what is the very core of our spiritual being. The following passage from Very Reverend Father General's circular letter[80] perfectly sums it up, if we take the trouble to relate it to the context whence it was taken, namely: our life of union with Christ and with Mary Immaculate.

"It is clearly indicated in the Rules. That which definitively establishes us in our special vocation is that *our commitment to the service of God and souls is unconditional, it is absolute.* It is a kind of 'reckless' giving of ourselves to the glory and service of God, to the ministry and his infinite love and mercy. It is a holy and impulsive giving, without restraint, a unique intensity of priestly charity, of zeal for the most difficult undertakings. It is – and these are the strongest terms we can find – such *an unreserved oblation of ourselves* that it can truly be said of us, 'these are the Oblates. They surpass all others *in the completeness* of their oblation.'"

Eugene de Mazenod – A Total Offering of Self to God Through His Priesthood

From his 1812 retreat notes one can conclude that Eugene sought to follow Jesus Christ, who was fully consecrated to his Father. Like Jesus and with Jesus, he wanted to be the perfect worshiper of the Father:

As a model of the devotion which I owe to God, I will take the example of his adorable son, Jesus Christ, our loving Saviour, for whom I shall strive to have the most tender devotion and the most ardent love . . . . And recognizing that I am both incapable and unworthy of loving him as I ought, I will ask him for that grace every day during the Holy Sacrifice and a hundred times daily will I say the ejaculatory prayer, "My Jesus, give me your love." Oh, I will have gained everything if I attain such a devotion to Jesus Christ, one which must be the devotion *par excellence* of a priest.[81]

We readily see that the young priest's attitude was that of offering himself totally to God. It was probably why he chose to make his own the prayer of St. Ignatius – remember that there were some notable similarities between Ignatian and French School spirituality:

Take, O Lord, into your hands my entire will; receive my memory, my understanding and my whole will. All that I am, all that I have, you have given me, and I give it back to you, to be disposed of according to your

---

[80] Father Leo Deschâtelets, O.M.I., *Our Vocation and Our Life of Intimate Union with Mary,* pp. 26-27.
[81] Rambert, vol. 1, p. 107.

good pleasure. Give me only your love and your grace: with these I am rich enough, and I desire nothing more.[82]

On the day of his ordination, December 21, 1811, he wrote the following to his mother in Aix:

My dear sweet *Maman*: the miracle has taken place. Your Eugene is a priest of Jesus Christ! Those few words say it all. It is with the deepest humility, with my face pressed down in the dust, that I announce that such a great marvel has been done unto so great a sinner as I. Dear *Maman*, it is beyond my power to say more. These joyful moments, given to me through the grace of so great a sacrament, are precious beyond words and I must remain completely recollected so that I might savour the happiness and consolation which the good God is pleased to send me . . . . What can I say? My tears flow, or rather, they fall in torrents. By right they should never cease, for they spring from the tenderest of love and are simply the expression of gratitude that I shall take with me into eternity.[83]

Throughout his priestly life Eugene de Mazenod celebrated the anniversary of his ordination as a very special day. On December 20, 1855, when he was already 70 years old, he wrote to Father de l'Hermite:

I could not finish my letter yesterday, and today I foresee that it will be difficult to complete it, and that is why I come to give you my affectionate greetings before going to the Capuchin nuns where you know I go on this day to say Mass within the community. In that shrine's atmosphere of recollection I will celebrate the anniversary of my priestly ordination and have the fervent prayers of those earthly angels help me in giving thanks to the Lord. I shall remain on retreat for the remainder of the day to prepare for the ordination I will perform tomorrow. You will be pleased to learn that I will ordain two of our men to the priesthood, Brother Mauran and another whose name escapes me at the moment, as well as seven deacons.[84]

The Missionary Oblates – A Priestly Congregation

What about the character of the congregation that Saint Eugene founded? To begin with, he made it clear that all Oblates are on an equal footing. The way they live their oblation draws its inspiration from the priestly attitude of Jesus, as presented to the Oblate Founder by the French School of Spirituality at St-Sulpice. He saw it as a unifying factor that helps all Missionary Oblates together to be faithful to their vocation and to enrich their spirituality through the experiences of their apostolate.

---

[82] Oblate Prayerbook *(English edition)*, p. 126.
[83] Postulation, FB I-7, Oblate General House, Rome, and Leflon, vol. 1, p. 392.
[84] *Oblate Writings*, vol. 11, n. 1303, p. 298.

The Oblate congregation is priestly, that is, Oblates are to live the priesthood of Jesus. Living such a priesthood can take several forms, yet it is important to note that in its totality – priests and brothers – the Oblate congregation is dedicated to the Father in the likeness of Jesus the Priest and the apostles.

Priests and Brothers

Father de Mazenod answered the call of the Church and fulfilled his lifelong missionary vocation through his exercise of the ministerial priesthood. Today the Oblates' main commitment continues along the same line, with Oblate brothers having their own responsibility. They, too, are animated by the priestly charity of the preface to the rule:

> Wherefore, while pledging themselves to all the works of zeal which priestly charity can inspire – above all, to the work of the missions which is the main reason of their union – these priests, joined together in a society, resolve to obey the following Constitutions and Rules; by living them they hope to obtain all the benefits they need for their own sanctification and for the salvation of souls.[85]

To help position the brothers within the Oblate priestly and apostolic vocation we quote Rule 3 of the present Oblate Constitutions. It is new, written 160 years after Saint Eugene's original work, written in the light of post-Vatican II theology, yet it continues to breathe the Oblate Founder's spirit:

> Oblate brothers share in the common priesthood of Christ. They are called to cooperate in their own way in reconciling all things to him (*cf.* Colossians 1:20). Through their religious consecration they offer a particular witness to a life inspired by the Gospel.
>
> Brothers have an important missionary role to play in building up the Church everywhere, but especially in those areas where the Word is first being proclaimed. Through their technical, professional or pastoral service they are often able to exercise a fruitful ministry in situations not always open to the priest.

The theology of Rule 3 is very simple: the priesthood of Jesus Christ is unique. All who are in Christ form a part of that priesthood, but in distinct ways, each according to his or her vocation. The Oblate brother has his particular way of sharing in it through his particular religious consecration, his life centred on God and on persons in the same way as Christ, who in his priesthood lived totally for God and totally for humankind. The energy required comes from "the love of God (which) has been poured into our hearts by the Holy Spirit" (Romans 5:5). The entire Oblate congregation is

---

[85] *Preface of the Rule* (English), p.13.

priestly, that is, it is totally dedicated in the likeness of Jesus and of the apostles.

The Founder's Charism in Every Oblate

Frequently Eugene de Mazenod referred to his love as that of a father for his sons. Oblate canon lawyer and spiritual theologian Father Francis Demers says that the words *father* and *sons,* used so often by the Oblate Founder, are not mere figures of speech but refer to a profound reality, a mystery that deepens with the living out of the Oblate life. To understand this concept, he says, we must see a father in the same light as a mother – as God's instruments for transmitting life. In that sense, Eugene de Mazenod, by virtue of his vocation as founder, was in a birth-giving capacity, and thus was a life-giver, or a father. This he is, even today, by passing on the charism, which is the particular Oblate way of living out gospel values.

All the gospel values in the Church are the same for every believer, yet when a founder's special religious experience – his charism – is transmitted to the community which he establishes, a new life comes about – a new family genetic code, as it were, is introduced into the Church. We can define a charism as *a new way of life introduced into the church by a founder under the inspiration of the Holy Spirit.* It is, furthermore, *a series of graces which make up a number of elements that enter into the life of a founder and come to completion in the formation of a community.*

Ingredients of a Founder's Charism, Applied to Eugene de Mazenod

Father Demers points out that six ingredients can be found in the makeup of a founder's charism. Here is how he applies them to the Oblate Founder.

Experience of Christ

Recall Eugene's special grace of Good Friday, 1807, when he experienced God's infinite love – a love that did not stop short of death for us – not just for all humankind but for him personally.

Complete Conversion

In 1814 Eugene had written to his friend Forbin Janson, telling him that perhaps the Lord was calling him away from the world to a monastic life. Yet, a year later, he again wrote to Forbin Janson to say that for the *second* time in his life – the first time being Good Friday 1807 – he felt an "impulse from without" that gave him the incredible vitality and energy to form a society of missionaries. His exact words in French were a *"secousse étrangère,"* meaning a strong jolt from outside himself. By this experience of establishing his community *he was converted to a new way of life.*

A Changed Person

Eugene could see things clearly now through the eyes of faith, and it showed him how badly the world around him needed the Saviour whom he had personally experienced.

Discovering Needs

There is a direct connection between Eugene's conversion and his being perceptive to the needs around him. Looking at the world through the eyes of faith – through the eyes of the crucified Christ – he could discover needs that others did not see and hear voices and cries that others could not hear. He began to distinguish clearly who were the most abandoned and what were their needs.

Responding to the Needs

He set out to respond to those needs by serving and evangelizing the poor, the youth and prisoners through preaching, teaching, through the ministry of reconciliation and compassion and through whatever means that the needs demanded.

Founding a Community

After his near-fatal bout with typhus, Eugene realized that alone he could not respond to the needs he saw among the most abandoned. The next step, and the final ingredient in his founder's charism, was establishing a community with a group of like-minded priests.

Ingredients of the Founder's Charism Applied to the Oblates

On the day he makes his vows, the Oblate receives in a special way the seal of the congregation's charism, that life-giving grace of the Holy Spirit enabling him to share intimately in the Founder's experience. He has been led to that point through a series of steps:

Experiencing Christ

Through his formation, the Oblate comes to experience Jesus Christ as Saviour. Just as not every Christian is converted by being knocked off a horse like a St. Paul, not every Oblate experiences the conversion that so profoundly affected Eugene de Mazenod on Good Friday, 1807. Nonetheless, his formation and spiritual journey will bring him to his own conversion wherein he realizes, like the Founder, that Jesus is his personal Saviour.

A Complete Conversion – A Changed Person

Through reading, study and spiritual guidance he continues the work of his conversion. Conversion is a lifetime process.

Discovering Needs

With the community and through the faith-filled eyes of the crucified Christ, he discovers the needs of the Church, seeing things that others do not see, hearing things that others cannot hear.

Setting Out to Respond to the Needs

In concert with the community, he responds to those needs, preferentially going to the poor and the most abandoned, using the means which the needs dictate.

Father Demers concludes by pointing out that Eugene de Mazenod's charism – the Oblate charism – must lead the Oblate to a life of holiness and ministry. Holiness is a value in itself that contributes immeasurably to ministry and makes it fruitful.

Oblation, the Life-Blood of Saint Eugene's Congregation

That the Oblate congregation took on an international dimension and that it is still alive today is a consequence of its religious consecration – its *oblation* – as understood by Saint Eugene de Mazenod. That oblation maintains authentic spirituality as well as the congregation's original thrust. Suffice it simply to recall the disappearance of the *Missionnaires de France*, by far a much stronger and more "distinguished" society of preachers in France in the early 19th century than Eugene de Mazenod's motley little band. The difference would appear to be found in the life-giving strength of the Oblate apostolic spirituality – being *given totally* to Christ as Christ was to the Father, and as the Twelve were to him – and then to be *sent* to proclaim the Good Tidings to the poor.

Father Mike Rodrigo's Oblation

In this chapter we have spoken at length of the Oblate Founder's oblation and what oblation should mean to all Oblates. Sixty-year-old Father Mike Rodrigo of Sri Lanka had been an Oblate for 39 years and a priest for 33. He dedicated his life to Christ in the person of the poor sugar cane cutters on the plantations in the interior of his native island and was revered by them. On November 10, 1987, he was just finishing the eucharistic celebration in his mission of Buttala when assassins entered the church and shot him. As he slumped over the altar, his blood literally flowed into the chalice. Years before, he had put on paper the oblation he was to live. Here is what he wrote:

Lord Jesus, I give you my hands to do your work,

I give you my feet to go your way,

I give you my eyes to see as you do,

I give you my tongue to speak your words,

I give you my spirit that you may pray in me.

Above all, I give you my heart

so that in me you may love your Father and all mankind.

I give you my whole self that you may grow in me,

so that it is you, Lord Jesus, who lives and works and prays in me.

Some of Eugene de Mazenod's Preferred Biblical Texts

To live in Christ

Lk 4:16-30 — Jesus' mission
1 Cor 1:18 — 2:16 — The wisdom of the cross
1 Cor 3:9, and I Thess 3:2 — Cooperators with
the Saviour

In the footsteps of the Apostles

Acts 2:1-4 — The gift of the Spirit
Acts 2:14-41 — Wonders of the apostolate

Seeking the glory of God

1 Cor 4:1 — Stewards of the Godps mysteries
1 Pt 4:11 — That God be glorified in all

Accepting the will of God

Job 1:21 and Mt. 6:10 — Death of Oblates
Mt 26:36-46 – Gethsemane
Mt 6:25-34 — Trust in divine providence

Qualities of an Apostle

2 Cor 2:17 — Truthfulness
2 Cor 3:12 — Daring
Lk 9:62 — Fidelity

Prayer for vocations

Mt 9:38

Charity

Jn 13:34; 15:12; and Acts 4:32 — The commandment of love
Gal 4:19 — Spiritual fatherhood
Phil 1:3-11, and Jn 4:10 — Love for the Oblates

IX

Oblate of Mary Immaculate

The Immaculate Conception

"The most blessed Virgin Mary, in the first instant of her conception, by a singular grace and privilege granted by Almighty God, in view of the merits of Jesus Christ, the Saviour of the human race, was preserved free from all stain of original sin" – this is the dogmatic formula in Pope Pius IX's decree *Ineffabilis Deus,* by which the Immaculate Conception of Mary became an article of faith. The definition made it clear that the person of Mary, not just her soul, was immune from original sin. *Lumen Gentium* of Vatican II incorporated the phrase "was preserved free from all stain of original sin," reiterating that Mary's grace and the privilege were absolutely unique in all of humankind.

Bishop de Mazenod went to Rome expressly to attend the solemn promulgation of the decree on December 8, 1854. Five years earlier, in 1849, he had been one of the prelates and theologians consulted by the pope. In regard to that survey he had written to the pontiff:

> (It is the) ardour of everyone's desire to at last see a definitive and solemn decree from the Apostolic See stating that the Most Holy Mother of God, the loving Mother of us all, the Immaculate Virgin Mary, was conceived without original sin. The members of the Congregation of the Oblates of the Most Holy and Immaculate Virgin Mary felt an immense joy impossible to describe.[1]

Bishop Jeancard accompanied the Founder to Rome and wrote: "I have never seen him happier. His joy upon seeing her (the Immaculate Virgin) honoured amidst such splendour and under the same title given to his own Congregation showed itself constantly in his conversation."[2]

While in Rome awaiting the solemn promulgation of *Ineffabilis Deus,* Bishop de Mazenod wrote in his diary November 18, "My heart overflows with Catholicism."[3] Three days before the ceremony in St. Peter's his diary

---

[1] Letter to Pope Pius IX, April 28, 1949, in *Missions,* 1904, pp. 247-248.
[2] Jeancard, *Mélanges,* p. 296.
[3] *Missions,* 1873, p. 21.

shows that he wanted his Oblates "to know what their father thought and did on this most glorious occasion." "It is one of the most interesting accounts. In it, one sees in full swing, the faith, the piety, the intelligence, the heart, the unlimited devotion to the Church, to which he gave vent during his sojourn in the Eternal City, a sojourn, alas! which would be his last."[4]

On December 8, 1857, three years after the pope's promulgation of the dogma, Bishop de Mazenod dedicated a monument in Marseilles to the Immaculate Conception. Originally it stood at the end of the boulevard d'Athènes – a statue of the Virgin, atop a victory column, looking across the ancient city toward its colourful port. Its inauguration was the occasion of gala festivities. After a two-hour-long procession, Bishop de Mazenod celebrated a solemn Mass at the foot of the column. His journal entry shows that even while honouring the Virgin, the emphasis of the celebration was on Christ and the eucharist: "What a Mass that was! . . . When I raised the host to show our Lord to his huge family . . . I kept it raised on high at least a full minute so that it reigned in dominion over all his people."[5]

When the central railway station was built at the turn of the century, the site became its esplanade with a monumental stairway leading to the street below, and the statue with its column was moved. It now stands at the intersection of the boulevards Flammarion and National, at the end of a ramp to the left of the station as one leaves by the main doors.

A Brief History of the Dogma

Belief in Mary's Immaculate Conception goes back at least to patristic times, although there is no explicit mention of the privilege in Sacred Scripture. The papal definition of the doctrine holds that it is implied in Genesis 3:15 ("I will put enmity between you and the woman and between your offspring and hers"), Luke 1:28 ("Hail favoured one, the Lord is with you.") and Luke 1:42 ("Most blessed are you among women and blessed is the fruit of your womb").

Historically, there is a clear emergence of the belief in tradition by the fourth century. The earliest explicit testimony comes from St. Ephraem in the *Nisibene Hymns*: "Certainly thou alone and thy Mother are from every aspect completely beautiful, for there is no blemish in thee, My Lord, and no stain in thy mother." And St. Ambrose wrote: "Adopt me, not from Sarah but from Mary, so that it might be an incorrupt virgin, virgin by grace free from all stain of sin."

---

[4] Rey, vol. 2, p. 510.
[5] Aimé Roche, O.M.I., *Eugene de Mazenod*, Lyon, 1961, n. 88.

St. Maximus of Turin, in the sixth century, spoke of "original grace," juxtaposing it to original sin, thus making Mary a suitable dwelling place for Christ. In the East the idea of Mary's special holiness progressed to her complete holiness. Theoteknos of Livias spoke of Mary as "all fair," "pure and without stain," "from pure and immaculate clay." In the Eastern Church, too, the feasts of Mary's Immaculate Conception and Nativity can be found in the fifth century.

In the Western Church indications are that the feast was celebrated in Ireland during the seventh century. However the first incontrovertible evidence in the West is found in England around 1050. It disappeared with the Norman invasion of 1066 but soon revived and spread to the continent through Normandy, thence south and north in France. It soon crossed into Germany and Belgium and then into Spain. The importance of the feast provided the *sensus fidei* – the conviction of the faithful – which is always indispensable in developing a doctrine.

Problems in the Middle Ages

It appears almost incredible that belief in the Immaculate Conception survived against the teachings of many – perhaps most – of the era's great theologians. St. Bernard of Clairvaux and St. Anselm denied the belief, but both conceded that in Mary's holiness there was, as Anselm wrote, "a degree of purity so great that, apart from God, no greater can be imagined." St. Albert the Great, although denying Mary's Immaculate Conception, conceded that she was probably sanctified in her mother's womb, a view shared by St. Bonaventure. St. Thomas agreed to sanctification in the womb, but flatly rejected Immaculate Conception.

The problem that plagued all those great thinkers was the universality of redemption. In general terms their argument went thus: if Mary were conceived without original sin she would have had no cause or need to be redeemed, but Jesus came to redeem all humankind without exception. Therefore, St. Thomas argued, Mary could not have been conceived without original sin. It took Duns Scotus, "the subtle doctor," to skirt the dilemma that stumped the great scholastic theologians. Centuries before medicine ever spoke of immunization, Scotus referred to maladies that are cured and those that are prevented. In both cases, he said, they require the intervention of the physician. In Mary's case, he argued, sin was prevented before the fact, and because of that divine intervention she, too, was subject to Christ's redemption. Scotus' teaching contributed to the definition of the doctrine in *Ineffabilis Deus,* by giving special meaning to the phrase "a singular grace . . . in view of the merits of Jesus Christ, the Saviour of the Human race."

Controversies continued, but with a series of decrees in 1477 Sixtus IV approved the Mass of the Immaculate Conception. By 1497 the University of Paris decreed that anyone admitted for degrees must take an oath to defend the belief. The Council of Trent discreetly pointed to the ultimate solution, yet between 1627 and 1644 the Inquisition of Rome forbade the term "Immaculate Conception," decreeing that supporters of the doctrine could not go beyond speaking of the conception of the immaculate Virgin.

Advances Toward the Definition

Despite such measures, defenders of the doctrine produced an enormous volume of literature. Between 1550 and 1800 the Jesuits alone issued over 300 works on the Immaculate Conception. The Inquisition relented when St. Pius V renewed the decrees of Sixtus IV with his Bull *Super speculam* (1570). Paul V followed suit with *Regis Pacifici* (1616) and *Sanctissimus* (1617), as did Gregory XV with his Bull of the same name, *Sanctissimus* (1622).

After Alexander VII's decree *Sollicitudo omnium Ecclesiarum* (1661), which gave the doctrine papal protection (and was the basis for the 1854 declaration of the doctrine), opposition virtually died out. In 1695 Innocent XII promulgated the Mass and Office of the Conception of the Immaculate Virgin Mary for the Universal Church and in 1707, by the Constitution *Commissi nobis,* established the feast as a holy day of obligation. Marian theology deteriorated greatly during the Enlightenment and the French Revolution. Indeed, it was not until 1830 that a revival came about – and then, from an unexpected source, the apparition of the Miraculous Medal. The accompanying revival of Marian prayer featured the formula "O Mary conceived without sin, pray for us who have recourse to thee."

When Pius IX defined the dogma of the Immaculate Conception on December 8, 1854, the defining formula was:

> Accordingly, by the inspiration of the Holy Spirit, for the honour of the holy and undivided Trinity, for the glory and adornment of the Virgin Mother of God, for the exaltation of the Catholic Faith and the furtherance of the Catholic religion, by the authority of Jesus Christ Our Lord, of the Blessed Apostles Peter and Paul and our own, We declare, pronounce and define that the doctrine which holds that the most blessed Virgin Mary, in the first instant of her Conception, by a singular grace and privilege granted by Almighty God, in view of the merits of Jesus Christ the Saviour of the human race, was preserved free from all stain of original sin, is a doctrine revealed by God and therefore to be believed firmly and constantly by all the faithful.

Devotion to the Immaculate Conception in Aix

We do not know precisely when belief in the Immaculate Conception initiated special devotion in Aix, but it must have been around the millennium, soon after the doctrine first arrived in France. The first tangible proof of its presence is to be found in the ancient chapel of Notre-Dame de la Seds, hidden away on the north-east outskirts of the city, beyond the ancient Roman walls. On the floor worn by centuries of pilgrims' feet there is a prominent flagstone with the inscription:

> Hic Anno MCCCXXI Petrus Aureolus Arch.
>
> in Immaculatam Conceptionem Mariae Virginis
>
> ecclesiae Aquensis fidem declaravit.[6]

Peter Aureolus, born in the north of France in the late 13th century, became a Franciscan and studied under Duns Scotus at the Sorbonne. For a while before he went to teach theology in Toulouse, Aureolus even took the great master's place lecturing there. At Toulouse he organized a series of solemn conferences to explain his faith in the Immaculate Conception and in 1314 composed a *Tractus de conceptione Beatae Mariae Virginis* (Treatise on the Immaculate Conception of the Blessed Virgin Mary), the first *ex professo* treatise on the subject.[7] He was elected Archbishop of Aix and received his episcopal ordination on June 14, 1321 at the hands of Pope John XXII, the second of the Avignon popes. Peter Aureolus died on January 10, 1322, just months after that flagstone was inscribed on the chapel floor in Aix.[8]

By Eugene de Mazenod's time devotion to the Immaculate Conception was a deeply rooted tradition in Provence, especially in Aix. The city's 1770 catechism even had a lesson devoted to the Feast of the Immaculate Conception, and as early as 1738 we find the following article in the archdiocesan catechism published by Archbishop de Brancas:

> *Question*: What do you understand when you say that the Conception of the Blessed Virgin was immaculate?
>
> *Answer*: I understand that the Blessed Virgin Mary was conceived without original sin; as a result she was never, in any instant of her life, a slave to sin or under the demon's power, since she was predestined to be the Mother of God.[9]

---

[6] Translation: Here, in the year 1321, Peter Aureolus, Archbishop, proclaimed the faith of the Church of Aix in the Immaculate Conception of the Virgin Mary.

[7] *Dictionnaire de Spiritualité*, vol. 12, col. 1505-1508.

[8] *L'Épiscopat d'Aix*, Macaire, Aix-en-Provence, 1863.

[9] Abbé M. Davin, *L'Immaculée Conception honorée dans la ville d'Aix*, Aix-Makaire, p. 53.

We know that from very early on in his life, Eugene had a strong devotion to Mary, like many of his contemporaries in Aix. Certainly, in his case, much of it must have been passed on to him from his mother whose Marian piety was well known.

Marian Devotion in the French School of Spirituality

Just as Eugene de Mazenod was influenced by the French School's way of seeing Jesus as the perfect worshiper of the Father, his spirituality must certainly have been affected by the Sulpician view of Mary. Both Cardinal Pierre de Bérulle, the father of the French School, and the Abbé Jean-Jacques Olier, founder of St-Sulpice and the Sulpicians, spoke clearly about the Immaculate Conception. Concerning that unique gift and privilege, Bérulle wrote, "The same moment (conception) gave her natural existence, the state of grace and life and movement toward God."[10] Olier, too, held that Mary had been conceived without original sin: "[B]esides being preserved from the crime of origin, she was all filled from the first instant of her conception with the Holy Spirit and his graces."[11]

Eugene's Provençal roots already provided him with an established devotion to the Immaculate Conception. It is not difficult to see how St-Sulpice would deepen and broaden that love. There, Mary was seen as the sanctuary of the Holy Spirit, mother and handmaid of the Son and spouse of the Father. It was taught there that through the birth of Jesus a spiritual bond ties Mary's motherhood to us – she forms Jesus in us. It was at St-Sulpice that Eugene de Mazenod learned the prayer *O Jesu vivens in Maria* – O Jesus living in Mary – adapted by Father Olier from a formula composed by the Sulpicians' other founder, Father de Condren, with many of its elements traceable to Cardinal Bérulle himself.

> In *The Society of Jesus and Mary,* (Olier) considered gospel episodes such as the Finding in the Temple, and Jesus' replies to words about his Mother and ends with a doctrine of Mary and the Church, that post-conciliar theologians can value. It provides an opportunity to prepare a new application of the bridal concept – the espousals of Mary and Jesus. This is brought out in the chapter on Mary on Calvary when "the Church, in the person of Mary, espouses Jesus Christ on the Cross."[12]

---

[10] M. Rigal, *Les Mystères de Marie,* from Coll. *Les Lettres chrétiennes,* Paris, 1961, p. 200.

[11] *Vie Intérieure de la Très-Sainte Vierge, ouvrage recueilli des écrits de M. Olier,* Rome, 1966, Michael O'Carroll, C.S.Sp., in *Theotokos,* Dominican Publications, Dublin, 1982, p. 273.

[12] Michael O'Carroll, C.S.Sp. in *Theotokos,* Dominican Publications, Dublin, 1982, p. 273.

Mary at the foot of the cross would deeply influence Eugene's devotion.

Oblate of Mary Immaculate

Mary in the Early Life of the Founder

Eugene de Mazenod grew up in a household of traditional Marian devotion. While he was exiled in Venice, that devotion deepened under the tutelage of the saintly Don Bartolo. Each morning for three years, the two prayed the Little Office of the Blessed Virgin, and each evening they recited the rosary with the Zinelli family. In Palermo, when the youth appeared to be distancing himself from his boyhood ideals, a worried Don Bartolo wrote him a reminder: "Nothing against God; nothing against Mary . . . . Be a good young man, all for Jesus, all for Mary." It was one of the last admonitions that Eugene received from him.

Eugene at St-Sulpice

Even a cursory examination of the French School's Marian theology helps us to understand the place of Mary in Eugene de Mazenod's spirituality. Olier repeatedly emphasized the interior states of Jesus and Mary: "The innermost being of Mary is Jesus living in her." The bridal motif, which we see time and again in Eugene's writings, is constant with Olier. Since Mary was conceived as sinless, Olier analyzed at length her state of soul after being been presented in the Temple: "The Word of God, through the love he bore the most holy Virgin, advanced the time of his marriage with the Church. For Mary cried out and longed for the Messiah with power exceeding that of all the prophets."[13] St-Sulpice energetically stressed the Immaculate Conception. We see Eugene's spiritual director, M. Duclaux approving of Eugene's fast on the vigil of the Immaculate Conception. And to his sister, Eugene wrote in December, 1808: "I am in a hurry to get over to St-Sulpice where we are celebrating the Immaculate Conception with special solemnity."

The birth of Jesus prompted Olier to express his opinion on the spiritual motherhood of Mary, namely, that she forms Jesus in us. In the chapter "The Society of Jesus and Mary" he concluded from Gospel episodes a doctrine that put a new face on the relation of Mary and the Church – a new application of the bridal concept: the espousals of Mary and Jesus. This is in his chapter on Mary at Calvary and it has its echo in Eugene's contempla-

---

[13] Michael O'Carroll, C.S.Sp. in *Theotokos,* Dominican Publications, Dublin, 1982, p. 273.

tion of Mary at the foot of the cross: "The Church, in the person of Mary espouses Jesus Christ on the Cross."[14]

Virgin and Mother – Mary in the Christian Youth Sodality

When Eugene de Mazenod established his youth apostolate in Aix, it was consecrated to the Blessed Trinity under the patronage and mediation of Mary Immaculate:

> We, the undersigned members of the Congregation of Christian Youth, founded in Aix under the patronage of the Immaculate Conception of the Most Holy Virgin Mary, testify by those here present, as members of the said Sodality, to consecrate ourselves perpetually to the Most Holy Trinity . . . to whom we offer this gift of our entire being through the hands of the Most Holy and Immaculate Virgin Mary, our Mother and Patroness; to her service, we likewise devote ourselves with all our heart.

Recall, too, how without fail at the end of each meeting the group heartily sang a Provençal hymn to Mary Immaculate.

At about the same time, in the 1814 retreat notes we read: "Now that I am admitted to the Sanctuary, you, my Patron Saints, my Guardian Angel and you, Holy Virgin, continue to protect me, and in virtue of the Sovereign Mediator's merits, obtain from him that my good works, despite my blameworthy sterility, may nourish not only my soul but the entire Church, as well."[15] This prayer was written at the end of the year when, after volunteering to serve the needs of Austrian prisoners-of-war in Aix, Eugene contracted typhus from them and nearly died. Remember how the members of the youth sodality stormed heaven with special novenas to Our Lady of Grace in the Church of the Madeleine and how, upon recovering his health, Eugene and the sodality celebrated a Mass of thanksgiving there, honouring the Virgin whom they considered responsible for his near-miraculous recovery.

Mary in the First Moments of the Oblate Congregation

We have seen how, on January 25, 1816, Eugene de Mazenod founded a society of secular priests dedicated to evangelizing the most abandoned. There is no document to tell us what role the Immaculate Conception played in that foundation. However, six months later, to judge from his retreat, Mary certainly had a privileged place in his heart. Among the retreat

---

[14] *Vie intérieure de la très-Sainte Vierge d'après les écrits de M. Olier,* vol. 2, Paris, 1875, Ch. 13, p. 85

[15] Retreat Notes, December, 1814, 4th day, Arch. Post. Rome.

resolutions was one that committed him each day of his life to pray, *"Dignare me laudare te Virgo Maria."*

And in his retreat notes of 1818 – the retreat that ended in the first general chapter after acceptance of the rule – not only does he refer to Mary as his "good Mother" but, by calling on her ever more often, he asks her to help him intensify and deepen his prayer life day by day:

> Virgin Mary, my good Mother, if I called upon you more often I would have less cause to groan inwardly. Help me, O my Mother, by your powerful intercession to carry out better than heretofore all the obligations your dear Son imposed upon me so that, with your help, my reward is to conscientiously carrying them out. And as I grow less unworthy, I promise to strive toward and to enter into the still greater reward which awaits me in heaven.[16]

That quotation is the only document extant on Eugene de Mazenod's interior disposition toward Mary, until the special grace of August 15, 1822. It shows how he sought to strengthen the ties binding him to her as his mother. However, we can surmise that, as difficulties grew, he increasingly felt the necessity of seeking his heavenly Mother's help.

> The heaviest crosses were laid upon him by the pastors of Aix. Aged, Jansenist, faithful to Napoleon, smugly satisfied to carry out their daily humdrum activities, they cast a malevolent eye, from the very outset, on that little company of young priests who propounded the moral theology of St. Alphonsus Liguori and who chose to exercise their apostolate outside the parish framework, ministering to the youth and preaching popular missions.[17]

The faithful, especially young people, crowded the Mission Church in Aix. It became a lightning rod attracting the wrath of entrenched old-school pastors' against the missionaries, and brought accusations that the missionaries were distancing the faithful from their parishes. There is no immediate testimony that Eugene recurred to Mary in this situation. Nevertheless, a letter he wrote to Father Tempier from Rome on March 20, 1826 is enlightening. In the letter he comments at length on the vicissitudes experienced by St. Alphonsus. The Oblate Founder's admiration for the saint is obvious. What makes this letter even more significant is that Alphonsus was beatified in 1816 and became one of Eugene's favourite patrons, one to whom he could relate spiritually. Indeed, he even got his own father to translate Giattini's biography of the saint from Italian into

---

[16] One-day retreat, during the community retreat of the Rule, October 30, 1818.
[17] Y. Beaudoin, O.M.I., *Itinerario spirituale di Mons. CJE de Mazenod,* 1986, p. 8.

French.[18] Eugene was well-versed in the Marian devotion of Alphonsus, who said of his "good Mother," "She told me so many beautiful things!" Eugene de Mazenod hoped that just as Mary showed Alphonsus the way for his congregation, she would point out the path for the Missionaries of Provence as well. And like the Redemptorist founder, Eugene went frequently to seek help from his "good Mother."

Mary on August 15, 1822

Something happened to Saint Eugene de Mazenod on August 15, 1822, that would profoundly influence his spiritual life and his attitude to Mary Immaculate. Some have noted a certain similarity between this experience and that of Alphonsus. Unfortunately, there are no documents that could truly reveal anything definite on the subject. On that day the statue of the Immaculate Conception, which now stands in the General House chapel in Rome, was dedicated in the Mission Church in Aix. Oblate tradition affirms that "our venerated Founder . . . with great fervour before a statue of the Immaculate Conception, asked for a grace to which he attached great importance, a grace, it is said, that dealt with his own and the Congregation's future."[19]

The Founder's own somewhat cryptic testimony is to be found in a letter written from Aix to Father Tempier at Notre-Dame de Laus on the very evening of the occurrence:

> The ceremony has just finished, my dear and best brother. Silence reigns in the house. It is broken only by the sound of a distant bell that announces the departure of the great procession. Overflowing with the sincere tributes we just finished rendering to our Mother at the feet of the beautiful statue we installed as a remembrance of her in our church, I am letting the others take care of honouring her with the external pomp of a procession which really would not add anything to my already over-demanding devotion. Let this interlude be used to talk with you, dear friend, in a sweet outpouring of the heart. Would that I could share with you all that I experienced in the way of consolation on this beautiful day devoted to Mary our Queen!

> Not for a long time had I felt as much joy in speaking of her grandeur and in encouraging our Christians to put all their confidence in her as I did during the instruction given to the Sodality this morning. I would like to think that I was understood and can well believe that all the faithful who came to our church this evening shared the fervour that inspired me at the sight of the *image* of the Holy Virgin, and greater still, the graces which, I

---

[18] The manuscript of his father's translation is preserved in the archives of the Oblate General House, Rome, DM I 8.

[19] Edmond Dubois, *Positio super introductione causae*, p. 716.

dare to say, she obtained from her divine Son while we were calling upon her with so much affection because she is our Mother. I also believe that it is to her that I owe *a special experience* I felt today; I will not go so far as to say more than ever, but certainly more than usual. I cannot describe it too well because it comprised several things but all are related to a single object, our dear Society It seemed to me that what I saw, what I could put my finger on, was that within the Society lies the germ of very great virtues and that it can achieve great good. I discovered our Society's worth; everything about it pleased me; I cherished its rules, its statutes. Its ministry seemed sublime, as indeed it is. At its heart I found the sure, even infallible, means of salvation.[20]

What Mary revealed to Eugene was the value of his congregation for the ministry to the poor and for the sanctification of its own members. From the beginning of his formation he had always looked upon the Virgin as his mother. On this day, however, he felt the full impact of that maternity and wrote the word *Mother* with a capital *M*. He described his feelings, yet said nothing about what had happened outwardly. Tempier was ever his confidant and to him he confessed that evening that "the sight of the *image* of the Holy Virgin" was a *"special experience"* inspiring him with extraordinary fervour.

Around those words, *image* (which in French can also mean *a vision*) and *a special experience*, an oral tradition grew in some parts of the Oblate congregation. The tradition holds that the statue of the Virgin inclined its head in an approving nod toward the Founder of the Oblates that evening. However, no one ever claimed to have heard the Founder tell of such a miracle, nor did he himself ever make such as claim. Nor did Father Rambert in his biography, although he saw the event as a special grace presaging papal approbation of the congregation.

The tradition of the Virgin's "miraculous inclining of the head" was first mentioned by Father Emile Lamblin in an article entitled *"The Immaculate Conception and the Congregation of Christian Youth"*:[21] "According to oral tradition, so carefully gathered and preserved, the statue opened its eyes and nodded its head as an approving sign while (the Virgin's) zealous servant asked her for a favour. This extraordinary feat never appeared in any written report."[22] Lamblin's account – although he put it in the wrong year (1823) – fuelled the writings of other biographers, notably Fathers Eugene Baffie and Marcel. The three put the Founder kneeling before the statue

---

[20] *Oblate Writings*, vol. 6, 1822, pp. 92-93, n. 86.
[21] *L'Immaculée Conception et la Congrégation de la jeunesse chrétienne*, in *Missions*, 1904, pp. 465-477.
[22] Ibid.

while the procession was going on outside, something that is patently contradicted by de Mazenod's own letter to Tempier. Despite such discrepancies, however, the "miraculous nod" became a tradition, not just among the Oblates of France but with the diocesan clergy of Aix as well. Writing about the closure of the Oblate chapel in that city because of the general expulsion of religious orders and congregations from France, the Abbé M. Davin stated that it was "the Church of the Immaculate Conception, where, we are assured, her statue inclined its head, surrounded by a cloud of stars, toward the Abbé de Mazenod."[23]

Somewhere, much later, a further tradition sprung up that the Virgin had actually smiled at the Founder. This may have been inspired by the accounts of Saint Therese of Lisieux who wrote that during her illness, "suddenly the Blessed Virgin appeared to me as beautiful – so beautiful that I had never seen anything to compare . . . but what really touched me to the depths of my soul was *the Blessed Virgin's ravishing smile*."[24]

Traditions aside, the fact is that the precious moment in Eugene de Mazenod's life spent kneeling before the statue of the Virgin in the chapel at Aix was an instant of great mystic grace filling him with extraordinary fervour and prompting him to fight against all odds for the survival of his little society of missionaries. What greater miracle do we need than the miracle of such grace?[25]

Arriving at the Name "Oblates of Mary Immaculate"

It was Eugene de Mazenod who requested a name-change. Writing to Father Tempier from Rome on December 9, 1825, Father de Mazenod stated that the previous day he had drafted the text of a four-page petition to Pope Leo XII.[26] Part of it read as follows: "In the letter of approbation that the missionaries beg of you, we beseech Your Holiness to consent to give them the name of Oblates of the Most Holy and Immaculate Virgin Mary."

When the Oblate Founder finally got to see the pope on December 20, recall how he impressed the pontiff by recounting the Oblates' missionary ex-

---

[23] Abbé M. Davin, *L'Immaculée Conception honorée dans la ville d'Aix*, Aix-Makaire, p. 98.
[24] *Manuscrits autobiographiques de Ste-Thérèse de l'Enfant Jésus*, ed., Office central de Lisieux, 1957.
[25] For a detailed description of this happening, see Kazimierz Lubowicki, O.M.I., in *"Marie dans la vie du Bx Eugène de Mazenod et de la Congrégation"* in *Vie Oblate Life*, vol. 88, p. 13.
[26] *Oblate Writings*, vol. 5, p. 209.

ploits among the poor. Pressing his good fortune, Eugene put four questions to Pope Leo from the petition he had written 12 days earlier. The first three were of a canonical and jurisdictional nature and were answered in the affirmative. The fourth question, as he wrote to Father Tempier on December 22, was this:

> "Does your Holiness approve that the Society take the name of *Oblates of the Most Holy and Immaculate Virgin Mary* instead of that of *Oblates of St. Charles* which it had taken previously?" The pope said neither yes nor no. I think I understood him to say that it should be put in the report. I did not insist on explaining the matter further . . . .[27]

Apparently the Founder's petition did not go unheeded. The pontiff's apostolic bull of approbation gave the little society the name its Founder had asked for and more: "We hereby, with a ready and willing mind, establish (the Congregation) and wish it to be known by the name of the Congregation of the Missionary Oblates of the Most Holy Virgin Mary, conceived without sin." Leo XII added *Missionary* to Father de Mazenod's request for a name change. After that, the Founder could only comment: "It is the Church which has given us this beautiful name; we receive it with respect, love and gratitude."[28]

Mary's Place in the Congregation

The pope's approbation put the Missionary Oblate congregation under Mary's direct patronage and filled the Founder with unspeakable joy. He made it very clear, however, that the Oblates were not approved just to proclaim the glories of Mary. They are *missionaries* under the *patronage* of Mary Immaculate, but *consecrated to God in his poor* whom they must see through the eyes of the crucified Lord:

> Does it not appear to be a sign of predestination to bear the name Oblates of Mary, that is, *consecrated to God* under the patronage of Mary, the name the Congregation bears as its family name in common with the most holy and immaculate Mother of God? It is enough to make others jealous. But it is the Church who has given us that beautiful name; we receive it with respect, love and gratitude, proud of our dignity and of the rights it gives us to the protection of her who is all-powerful in God's presence. Let us delay no longer in taking upon ourselves that beautiful name . . . .[29]

De Mazenod's Directives About Mary

Popular devotion to Mary must be faithful to Church doctrine:

---

[27] *Oblate Writings,* vol. 5, p. 220.

[28] Ibid., vol. 7, p. 63.

[29] Ibid., p. 63.

Mary's power of intercession and maternal love are acclaimed everywhere
. . . . We never give too much honour to the Blessed Virgin provided
devotion to her is understood and practised in the limited sense of what is
due to a creature, however great and sublime she may be. We must be
careful, however, lest we pay to ordinary images of God's mother a
veneration whose external signs seem to obscure those required by the
presence of Jesus Christ. On the contrary, the devotion which our faith and
love address to the adorable Eucharist must be, proportionate to our
humble means, far superior to what we generally entertain and practice for
Mary Immaculate.[30]

Oblates are to put themselves under the protection of Mary. Their Founder
made that clear in a letter to the first missionaries in Canada: "May the
Blessed Virgin conceived without stain be your guide and patroness. Bear in
mind that to propagate devotion to her everywhere is a special duty of our
vocation."[31] Oblates are to share his implicit trust in our Mother. When he
appointed Father Jean Verdet head of the Texas mission, he wrote, "Before
you leave the Sanctuary (Notre-Dame de Bon Secours) pray fervently that
the Most Holy Virgin obtain for us the light that we need in order to make a
decision in harmony with the will of God, the edification of the Church, the
salvation of souls and your own sanctification."[32]

Mary, Sign of Redemption

When Saint Eugene spoke of the Immaculate Conception he, like his
contemporaries, meant that Mary was conceived without original sin. Yet
for him it was more than just the absence of sin, for he referred to her special
privilege in positive terms, much as the Second Vatican Council did over a
century later, as "redeemed in a more exalted fashion by reason of the merits
of her Son, and united to him by an indissoluble tie."[33]

Mary, Bearer of the Holy Spirit

Though he did not say so in as many words, Eugene de Mazenod appeared
to see Mary as the *pneumatophore*, the "Bearer of the Holy Spirit." That
would be very much in line with the teaching of the French School.
Accordingly, when the Founder admired the beauty of Mary and
contemplated the marvelous form that redemption takes in her, he was
praising Christ for the marvel of his redemption.

---

[30] *Pastoral Letter of December 21, 1859, Selected Texts*, pp. 130-131, n. 109.

[31] *Oblate Writings*, vol. 1, p. 156, n. 78.

[32] Ibid., vol. 2, p. 25, n. 153.

[33] *Lumen Gentium*, no. 53.

Theologians such as René Laurentin have stated that during the 19th century, Western Church theology was at a low and the Holy Spirit was all but forgotten. Moreover, according to Laurentin, many of the Spirit's attributes were frequently misapplied to Mary:

> The first thirty years of the nineteenth century are perhaps the most barren in the history of Marian literature. Books are rare and mediocre. And yet the impulse springs up again and again, suddenly, in new and surprising forms.
>
> First, there is an apparition in 1830, the first in a long series that will characterize the nineteenth century. The Virgin Mary gave the image of the Miraculous Medal to Catherine Labouré. The fact remained hidden but it led to a vast movement of devotion and conversion. . . . This medal – the Virgin "conceived without sin," with arms outstretched downward – seemed to set forth the program that was to guide the Marian movement for a whole century: Mary's Immaculate Conception and her Mediation.
>
> Inaugurated by an apparition, the period was prolonged in a definition. In 1854 the Immaculate Conception was declared a dogma of the faith. The infallible pronouncement came upon a theology that had not yet shown any sign of renewal. The effort of the seventeenth and eighteenth centuries seemed to have been forgotten for the while and that of the nineteenth century was still negligible. . . . Theology remained enfeebled, with the exception of trailblazers unrecognized in their day: Newman in England (1866) and Scheeben in Germany. It is disappointing to read today the Mariologists who were then in vogue. Even the widely read Msgr. Malou startles one when, for example, he calls Mary a "divine person," or "the fourth person of the Holy Trinity" – all that "according to the Fathers," without any reference being given. And one readily understands why not.[34]

Be all that as it may, it was certainly not the case with Eugene de Mazenod. The Oblate Founder may have been one of the few who gave the Spirit its due, for he seemed intuitively to see a link between Mary and the Spirit. For him she was the Spirit's masterpiece in whom we honour God's power through Jesus:

> It is God whom we glorify in the masterpiece of his power and glory; we praise him because among all the marvels of his power that prove his infinite greatness, he produced someone who sums up in herself alone, better than in all other persons put together, his adorable perfections. Furthermore, the greatness of the Blessed Virgin consists especially in her dignity as Mother of God. This is the reason for all the prerogatives with which she is endowed and for the greater devotion we pay to her.[35]

---

[34] Laurentin: *A Short Treatise on the Virgin Mary,* Ami Press, 1991, pp. 135-137, translated from *Court traité sur la Vierge Marie,* Les éditions OEIL, Paris.

[35] *Selected Texts,* p. 129, n. 107.

What he wrote in the preceding passage is completely in line with the pronouncements of Vatican II: Mary was "redeemed in a more exalted fashion by reason of the merits of her Son, and united to him by a close and indissoluble tie . . . ."[36]

Mary at the Foot of the Cross

One can see how important for Saint Eugene was the contemplation of Christ's love on Good Friday, 1807 – the realization that Christ's blood was the symbol and proof of his limitless love. In the lamentations of Holy Week's divine office, in which Jerusalem is presented as a mother mourning the death of her children, the young de Mazenod came to an awareness of how that mourning symbolized the Church of his day – his mother, mourning so many defections. This awareness was to influence the content of the preface to the rule which he would later write: "The Church, that glorious inheritance purchased by Christ the Saviour at the cost of his own blood, has in our days been cruelly ravaged. The beloved spouse of God's only-begotten Son is torn with anguish as she mourns the shameful defection of the children she herself bore."

For Eugene de Mazenod the presence of the Immaculate Conception at the foot of the cross becomes vital: "Seeing his mother and the disciple he loved standing near her, Jesus said to his mother, 'Woman, this is your son.' Then, to the disciple he said, 'This is your Mother.' And from that moment the disciple made a place for her in his home" (John. 19:25-27). Part of the Founder's charism, as the loving servant of his brothers and sisters in the world, will always be the Oblate's task: to bring God's sons and daughters back to the bosom of the Mother of Mercy.

When Saint Eugene brought together the Immaculate Conception and Mary, standing at the foot of the Cross, he saw her, the marvel of the redemption, taking part in the salvation of all humankind, sharing her Son's limitless love. How the Founder viewed the presence of Mary at the foot of the cross comes through clearly in his pastoral letter, issued on July 8, 1849, to introduce the see of Marseilles to Pope Pius IX's encyclical on the Immaculate Conception:

> Next to that which directly concerns God, nothing is more precious for truly enlightened piety than that which concerns the honour of the Blessed Virgin Mary. Here we encounter all that exists in a son towards his mother. And what a Mother! To us she gave her Son, the world's life and salvation; she engendered all of us spiritually at the foot of the Cross through the pangs of the passion and death of the God-Man, the blessed

---

[36] *Lumen Gentium,* no. 53.

fruit of her womb. She is rightly called the new Eve and the co-redemptrix of the human race.[37]

We can see the vital synthesis which the Oblate Founder made: Mary was redeemed in a more exalted fashion; her vocation was to participate in Christ's work of redemption through her maternal love, and then through her even greater love beneath the cross: "One can have no greater love than to lay down one's life for one's friends" (John 15:13).

At the centre of it all was Mary's "fiat" which the Oblate missionary must make his own. We can, perhaps, diagram Mary's *fiat* and oblation as follows:

Mary   **Mary**

redeemed in a privileged fashion   united with the redemption at
                                          the foot of the cross

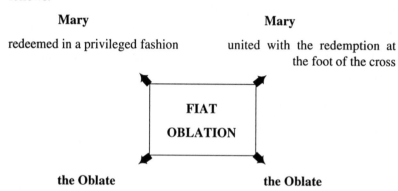

FIAT

OBLATION

the Oblate   **the Oblate**

called by Christ in a privileged way   co-worker with the Saviour,
                                          redeemed in a privileged
                                          way by his oblation

Granted, much of the foregoing goes beyond Saint Eugene's explicit writing. Nonetheless, from what he said, from the way he spoke and wrote of Mary, one can come to thus understand the Oblates' name and their very being in the Church. With this title Mary proclaims that redemption is the greatest of marvels; the most striking manifestation of God's love – and Missionary Oblates of Mary Immaculate are at its service.

Mary and the Oblate Charism

Mary's Place in the Oblate Apostolate – *Praying with Mary*

The 1826 Constitutions and Rules state that "all the members of the Society will cultivate a particular and affectionate devotion towards Mary, to whom

---

[37] *Selected Texts*, p. 128, n. 107.

they will always look as their Mother." A more literal translation would be "... towards sweet Mary whom they will always have as their Mother." The word *sweet* comes from the original French and Latin and is understood in the biblical sense. In Latin there are two words that signify *sweet* or *meek*. They are *dulcis* and *mitis* and are applied to the poor.[38] It is said that God is *sweet*, especially in regard to the poor,[39] so they will be happy in the Lord.[40] And Jesus said, "Learn from me, for I am meek and lowly of heart" (Matthew 1:29).

Praying with the Bible in Latin, as the early Oblates were accustomed to do, they used the same term *sweet* to designate *the poor, God* and *Mary*. For them, Mary became the option of "the little ones." *Dulcem Mariam* was not simply an expression of pious sentimentality, but a title of deep biblical meaning, an expression of faith in the maternal tenderness of their mother, the Virgin Mary. The title took them back to one of the oldest liturgical prayers, the *Salve Regina*.

Mary, Model of Faith Today

Time and again we have seen how important for Eugene was the Saviour aspect of Jesus Christ. Redemption – the precious blood of Jesus shed for love of humankind – overrode every other consideration in his life. And Mary was an integral part of the equation. He wrote, "She is the dawn of our Redemption, the ineffable moment when the promises began to be fulfilled."[41] Other images of Mary's Immaculate Conception and redemptive role repeatedly entered his vocabulary, as in the following: "It is a seed of immeasurable grace, a living cell bearing great fruit . . ., a pure spring which flows in all freedom."[42] For Eugene de Mazenod, admiring the beauty of Mary meant praising Christ for the marvel of that redemption: "It is the Son whom we honour in the person of the Mother and that is why, in our homage to Mary, it is impossible to overstep the limit, provided we consider her a creature, because God then always remains the supreme end of all that homage."[43]

---

[38] Cf. the third Beatitude: "Blessed are the meek" (King James).

[39] Psalm 25 (24): 8 – "Sweet (dulcis) and upright is the Lord."
I Peter 2:3 – "You have tasted that the Lord is sweet (dulcis)."
Psalm 21 (20): 4 – "You prevent him with the blessings of sweetness (in benedictionibus dulcedinis)."

[40] Isaiah 29:19 – "The meek (*mites* in Latin) also shall rejoice in the Holy One of Israel."

[41] August 1, 1854.

[42] From the Founder's notebook.

[43] *Pastoral Letter*, July 8, 1849, *Selected Texts*, p. 129, n. 107.

Truth has not changed, but often the way of expressing it has. Constitution 10 of the 1982 Oblate Constitutions and Rules echoes the Founder today when it states:

> Mary Immaculate is the patroness of our Congregation. Open to the Spirit, she consecrated herself totally as lowly handmaid to the person and work of the Saviour. She received Christ in order to share him with all the world whose hope he is. In her we recognize the model of the Church's faith and of our own.
>
> We shall always look on her as our mother. In the joys and sorrows of our missionary life we feel close to her who is the Mother of Mercy. Wherever our ministry takes us, we will strive to instil genuine devotion to the Immaculate Virgin who prefigured God's final victory over evil.[44]

How is Mary a model of the Church's faith in the modern world? How are Oblates of Mary Immaculate in the 20th and 21st century to make their mother known, to instil genuine devotion to her in a world where meekness is frequently despised as weakness? Well, if we look at Mary as she really is, and not simply as a shy and pale facsimile of the real person, a number of possibilities present themselves:

Mary Welcomes God in Whatever Way He Chooses to Come

God chose his own way to come to Mary. It was Bethlehem instead of Nazareth, a cave instead of a home, her son executed in the prime of life instead of being proclaimed a king by an angel. In his homily at Ephesus in 1979, Pope John Paul II stressed that "Mary went through difficult moments of darkness." What a model she is for anyone on the brink of doubt or unbelief! "She had also heard the words, 'he will be great and the Lord God will give to him the throne of his father, David . . .' and now, standing at the foot of the cross, Mary is the witness, humanly speaking, of the complete negation of those words."[45]

Silent Faith That Contemplates the Marvels of Her Own Destiny

In that contemplation Mary discovered God's plan for the poor. Mary's faith is not limited to herself, but is a source of light revealing the divine plan. It is in giving thanks for her own destiny that Mary discovers God who "exalted the lowly." She discovers God's faithfulness to his promises "to Abraham and his descendants forever."

---

[44] *1982 Constitutions and Rules,* Const. 10 (English), p. 22.

[45] *Redemptoris Mater,* no. 18.

Silent Faith That Listens to God Through the Poor

Mary, the model of the Church's faith, was attentive to Elizabeth at the time of the Visitation. She herself said nothing special, leaving it to the once-barren Elizabeth – the "poor" woman – to speak the name of the Lord while she listened to the message (Luke 2:25).

In Bethlehem, she listened to the poor and despised shepherds, who had received God's announcement of the Saviour and who "repeated all they had been told about the baby." Mary listened as they, the poor, proclaimed the mystery of God, Jesus the Saviour (Luke 2:17). She was evangelized by the poor. Her example of listening to them in order to hear God refers the Oblate directly to his own Rule 8: "Let our lives be enriched by the poor."

Active Faith That Collaborates in the Work of Salvation

At Cana Mary introduced the disciples to faith in Christ. "The Good News is the power of God saving all who have faith" (Romans 1:16). Mary shows the Oblate how the faith of the poor is powerful enough to cooperate in salvation. The last image of Mary in the New Testament is of her in prayer with the apostles as they await the coming of the Paraclete (John 2:1-11). Thus, just as she was an active participant in the birth of Jesus the Saviour, she was active at the birth of the Church by her prayer of faith. We see that she constantly leads us to Jesus.

Faith Unites Mary to Christ's Sacrifice

At the presentation, Simeon foretold, in reference to Jesus' destiny, that a sword would pierce Mary's soul (Luke 2:34). Those who, like Mary, take part in evangelization, will also have their heart pierced by the sword of contradiction. They want to be and are peacemakers, yet while they denounce injustice, sin and evil, they meet opposition – their heart is pierced. Jesus came to bring the fire of love to the earth (Luke 12:49), but his unsettling message also brought the sword of division (Luke 12:51). Mary was the first member of the prophetic Church to experience the pains of evangelization. At the foot of the cross, when Jesus was reviled and rejected, Mary was not ashamed of him (John 19:25-27). Indeed her presence proclaimed staunchly: I do not understand what is happening here but *this is my son*. Jesus entrusted her to the beloved disciple and, through him, to all humankind. To the Missionary Oblate whose vocation it is to announce the Good News to the poor, this has special meaning. Constitution 10 of his rule tells him, "She received Christ in order to share him with all the world."

Marian Devotion Today

We are challenged today not to imitate Saint Eugene de Mazenod, not to try to do things exactly as he did them, but we are challenged by the grace of his charism; challenged by his conversion, challenged to see the world as Saint Eugene saw it, through the eyes of its Saviour, the crucified Christ. We are challenged to let the Spirit move us today, as Saint Eugene let the Spirit move him in Marseilles and to the ends of the earth, challenged to seek out today's most abandoned, wherever they be, as he did in his day, challenged to make Mary Immaculate, "our Mother," known and loved today in our world, as Saint Eugene did 150 years ago in his.

Several passages from Pope John Paul II's encyclical, *Marialis Cultus*, can help show the way to a positive contemporary Marian devotion in keeping with the charism that the Oblate congregation received from its Founder. Here are a few examples to help meet the challenge of presenting Mary today:

Renewing the Devotion

> The piety of the faithful and their veneration of the Mother of God has taken on many forms according to circumstances of time and place, the different sensitivities of peoples and their different cultural traditions. Hence, it is that the forms in which this devotion is expressed, being subject to the ravages of time, show the need for a renewal that will permit them to substitute elements that are transient, to emphasize the elements that are ever new and to incorporate the doctrinal data obtained from theological reflection and the proposals of the Church's Magisterium.[46]

Respecting the Devotion

There are certain persons concerned with the care of souls who scorn, a priori, devotions of piety which, in their correct forms, have been recommended by the Magisterium, who leave them aside and in that way create a vacuum which they do not fill.[47]

Devotion Consonant with Today's Mentality

Devotion to the Blessed Virgin must also pay close attention to certain findings of the human sciences. That will help to eliminate one of the causes of difficulties experienced in devotion to the Mother of the Lord, namely, the discrepancy existing between certain aspects of this devotion and mo-

---

[46] *Marialis Cultus,* no. 24.
[47] Ibid., no. 31.

dern anthropological discoveries and the profound changes which have occurred in the psycho-sociological field in which modern humans live and work. The picture of the Blessed Virgin presented in certain types of devotional literature cannot easily be reconciled with today's lifestyle, especially with the way women live today.[48]

Mary Stands Out Among The Poor

The modern woman will note with pleasant surprise that Mary of Nazareth, while completely devoted to the will of God, was far from being a timidly submissive woman or one whose piety was repellent to others; on the contrary, she was a woman who did not hesitate to proclaim that God vindicates the humble and the oppressed and removes the powerful people of this world from their privileged positions. The modern woman will recognize in Mary who "stands out among the poor and humble of the Lord"[49] a woman of strength who experienced poverty and suffering, flight and exile. These are situations than cannot escape the attention of those who wish to support, with the Gospel spirit, the liberating energies of humankind and society.[50]

Trust in Mary, An Oblate Characteristic

We have noted how in his writings the Oblate Founder often called Mary "our Mother" or "my Mother," expressing his confidence and love. Recall what he wrote from Rome to his tiny congregation in Aix just after papal approval:

> May we understand well what we are! I hope that the Lord will give us that grace, with the assistance and by the protection of *our holy Mother*, Mary Immaculate, for whom we must have a great devotion in the Congregation. Does it not seem to you that it is a sign of predestination to bear the name of Oblates of Mary, that is, consecrated to God under the patronage of Mary, a name the Congregation bears as a family name held in common with the most holy and immaculate Mother of God? It is enough to make others jealous; but it is the Church who gave us this beautiful name. Thus, we receive it with respect, love and gratitude, proud of our dignity and of the rights it gives us to the protection of her who is all-powerful in God's presence.[51]

---

[48] *Marialis Cultus,* no. 34.
[49] *Lumen Gentium,* no. 55.
[50] *Marialis Cultus,* no. 37.
[51] *Oblate Writings,* vol. 7, p. 63, n. 231.

In relinquishing the reins of the Oblate congregation, outgoing superior general Father Leo Deschâtelets told the 1972 general chapter:

> I believe in our Congregation, in its life and its aims, in its apostolic charism and in that of its members, above all, because of its attachment to the Virgin Mary. The 1966 Chapter expressed its faith in her, the Patron and Mother of our Institute in various articles where our devotion and our filial affection, as well as her protection over us, are forcefully asserted.[52] It is impossible that we degenerate, that we weaken, that we become useless to the Church and to the glory of God, as long as our whole life will be inspired by Mary Immaculate, the patroness of our Congregation, as long as we are open to the Spirit as she was, as long as we recognize her as our mother in the joys and sorrows of our apostolate, as long as we see in her a model of the faith we are sent to witness to the world . . . .

In that excerpt from his ringing address to the general chapter Father Deschâtelets paraphrased the article from the 1966 experimental Oblate rule, later adopted verbatim as Constitution 10 of the definitive 1982 rule. It was the last time he addressed the assembled Oblates. Those privileged to be present had the distinct feeling that Father Deschâtelets was leaving us his testament, and indeed, he died a year and a half later. But more, we felt that Eugene de Mazenod was speaking to us through him.

Saint Eugene De Mazenod, A Son Of Mary

Throughout his life, St. Eugene de Mazenod had a deep-rooted devotion to Mary Immaculate, his mother. And it is only fitting that he died hearing the *Salve Regina* that his Oblate sons were prayerfully chanting around his bed. In his will he had written:

> I invoke the intercession of the Most Holy and Immaculate Virgin Mary, Mother of God, daring to remind her in all humility, but with consolation, of the filial devotion of my whole life and of the desire I have always had to make her known and loved, and to spread her devotion everywhere through the ministry of those whom the Church gave me as children, who have the same desire as I.[53]

---

[52] *Administrative Circular 247*, April 11, 1972, p. 63.
[53] *Selected Texts*, p. 130, n. 108.

317

Epilogue

What Is a Miracle?

"Si, soy católico, pero no soy fanático" – Yes, I'm a Catholic, but I'm not fanatic about it. In Mexico, when a man makes that oft-repeated statement, it means that he was baptized, that he received the eucharist (once, at least), perhaps that he even got married in the Church, and that he intends somehow to come to terms with the Lord scant seconds before his last breath. That, aside from the rare visits made to a church for some social event or for a patronal *fiesta,* may well sum up his Catholic practice. It may sound contradictory, but there is a deep underlying faith there. In some ways it is a situation probably not very different from what Saint Eugene de Mazenod and his little band of missionaries encountered when they set out to re-evangelize Provence in 1816. Perhaps that is why the Founder of the Oblates, long after his death, took a special interest in changing the life of a humble Mexican.

Jesús Hernández Serrano is that Mexican. He was born in Mexico City in 1932 to parents who had fled the rural poverty that was the lot of so many in the revolution-ravaged state of Michoacán. He grew up in the city's then-chaotic Ampliación Providencia district. In 1949 he married Marcelina Hernández and the couple had two daughters, María Guadalupe and María de la Luz. Life in Ampliación Providencia was a constant struggle for something better. To most *barrio* dwellers – and Jesús Hernández was no exception – the "better" life in the megalopolis meant throwing together a hovel with whatever materials he could find, tapping dangerously into the electricity from nearby high tension power lines; it also meant that his wife and children had to go up the cluttered street to bring cans and buckets of questionable water from a common tap – water for drinking and cooking, water for washing the family's few clothes each day on the stone scrubboard. In the September rainy season, Marcelina's frequent early morning task would be to carry her children through the morass of unpaved, unlit streets to where the pavement began so that they would not arrive at school with their only shoes all muddied. As for Jesús himself, he eked out a living doing clean-up work whenever and wherever he could find it.

The Oblates in Mexico – With the Most Abandoned

During all that time Oblate missionaries were there in Ampliación Providencia, helping the people create church, accompanying them as they organized their communities, cooperatives and literacy classes. Slowly conditions improved. San Mateo Apostol became a thriving parish; the streets were paved and lit, life in the barrio became more stable, more human. While certainly not affluent, the neighbourhood was a far cry from what the Oblates had found when they arrived. Indeed, almost all of the half-dozen parishes that they had set up in the city's northeast district had become self-sufficient to the point where they were eventually handed over to the archdiocese. The Oblates then went elsewhere to look for other desperate newcomers. In Santa Cruz Meyehualco they still accompany over 180,000 poor people in their search for dignity. Like their Founder, Mexico's Oblates keep looking for the most abandoned. In the northeast only one parish still remains in Oblate hands – San Mateo Apostol, the parish of the Hernández family.

Over the years Jesús Hernández also saw a marked improvement in his own life. He turned his tiny shack into a real house. Increasingly, he found work as a truck driver, and as his daughters grew and married, living was no longer the struggle it had once been. Like many of his *compadres* he was *macho* and drank a lot to assert himself, especially on weekends or in fiestas when he was quite capable of getting roaring drunk. He also smoked a lot, but so did everyone else. And, of course, he was Catholic, "but not a fanatic about it."

It was in March, 1987, that Jesús' life began to come apart. At first he thought that the stomach aches, the bloating, the loss of appetite, the debilitating fevers that made him break out in an intense sweat were possibly brought on by something he had eaten at a fiesta. Perhaps if he quit drinking . . . . The symptoms persisted, however, and when he lost over twenty-two kilos – fifty pounds – in six weeks, he knew something was definitely wrong.

Admitted to hospital in May, Jesús' yellowing complexion made Doctor Francisco Manzano suspect hepatitis B or some type of salmonella infection. Tests, however, turned out negative, so the doctor brought in three specialists who performed a liver biopsy. Nurse Sara Rosales, who assisted at the operation, recounted:

> When Doctor Izcoa Vives opened the patient he commented, in my presence and in the presence of the other surgeons, "This is cancer." Then, since he knew I was a friend of the family, he said, "You know, girl, this

guy is not going to make it but, no matter, we'll have to take a sample for a biopsy. . . . We'll have to talk with Doctor Manzano so he breaks it to the family."[1]

The verdict was calangiocarcinoma, a well-advanced example of a rather rare but extremely aggressive form of liver cancer – the prognosis: death was probably a few scant months away. Commenting on her reception of the chilling news, Jesús' wife, Marcelina, later testified:

> The doctors told me he probably had two months to live. Lest he react badly we hid the truth of his illness from him. There was no hope that he might pull through, so we decided to let him live those months peacefully.[2]

Jesús had no insurance and the operation had left him without the money needed to remain in hospital. In considerable pain, he returned home to die. When a subsequent series of emergency tests confirmed the perniciousness of the cancer and that death was indeed imminent, the family was left with but one recourse: prayer. By then, Jesús did not have to be told – he knew it was time to settle things with God. Oblate Father Santiago Lyons gave him the sacrament of the sick as Marcelina and the Hernández daughters stood at the bedside, tearful and distraught. Padre Santiago, along with Padre Roberto Ward, his assistant in the parish, suggested a novena to Blessed Eugene de Mazenod. The novena was announced to the parishioners on June 7 and begun at the morning Masses while in the Hernández home a prayer ministry group entreated the Oblate Founder's help as the agonizing Jesús screamed in pain.

We cannot help but remember Eugene de Mazenod visiting the poor in their last moments or the needy crowding into his residence in Marseille, asking for favours 150 years earlier. There was one big difference, however: the parishioners of San Mateo Apostol were not just asking for a little handout to alleviate the moment's sufferings and ills, as petitioners did then. What they were asking of the Founder was a complete cure, a full-blown miracle. Jesús, only half conscious and in terrible pain, was frankly sceptical. Undaunted, the Oblates and their parishioners stormed heaven, much as Eugene's youth sodality had done in 1814 when their founder was at death's door with typhus.

---

[1] *Fattispecie cronologica: Canonizationis Beati Caroli Josephi Eugenii de Mazenod,* p. 143, n. 3. In Spanish, the doctor referred to the nurse as "hija" – daughter or girl, and to the patient as "este cuate" – this guy.

[2] *Fattispecie cronologica: Canonizationis Beati Caroli Josephi Eugenii de Mazenod,* p. 87, n. 3.

Miracle!

The nine days of the novena ended on the night of June 16, 1987. The next morning an incredulous Jesús told his wife the pain had disappeared! This is how he later described it:

> I always tried not to think about the pain, for whenever I moved it came, along with the fever. So I remained rigid and had grown accustomed to not moving, to not even thinking about it, hoping the pain would not keep coming back. That day when I awoke it was almost comical. "Where am I?" I said – it was like I didn't recognize my own room. But I stayed rigid and would not even think about it because I was sure the pain would return. But then I moved – my arms first – and felt all sweaty and wet from the fever. But soon I felt dry, dry, dry and I was afraid. . . . My wife always asked me, "How do you feel?" or "What would you like?" or "Does it hurt?" and I kept telling her, "Stop asking me all those questions – I feel rotten." . . . That day I told her, "You know what? I feel really strange." But she didn't pay any attention. Then I repeated, "I feel really strange. I'm dry, no longer perspiring and I feel very well." After that she asked me if I wanted something to eat because I had only been taking liquids.[3]

When Nurse Rosales phoned in the afternoon to check on Jesús, she was speechless at the news that he was up and walking. Only the day before she had been almost certain he would not make it through the night. Indeed, she could not turn him in bed because of the excruciating pain that not even a massive dose of Demerol could numb!

In the following days Jesús felt his appetite quicken and his weight begin to return. A week after the miracle, on the Feast of the Sacred Heart, he and his family went to Mass to give thanks to the Lord. Soon he was back at work. But a nagging question remained: was he really cured or was this just some cruel joke, a remission that left his cancer hanging over his head like a sword of Damocles, ready to come crashing down upon him again at any moment? When his daughter Guadalupe made him a gift of the Christmas bonus from her job he decided to use it to undergo new medical tests. He was carefully re-examined and absolutely no trace of his cancer was found. At that point, Padre Santiago reported the cure to his Oblate superiors. An official inquest was initiated from Rome and more minute medical tests were made. The results were the same – a complete and physically unexplainable cure.

The process of recognizing a miracle is long and thorough, but on March 24, 1994, five medical experts in Rome approved the miraculous cure of Jesús Hernández Serrano as attributable to the intervention of Blessed Eugene de

---

[3] *Fattispecie cronologica: Canonizationis Beati Caroli Josephi Eugenii de Mazenod*, pp. 75-76, n. 33.

Mazenod. The way was now open for the Oblate Founder's canonization. Soon that stormy Provençal *mistral* who reached inner peace through being ground in the mortar of obedience and refined in the crucible of faith – that apostle who let himself be led by the Spirit to work for the glory of God and the salvation of souls – soon he would be *Saint* Eugene de Mazenod. That, too, was miracle of grace.

What Is a Miracle?

Jesús Hernández Serrano's cure has been recognized by the Church as miraculous, and so it should be. But an even greater miracle took place in San Mateo Apostol parish. Jesús Hernández no longer refers to his non-fanatic Catholic faith. On the contrary, the miracle not only cured him, it changed him. And not only him, but his family too. The family has become much closer, even as a whole new world of community stretches their horizons. They now take an active part in the faith life of the parish, even participating in preparation of the liturgy and in regular biblical studies to feed and liven their faith. Indeed, Jesús even invited his brother Máximo to bring his family and join in. The miracle keeps growing. At times parishioners are almost awe-struck by God's presence in their midst. He touched one of them – *actually came to their neighbourhood, to their parish, and touched one of them* through the intervention of Eugene de Mazenod! No wonder there is a new awareness of God's presence and a healthy devotion in the parish to the Oblate Founder. That's the real miracle – the miracle of God's grace working in his people.

There is an awe-inspiring mystery in the realization that God's grace began working in the life of his people from all eternity, that he chose us –you and me – "by his grace to reveal his Son in (us)" (Galatians 1:15). Revealing his Son *in* us – not just *to* us – means that like that Son we are eucharistic: taken, blessed, broken and given. From the moment of his fateful Good Friday conversion in 1807, Eugene de Mazenod lived more and more in the realization of being taken – being chosen – chosen by God; not chosen over others, but chosen to better recognize the chosenness of others. He felt God's blessing profoundly and sought to bring the most abandoned and marginalized into that blessing, to make them realize that they, too, are chosen:

> You are the children of God, the brothers and sisters of Jesus Christ, the co-heirs of his eternal kingdom, the cherished portion of his inheritance; you are, in the words of St. Peter, the holy nation; you are kings, you are priests, you are, yes, in a certain way, gods. . . So lift up your heads, let your spirits rise! Stop grovelling on the ground and raise yourselves

toward heaven where you were meant to attain what should be your most normal relationship. . . For once let your eyes look inward and see through the rags you wear. There, within you, is an immortal soul, created to the image of God whom it is destined one day to possess – a soul redeemed at the cost of the blood of Jesus Christ. . . Therefore, O Christians, recognize your dignity.[4]

And, yes, Eugene de Mazenod was broken, and the more he acknowledged his brokenness, the greater were his peace and serenity, the greater his strength. By embracing his brokenness and coming to terms with it, he became, in the footsteps of his eucharistic Saviour, a gift of God to humankind, not just in his generation but for generations to come.

Eugene de Mazenod is a saint for our times, a saint who had to face so many of the hurdles before us today: alienation, a dysfunctional family in dysfunctional times, divorce, rejection, unfair treatment – the list goes on. Often today we feel overwhelmed by our own brokenness, a brokenness that makes us feel anything but chosen, that makes us feel cursed, not blessed – the brokenness of anger, rage and resentment, the brokenness of jealousy, abuse, hurtfulness and revenge. And then a saint like Eugene comes along to show us that, yes, life is a struggle, that, yes, life can appear to deal us a rotten hand at times, that, yes, brokenness is a fact, but that we have been truly chosen and that no matter how bad the outlook, if we embrace our brokenness, if we take up our cross of brokenness and put it under the blessing of God – if we celebrate God's goodness – we begin to discover that somewhere deep within that brokenness lies our real and beautiful self, a self of confidence and assurance and love, a self at peace with itself and with the Lord, a self living in the Spirit. Only then, like our eucharistic Lord and like Saint Eugene, can we be given as a gift from God to serve our broken sisters and brothers truly. Saint Eugene's life shows that it is not easy, but that we can do it and that it is worth the effort.

In very deed, the lifelong process of Eugene de Mazenod's sanctification demonstrates what God's blessed grace could achieve in such an impetuous, explosive, volatile, imperfect and completely generous soul – a miracle that God can repeat in each of us if we give the Spirit space in our lives to do so. Eugene showed us how to live our personal Pentecost daily, how to let the Spirit lay hold of us, strengthen us, purify us, give us peace in the midst of turmoil or adversity, so among our brothers and sisters everywhere – among today's most abandoned – we can be given and bear witness to the kingdom of God here on earth as we joyfully await Jesus' coming to take us to his eternal kingdom. What a glorious experience! What a privilege!

---

4   Saint Eugene's Lenten instruction for the poor on the first Sunday of Lent, 1813.

Through Eugene de Mazenod's life and struggles we see how the ever-faithful presence of the Spirit can inspire generous persons in any age. His life lets us discover that the Spirit is always here in our midst. Thus, the obvious question each of us must ask ourselves is searching and blunt: if the Spirit is here, where am I?

At the time of Eugene de Mazenod's beatification in 1975, Oblate Father Aimé Roche wrote:

> We can affirm that this impassioned witness of God, Eugene de Mazenod, was in no way a prisoner of his era. His mission spilled over far beyond the boundaries of time and space surrounding him.
>
> Isn't that the way with all saints?
>
> Today's Church, moreover, continues to honour saints regardless of the epoch in which they lived. Indeed, we can well ask ourselves what the Gospel would have become without them. A dead letter, perhaps? Or might it not have come to a petrified ending?
>
> Instead, such creatures of flesh and blood *lived* the Gospel. They were sinners like us, yet sinners transformed by the Spirit of God into living witnesses of his tenderness. Thanks to such persons, therefore, the Gospel lives constantly and answers the needs of all times, whatever the deep changes that take place.

Now, as we celebrate the canonization of Saint Eugene de Mazenod, those words apply as never before.

Alfred A. Hubenig, O.M.I.

BIBLIOGRAPHY

Bérulle and the French School. Compendium, several authors, Paulist Press, New York, 1989.

Blessed Eugene de Mazenod. Aimé Roche, O.M.I. Translated by A. A. Hubenig, O.M.I., Éditions du Chalet, Lyon, 1974.

Blessed Eugene de Mazenod, His Life and Work. The beatification cause, Angelo Mitri, O.M.I., General Postulation, Rome, 1979.

The Complete Parallel Bible. Oxford University Press, Oxford and New York, 1989.

Cristo crocifisso e la Chiesa abbandonata. Angelo d'Addio, O.M.I., publicazioni Missioni O.M.I. Roma.

Ecrits spirituels O.M.I. 1812-1856. From the collection *Ecrits oblats,* I, 15, O.M.I. Postulation publication, Rome.

Elisabeth de la Trinité, oeuvres complèts. Édition critique réalisée par le Père Conrad de Meester, Éditions du Cerf, Paris, 1991.

Entretiens spirituels aux missionnaires. André Dodin, Seuil, Paris, 1966.

Eugene de Mazenod, Bishop of Marseilles, Founder of the Oblates of Mary Immaculate. Four volumes, Jean Leflon. Translated by Francis D. Flanagan, O.M.I. Fordham University Press, New York, 1961.

Fattispecie cronologica: Canonizationis Beati Caroli Josephi Eugenii de Mazenod. James Fitzpatrick, O.M.I., O.M.I. Postulation publication, Rome, 1993.

First Roman Journal, 1825-1826. C. J. E. de Mazenod. Translated by J. W. Mole, O.M.I. O.M.I. publication, Rome, 1952.

Flight Into Italy, 1792-1802. The Oblate Founder's boyhood reminiscences. Translated by J. W. Mole, O.M.I., O.M.I publication, Rome, 1952.

France, 1848-1945. Theodore Zeldin, Two volumes. Clarendon Press, Oxford.

François de Paule Henri Tempier. Yvon Beaudoin, O.M.I. Translated by Ronald Zimmer, O.M.I. From the collection *Oblate Writings* 2. General Postulation O.M.I., Rome, 1991.

François de Paule Henri Tempier. Selected letters and various writings. Compiled by Yvon Beaudoin, O.M.I. Translated by Ronald Zimmer, O.M.I. From the collection *Oblate Writings* 2. General Postulation O.M.I., Rome, 1991.

General Norms for Oblate Formation. O.M.I. publication, Rome, 1984.

Histoire des Catholiques en France du XV siècle a nos jours. Sous la direction de François Lebrun, Eduard Privat, éditeur, Toulouse, 1980.

Histoire de France, Vol. 4: *Les Révolutions, 1789-1851.* Jean Tulard, Fayard, Paris, 1985.

Histoire de la spiritualité chrétienne. Abier, Paris, 1966.

Histoire de Mgr Charles-Joseph-Eugène de Mazenod, évêque de Marseille, fondateur de la Congrégation des Oblats de Marie Immaculée. Two volumes. Achille Rey, O.M.I., Rome-Marseille, 1928.

Histoire réligeuse de la France contemporaine, 1800-1880. Gérard Cholvy, et Yves-Marie Hilaire, Toulouse: Eduard Privat, éditeur, 1985.

Historia Universal. Vol. 10, Salvat, Barcelona, 1975.

Inquisitio historica de quibusdam animadversionibus in Servi Dei vitam et operositatem, ex officio concinnata. Angelo Mitri, O.M.I., O.M.I. Postulation publication, Rome, 1968.

Instruction of Our Venerated Founder on Foreign Missions. O.M.I. publication, Rome, 1936.

Jerusalem Bible. Doubleday and Company, Inc., New York, 1968.

La Europa de los nacionalismos, 1848-1898. Julio Aróstegui, Anaya, Madrid, 1989.

La Europa Revolucionaria. Javier Paniagua, Anaya, Madrid, 1989.

La Revolución Francesa, 1789-1848. Esperanza Yllán, Anaya, Madrid, 1989.

L'Eglise de France, face aux crises révolutionnaires. P. Pierrard, Éditions du chalet, Lyon, 1974.

L'image de piété en France, 1814-1914. Catherine Rosenbaum-Dondaine, Paris: Musée Galérie de la Sieta, 1984.

L'Immaculée Conception honorée dans la ville d'Aix. Abbé M. Davin, Aix-Makaire, 1904.

Manuscrits autobiographique de Ste-Thérèse de l'Énfant Jesus. Éditions office central de Lisieux, 1957

Missionaries in Today's World. 1986 General Chapter, English, O.M.I. publication, 1986.

Missions. March 1866. Translated by J. W. Mole, O.M.I., St. Paul's University, Ottawa.

My Name Is Eugene: Texts by Eugene de Mazenod. Selected and annotated by Hermenegilde Charbonneau, O.M.I. Translated by Francis Flanagan, O.M.I., Eastern Oblate Province, U.S.A., Boston, 1976.

Mystère et dynamique de l'amour dans la vie du Bienheureux Eugène de Mazenod. K. Lubowicki, O.M.I., O.M.I. publication, Rome.

XIX siècle, siècle de grâce. Cardinal Paul Poupard, éd. SOS, Paris, 1982.

Nouvelle Histoire de l'Eglise. Vol. 4: *Siècle des Lumières – Révolution, Restauration,* L.J. Rogier, G. de Bertier de Sauvigny and J. Hajjar, Éditions du Cerf, Paris, 1966.

Oblate Constitutions and Rules. English edition. O.M.I. publication, 1982.

Oblate Prayer Book. English edition, O.M.I. publication, Rome, 1986.

O.M.I., the Apostolic Man. Fernand Jetté, O.M.I. Translated by A. Kedl, O.M.I. and A. Lalonde, O.M.I., O.M.I. publication, Rome, 1992.

Oblate Necrologium. O.M.I. publication, Rome, 1988.

Oblate Writings. Letters and writings of Saint Eugene de Mazenod. Sixteen volumes. Translated by J. W. Mole, O.M.I., Peter C. Farrell, Michael Hughes, O.M.I., B. Rayappu, O.M.I., Lionel Desjardins, O.M.I., George Capen, O.M.I., Alois Kedl, O.M.I., Albert Lalonde, O.M.I., John Rheidt, O.M.I., Ronald Zimmer, O.M.I.; O.M.I. publication, Rome, 1978-1995.

Les Oblats de Marie Immaculée durant le premier siècle de leur existence. Two volumes. Théophile Ortolan, O.M.I., Paris, 1915.

Opuscule de la pieté. G. Rotureau, Aubier, Montaigne, 1944.

The Oxford Dictionary of Popes. J.N.D. Kelly, Oxford University Press, Oxford and New York, 1986.

Robespierre, ou le délir décapité. Pierre Alexandre Bourson, Buchet-Chastel, Paris, 1993.

Selected Oblate Studies and Texts. Volume 1. O.M.I. publication, 1986.

Selected Texts. Translated by B. Rayappu, O.M.I., O.M.I. publication, Rome, 1984.

A Short Treatise on the Virgin Mary. René Laurentin. Translated by Charles Neumann, S.M., Ami Press, Washington, New Jersey, 1991.

The Spiritual Journey. Critical Thresholds and Stages of Adult Spiritual Genesis. Maria Theresa Coombs and Francis Kelly Nemeck, O.M.I., Michael Glazier Inc., Wilmington, Delaware, 1988.

Theotokos, a Theological Encyclopedia of the Blessed Virgin Mary. Michael O'Carroll, C.S.Sp., Michael Glazier, Inc., Wilmington and Dublin, 1982.

L'Univers. Paris, July 7, 1848 and February 12, 1849.

Vie de Mgr Charles-Joseph-Eugène de Mazenod, évêque de Marseille, fondateur de la Congrégation des Missionnaires Oblats de Marie Immaculée. Two volumes. Toussaint Rambert, O.M.I., Tours, A. Mame et Fils, 1883.

Vie Oblate Life. Volumes 36-52, St. Paul's University, Ottawa.

Witnessing the Apostolic Community. 1992 General Chapter, O.M.I. Publication, Rome, 1992.

MARQUIS

PRINTED BY
IMPRIMERIE D'ÉDITION MARQUIS
IN OCTOBER 1995
MONTMAGNY (QUÉBEC)